Shakespeare's Sugared Sonnets

Shakespeare's
Sugared Sonnets

Katharine M. Wilson

London
George Allen & Unwin Ltd
Ruskin House   Museum Street

First published in 1974

© Katharine M. Wilson 1974

ISBN 0 04 820014 X

Printed in Great Britain by
Willmer Brothers Limited
Birkenhead

'Satire is the last flicker of originality in a passing epoch as it faces the onroad of staleness and boredom.'

A. N. Whitehead, *Adventures of Ideas*

CONTENTS

I

INTRODUCTORY

I. THE SONNET TEXTURE

In his *Palladis Tamia* Francis Meres gives a contemporary
report on Shakespeare's sonnets:

> As the soul of Euphorbus was thought to live in Pythagorus :
> so the sweet witty soul of Ovid lives in mellifluous and honey-
> tongued Shakespeare, witness his *Venus and Adonis*, his
> *Lucrece*, his sugared sonnets among his private friends.

This was written in his section on a 'Comparative discourse of
our English poets, with the Greek, Latin and Italian poets'.
Meres thinks they stand up well in comparison. Of Shakespeare in general he writes :

> I say that the muses would speak with Shakespeare's fine
> filed phrase, if they would speak English.

The two things which he specially appreciated in Shakespeare
were the musical quality of his verse, that it was 'mellifluous
and honey-tongued', and the 'fine filed phrase', the wit; he
calls Shakespeare's sonnets 'sugared'. These are contemporary
judgements. We have become much less sensitive to the
'mellifluous' in verse, its flowing melody, its song quality. But
the early poems of Shakespeare certainly have this, and his
contemporaries were more song-conscious than we are. So also,
we think little of the 'fine filed phrase'. Nor is 'sugared' an
epithet we should apply to his sonnets, perhaps not one he

would either. But 'sugared' was often used by the sonneteers of
their love talk. Sidney says to his muse that whereas he has 'oft
craved' that it might 'With choicest flowers, my speech to
engarland' he now means,

No other sugaring of speech to try.[1]

Giles Fletcher apostrophises thus:

Oh sugared talk! wherewith my thoughts do live.[2]

Watson in his *Passionate Centurie of Love* curses the day when
'the sugared speech and siren's song'[3] bewitched him, and
Richard Linche, one of the very minor sonneteers, actually
couples Meres' epithets in *Diella*:[4]

What sugared terms, what all persuading art,
What sweet mellifluous words . . .

We might define 'sugared' as 'sweetened by artifice'. Meres
notes that the 'sweet witty soul of Ovid' is in Shakespeare; the
sugared quality is a sort of wit, a 'liveliness of fancy' to use one
of the *Oxford English Dictionary* definitions of 'wit'. It is not
that they thought of imagery and the play of the mind as
decorating what was said, like sugar sprinkled onto it, but that
the texture of the poetry was itself of this sort, a lace or brocade
so to say, that the sonnets were made of, and that was itself a
thing of art and beauty.

These attributes of the Elizabethan sonnet, its song quality
and its texture, can be traced to three ancient sources—
primitive song, a chivalric convention and Platonic theory.

Troubadour song[5] has been traced to carols sung to Venus
by peasant girls of Poitou and Limousin in May festivals. They
sang and danced in a ring and it looks as if this may have been
a survival of spring festivals from possibly prehistory. Out of
this spring-time love and the glorification of women the
troubadours developed their conventions of love. Love enters
by the eyes and penetrates the heart, where it dwells, and it
does so in an atmosphere of flowers and bird-song. The poet
worships his lady and asks to be accepted only as her servant.

But she does not favour him and he calls her proud and pitiless, even cruel and savage. Here is a translation from a courtly lover :[6]

> Bitter the breeze that strips the forest boughs
> Whose leafage once with sweetness was fulfilled,
> And strikes the beak of every bird on branch,
> Mated and single, to stammer or be mute.
> Why have I striven word and deed to please,
> In all, that she who has my high estate brought low.
> Of which I die unless she end my grief?

The prosaic answer to this question is because the lady might well be the wife of the troubadour's overlord. He sang as much out of compliment as out of love, and had to take the attitude of suffering from her invincible chastity. She might be his inspiration, his guide, even his saint, but she could not reward her poet, who suffered in lonely misery, unworthy and rejected. Troubadour songs of the eleventh and twelfth centuries make the warp of the love-song to the aristocratic lady that persisted unchanged until the time of the Elizabethan sonnet at the end of the sixteenth century.

Across this warp, the twelfth-century French poet, Chrétien de Troyes,[5] wove an intricately patterned woof out of chivalric ideals in long romantic poems that were no longer sung. He developed the old warp a little but did not change it in any essential. Thus love may not only come into the lover's heart; the poet may add the sophistication of sending his heart to his lady. He trembles as she looks at him; he cannot confess his love for fear of her, or sleep. When he is absent her image still dominates him. He is sick for love and like to die.

All this was created on the background of women's play. The peasant dances to Venus expressed attitudes that did not belong to the actual life of the women, who once a year sang of what they wanted and complained of the husbands they had. Similarly the troubadours' songs made art of a play for courtly ladies, the most important of whom, and therefore the most beloved, held courts of love for which they made rules that their 'servants', the knights who loved them, must keep.

The most famous of these was Queen Eleanor of Aquitaine, the mother of Richard, Coeur de Lion, who held court at Poitiers from 1170 to 1174.[7] One of her daughters held a similar court at Troyes, and Chrétien's romances were written for her.

We know much about the love-play at Troyes and its conventions from a treatise on *The Art of True Love* (*De Arte Honesti Amandi*) written by a monk, Andreas Capellanus,[8] between 1184 and 1186, in which he first gave examples of all the different ways in which a lover might approach his lady according to her rank and her relationship with him, and then codified the rules of love. We could describe it as a book on the etiquette of courtly love. But it ends with arguments against such love, denigrates women and points out that if you give up your allegiance to the King of Love, 'the Heavenly King will be more favourably disposed to you'.[9] Whatever his real intention may have been in writing his book, Capellanus's rules were remembered, and the advice tacked on at the end forgotten. His rules came to be thought of as decrees of King Arthur, and they guided poets and romancers of chivalric love until the fashion for it died.

Andreas Capellanus introduced the rules in a story of Arthurian adventure. His lady sends a knight in quest of the parchment on which the King of Love has written rules for lovers. After due tests he receives this parchment in the court of King Arthur.[10] Here are some of the rules[11] that are still relevant to the courtly lovers of Elizabethan sonnets : He who is not jealous does not love, and jealousy is good for love since it increases it; love easily attained has little value, but if it is difficult to attain, it is valued greatly; if the lover suspects his love's faithfulness his love will intensify. The lover can neither eat nor sleep. He thinks nothing good unless it pleases his lady; he can deny her nothing; he is possessed by the thought of her at all times and without rest. The woman may have more than one lover, but the lover adores her alone, although he may forsake her as a lesser love, if he finds a greater. Capellanus ends his story with all lovers being ordered to keep the rules faithfully under

> threat of punishment by the King of Love . . . . Every person who had been summoned and had come to the court took

home a written copy of the rules and gave them out to all lovers in all parts of the world.[11]

No wonder they became legendary and held the imagination of all true lovers in many generations to follow.

So much for the patterning of feudal France. When troubadour poetry came to Italy[12] although it retained the basic attitudes of the lover—his absorption in his lady, his serving her, trembling before her, dreaming of her or spending sleepless nights, sending his heart to her and so on, and all in vain because of her heartlessness—it breathed in a renaissance rather than a feudal atmosphere, for it now flourished in a city or university society, not a feudal one. Its basic philosophy became Platonic.

Plato in his *Symposium*[13] distinguished between two sorts of love—common love and heavenly love. The first was physical, demanding, selfish, even debasing. Most love for women and for boys was of this sort. But there was a heavenly love that could spring up between men, which was rational, not self-seeking or physical and which was conducive to spiritual development. The love of a noble nature is constant and endures throughout one's life. This constancy makes one of the tests by which you can recognise heavenly love. Plato advised any youth who was loved, to flee and reject his lover until his constancy was tested. Among other qualities of this heavenly love, we may note that one who loves wants to be indissolubly united with the beloved. But Plato is not sentimental about love. He makes Socrates say that the lover is always poor, feels deprived, is weather-beaten and homeless, scheming to get what is beautiful and good, for what heavenly love seeks is beauty and truth. He then discusses how this heavenly love begins and develops. It begins with admiration of physical beauty, and with falling in love with one particular beautiful person, and it proceeds from love of particular beautiful things and persons to a delight in beauty itself. The lover comes to think 'beauty of soul more valuable than beauty of body'. By contemplating this spiritual beauty which is eternal (for beauty is an 'absolute', one 'substance' which all beautiful things partake of) one will be in contact not with its reflection in particular things or people, but with truth itself.

The *Phaedrus*[14] deals with love as a madness :

The greatest blessing comes to us through madness when it is sent as a gift of the gods.

One freshly initiated into beauty, when he sees a godlike face or form, shudders in awe. The beauty has entered through the eye and the soul is filled with joy. It rages with pain and joy alternately, and is 'troubled by its strange condition'. It is

perplexed and maddened and in its madness it cannot sleep at night or stay in one place by day, but it is filled with longing and hastens wherever it hopes to see the beautiful one.

And when it sees him it enjoys 'the sweetest of pleasures'. It becomes his slave, finding in him 'the only healer of its greatest woes'.

Each one chooses his love ... and he fashions him and adorns him like a statue as though he were his god, to honour and worship.

That is to say the lover attributes to his love the qualities he most wants to have himself, and thus gives him the perfection of a god. So when he sees his beloved he is afraid and retreats in reverence. Then he follows 'in reverence and awe'. But gradually desire awakens between the two. 'The stream of beauty passes ... through the eyes, the natural inlet to the soul.'

Like one who has caught a disease of the eyes from another, he can give no reason for it, he sees himself in his lover as in a mirror.

However, he is not aware that it is his own reflection that he sees. If the better element in love prevails, the lovers recover from their disease and live a self-controlled and orderly life as friends. Plato ends by discussing what sort of madness love is. There are two sorts of madness, one arising from disease, the other 'from a divine release from the customary habits'. The four divine madnesses are prophecy inspired by Apollo, religious phrensy inspired by Dionysus, the poetic madness inspired

by the muses, and love inspired by Aphrodite and Eros. Of
these love is the best. Common to all is unreason. Love can be
either good or bad, or rather it has a good side and a bad
side.

The *Timaeus* is most relevant also, although its theme is not
love. The system of creation that Plato puts forward was
accepted in the renaissance. Everything is made from the four
elements, earth, air, fire and water.[15] The creator puts reason
within the soul, which is made before the body, as its mistress
and ruler.[16]

All this came to be interwoven in the traditional texture of
love poetry. Some of it corresponds in the most startling way
with troubadour poetry. This may be because it describes
common experience. Thus in most first love the lover is struck
dumb, he experiences an exclusive adoration, he desires to
serve, and has a sense of his own worthlessness. Similarly
perhaps the idea that love enters by the eye and lodges in the
heart is a universal experience. But one would like to know
whether this appears in the poetry of other traditions. If not,
we must presume a very early Platonic influence in the pre-
sonnet tradition. It is not just that common experience might
explain the similarities. Common experience often goes un-
noticed. What is striking is Plato's conscious observation of
love. Margaret Schlauch notes[17] that Plato's influence on
western philosophy can be seen in the time of Charlemagne.
Indeed I think we must presume it influenced troubadour
song, even if the actual source is not established, for there are so
many resemblances between them. For the rest we can say that
this philosophic stream flooded into the Italian poetry that
developed from the troubadour tradition. Lu Emily Pearson[18]
says it was Guido Guincelli who first gave it this Platonic bias,
and only after him, Dante and Petrarch.

It is interesting that the troubadours and particularly Dante
and Petrarch should have found that Plato's philosophy of the
experience of love between men fitted their love for a woman.
Considering, however, that certainly the Italian poets wrote of
a love that could never have a physical goal and that Plato's
heavenly love has this character, the correspondence is not
unnatural. Indeed one can say of the Italian sonneteers that

since they had not the chivalric motive of a deep feudal allegiance, they probably needed some such spiritual or heavenly love to give depth to their sonnet game. No doubt Dante and probably Petrarch[19] experienced this quality in their own personal love and worshipped their ladies as if they were their own soul, their not yet realised self, as Plato suggests, mirroring their deepest desire for their own development. But Petrarch's followers cannot all be said to write out of personal experience like this. It is rather that they presume this quality to be of the nature of the sonnet love they are expressing; that is to say they accepted it as a convention.

Both the Italian and the French sonneteers write in this convention. Petrarch fixed the sonnet stanza he found in Dante and wrote in this traditional poetic texture which his Italian and French followers kept true to its nature. The Platonic influence gave it a seriousness and depth. Poets can now write of constancy as a moral beauty. They promise their beloved immortality. They also add a sophistication. Thus all seem fascinated by the idea of their lady seeing herself in a mirror as Petrarch's Laura did. The old images too, become more 'conceited', more sugared. Thus the poet may now have a dialogue with his eyes, or with his heart as did Petrarch; or eyes and heart may even confer with each other; complex situations between them may develop. Fresh images also appear, to be accepted as commonplaces, like the ship in storm, tossed in tempest, driven on the rocks.

Horace to some extent, and particularly Ovid also contributed to the richness of the sonnet brocade. Blair Leishman in *Themes and Variations in Shakespeare's Sonnets* and Claes Schaar in *An Elizabethan Sonnet Problem* and in *Elizabethan Sonnet Themes and the Dating of Shakespeare's Sonnets* illustrate this fully, as likewise the common texture of the love sonnet in Italy, France and Tudor England. I should like to mention only Horace's ode with its monument more enduring than brass, and Ovid's stress on time, the devourer, which became sonnet commonplaces and are important in Shakespeare's sonnets. The poet integrated such ideas with his sonnet love, which became fused with his ambition as a poet. One of his motives was to build an eternal monument by his verse, in which he made himself as well as his lady immortal. So he felt as impelled by fear of time the devourer as by his unsatisfiable worship of his cruel goddess.

II. ENGLISH SONNETEERS[20]

It was as court literature and as a sort of song that the English sonnet came into being, no matter that its texture was determined by foreign models, that it got its shape from Petrarch and that it was not written to be sung. We have an almost contemporary view of the first sonneteers in Puttenham's *Arte of English Poesie* :[21]

> In the latter end of the same king's [Henry VIII] reign sprang up a new company of courtly makers, of whom Sir Thomas Wyat the elder and Henry Earl of Surrey were the two chieftains, who having travelled into Italy, and there tasted the sweet and stately measures and style of the Italian poetry as novices newly crept out of the schools of Dante Ariosto and Petrarch, they greatly polished our rude and homely manner of vulgar poetry . . . and for that cause may justly be said the first reformers of our English metre and style.

Puttenham no doubt meant what he said when he gave Wyatt and Surrey credit for being reformers of English metre and style, for the pronunciation of Chaucer's age had so changed by this time that his smooth and polished rhythms were not discernible. But his statement does not mean that the Elizabethans failed to recognise Chaucer's quality as a poet of courtly love, deeply influenced by the great Italian love poems. Nor should we forget Malory when thinking of this tradition, whose *Le Morte D'Arthur* was made by translating from the French prose romancers who stemmed from Chrétien de Troyes. His tales were felt to be thoroughly English, at least to the extent that Arthur was accepted as the great English hero, the obvious king to rule over Spenser's epic, *The Faerie Queene,* and to merit consideration, if also rejection by Milton as the hero for his epic. Puttenham was thinking of court song, which was sparrow-verse compared with such eagle-poetry, and would be considered such by the Elizabethans.

We can understand what Puttenham is saying if we

compare Tottel's Miscellany of *Songes and Sonettes*, in which
Wyatt and Surrey's sonnets were first printed, with the Fairfax
Manuscript of early Tudor songs.[22] The Fairfax Manuscript,
like Tottel's collection, is a miscellany of court songs. It dates
from the opening of the sixteenth century. Its themes have
been summed up thus:[23]

> They elaborate the time-honoured chivalric themes of
> absence, desertion, 'departure', service. 'Absens of you
> causeth me to sygh and complayne' is the tone of dozens.
> The lover goes through all the stages recommended by the
> 'rules' of courtly love 'from wo to wele, and aftir out of
> joie.

It would be truer to say that they are bits and pieces of this
tradition than that they elaborate it. It is rather that we can
recognise where they have come from, than that they tell us
much about it. Here is a sample.[24]

> To complayne me, alas, why shulde I so?
> For my complayntes it did me nevir good;
> But be constraynt, now must I shew my woo
> To her only which is myn yes fode,*
> Trustyng sumtyme that she will chaunge her mode
> And lett me not allway be guerdonless,
> Syth for my trouth she nedith no wittness.

It is interesting that many of the Fairfax Songs are in rhyme
royal, so establishing an association of this stanza with song.
The poems in Tottel's Miscellany have this association also.
That the Nott manuscript of Tottel should contain twelve
tunes for its songs[25] makes clear that 'Songes' in its title does
not mean just lyrics. Here we find the first English sonnets, and
they are coupled with songs. Indeed the word 'sonnet' was at
first used in England as synonymous with song. Some of the
Elizabethan sonnet sequences include lyrics not in the least like
what we mean by a sonnet. So also of the four 'sonnets' in
Love's Labours Lost, only one is strictly speaking a sonnet. We
do not find sonnets in the Fairfax song-book however. They
appear first in Tottel.

* eye's food

The less polished and sophisticated song, which we find in
the Fairfax song-book, persisted throughout Henry VIII's
reign into Elizabeth's. Indeed, Henry himself wrote songs of
this type; that is to say he composed both words and music.[26]
But he was at the end of the chivalric era. Already in his reign
Italian culture was making an impact. Italian secretaries and
tutors became fashionable. His second wife, Anne Boleyn, had
been at the court of Margaret of Navarre, where she must have
come in contact with Platonic ideals, for there Cardinal Bembo
taught that man may attain to God through contemplation of
beauty and the 'spiritual love' of a woman.[27] Surrey was her
friend and Wyatt may have been in love with her.[28] We know
that Wyatt was in Italy in 1527, where he learnt to write the
Petrarchan fourteen-lined stanza with the abba, abba rhyme
scheme for the octave. Surrey invented the Elizabethan
alternately-rhymed octave. Surrey's attitude, however, may be
more Petrarchan, more Platonic than that of Wyatt, who has
quite a dash of English common sense, and after much provo-
cation even ends by telling his lady to go hang.

Wyatt and Surrey wrote their sonnets between about 1530
and 1540, although they were first printed by Tottel in 1557.
We have seen that their sophisticated art was appreciated, but
their sonnets remained as songs in Tottel's Miscellany, not
stimulating others to write sonnets proper. Nor did either
publish a book of sonnets. It was not till a quarter of a century
later in 1582 that Thomas Watson translated French and
Italian sonnets in his *Hekatompathia or Passionate Centurie of
Love*, and followed with sonnets of his own in *Tears of Fancie*,
which though not actually translations reflect French and
Italian models pretty closely. Although Watson's sonnets were
not printed till 1593, a year after his death, they had circulated
in manuscript, and he could be called the real father of the
Elizabethan sonnet. He started off a stream that was eventually
to break into a spate after the printing of Sidney's Sonnets in
1591.

Between Tottel and Watson there had been a rich development of French sonnets, to add to the Italian. In his *Passionate Centurie of Love*, as Sir Sidney Lee[29] calculated, Watson
translated eight sonnets from Petrarch, four from Ronsard, not
quite as many each from a variety of lesser Italian and French

poets, and quite a number of poems from Latin. He does not use the fourteen-lined sonnet, however. Most of the poems have three stanzas of six lines each—an alternately rhymed quatrain followed by a couplet, which he indents, thus emphasising the shape. His own sonnets in the *Tears of Fancie* have fourteen lines made up of three alternately rhymed quatrains ending in a couplet. As in the poems of the *Passionate Centurie*, the meaning of his sonnets tends to break in three waves. This is not Petrarchan, but it is very English. And certainly Watson's sonnets must have contributed to this becoming the typical Elizabethan or Shakespearean stanza. In a previous book[30] I suggested that this form arose because the poet was really thinking in English song tunes, the alternately rhymed quatrain being a common stanza in English song.

Sidney, although he may have been influenced by Watson, was a man of quite a different type. He was not a translator or man of letters, but belonged in the tradition of courtier love. He wrote his first sonnets for *Arcadia*, a novel in the vein of courtly love. One does not have to read very far into it to find love recognised by the conventional symptoms:[31]

> his eyes sometimes even great with tears, the oft changing of his colour, with a kind of shaking unstayedness over all his body, he might see in his countenance some great determination mixed with fear; and might perceive in him store of thoughts, rather stirred than digested; his words interrupted continually with sighs . . . and the tenour of his speech . . . not knit together to one constant end, but rather dissolved in itself, as the vehemency of the inward passion prevailed.

Yes, this is Plato's madness. And here[32] is a lover complaining, 'I am sick, and sick to the death; I am a prisoner, neither is any redress, but by her to whom I am slave'. In more cheerful mood we find,[33] 'The clouds gave place, that the heavens might more freshly smile upon her; at the least the clouds of my thoughts quite vanished'. Sidney, however, was a man of the world, a soldier, a realist. He can laugh at the unreality as he does in the qualifying sentence in the last quotation. Or again, there is the knight who took[34] love upon him like a fashion; he courted this Lady Artesia, who was as fit to pay him in his own money as might be. For she thinking she did wrong to her beauty if she were not proud of it, called her disdain of him chastity, and placed her honour in little setting by his honouring her.

Sidney makes mirth also out of such complicated and ridiculous situations as that created by Zelmane, the Amazon who is really a knight disguised so that he may get access to the lady he worships. When she remains cold and apparently unaware that he is a man, her mother, more perceptive, falls in love with him, as also does her father, thinking him a woman.

Sidney's sonnet sequence, *Astrophel and Stella,* has this two-faced approach. The poet in him writes under the influence of Italian and French sonneteers, adopts the correct poses and suffers the correct agonies, but the soldier, the man of physical passion, the realist in love with an actual woman, at times sticks out from the polite convention. It was awkward too of the lady to have dark eyes. However he gets out of that difficulty quite neatly. In his sonnets we see what may happen when the real man in a real-love situation has something to say that does not fit the convention. Sidney's sonnets were not published till 1591, six years after his death, but they had circulated in manuscript.

Fulke Greville the exact contemporary and lifelong friend of Sidney wrote love sonnets under his influence, some of them as roughened by crude reality as Sidney's. They belong to this early date, although not published till 1633, along with others of a different character.

Daniel was a tutor in the household of Sidney's sister, the Countess of Pembroke. Twenty-eight of his sonnets first appeared in an appendix to a pirated edition of *Astrophel and Stella* in 1591, but were omitted from the authentic edition of the same year. His own sequence, *Delia,* was printed a year later. Although only eight years younger than Sidney, we might say that Daniel belongs to the next generation of writers. His *Delia* is always said to be very imitative, which is as much as to say he was well soaked in the sonnet stream. Claes Schaar,[35] from his most painstaking and detailed comparison between parallels in Shakespeare and Daniel, shows that they belong in the convention, mostly traceable to foreign models.

Drayton, a contemporary of Daniel, resembles him in many respects. Although his *Idea's Mirrour* was not published till 1594, he could have written it earlier.[36] Anne Goodere, his sonnet love, was the daughter of Sidney's friend, Thomas Goodere. Like Daniel he has the reputation of copying others, and because he also was soaked in sonnet literature. He is not known to have been in London in 1591.[37]

Barnabe Barnes and Constable also, can be thought of rather as Shakespeare's contemporaries than Sidney's. Both were courtiers. Barnes dedicated his sonnet sequence, *Parthenophil and Parthenophe* to his 'dearest friend', William Percy, the son of the Earl of Northumberland, but at the end of his book he adds dedicatory verses to among others, Sidney's sister, the Countess of Pembroke, and Shakespeare's patron, the Earl of Southampton. He fought in France with Essex, but returned to London in October 1591.[38] Although his sonnets were not published till 1593 it is reasonable to suppose that they circulated in manuscript before. He was not a good sonneteer, but he has peculiarities and is interesting from Shakespeare's angle.

Constable[39] travelled about but probably spent 1588 and 1589 at court. He also fought in France with Essex, but had probably written his sonnet sequence, *Diana*, by the end of 1590, although it was not printed till 1592. Joan Grundy, a recent editor, concludes [40] that of the 76 sonnets in *Diana* only 27 are certainly by him. Such a conglomeration of sonnets by different poets published under one man's name suggests that they were at least circulating among the same people, and as eight of those in *Diana* were certainly Sidney's, we may perhaps conclude that he was in the circle with Pembroke connections. Incidentally, apart from those by Sidney, I shall make no attempt to distinguish what is genuinely Constable's and what not, since it makes no difference to my argument.

The history of Spenser as a sonnet writer is unusual. His earliest poems were sonnets, *The Visions of Bellay* and *The Visions of Petrarch*. But they hardly belong in the English stream. They reflect his study of foreign language as a young man rather than are youthful love sequences. He was introduced to Sidney by Gabriel Harvey and owed much to him;

incidentally he dedicated his first book to him and his *Ruines of Time* to his sister, the Countess of Pembroke. Since he was resident in Ireland he possibly did not read Sidney's sonnets and those circulating in manuscript till the end of 1589 when he came to London, where he remained till the spring of 1591, apart from a short absense in 1590.[41] His *Amoretti*, which was registered in Stationers' Hall in November 1594 seems likely to have been stimulated by the sonnet-reading going on about the time of his London visits. If this is so, he was certainly not writing as a young man, for he was forty in 1592. He was enough in the courtly tradition, nevertheless, to dedicate *The Faerie Queene* to Elizabeth. Although she can hardly have taken him as a lover, there was something of this game in the compliments of poets and musicians who thus honoured her as their virgin Queen.

During the years before 1591, and round about then, the sonnets of all these poets almost certainly circulated among their 'private friends', to use Meres' phrase. It is also reasonable to suppose they were the same private friends, as this sudden concentrated creation must have depended on a reciprocal stimulus. Apart from Watson these sonneteers were either courtiers or had connections with the court, or with courtiers. Most are known to have had some connection with the Pembroke circle. A striking number of them at least visited London during this period, and London was by our standards a small town, with a tendency for talent to gravitate to the court. It would not be surprising if Shakespeare were familiar with them all, as he has been proved to be with some.

II

THE SONNET IN
SHAKESPEARE'S PLAYS

Shakespeare was neither a courtier nor a knight. He did not
grow up in any such atmosphere. Although as a person he
seems to have been respected, his status as an actor would not
qualify him to be called a gentleman. It is said that the
Countess of Pembroke in a letter unfortunately lost and therefore not having the best credentials, referred to him as 'the
man Shakespeare'. However, he was certainly designated as a
gentleman later in life, and his humble origin has been
exaggerated. His mother's family owned a farm or a small
estate and his father was a prominent tradesman. Nor was he
without education. His plays by themselves prove this; it is how
much he knew rather than how little that surprises us. The best
education available would have been that at Stratford
Grammar School, and as it was among the better sort of
Grammar School[42] he would have covered some of the ground
studied in the universities. That is to say he must have had a
grounding in grammar, rhetoric and logic—the medieval
trivium. Incidentally it is astounding how long this discipline
survived, for in what was one of the first schools in Scotland to
send girls to the university, they taught it up to about the very
end of the nineteenth century, only with English as the
language studied not Latin, and in a *Grammar,* a *Rhetoric*
and a *Logic* all compiled by the philosopher Alexander Bain.
In Shakespeare's day it involved a thorough grounding in
Latin, including Cicero, Horace, Virgil and particularly
Ovid.[43] They also studied some Greek including Homer and

Hesiod. 'Town' boys like Shakespeare learnt alongside the sons of squires, knights and even noblemen.[44] So we need not presume that Shakespeare arrived in London a country bumpkin. He is much more likely to have been well educated and accustomed to mixing with cultured youths.

In London Shakespeare could have continued his studies. He could have learnt Italian and French, but we have not evidence of it. *Love's Labours Lost* shows that he must have picked up some very elementary French and Italian, and suggests that he might have at least looked into a book used in teaching Italian, although he may only have heard youths talking about it. There is the most frail evidence that he might have read a French sonnet or so. But until a thorough research into this question has been done, we must assume that his knowledge of foreign literature was confined to that in translations, with Latin, perhaps even Greek, as a possible exception. When similarities between Shakespeare's sonnets and those of other sonneteers appear to come from the same French models, the inference should be that they borrowed from the French models, and Shakespeare from them. Certainly at this moment in history, that seems what should be assumed.

For the rest we can be sure that Shakespeare was at least in touch with literate young men of his day, and must have known what they thought about and were interested in. It was to London rather than to the universities that most young men, even of noble families, came to be educated.[45] Queen Elizabeth encouraged her nobles to attend court so that she could keep an eye on them, and London catered for the sons of the lesser nobility, who did not have their own tutors for their children. There was a real enthusiasm for education at this time, and there were not only good schools for boys in London, but classes for older youths in such things as foreign languages.[45] The Inns of Court gave many of the advantages of a university, with Gray's Inn specially catering for the aristocracy. Shakespeare wrote for this enthusiastic, highly educated, aristocratically dominated audience.[45] And he must have been educated to do so. It was not an exclusive audience, however, for even the ordinary man enjoyed his Tottel, as we can see from Slender's saying in *The Merry Wives of Windsor,*

I had rather than forty shillings I had my Book of Songs and
Sonnets here.

Incidentally, a copy of Tottel which Shakespeare gave Robert
Brome of Lichfield still exists.[46]

In *Love's Labours Lost* Shakespeare makes fun of the
educational background of young men of his day, assessing its
weaknesses in human terms. It is most relevant from our point
of view since the sonnet fashion stands in the foreground.
Indeed it could be described as a play about young sonneteers
against the background of their academic education. The title
page of the earliest printing in 1598 states that this is the play
as 'presented before her Highness this last Christmas. Newly
corrected and augmented'. This implies an earlier play of
which we have no copy. But it is evident that it must have been
written when sonnet writing had a topical interest. We do not
know the date when this earlier version was written, but there
are certainly arguments that it was early enough for a not too
distant comment on the sonnet fashion of about 1590–1. The
sonnet criticism in the play itself makes the best evidence for
this.

In Florio's *First Fruits,* a textbook used in the teaching of
Italian by dialogue, many of the young men in Shakespeare's
audience must have read :

We need not speak so much of love, all books are full of
love; with so many authors, that it were labour lost to speak
of love :[47]

The last words of this quotation seem to have given Shakespeare his title, the 'labour lost' of speaking of 'love'. Since the
speaking of love in the play includes sonnet writing, this is one
of the lost labours. The joke made by Florio is likely to have
been remembered. Not only so, one of the themes for discussion
in *Second Fruits*[48] was the question whether the Petrarchan
ideal of women or something quite the opposite was the real
truth about them. And finally a parody of Florio was published in April 1593; so if it is possible that *Love's Labours
Lost* was written in that year, Shakespeare would be exploiting
a topical interest.[49]

The setting of the play in the court of Navarre has made a puzzle. It has been suggested that it implies an earlier play that might account for this and other anomalies. On the other hand it is at least an interesting coincidence that both Constable and Barnes had been soldiers at the court of Navarre and returned to England sonnet-writers. Whether this was the fact is no matter, provided it seemed so. Or there may have been an association between Navarre, sonnet writing and Platonic ideals in the minds of Shakespeare's audience. The court of Navarre might seem a suitable scene for the philosophic and chivalric ideals that gave a background to sonnet writing.

The suggestions of the title and of the setting are followed out in the play. The main plot of *Love's Labours Lost* has love and sonnet writing as its theme. The courtiers fall in love and the immediate, and Shakespeare suggests, inevitable result is sonnet writing; this is what you do if you fall in love. So also does the shadow knight, Armado, write a sonnet when he falls ridiculously in love with even so unpoetical a lady as Jaquenetta. The next step is taken when their sonnets make it apparent to everyone that all of them—king and three courtiers—are in love. It remains to prove that their talking of love is lost labour.

The comic scenes range wider than love and sonnet writing, but they are integrated into the main plot by the sonnet. Armado's fantastic, chivalric love makes the sonnet love absurd at once. Holofernes and Sir Nathaniel, although for the most part they stand outside the main plot, are at first integrated into it by Berowne's sonnet falling into their hands. They comment, and Holofernes promises to pull it to pieces at a dinner to which he is going, and to which he invites Sir Nathaniel. When 'the gentles are at their game' of deer-hunting, he says, 'we will to our recreation', which Moth later describes as eating words. When next we see them, they are discussing Armado, whom Sir Nathaniel has 'conversed with' recently. Moth sums it all up : 'They have been at a great feast of languages, and stolen the scraps'.

In this sort of way, the sonnet magnet draws into its field the whole educational background of Elizabethan youth. Shakespeare makes fun not only of artifices of speaking, of Armado's chivalry and his fantastic speech, but also of the pedantry of

Holofernes and Sir Nathaniel. So he creates young man laughter. Although education included other things which he laughs at, like arithmetic and astronomy commonly studied at the universities, it was largely a matter of language study, of spelling, pronunciation, grammar, rhetoric, logic and philosophy. This made the mental background of young men, which their tutors and schoolmasters and parents—everyone in authority—had been conditioning them to think important. And Shakespeare makes fun of it. Similarly his love talk is about sonnet love, courtly love, Platonic love, in fact literary love, the young courtier poets' fashionable game. This also was in the young men's background. I take it he is not making a personal attack on any one teacher or group of philosophers, although this has been suggested. The mood of the play is not censorious, and the oddities he guys are largely those of education or fashion in general, with perhaps some minor exceptions. It is laughter-provoking rather than a matter of serious criticism. But let us look at it in more detail.

Love's Labours Lost opens, not as one might expect, with love. Shakespeare makes an important point at once, for the real motive of the sonneteer, as of the whole genus poet, is fame; and this is the theme he begins with :

> *King*   Let fame, that all hunt after in their lives,
> Live registered upon our brazen tombs,
> And then grace us, in the disgrace of death;
> When, spite of cormorant devouring time,
> The endeavour of this present breath may buy
> That honour which shall bate his scythe's keen edge,
> And make us heirs of all eternity.

Since fame is what they want, or more particularly since they want to be poets, the young men forswear women; they will 'war against' their own affections or feelings, and the world. The King continues,

> Our court shall be a little academe,
> Still and contemplative in living art.

Like Horace and Ovid whose words they have borrowed, they are to practise 'living art', the art that defies death and will make their names live for ever. There was a fashion for 'little academes'. Puttenham in his *Arte of Poesie*,[50] which no doubt the young poet would know well since it teaches his art, has this bit of 'history':

> For the better execution of that high charge and function [of being a poet, the first poets lived] chaste and in all holiness of life, and in continual study and contemplation; they came by instinct divine, and by deep meditation, and much abstinence . . . to be made apt to receive visions, both waking and sleeping.

This is the model for their academe, for they are all by nature poets, potential sonnet writers. The play tests the rationality of it. It breaks down first because women cannot be shut out like this. Practical necessity, a very good philosophical cause, brings them into contact. By natural and inevitable steps they fall in love and are led on by degrees to the entry of the death they have defied. It proves the big words of the opening, and which the King has borrowed from among the greatest Latin poets, to be nonsense.

Berowne is the play's first critic, the chorus who comments. He begins by attacking the contemplative basis, and particularly the study they are to devote themselves to:

> Oh, these are barren tasks, too hard to keep,
> Not to see ladies, study, fast, not sleep.

Adopting the philosopher's method, he asks, 'What is the end of study?' This was the sententious question of philosophy, concerned first of all with the purpose of things. The question here is therefore a joke, and the answers of the courtiers quite unsatisfactory. He concludes,

> Small have continual plodders ever won,
> Save base authority from others' books.
>
>   .   .   .   .   .
>
> Too much to know is to know nought but fame.

So, says Berowne,

Study me how to please the eye indeed,
    By fixing it upon a fairer eye,
Who dazzled so, that eye shall be his heed.
    And give him light that it was blinded by.

And this is precisely what every sonneteer does. There is a
theory that Shakespeare had Chapman in mind and that
Berowne mocks him. But everything he says is applicable to the
sonneteering poets of the day and more generally applicable to
them than to the one poet Chapman.

Berowne then reminds the King that the French Princess is
coming to negotiate on behalf of her sick father. So he points
out that study,

While it doth study to have what it would,
It doth forget to do the thing it should.

Then, in the language of the schools he proves that they will be
forsworn 'on mere necessity'.

When they all fall in love, Berowne too takes this fall. It
hurts him worst because it undermines his confidence, his sense
of being in command of himself. We have already seen love
natural in Costard and fantastically phrased in Armado. This
comic introduction makes Berowne's falling into its power all
the funnier. But he does not try to get back his self-respect by
self-deception as Armado does, making himself ridiculous by so
doing. Berowne is the genuine man among the courtiers, as
Costard is among the comics; indeed we could call him the
courtier jester. He makes the same comment on himself as on
others, and accepts the truth however much he dislikes it. So
far from trying to excuse himself by finding heroes in his plight
like Armado does to get back his dignity, he kicks himself :

What I! I love! I sue! I seek a wife!

But he submits to his fate :

Well, I will love, write, sigh, pray, sue and groan.

The lot! When next he enters he is still in this typical sonnet
mood :

By heaven, I do love, and it hath taught me to rhyme,
And to be melancholy . . . Well,
She hath one o' my sonnets already.

Clearly, love is there not only to prove study and philosophy nonsense, but to provide a target. The hilarity gathers as one after another of the court party enters with his sonnet, and each ashamed to acknowledge that he has fallen. It reaches a climax when Berowne's disgrace is revealed.

The sonnets in the play say what all sonnets do. They need nothing more to be comic than to be characteristic of the fashion. The King has :

So sweet a kiss the golden sun gives not
To those fresh morning drops upon the rose,
As thy eye-beams, when their fresh rays have smote
The night of dew that on my cheeks down flows.

Her face shows like a moon in his tears. Then to cap the absurdity—but it is not more absurd than the fancy of some serious sonneteers :

No drop but as a coach doth carry thee,
So ridest thou triumphing in my woe.

He begs her not to keep his tears for glasses (in which she can see herself).

Longaville has caught the authentic note too. Indeed his is in the typical fourteen lines :

Did not the heavenly rhetoric of thine eye,
'Gainst whom the world cannot hold argument,
Persuade my heart to this false perjury?
Vows for thee broke deserve not punishment.
A woman I forswore, but I will prove,
Thou being a goddess, I forswore not thee.
My vow was earthly, thou a heavenly love.
Thy grace being gained cures all disgrace in me.

She is not only, as is usual, a goddess but again as usual, her grace cures his disgrace. Countless sonneteers have said this

B

with less clarity, and without the excuse of a broken oath. Berowne comments :

> This is the liver vein, which makes flesh a deity,
> A green goose a goddess—pure, pure idolatry,
> God amend us, God amend us, we are much out of the way.

Taken seriously sonnet talk would be blasphemous. Berowne points this out with his mockery. The poet being in disgrace with his lady is as common as the woman being a goddess. It is also common form to feel worthless when one is in love. But if the lady is kind then she cures all hurts, among them this disgrace.

Dumaine's song is even commoner :

> On a day, alack the day!
> Love, whose month is ever May.

So on it trips. Katharine characterises it as,

> A huge translation of hypocrisy,
> Vilely compiled, profound simplicity.

The King who has heard most of their attempts from his hiding place says,

> 'Ay me', says one! 'Oh Jove' the other cries!
> One, her hairs were gold, crystal the other's eyes.

Berowne when he knows they are all in it, gives unashamed vent to his passion in the approved sonnet terms. He is 'blinded' by Rosaline's 'majesty'. (She did not seem very majestic playing with Boyet). But he is irrepressible :

> Oh! but for my love, day would turn to night!

He says her eyes are the sun that makes 'all things shine'. The King laughs :

> By heaven thy love is black to ebony.

But Berowne retorts,

Is ebony like her? Oh wood divine!

Dumaine and Longaville comment, 'To look like her are chimney-sweepers black', and 'since her time are colliers counted bright'. This is an obvious skit on Sidney's defence of his dark love which Shakespeare parodies also in his sonnet sequence. But Berowne is undaunted :

I'll prove her fair, or talk till doomsday here.

He falls into a rapture on love :

It adds a precious seeing to the eye;
A lover's eyes will gaze an eagle blind;
A lover's ears will hear the lowest sound,
When the suspicious heed of theft is stopped;
Love's feeling is more soft and sensible
Than are the tender horns of cockled snails;
Love's tongue proves dainty Bacchus gross in taste.
For valour, is not love a Hercules,
Still climbing trees in the Hesperides?
Subtle as Sphinx, as sweet and musical
As bright Apollo's lute, strung with his hair;
And, when love speaks, the voice of all the gods
Make heaven drowsy with the harmony.
Never durst poet touch a pen to write,
Until his ink were tempered with love's sighs;
Oh, then his lines would ravish savage ears,
And plant in tyrants mild humility.
From women's eyes this doctrine I derive:
They sparkle still the right Promethean fire—
They are the books, the arts, the academes,
That show, contain, and nourish all the world;
Else none at all in aught proves excellent.

This is the real tune and tempo of love, not something clipped to fit the fixed sonnet structure. Ardour and passion drive Berowne along in a gale of boisterous feeling, that makes the sonnet progress seem mincing. It is as if Shakespeare gives the final blow to sonnet love by this spontaneous outburst. But we may notice that it is not less ridiculous than the sonnets. Berowne has substituted love for contemplation and the pursuit of fame. And in its turn, Shakespeare will overturn this unbalanced enthusiasm also.

The comic plot, if 'plot' does not suggest too much action, is integrated into the main theme in the first scene. The King introduces Armado and describes him as a 'refinéd traveller of Spain'—

> A man in all the world's new fashions planted,
> That hath a mint of phrases in his brain.

He will tell them

> In high-born words the worth of many a knight.

Berowne calls him, 'A man of fire-new words, fashion's own knight'. Immediately on this, Dull the constable enters. One of his language contributions is malapropisms. In this the clown Costard does his part too. Dull has come with a letter accusing Costard, who explains :

> Sir, the contempts thereof are as touching me.

Berowne says,

> How low soever the matter, I hope in God for high words.

Costard's function here is to present both love and high words as absurd. His speech makes fun of exalted talk and his love is absurdly natural—at the extreme from sonnet-love which is purely an intellectual play. He introduces it as if he were clarifying some legal point—'in the manner and form following'. Armado's letter has a similar analytic formality. He explains that he witnessed the 'crime'.

> When? about the sixth hour, When beasts most graze, birds best peck, and men sit down to that nourishment called supper: So much for the time when. Now for the ground which?

So much for the grammar of the situation. And for the diction-ary aspect we have, the ebon-coloured ink, which here thou viewest, beholdest, surveyest, or seeth.

This is sufficiently ridiculous in itself, but it is made more so by Costard bringing high-falutin phrases down to his most natural self. The letter continues,

> There did I see that low-spirited swain, that base minion of thy mirth.

Costard: Me?

We then have the comic juxtaposition in reverse. Armado has seen Costard with a ... Costard interrupts, 'With a wench'. Armado continues,

> with a child of our Grandmother Eve, a female; or for thy more sweet understanding a Woman.

When he hears his sentence, Costard protests,

> I suffer for the truth sir; for true it is I was taken with Jaquenetta, and Jaquenetta is a true girl.

So indeed it is. This is the first plain fact in an artificial world. Not only so, Costard's naturalness throws up the falseness of the sonnet-love situation, and his genuineness Armado's unreality. To Moth Armado says,

> Boy, what sign is it when a man of great spirit grows melancholy?

He 'confesses' he is in love—and with Costard's wench. In keeping with his great spirit he looks for other great heroes who have been in love. He complains as the poets do :

> Love is a familiar; love is a devil. There is no evil angel but love.

So after their manner he goes about sighing and calling,

> Assist me some extemporal god of rhyme, for I am sure I shall turn sonnet. Devise wit, write pen, for I am for whole volumes in folio.

His sonnet written, he gives Costard 'a remuneration' for carrying it. Bringing his language to the test of common reality, 'that's the Latin for three-farthings', says Costard. To get the two plots intertwined, Shakespeare makes Berowne send Costard on the same errand with, 'There's thy guerdon'. Costard calculates:

> Gardon, oh sweet gardon! better than remuneration, eleven-pence farthing better.

Of the comics, Holofernes and Nathaniel are not very carefully knit into the play. They suddenly walk on and talk, just talk in the fantastic manner of pedants. Dull's stupidity acts as their foil. They are clever and foolish and he is stupid but sensible. He guys their pomposity by insisting on the plain and obvious fact:

> 'Twas not a *haud credo*, 'twas a pricket.

He insists on it, and returns to it long after everyone else has gone on to something else:

> And I say beside that 'twas a pricket that the Princess killed.

He thus insists on his correctness, just as the schoolmaster insists on his correctness, and equally ridiculously. Nathaniel finds excuses for him.

> Sir, he hath never fed of the dainties that are bred in a book. He hath not eat paper, as it were; he hath not drunk ink.

A later bout of words strikes Dull dumb, and to Holofernes' comment of, 'Via, good man Dull! Thou hast spoken no word all this while', he replies, 'Nor understood none, neither, sir!'

I need not illustrate the uproarious nonsense of the talk about language that follows, in all its pedantry, with Holofernes laying down the law and demonstrating his superiority. He well deserves to meet his match in Berowne's baiting at the end, when at last he is put out. Shakespeare gives him the schoolmaster's final word:

This is not generous, not gentle, not humble,

followed I do not doubt by the audience's delighted laughter, for they must have recognised in its appeal to their better nature, the superior being giving the mature protest at their childish thoughtlessness. 'Alas, poor Maccabaeus, how hath he been baited!' even his final word turned to laughter. Only the Princess feels sympathy for him. But it has been done in the festive spirit; oppressed youth has got its own back in this holiday mirth.

A great many of the absurdities in the comic scenes have been shown to be easily recognisable hits at topical education or educators, or at fantastic learning. Florio was probably the young Earl of Southampton's tutor. Dover Wilson suggests that the play may have been written first for Southampton's friends. This seems a good guess, although it is just a guess. There have been attempts to identify the comic characters as parodies of particular people. But they are types, many of them common types. Their oddities are not those of one particular person. It does not look as if Shakespeare has chosen targets because he had anything against some particular man, but guyed things that were ridiculous in themselves wherever he found them. Thus although the play certainly has topical references, and left quite a number of books and people with darts sticking in them, it is less personalities that Shakespeare laughs at than absurdities of talk. In this the comic scenes resemble those of the main plot. The whole play is lighthearted. This is not the voice of malice; it is not even a moral comment; it makes laughter at what is ridiculous in itself if one has the detachment to see it. Just as Shakespeare found speaking of love was like a great meadow where he found many different flowers to laugh at, so in the comic scenes he chose from a large field. He shows how the ridiculous proliferates in this sort of soil.

Enter the Princess. This is an electrical moment in sonnet history. The lady of the sonnets has not come onto the page before. We have seen her only through the 'madness' of her lover, as his goddess or his devil—a shifting image in a raging fever. Very often she has not existed at all outside the poet's imagination, and when she seems to have been an actual identi-

fiable woman there has always been someone to doubt it. Now
here she is. She states her point of view, and gives a judgement
on the situation. It is sane, unprejudiced, but very critical.
Indeed she would be too critical, were this not the precise
function for which Shakespeare has created her. She begins by
snubbing Boyet's flattery, the sonnet commonplace that nature
'did starve the general world beside' and gave her all the
graces. To this she replies,

> I am less proud to hear you tell my worth
> Than you much willing to be counted wise
> In spending your wit in the praise of mine.

That is a quite devastating truth about sonnet talk. 'Avaunt
perplexity!', she says in the last act when he reflects this aspect
of sonnet style. She puts exaggeration in perspective; when
Maria describes Longaville as having a wit, 'Whose edge has
power to cut,' and wills to spare none, she comments, 'Some
merry mocking Lord, belike,' and 'Such short-lived wits do
wither as they grow'. Her ladies are soon in love, and she with
them. She enters at the beginning of act IV asking,

> Was that the King that spurred his horse so hard
> Against the steep-up rising of the hill?

In the deer-hunt she is the sonnet lady who wounds her lover
—one of their common images, to which the sonneteers
respond in various ways, as often as not wishing she would kill
them outright. This is where the princess now stands. Like all
the sonnet ladies she has been placed there by those who serve
her, and given bow and arrow. It is her function to kill the
deer. But she does not know whether she can, and considers
what attitude she will assume if she manages to, and what if
she only wounds :

> now mercy goes to kill,
> And shooting well is then accounted ill.
> Thus will I save my credit in the shoot:
> Not wounding, pity would not let me do't;
> If wounding, then it was to show my skill,

That more for praise than purpose meant to kill.
And, out of question, so it is sometimes:
Glory grows guilty of detested crimes,
When, for fame's sake, for praise, an outward part,
We bend to that the working of the heart:
As I for praise alone now seek to spill
The poor deer's blood, that my heart means no ill.

Love does not come into this. She, like the King, acts out of a desire for fame, for praise is a sort of feminine fame,

—and praise we may afford
To any lady that subdues a lord.

This is immediately followed by the arrival of Armado's letter to Jaquenetta, and so by the information that Berowne has been wounded by Rosaline. Then follow smutty exchanges between Boyet and the ladies. This sort of banter is quite uncharacteristic of Shakespeare. He can be coarse enough; his women are not prudish. Rosalind in *As you like it* is far from being a Victorian ignoramus, but the ladies in *Love's Labours Lost* have sex—sex not the love situation—as the one target of their wit. Their interest plays around it; this seems what is chiefly in their minds. The joke is obvious enough. Shakespeare seems to say : Here are your ladies, whom you represent in your sonnets as too chaste to give you any encouragement, as they really are, enjoying flirting with impurity. The Princess has more dignity than her ladies, but she accepts it all. Her aim is Shakespeare's—if we may put it like that—to get as much fun out of the situation as possible. Lovers are to be laughed at. This makes part of the recognised love-game. She has some reserve, however, for contrary to what the sonneteers say of her she is tender-hearted; she did not kill the deer for fun. It is Rosaline who says,

They are worse fools to purchase mocking so.
That same Berowne I'll torture ere I go.
Oh, that I knew he were but in by the week,
How I would make him fawn, and beg, and seek,
And wait the season, and observe the times,
And spend his prodigal wits in bootless rhymes,

And shape his service wholly to my hests,
And make him proud to make me proud, that jests!
So planet-like would I o'ersway his state
That he should be my fool, and I his fate.

In fact she would make him into a sonneteer. The Princess
comments on the criticism, acting as chorus for Shakespeare's
own opinion.

> *Princess:* None are so surely caught, when they are catched,
> As wit turned fool. Folly, in wisdom hatched,
> Hath wisdom's warrant, and the help of school,
> And wit's own grace to grace a learnéd fool.
> *Rosaline:* The blood of youth burns not with such excess,
> As gravity's revolt to wantonness.
> *Maria:* Folly in fools bears not so strong a note
> As foolery in the wise, when wit doth dote:
> Since all the power thereof it doth apply,
> To prove, by wit, worth in simplicity.

This throws up the unity of *Love's Labours Lost* where the
sonnet-folly and the pedants' folly belong together. All 'clever-
ness' is childish. Maria ends with one of the positive ideas in
the play, that of 'worth in simplicity'.

Boyet enters promising more mirth, for the courtiers are
about to come masked as Russians—a childish approach as the
ladies think it. He describes the preparation which he has
overheard. The King was giving instructions to their herald, 'a
pretty knavish page' :

> 'Thus must thou speak', and 'thus thy body bear';
> And ever and anon they made a doubt
> Presence majestical would put him out:
> 'For,' quoth the King, 'an angel shalt thou see;
> Yet fear not thou, but speak audaciously.'
> The boy replied, 'An angel is not evil;
> I should have feared her had she been a devil'.

That is another sonnet hit. The Princess arranges to cross
them, for she sees the real truth of the situation :

> They do it but in mockery-merriment,
> And mock for mock is only my intent.
>
> . . . . . .
>
> So shall we stay, mocking intended game,
> And they, well mocked, depart away with shame.

After the Russian fiasco the Princess comments that there is most mirth 'When great things labouring perish in their birth', and Berowne admits, 'A right description of our sports'. He now takes over again as critic. Boyet pandering to both sides, tries to laugh with the courtiers by saying in a meaningful way, perhaps with a wink, that he knows the Princess will receive them. Berowne expresses disgust :

> This gallant pins the wenches on his sleeve.
> Had he been Adam, he had tempted Eve.
>
> . . . . . .
>
> This is the ape of form, monsieur the nice,
>
> . . . . . .
>
> This is the flower that smiles on every one,
> To show his teeth as white as whalës bone.

It is the severest criticism of Boyet, and he deserves it, although everyone else in the play, like him, has as their real aim, to display themselves. The Princess and Berowne stand out only because they recognise their own weakness. Berowne comes to think he has learnt his lesson. He confesses to Rosaline,

> Oh, never will I trust to speeches penned,
>   Nor to the motion of a schoolboy's tongue,
> Nor never come in vizard to my friend,
>   Nor woo in rhyme, like a blind harper's song.
> Taffeta phrases, silken terms precise,
>   Three-piled hyperboles, spruce affectation,
> Figures pedantical—these summer-flies
>   Have blown me full of maggot ostentation.
> I do forswear them, and I here protest,
>   By this white glove (how white the hand, God knows!)
> Henceforth my wooing mind shall be expressed
>   In russet yeas and honest kersey noes.
> And, to begin, wench—so God help me, la!—
>   My love to thee is sound, sans crack or flaw.

Rosaline picks him up on 'sans', and he admits it. Certainly one of the lessons of *Love's Labours Lost* has been learnt. We have a sense of approaching the end. And here again we may notice that Shakespeare links together poet and pedant. He implies that we all make ourselves important in similar ridiculous ways, and when we do, the intelligent man's folly is more stupid than the foolishness of the simple. The Princess was aware of this from the beginning. She sees it in herself. She is gentler with herself than Berowne with himself, and so she is gentler in her criticism of others. The lesson of the play is learnt when this comment comes to the fore and is accepted. We are now ready for the end.

Death that puts an end to the play makes a surprising conclusion. We do not expect this of a comedy. Even in a tragedy it has to be prepared for. Actually *Love's Labours Lost* makes a formal preparation for it. The *hubris* of the opening perhaps should have warned us, but we are accustomed to the full-toned bombast of the opening lines. The young scholar takes it as memorable Latin verse and does not consider it seriously, or he would tremble for it as tempting fate. But Shakespeare has given a genuine response to it in all seriousness. This may be something we should not forget about him—that he takes the statements of poetry seriously. There are other warnings of death also. Thus the Princess is here to represent a father too ill to cope with the situation. The end should be expected. The King opened the action by proclaiming that they will get the better of death by making themselves famous as poets. It ends by death having the last word about this and everything else.

The function of death in this comedy is not so very dissimilar from its function in tragedy, for death cannot make a comic conclusion except in melodrama. We could say its function in *Love's Labours Lost* is to make a sort of purgation, a *catharsis* of unrelieved wit. It does so by shattering all the shams in the play. Even the Princess, the one genuine character in the main plot, always steady and balanced, now speaks 'Out of a new-sad soul'. She has a new humility; she begs forgiveness for 'The liberal opposition of our spirits', or in plain prose her free indulgence in contradicting. Instead of blaming the courtiers' game, or answering it in mockery, she would now excuse her faults as due to their gentleness. And she excuses her own plain speech :

A heavy heart bears not a nimble tongue.

This could be taken as implying that the nimble-tongued sonnets have no depth of feeling. But Shakespeare's own change of mood has touched a new depth too. Death has swept the whole artificial world away; there is no longer any point-scoring. The Princess is too stunned to think of anything else. She cannot take in what the King is laboriously trying to say. And here Shakespeare intends criticism. 'I understand you not,' she says. (Perhaps just as well considering the egoism he has shown.) Berowne rushes in :

Honest plain words best pierce the ear of grief.

But his speech is quite as egoistic and quite as laboriously expressed as the King's. To put it shortly he says their 'unbefitting strains' are the fault of the Princess and her ladies :

Our love being yours, the error that love makes
Is likewise yours.

This is typical sonnet logic. The Princess replies with dignity, 'We have received your letters' and 'rated them At courtship, pleasant jest, and courtesy'. The ladies have

A time methinks too short
To make a world-without-end bargain in.

But if at the end of the year the King returns and challenges her, she will have him. Till then she will mourn her father. Her ladies follow suit and give tests to their lovers. Berowne's discipline of visiting the sick and talking with 'groaning wretches' will teach him the value of wit :

A jest's prosperity lies in the ear
Of him that hears it, never in the tongue
Of him that makes it.

Armado now enters to bind all together. He too will come down to earth for three years to win Jaquenetta. Boaster and coward, he can at least do this, although his chosen work is still ridiculous.

For the most part in the play Shakespeare has shown what is absurd by laughing at it. He gives a serious answer at the end, by making reality the test of truth. Life has situations of hurtful reality. One of them teaches the Princess humility. She has seemed an adequate judge before, but now she apologises for her faults. By jest and laughter Berowne has made the right comments, but now he is sent to test the value of jesting against the ultimate horrors of life. When the plague is in your street nothing false or superficial stands. This is a play of gradually deepening layers of meaning. It begins with parodying sonnet attitudes; it widens to include all sorts of ridiculous fashions in language study and usage. At length we become aware of the self-deception not only of the pedants, of Armado and the other comics, but of everyone in the play without exception. We all make ourselves important, perhaps to protect ourselves against death. The play can be read like that. But when death enters we learn that it must be allowed the last word. It reduces us to the final truth about ourselves. It has all turned out to be much more than a comment or a skit on sonnet writing although no doubt the great oak was all there in that seed about fame in the opening lines. This was an extraordinarily mature play for a young man to write. It has a wisdom, even a profundity we do not expect from what in some respects resembles a college rag. Perhaps however, it was written during the plague years, and this may be enough to account for it.

Love's Labours Lost sprang out of poetry. The sonnet is its formal theme. It is therefore appropriate that it should end with two silly little songs. They make as surprising a bathos as the sudden entry of death was unexpected. They sing a mimi-cry of the play. 'When daisies pied and violets blue' with its piping shepherds and maidens bleaching summer smocks, and its pretty springtime love, is followed by a shattering parody, made out of the indignities and hardships of the menial situa-tion with Marion's nose red and raw, and greasy Joan keeling the pot, Shakespeare faces the unreality with stark reality. He does in little what the play has done in a wide sweep—shows the falseness of these pretty love songs by juxtaposing the truth. In the play he put the love sonnet in its context of poetic artifices, gave the poets pedants for partners in the language game, and the fantastic knight as their partner in love. The sonnet speaking of love and the pretty love ditty belong with all useless things, all lost labours. But this is not all. It is not just poetry that fails life. Even Costard had not the rights of it, for Jaquenetta did not prove a true girl to him. Even jesting is not fit for all occasions. The only thing that remains is 'honest plain words' and simple truth, and the hope that the passing of time, which the courtiers began by decrying, may do more for them all than give Dumaine a beard. Just as the young men who defied death and love ended by submitting to the judgements of both, so the game of the May Day song is answered by the undignified parody.

The final words—'The words of Mercury are harsh after the songs of Apollo'—have puzzled critics. One thing we may be certain of, if we cannot find a relevant meaning in them, then our interpretation of the play must be wrong. If the interpretation I have given is accepted, there in no difficulty. Indeed the end corroborates it. Apollo is the god of poetry. Mercury as identified with Hermes, is the messenger who conducted dead souls to the underworld. The words of Mercury summoning one to death are harsh after the poets' songs. Or there may be a more specific reference to the play. It started with a song of Apollo making a confident claim of defeating death's oblivion, but when at the end of the play death had the last words 'after' the songs of Apollo, they were harsh indeed. So here, after the two little songs, come the harsh words of Mercury. The triple coda repeats the argument of the play. After the sonnets were mocked, then death entered. So after the springtime song is mocked, we are reminded that Mercury speaks harshly after the songs of Apollo.

Whenever Shakespeare mentions sonnets in his plays he does it as a joke—this without exception. In his early days he seems to have given much thought to the attitudes they presume, and to have considered them puerile. We can see this in *The Two Gentlemen of Verona*, a play of which it is not really too much to say that although it contains memorable stuff, it can be sensibly interpreted only on the supposition of being a calcu-

lated farce. Derek Traversi put it respectfully as 'a revelation
of the limitations of the romantic attitude to love',[51] its aim
being 'to free valid human attachments from excess and empti-
ness, restoring them to a sane and balanced conception of life'.
Silvia and Julia 'oppose to corrupt convention their own firm
and clear-eyed view of reality'. Another way of putting it is to
say that both Valentine and Proteus are quite unconvincing as
persons. They are cardboard figures cut to literary poses, for
they have literary poses rather than anything so real as a
corrupt way of life.

The play is about their Platonic friendship and sonnet love.
It opens with the friends saying farewell. Proteus has been
trying to persuade Valentine to stay at home but he will not
live 'sluggarised'. Proteus is held by his love for Julia, which
is described in sonnet terms and presented as foolish, an
immature pose. He does not love her at all, but has learnt the
art of love from books. Valentine sees this and accuses him. He
answers,

> Yet writers say; As in the sweetest bud
> The eating cancer dwells, so eating love
> Inhabits in the finest wits of all.

Valentine mocks, 'And writers say; ...' This is really all the
youths know about love. Proteus has learnt to be the sort of
sonnet lover the courtiers are in *Love's Labours Lost*, only he
is more callow. Julia, he says,

> Made me neglect my studies, lose my time;
> War with good counsel; set the world at nought;
> Made wit with musing weak; heart sick with thought.

When he is forced into absence he complains in sonnet
imagery:

> Oh, how this spring of love resembleth
>   The uncertain glory of an April day,
> Which now shows all the beauty of the sun,
>   And by and by a cloud takes all away.

Valentine too, when he later falls in love has sonnet signs, as
Speed reports them :

> to relish a love-song . . . to walk alone . . . to weep . . . . to fast . . .
> to watch.

He twits his master :

> *Speed:*   If you love her, you cannot see her.
> *Valentine:* Why?
> *Speed:*   Because love is blind.

Again he says,

> Ay, but hearken Sir: though the chameleon love can feed on
> air, I am one that am nourished by my victuals.

Julia is Proteus' first love whom he may forsake for a finer
love without infringing the rules. He does so by falling in love
with Valentine's lady. This also is a permissible situation. The
lady may receive the love of as many lovers as she likes. She is
'mistress' of all her 'servants'. Shakespeare mocks the situation.
He makes Silvia play the game with her lovers with a conscious
affectation, in contrast with their serious and self-deceptive
posing. The scene where Valentine introduces Proteus to her
opens :

> *Silvia:*   Servant.
> *Valentine:* Mistress !

He introduces Proteus :

> > This is the gentleman I told your ladyship
> > Had come along with me, but that his mistress
> > Did hold his eyes locked in her crystal looks.
> *Silvia:*   Belike that now she hath enfranchised them
> > Upon some other pawn for fealty.
> *Valentine:* Nay, sure, I think she holds them prisoners still.
> *Silvia:*   Nay, then he should be blind—and, being blind,
> > How could he see his way to seek you out?

So on it goes, Silvia mocking. He presents his friend so :

Valentine: Sweet lady, entertain him
                   To be my fellow-servant to your ladyship.
Silvia: Too low a mistress for so high a servant.
Proteus: Not so, sweet lady, but too mean a servant
                   To have a look of such a worthy mistress.

                   .   .   .   .   .

Valentine: Sweet lady, entertain him for your servant

             .   .   .   .   .

Silvia: Servant, you are welcome to a worthless mistress.

             .   .   .   .   .

                   Once more, new servant, welcome.

The lovers express no love that is not in sonnet imagery.
Thus the lover's being enfranchised by some other pawn when
he changes his lady is a reference to Barnes' sixth sonnet where
his new love offers herself as a pawn to liberate the poet's heart
in love with his first lady. Indeed we could almost say that
their love *is* sonnet imagery. Thus Proteus asks Silvia for her
portrait :

> Vouchsafe me yet your picture for my love,
> The picture that is hanging in your chamber:
> To that I'll speak, to that I'll sigh and weep:
> For since the substance of your perfect self
> Is else devoted, I am but a shadow;
> And to your shadow—will I make true love.

This shadow-substance, with the shadow sometimes a portrait,
is a sonnet commonplace derived from Plato's theory of
created things being imperfect reflections or shadows of the
ideal uncreated substance or essence. What he is saying is that
since she is vowed to Valentine, he is only a shadow, but he will
make love to her portrait which is a shadow of her perfection.
Valentine uses the same imagery when he suffers the common
fate of sonneteers in being banished from his lady—a fate
almost 'prescribed' for the sonnet lover :

> What light is light, if Silvia be not seen?
> What joy is joy, if Silvia be not by?
> Unless it be to think that she is by,
> And feed upon the shadow of perfection . . .
>
> .   .   .   .   .
>
> She is my essence—and I leave to be,

If I be not by her fair influence
Fostered, illumined, cherished, kept alive ...

If we are in any doubt about this sonnet-talk being intended to seem unreal, we can be sure of it from Proteus' advice to Trurio on how to woo Silvia :

You must lay lime to tangle her desires
By wailful sonnets, whose composéd rhymes
Should be full-fraught with serviceable vows.

It is presented as a technique. The sonnets are 'wailful' rather than expressions of real agonies. They are 'composéd' rhymes, rather than natural. The ship makes a common sonnet image, and this is suggested in 'full-fraught'. How are we to interpret 'serviceable'? Possibly we are intended to notice the double sense, the pun. The vows protest service, but if Silvia falls for this, then they will have served Trurio well. Proteus even tells him what to say :

Say that upon the altar of her beauty
You sacrifice your tears, your sighs, your heart:
Write till your ink be dry: and with your tears
Moist it again: and frame some feeling line
That may discover such integrity ...
For Orpheus' lute was strung with poets' sinews—
Whose golden touch could soften steel and stones;
Make tigers tame and huge leviathans
Forsake unsounded deeps to dance on sands ...

Trurio, who has now learnt his lesson and recognises that there need be no personal feeling, thinks he has 'a sonnet that will serve the turn'. This is a cynical situation of course, but the cynicism reflects on the sonnet convention.

In order to demonstrate the flimsy basis of the sonnet love Shakespeare brings it into conflict with the Platonic friendship of the two gentlemen. Platonic love as being by definition the nobler love dominates. Thus Valentine, the hero who always does the right thing, has to end by sacrificing his lady for his ideal. Proteus the villain brings both ideals into disrepute by loving only himself, being constant only to his own interest.

Since the love of woman is a lower ideal than that of Platonic friendship the women are naturally sacrificed to it, although in reality they count for no more in the sonnet ideal. The men never consider the women's feelings or attitudes at all. The two worlds, the real and the ideal run their course without fusing, unless we are supposed to assume this might happen after the play ends. But there is no indication of what to think of that; it is possibly irrelevant to consider it.

Let us look at what happens in the play. Valentine as a typical sonnet lover does penance for condemning love before he loved Silvia; he fasts and says,

> with penitential groans,
> With nightly tears, with daily heart-sore sighs,
>
> .   .   .   .   .
>
> Love hath chased sleep from my enthrallèd eyes.

To Proteus' question whether Silvia was 'the idol that you worship so', he replies, 'Even she; and is she not a heavenly saint?' But he also thinks it important to ask forgiveness of Proteus, 'that I do not dream on thee'. Similarly when Proteus falls in love with Silvia, it is not Julia he has on his conscience, but Valentine :

> Methinks my zeal to Valentine is cold,
> Oh, but I love his lady too-too much.
>
> .   .   .   .   .
>
> There is no reason but I shall be blind.

Thus Shakespeare stresses the double treason in Proteus; his love for Valentine is as baseless as that for Julia. He says, 'I to myself am dearer than a friend'. We are now prepared for his treachery to Silvia. If he betrays his friend, we perhaps should not be more horrified that when he realises he cannot win Silvia's love he threatens to force it; there is nothing at all to be said for him either as a lover in the sonnet convention or a friend in the Platonic. Finally he is discovered, and gets himself out of the trap by repenting. To this Valentine acts as the ideal friend. To forgive is something that a friend should surely do. Fair enough! But more is needed in Platonic love. If one's friend loves the same lady as oneself, Plato's ideal lover must surely let him have her; so Valentine says he will relinquish Silvia to Proteus, 'that my love may appear plain and free'. Now the dramatist is in a tangle, for he has landed himself with both the women sacrificed and only the villain rewarded. Shakespeare gets out of it by making Proteus suddenly recognise Julia, who has been serving him in disguise, and announce that he loves her best after all. On this happy note the comedy ends.

What an escape! The play nearly ended with the noble ideals of sonnet love and Platonic friendship resulting in misery for everyone except the man who in reality loves no one but himself. Can we suppose that Shakespeare meant us not to notice this, that he is recommending, or even accepting the Platonic and sonnet ideals as viable? Some readers suppose something of the sort. But taken seriously *The Two Gentlemen* would make a very bad play, for not only is the psychology absolutely incredible since it goes against human nature, but in that case Shakespeare must also have miscalculated the natural reactions of a theatre audience. That he makes the actions of Proteus and Valentine incredible surely indicates that he intended them to seem so. Indeed he encourages a natural reaction. Launce gives a pointer to Proteus' character early in the play :

I am but a fool, look you, and yet I have the wit to think my master is a kind of a knave.

There can be no doubt about this. But he is not recognised as a knave by Valentine his friend, nor is Julia revolted by him; her love remains unshaken. Shakespeare has followed out the implications of the literary ideals, not attempting to give them a basis in real feeling. They are a pose. There is nothing real about the two gentlemen at all. Neither the Platonic friendship nor the sonnet love counts for anything at all in one, and in the other they lead to an unnatural idealism towards his friend, and a cruel irresponsibility towards his lady. This is the point that Shakespeare makes, and he trusts to our natural reaction to see it. Their sonnet love, which purports to give unqualified dedication to the lady, in fact does nothing of the sort. Proteus forsakes Julia without a thought of her hurt—a common

enough attitude of the youth in that situation, which the
sonnet-tradition permitted, but not what we might expect from
sonnet protestations. Similarly Valentine hands over Silvia to
Proteus. Shakespeare must have meant us to notice the dis-
crepancy between the poetry he speaks and his actions.

In contrast with the men, the women in *The Two Gentlemen* are real characters with genuine feelings. This throws up
the falseness of the men. When the women follow the sonnet
convention they do so, aware of its unreality. We cannot say of
them, as I said of the men, that their love consists in their
sonnet language. Even Julia's serving woman has a strong
sense of reality. She cautions her mistress against taking sonnet
extremes as real :

> I do not seek to quench your love's hot fire,
> But qualify the fire's extreme rage,
> Lest it should burn above the bonds of reason.

When Julia plays the sonnet lady's game of rejecting her lover
with scorn, and has dismissed Lucetta with Proteus' letter un-
opened, she is sorry :

> How angerly I taught my brow to frown,
> When inward joy enforced my heart to smile!

We have already seen that Silvia only plays the convention.
Proteus receives her direct criticism of his perfidy; as he tells
us,

> Silvia is too fair, too true, too holy
> To be corrupted by my worthless gift.
> When I protest true loyalty to her,
> She twits me with my falsehood to my friend;
> When to her beauty I commend my vows,
> She bids me think how I have been forsworn
> In breaking faith with Julia whom I loved.

The women pass Plato's test of real love in being constant.
Although they each experience the utmost hurt from the men
they love, being sacrificed for a preferred love, and cannot but
see how far from ideal their loved one is, their love never
wavers. Moreover Shakespeare makes them feel for each other.

They are better friends than the Platonists. They are not only as human in their relationship with each other as their loves are human, it is a more natural and genuine relationship.

The *Two Gentlemen of Verona* is similar to *Love's Labours Lost* in showing up sonnet artificiality. In *Love's Labours Lost* Shakespeare concentrated on the false expression, in *The Two Gentlemen* on the basic unreality of the attitudes, where he shows that not only are Platonic friendship and sonnet love inconsistent with each other, both are unrelated with reality, being only literary poses.

In *As you like it* Shakespeare laughs at sonnet love as it appears in the pastoral convention. His way of doing so makes an interesting contrast with that in *Love's Labours Lost*. For one thing the general intention is much less clear; *As you like it* is ambivalent. It is of course a very close dramatisation of Lodge's *Rosalynde*, and we need to be careful not to take as Shakespeare what is Lodge, for he accepts Lodge's romance and identifies with it. His story is a cut version of Lodge's, a selection of the incidents, with the same characters, the pastoral scene, the sonnet love, and he even has some of the same phrases and the same names for his characters. But Shakespeare's title suggests a mocking answer to a similar clause in Lodge's preface. Lodge says, 'If you like it, so :' but, he continues, if any ass or any ignorant critic objects, he will throw 'the cockscomb over board to feed cods'. Shakespeare responds by saying, that his play is as Lodge liked it. But it cannot be without significance that he has *two* cockscombs to criticise it in Jaques and Touchstone. Of them there can be no doubt; they have no original in Lodge's romance. So far then, from Lodge being able to throw his critics overboard, Shakespeare had added two to the story.

Shakespeare stresses the artificiality of Lodge's pastoral scenes by playing them in a more natural mode. Lodge's pastoral is self-contained and self-consistent. If one accepts the convention, then it is not ridiculous for it all hangs together. Shakespeare destroys this coherence by setting the pastoral against a natural background. Thus his forest of Arden is of English oak and his shepherds approximate to real ones. Although Lodge's Rosalynde and the equivalent of Orlando have already a reality, they live comfortably within the con-

vention. Shakespeare makes their normality clearer by keeping
them a little distant from that convention. In general he does
not let us forget the real world we all belong to that prevents us
taking the pastoral romance seriously.

To illustrate: Lodge's runaway ladies know they have
arrived on the pastoral scene and that there must be shepherds
around, because they find love songs pinned to trees. That is: if
you want to find shepherds follow the trail of their madrigals.
Not so with Shakespeare. To signify the arrival of the stranger
in the country Celia says she found Orlando 'under a tree, like
a dropped acorn'. This is altogether different phantasy from
Lodge's. In Shakespeare the real forest makes the background,
and imagination plays on it. Celia goes on to say, 'There lay
he, stretched along, like a wounded knight.' The first images
make the facts—the oak, the sleeping man. And the chivalric
phantasy is played against it. Or again in the description of the
stag hunt, Jaques lay

> Under an oak, whose antique root peeps out
> Upon the brook that brawls along this wood.

And in that natural forest, the first Lord develops his emotion-
alised story of the stag, and tells how Jaques projected his
own sentimental imagery onto it. The forest and the stag
belong to the natural world, and the courtiers and Jaques
have come into it and see it with the eyes of phantasy. Of
course there is the lion to think what you will of, but by the
time it intervenes the play is nearly done. It ends in a sort of a
clutter anyhow—Lodge gone to pieces.

But it is Jaques and Touchstone who make sure that we
stand a little outside the play. Touchstone keeps showing nonsense up. Although this may not be Jaques' whole function,
he at least finds Touchstone a man after his heart, and he at
least prevents us from taking the Duke and his courtiers
seriously. He does not leave us long in doubt about this pastoral
idealism 'Under the greenwood tree' with 'No enemy, But
winter and rough weather'. He mocks: if anyone 'turn ass' and
leaves 'his wealth and ease',

> Here shall he see,
> Gross fools as he.

But it is not with the courtiers and Jacques that I am concerned but with Touchstone and the lovers. Touchstone makes the best of what life brings him, whether sham or real. He is at home anywhere, and at ease with everyone. He knows how to talk with the shepherd about the country :

> Now in respect it is in the fields, it pleaseth me well; but in respect it is not in the court, it is tedious.

He can mock town nonsense with Jaques. 'Your If is the only peace-maker; much virtue in If", he says when showing how far an aggressive swordsman can go in insulting someone, without having actually to fight. Of his marriage he says simply and charmingly to Audrey,

> To-morrow is a joyful day, Audrey. To-morrow will we be married.

And to the Duke he explains,

> A poor virgin, sir, an ill-favoured thing, sir, but mine own— a poor humour of mine, sir, to take that that no man else will; rich honesty dwells like a miser, sir, in a poor house, as your pearl in your foul oyster.

He plays the game of talking as others do, but he will act on his own judgement.

You could say of Shakespeare's love-story that in respect that it is real love he presents it with the charm that has delighted all unsuspecting audiences from his own day (presumably) to this, Rosalind being possibly the most lovable and convincing of all his heroines, and Orlando the right man for her. But in respect that it is pastoral and sonnet love, he laughs at it. In *Love's Labours Lost* he concentrated on the language or texture of sonnet poetry and left us with the tag in our mind of honest kersey and plain home-spun speech as the solution. But it is not; in *As you like it* he uses this plain speech, sets sonnet love in a natural setting, no artificial courtiers affect it, the shepherds work with real ewes and have dirty and work-hardened hands, and they talk in plain, unsugared verse. But as a result they throw up the absurdity of this sort of love all the more. Here is not ridiculous talk about love, but a ridiculous sort of love. Only the actual sonnets in *As you like it* are written in a ridiculous sonnet-like style, making a parody of the convention. There is no rhetorical artifice apart from them.

In pastoral a shepherd is almost by definition a man in love, or if not, he is defined by his attitude to love. Although Celia and Rosalind are not guided to Arden by finding a trail of sonnets, the first shepherds they meet are discussing love. Silvius is deep in it. The theme rings a bell in Rosalind. Touchstone comments what must be right for all of us by now, 'it grows something stale with me'. Just as Rosader (Lodge's Orlando) engraved his verse on a myrtle tree, so does Orlando pin his to the trees he finds here. This is Rosader's :

> Of all chaste birds the Phoenix doth excel,
> Of all strong beasts the lion bears the bell,
> Of all sweet flowers the rose doth sweetest smell,
> Of all fair maids my Rosalynde is fairest.
>
> Of all pure metals gold is only purest,
> Of all high trees the pine hath highest crest,
> Of all soft sweets I like my mistress' breast,
> Of all chaste thoughts my mistress' thoughts are rarest.
>
> Of all proud birds the eagle pleaseth Jove,
> Of pretty fowls kind Venus likes the dove,
> Of trees Minerva doth the olive love,
> Of all sweet nymphs I honour Rosalynde.
>
> Of all her gifts her wisdom pleaseth most,
> Of all her graces virtue she doth boast:
> For all these gifts my life and joy is lost,
> If Rosalynde prove cruel and unkind.

Orlando parodies this in a verse of short lines with every alternate line ending in 'Rosalind', and the other rhyming with it. Touchstone mocks it with nonsense in the same rhythm :

> If the cat will after kind,
> So be sure will Rosalind:
> Wintered garments must be lined,
> So must slender Rosalind.

This makes game of Orlando, so it is a parody of a parody. Celia enters with another verse she has found in the same rhythm, which Touchstone had described as 'the right butter-woman's rank to market'. It expresses one of the sonneteers' ideas of creation and ends with the devoted slavery that characterises them :

> The quintessence of every sprite
>   Heaven would in a little show.
> Therefore Heaven nature charged,
>   That one body should be filled
> With all graces wide-enlarged:
>   Nature presently distilled
> Helen's cheek, but not her heart,
>   Cleopatra's majesty,
> Atalanta's better part,
>   Sad Lucretia's modesty . . .
> Thus Rosalind of many parts
>   By heavenly synod was devised,
> Of many faces, eyes, and hearts,
>   To have the touches dearest prized . . .
> Heaven would that she these gifts should have,
> And I to live and die her slave.

Orlando does not talk in a sham tongue apart from in his sonnets. His exchanges with Rosalind are playful rather than poetic. They use natural prose and have what we could call the first degree of reality. (Real men can write ridiculous verse). Perhaps I should emphasise that Lodge gave both of them the qualities they have. It is just that Shakespeare has tipped a balance on the side of reality. Silvius and Phebe are of the next degree. They talk in verse, but it is not affected, though they talk of sonnet affectations, and they have absurd sonnet attitudes, attitudes which Lodge gave them. Silvius kneels to Phebe and pleads,

> Sweet Phebe, do not scorn me, do not, Phebe.

This parodies Lodge, the abject misery of whose lover is already very near the ridiculous. Shakespeare turns the balancing scale to the absurd by making the expression as naive and

abject as the attitude. Still following Lodge Silvius says that
Phebe is killing him. This habitual sonnet complaint normally
goes unanswered, but Shakespeare makes Phebe analyse it with
great sense. She ridicules its silliness :

> I would not be thy executioner,
> I fly thee, for I would not injure thee ...
> Thou tellest me there is murder in mine eye—
> 'Tis pretty, sure, and very probable,
> That eyes, that are the frail'st and softest things,
> Who shut their coward gates on atomies,
> Should be called tyrants, butchers, murderers!
> Now I do frown on thee with all my heart,
> And if mine eyes can wound, now let them kill thee;
> Now counterfeit to swoon, why now fall down,
> Or if thou canst not, oh for shame, for shame,
> Lie not, to say mine eyes are murderers!
> Now show the wound mine eye hath made in thee.
> Scratch thee but with a pin, and there remains
> Some scar of it: lean upon a rush,
> The cicatrice and capable impressure
> Thy palm some moment keeps: but now mine eyes,
> Which I have darted at thee, hurt thee not,
> Nor, I am sure, there is no force in eyes
> That can do hurt.

Silvius takes this analysis seriously, and answers it patiently and
intelligently, as no doubt many a poet may have had to do
with his verses. He says that if she could understand 'the power
of fancy' (that is, of imagination)

> Then shall you know the wounds invisible
> That love's keen arrows make.

It is all quite seriously taken. Rosalind deals with them in a
common sense way too. She asks why Phebe, who has no looks,
should be 'proud and pitiless', and insult and exult over her
lover; there is no sense in it. She asks Silvius why he should be
so silly as to love someone inferior to himself; he is a 'properer
man Than she a woman' :

> 'Tis not her glass, but you, that flatters her.

Then to her she says, 'thank heaven, fasting, for a good man's love'. She whispers common sense in her ear, for she dare not say it aloud in such a context:

> For I must tell you friendly in your ear,
> Sell when you can—you are not for all markets.

Good country sense! The humour lies not in direct parody (although Lodge's Phoebe indicated to her lover that she was not in his market) but in treating this artificial game as if its attitudes were natural ones, whereas in the heart of a pastoral situation they are not meant to be taken seriously. To do so is inappropriate and hence ridiculous. And so with Silvius. His style is unaffected; it expresses ridiculous attitudes in real country imagery:

> So holy and so perfect is my love,
> And I in such a poverty of grace,
> That I shall think it a most plenteous crop
> To glean the broken ears after the man
> That the main harvest reaps: loose now and then
> A scattered smile, and that I'll live upon.

This fawning, self-abasing attitude is ridiculous; the language in which it is expressed is more than adequate if the attitudes were sensible. Its common sense treatment shows that it has not a sensible basis.

As you like it is gay. Its laughter and wit are carefree. No death stops the play to give it seriousness; no villain remains a villain to the end to give it a moral tone; no one is baited. The characters except for Jaques, whose melancholy is perhaps affected, criticise because they are happy and like exercising their wit. 'It was a lover and his lass' passes without other criticism than Touchstone's, 'I count it but time lost to hear such a foolish song'. Jaques mocks as he sees lovers assembling:

> There is sure, another flood toward, and those couples are
> coming to the ark.

He calls Touchstone and Audrey 'very strange beasts, which in all tongues are called fools', but he commends him to the Duke.

The spirit of the whole play is Touchstone's. It accepts what it laughs at. We enjoy the joke of pastoral sonnet love because it makes us laugh, not laugh because it deserves to be censured. All of these plays criticise for fun, but in *As you like it* Rosalind and Orlando give it a charm. We are not quite clear whether Shakespeare meant us to enjoy Lodge's love story sentimentally, whether he himself fell in love with Lodge's Rosalind, or whether he presented their story genuinely merely to throw up the silliness of Silvius and Phebe, and Lodge's pastoral romance in general. But it is clear that the sonnet love is there to make fun of.

It is interesting to study *Romeo and Juliet* from our point of view. In it Shakespeare does not discuss or criticise sonnet love and talk. Only Mercutio scoffs at it when he laughs at Romeo for being in love and refers to the sonneteers' habit of citing famous heroines as being inferior to their loves :

> Now is he for the numbers that Petrarch flowed in. Laura to his lady was a kitchen wench—marry, she had a better love to be-rhyme her!—Dido a dowdy, Cleopatra a gipsy, Helen and Hero hildings and harlots, Thisbe a gray eye or so, but not to the purpose.

But what makes the play interesting from our point of view is not any such criticism of the sonnets. *Romeo and Juliet* is not a comedy, its function cannot be criticism. Nevertheless it reveals Shakespeare's continuing interest in sonnet style as a medium for expressing love, though in a positive way, by experimenting with it. It is almost as if, having criticised sonnet talk, he now sets himself the problem of writing of young love in a language that reflects the experience sensitively. He patterns his style to convey subtle changes in mood and attitude, using sonnet-talk for what is conventional and plain speech for intense feeling. This is best seen by following the lovers through the earlier acts of the play, concentrating on the expression. The actual details of the plot are taken without many significant changes from Brooke's *Romeus and Juliet* and therefore cannot show any deliberate planning of Shakespeare's. But a close study of the language does. In the first scene we hear of Romeo behaving in the approved sonnet way :

Many a morning hath he there been seen,
With tears augmenting the fresh morning's dew,
Adding to clouds more clouds with his deep sighs;
But all so soon as the all-cheering sun
Should in the farthest east begin to draw
The shady curtains from Aurora's bed,
Away from light steals home my heavy son,
And private in his chamber pens himself.

No one guesses the cause except Benvolio, and to him Romeo says he is

Out of her favour where I am in love.

Benvolio, apparently well aware of how sonnet ladies behave says,

Alas that love, so gentle in his view,
Should be so tyrannous and rough in proof!

Romeo talks of love :

Love is a smoke made with the fume of sighs:
Being purged, a fire sparkling in lovers' eyes;
Being vexed, a sea nourished with lovers' tears.
What is it else? A madness most discreet,
A choking gall and a preserving sweet.

He describes his lady :

She'll not be hit
With Cupid's arrow: she hath Dian's wit,
And, in strong proof of chastity well armed,
From love's weak childish bow she lives unharmed.
She will not stay the siege of loving terms,
Nor bide the encounter of assailing eyes,
Nor ope her lap to saint-seducing gold.
Oh, she is rich in beauty, only poor
That when she dies, with beauty dies her store.

This is in good sonnet tradition. Benvolio asks if she has sworn never to marry, and Romeo replies :

> She hath, and in that sparing makes huge waste:
> For beauty, starved with her severity,
> Cuts beauty off from all posterity.

This, with the previous statement 'That when she dies, with beauty dies her store' is interesting for it is not in sonnet reasoning at all, nor in the spirit of it. But we find it in both *Venus and Adonis* and in Shakespeare's own sonnets. I hope to show later where it came from and that it appears first in his sonnets, where it can be easily accounted for. It makes sense as an argument in *Venus and Adonis*. Here it is gratuitous, not related with anything else in the play and not contributing anything to it. I conclude that it is an echo of something that has become in Shakespeare's mind, an association now inhering in this situation.

To continue the story, Benvolio advises the course that Brooke's Romeus took, to go and see other ladies and so perhaps cure his love by comparison. Both Romeus and Romeo doubt the use of it. But as Shakespeare's hero is still arguing, a messenger comes and invites them to Capulet's feast. Rosalind is to be there, so Romeo will go, but not in order to discover, as Benvolio suggests he will, that his 'swan is a crow'. He answers with a sonneteer's ardour,

> When the devout religion of mine eye
> Maintains such falsehood, then turn tears to fires:
> And these who, often drowned, could never die,
> Transparent heretics, be burnt for liars.
> One fairer than my love! The all-seeing sun
> Ne'er saw her match since first the world begun.

This is the sonneteer's conventional attitude, on how little basis of reality we are soon to see. Shakespeare's purpose in stressing Romeo's faithfulness to his ideal is so that he may have a clear conscience when the greater love puts out the lesser on the best chivalric model. We have seen from *The Two Gentlemen of Verona* that Shakespeare does not take this defection lightly, that he thinks the woman should be considered. Brooke did so also. They both absolve their lover by stressing that his first love was impossible to win. We can also say that if the lady was sincere in her protestations, and neither Brooke nor Shakespeare suggest she was not, then she perhaps received no hurt, certainly none that she had not asked for. That this is taken care of by both writers shows that by now there was a literary public for romance of a more natural sort. Romeo and the Friar discuss the situation. The Friar comments,

> Is Rosaline, that thou didst love so dear,
> So soon forsaken? Young men's love then lies
> Not truly in their hearts but in their eyes.

But Romeo replies,

>   Her I love now
> Doth grace for grace and love for love allow:
> The other did not so.

The Friar expresses what we can be sure is Shakespeare's view :

>   Oh, she knew well
> Thy love did read by rote, that could not spell.

Juliet had no previous love. She is barely fourteen, and is not yet thinking of such things. Or at least so she says. Her mother asks,

> How stands your dispositions to be married?

and she replies,

> It is an honour that I dream not of.

If she could indeed be so much of a child that she had never thought about it, at least she considers that the thing to do is to obey. Asked to think of Paris, she replies in effect that she will do as she is told. Thus both young people, each in their own way, are bound within the convention of their society.

At the dance Romeo enters 'too sore enpiercéd' with love's shaft, so 'Under love's heavy burden', that he has no heart to dance. Love is rough, rude, boisterous 'and it pricks like thorn'. But when he sees Juliet the tune changes :

C

> Oh she doth teach the torches to burn bright!
> It seems she hangs upon the cheek of night
> As a rich jewel in an Ethiop's ear—
> Beauty too rich for use, for earth too dear!
> So shows a snowy dove trooping with crows,
> As yonder lady o'er her fellows shows.

A sonneteer might say this, but here the first hyperbole at least is not just wild fancy. Romeo sees the lady by the light of torches, which is a dim one. So the hyperbole, which he used in *Lucrece*, is here pinned to the situation.

Shakespeare makes the lovers meet in a sonnet. They literally make their first contact in this form, and also use the imagery of pilgrim, saint and prayer belonging to that convention. I take it Shakespeare intends us to notice that they have met in a conventional love game, and indeed at the end Juliet points this out. Romeo takes her hand :

(Romeo) If I profane with my unworthiest hand
        This holy shrine, the gentle pain is this :
        My lips, two blushing pilgrims, ready stand
        To smooth that rough touch with a tender kiss.
(Juliet) Good pilgrim, you do wrong your hand too much,
        Which mannerly devotion shows in this :
        For saints have hands that pilgrims' hands do touch,
        And palm to palm is holy palmers' kiss.
(Romeo) Have not saints lips, and holy palmers too?
(Juliet) Ay, pilgrim, lips that they must use in prayer.
(Romeo) Oh then, dear saint, let lips do what hands do,
        They pray : grant then, lest faith turn to despair.
(Juliet) Saints do not move, though grant for prayers' sake.
(Romeo) Then move not, while my prayer's effect I take.
        Thus from my lips by thine my sin is purged.
(Juliet) Then have my lips the sin that they have took.
(Romeo) Sin from my lips? Oh trespass sweetly urged !
        Give me my sin again.
(Juliet)   You kiss by the book.

The sonnet has included a hand clasp and a kiss. Shakespeare's audience would be likely to hear the sonnet tune and not miss its significance. They would take it as a love game such as was played in court dances in Tudor times,[52] something not too serious to be played in the open, but possibly with a promise of something more. However, Juliet's mother, who would have her eye on her daughter, does not miss it, and sends the nurse to take her away. But this sonnet ritual could also have a symbolic significance, the meeting in one sonnet expressing the oneness with each other that all lovers desire, what Keats described in different imagery in *The Pot of Basil* :

> Twin roses by the zephyr blown apart
> Only to meet again more close.

This may add a second meaning to their conventional game.

Romeo first expresses his true love in the orchard as he looks up at Juliet in her high window. Here Shakespeare interchanges conventional imagery with natural excited speech. When he sees Juliet come to the window, Romeo reacts with a sonnet convention :

> But soft! What light through yonder window breaks?
> It is the east, and Juliet is the sun.
> Arise, fair sun, and kill the envious moon,
> Who is already sick and pale with grief
> That thou, her maid, art far more fair than she.
> Be not her maid, since she is envious.
> Her vestal livery is but sick and green,
> And none but fools do wear it.

Then Juliet presumably leans over the sill and is no longer just a picture seen in its frame. It is she herself. Romeo responds :

> It is my lady, oh it is my love;
> Oh that she knew she were.
> She speaks, yet she says nothing. What of that?
> Her eye discourses: I will answer it.
> I am too bold: 'tis not to me she speaks.

This is not the language of the sonnets. It has a sudden reality. The rhythm and the plain everyday natural speech carry a depth of real feeling not there in the imagery of the sun and the moon, where imagination rather than feeling is active. As Romeo realises that it is not to him she speaks, she recedes again into something just seen, and once again imagination takes over with traditional imagery :

> Two of the fairest stars in all the heaven,
> Having some business, do entreat her eyes
> To twinkle in their spheres till they return.
> What if her eyes were there, they in her head?
> The brightness of her cheek would shame those stars
> As daylight doth a lamp; her eyes in heaven
> Would through the airy region stream so bright
> That birds would sing and think it were not night.

She leans her cheek on her hand and he responds with a natural desire :

> See how she leans her cheek upon her hand!
> Oh that I were a glove upon that hand,
> That I might touch that cheek.

By presenting the actual fact of her leaning her cheek on her hand Shakespeare has naturalized what may be two sonnet memories. Surrey's sonnet XI in Tottel's Miscellany opens with the poet thinking sadly of his love,

> When Windor walls sustained my wearied arm,
> My hand my chin, to ease my restless head.

Here is Juliet in the pensive love pose. But it is so natural that we do not think of Surrey. And Barnes in sonnet LXIII of *Parthenophil and Parthenope* writes,

> Would I were changed but to my mistress' gloves,
> That those white lovely fingers I might hide,
> That I might kiss those hands, which mine heart loves.

This is sonnet artifice. But Romeo's response is an natural as Juliet's attitude. There is a tenderness in his wish that he could just touch, not kiss, her cheek, suggested by the sight of her hand doing so. He could not touch her with her own hand. It is himself he wants to make the contact. To wish he were a glove is a natural association. If only he were a glove that could

touch her cheek without impertinence or irreverence, a glove
that she indeed rested her cheek on. Comparison with Barnes'
image shows very clearly the distinction between imagery that
is 'sugared', a fanciful idea, and imagery close to a natural
situation. Shakespeare's conveys the feeling natural in the
situation. Similarly when Juliet speaks again, Shakespeare
naturalises the convention:

> Oh speak again, bright angel, for thou art
> As glorious to this night, being o'er my head,
> As is a wingéd messenger of heaven
> Unto the white-upturnéd wondering eyes
> Of mortals that fall back to gaze on him
> When he bestrides the lazy-passing clouds
> And sails upon the bosom of the air.

The comparison with the angel is as natural as that with the
glove. Shakespeare stresses their physical relationship in 'being
o'er my head'. This is a prosaic relationship. She is like an
angel, which can be defined as a 'winged messenger of heaven',
since she is over his head. And his wondering eyes are in fact
upturned, showing the whites. One might suppose that these
factual explanations would take from the wonder. On the contrary, since the imagery arises from the facts of things seen, it
has a more convincing quality. When Romeo's pulse slows
down again he moves away from the reality of his love to the
fancy, also visually imagined, of the messenger bestriding the
lazy-passing clouds of his calm sky.

Juliet's language commonly has this direct quality. She is
more spontaneous than Romeo :

> Oh Romeo, Romeo! Wherefore art thou Romeo?
> Deny thy father and refuse thy name.

Then she says it is his name that is her enemy.

> What's in a name? That which we call a rose
> By any other name would smell as sweet.

Romeo meets her by playing on her theme. He says he will be
baptised anew. Then follows happy fun, the sort of imagina-

tive play or nonsense that love often uses. Juliet asks how he got into the orchard, for the walls are high, and he replies,

> With love's light wings did I o'erperch these walls
> For stony limits cannot hold love out.

This is not a poet seizing every opportunity to let his imagination get away. Romeo has come over a 'stony limit'. The submerged bird-imagery of 'wings' and 'o'erperched' give a visual suggestion of the speed and ease with which love took him over. Similarly the extravagant assertion about his enemies—

> My life were better ended by their hate
> Than death proroguéd, wanting of thy love.—

is a hyperbole based on the threatened fact, not just the lover's extravagance of death being better than life without her love. It is as much a comment on the actual danger in which he stands as a sonnet convention. In such ways Shakespeare chains the sonnet figures of speech and conventions to a contextual reality, and they are not destroyed by contact with it, as happens in *Love's Labours Lost* and *As you like it*. They therefore feel genuine. And again Romeo's conceit that he lent his eyes to love does not read like artifice. Juliet asked who directed him to her, and he answers,

> By love, that first did prompt me to enquire.
> He lent me counsel, and I lent him eyes.
> I am no pilot; yet, wert thou as far
> As that vast shore washed with the farthest sea,
> I should adventure for such merchandise.

The imagery lights up common love-nonsense, which gives it a reality. Juliet responds with a plain description of their situation and no imagery at all. Her love is too genuine to be anything but serious and straightforward:

> Dost thou love me? I know thou wilt say 'Ay',
> And I will take thy word...
>   ... Oh gentle Romeo,
> If thou dost love, pronounce it faithfully.

Or, if thou think'st I am too quickly won,
I'll frown and be perverse and say thee nay,
So thou wilt woo; but else, not for the world.
In truth, fair Montague, I am too fond,
And therefore thou mayst think my haviour light;
But trust me, gentleman, I'll prove more true
Than those that have more cunning to be strange.
I should have been more strange, I must confess,
But that thou overheardst, ere I was ware,
My true-love passion. Therefore pardon me,
And not impute this yielding to light love,
Which the dark night has so discoveréd.

There is no artifice of any sort in this. Romeo, with a lapse from his most true love, will swear his love by the moon that shines over them. It strikes a false note, and Juliet immediately tells him not to swear by the moon, which is inconstant:

> Do not swear at all:
> Or, if thou wilt, swear by thy gracious self,
> Which is the god of my idolatry,
> And I'll believe thee.

The god of her idolatry is quite in the sonnet tradition for the man. Juliet has the genuine feeling that the tradition originated in. Although she meets his play she ends by telling him not to swear:

> Well, do not swear. Although I joy in thee,
> I have no joy of this contract tonight:
> It is too rash, too unadvised, too sudden,
> Too like the lightning, which doth cease to be
> Ere one can say 'It lightens'. Sweet, goodnight:
> This bud of love, by summer's ripening breath,
> May prove a beauteous flower when next we meet.
> Goodnight, goodnight! As sweet repose and rest
> Come to thy heart as that within my breast.

She yields to the fact of the situation. But he wants to prolong the dialogue:

> Oh wilt thou leave me so unsatisfied?

She answers with the fact again :

What satisfaction canst thou have tonight?

She expresses her love in hyperbole because it is too great to be expressed without it :

My bounty is as boundless as the sea,
My love as deep: the more I give to thee,
The more I have: for both are infinite.

When she has to leave him to go to the nurse, Juliet does not indulge in fancy :

I am afeared,
Being in night, all this is but a dream,
Too flattering sweet to be substantial.

She then arranges how they may marry—quite wrong by the convention. She returns again from the nurse's interruption and calls him. They express their love for each other, using imagery from birds. She calls :

Hist, Romeo, hist! Oh for a falconer's voice
To lure this tassel-gentle back again!
Bondage is hoarse and may not speak aloud,
Else would I tear the cave where Echo lies,
And make her airy tongue more hoarse than mine
With repetition of my 'Romeo!'

The tassel-gentle is the noblest of hawks. She remembers, presumably, that she had wished him to change his name, that this was her enemy. She now dwells on it for she has accepted him without reserve. But she wishes she were not in bondage and could call his name not with a hoarse and breathy whisper but loud enough to tear open the cave of echo. The imagery is closely tied to the situation. She calls 'hist', which is the call of the falconer. It is her bondage that makes her have to call hoarsely. Romeo responds to the mood of her imagery and to the whispered, far-heard voice calling his name. She has regretted the quality of her voice. But he says,

It is my soul that calls upon my name.
How silver-sweet sound lovers' tongues by night,
Like softest music to attending ears!

The sound of music by night seems to have moved Shakespeare. But he is not decorating a theme. The image has a particular relevance here. It is the voice of Juliet that Romeo hears. It was a hoarse whisper, seemingly far off, not a daylight, conscious voice. Juliet calls his name again and he answers with 'my niess', using imagery from falconry, as she had done, but one geared to their prose situation, for a niess is the young bird in the nest; and this is Juliet to him, soft, desirable, young, innocent, but high up out of reach. They make plans. Then she keeps him talking:

Juliet: I have forgot why I did call thee back.
Romeo: Let me stand here till thou remember it.
Juliet: I shall forget, to have thee still stand there,
               Remembering how I love thy company.
Romeo: And I'll still stay, to have thee still forget,
               Forgetting any other home but this.

The dialogue of love includes no imagery at all; it is merely related to the situation of neither being able to part. Then Juliet recurs to the imagery of a bird, but now one in a cage:

'Tis almost morning. I would have thee gone,
And yet no farther than a wanton's bird,
That lets it hop a little from her hand,
Like a poor prisoner in his twisted gyves,
And with a silk thread plucks it back again,
So loving-jealous of his liberty.

The imagery is a close definition of the situation. She pictures it as of benefit only to herself, and of holding the bird a prisoner. He responds by saying he wishes he were that bird, that her love for him does not confine him in bondage but is what he most wants. This is a sonnet image, but Shakespeare has divided it between the lovers and so made it express a shared relationship. Juliet says it, pitying the bird she holds captive so cruelly. Romeo accepts it with joy. In the sonnet we have only one side, the poet complaining of his cruel bondage. In fact the lover chooses to be in this situation. So the image is false in the sonnet. It is as interesting to see the contrast between Romeo's parting and that of the sonneteer thinking only of his misery. Romeo's eyes are not on himself. He prays that Juliet may have sleep and peace; he does not complain of the agony he suffers in parting from her. He wishes for himself only to rest within her peace. And this is a thought that he picked up from Juliet herself when she wished him as sweet a repose and rest as she felt within her heart. And moreover it is secondary to his wish for her :

> Sleep dwell upon thine eyes, peace in thy breast!
> Would I were sleep and peace, so sweet to rest!

Here is a complete solution to the poetry of love.

Romeo and Juliet's way of talking to each other by using similar imagery such as that of the tassel-gentle and niess, the play on her forgetting why she called him back, the caged bird and so on, shows a close relationship. They each respond to the other's way of thinking by accepting the other's thought as their own and talking from that. They take part in an intimate image-dialogue, as if their minds were united in one imagination. This makes only a heightened form of what happens when people have a close relationship. It is an interplay that belongs naturally in love. It is not of course the only sort of love dialogue that Shakespeare uses. The opposite can be seen in the exchanges of Beatrice and Benedict, Berowne and Rosaline. Both are genuine expressions of a relationship, and both differ from sonnet expression which shows no contact, no interchange, no relationship. It would appear that Shakespeare must have been aware of this. Considering the attention he gave to the use of sonnet conventions to express love in *Love's Labours Lost* and the expression of sonnet attitudes in natural speech in *As you like it,* he can hardly have missed considering how to express love genuinely. In this scene the deepest, most intense feeling is expressed in plain 'unsugared' speech. Apart from this he uses two sorts of imagery, as we have seen, a conventional and his own fresh imagining. As he uses them, the sonnet as well as the natural imagery, carries the feeling because both are integrated with the facts of the situation. They are used not to swaddle the mind in a rapturous blanket but to give depth of feeling to the actual. This keeps them rooted in truth, honest. More than this, I have shown how in Romeo's soliloquy when he sees Juliet at the window, the conventional imagery and the plain, 'unsugared' language follow the fluctuations of his heart beat, and indicate it. When it quickens, all imagery disappears and leaves nothing but unstained pure statement. As it slows down, imagination takes over with a play of images. After this it is most interesting to note that the very ornate conventional imagery, which opens the next scene lowers the intensity to that of everyday life, as Friar Laurence collects his simples :

> The grey-eyed morn smiles on the frowning night,
> Checkering the eastern clouds with streaks of light:
> And darkness fleckéd like a drunkard reels
> From forth day's pathway, made by Titan's wheels:
> Now ere the sun advance his burning eye,
> The day to cheer and night's dank dew to dry,
> I must upfill this osier cage of ours . . .

This conventionally-structured verse shuts the door on the freshness of the young love we have been listening to.

Not only Shakespeare but the lovers, so to say, seem interested in love's language, as is evident in their next appearances. While Juliet waits for the nurse to return she says,

> Love's heralds should be thoughts,
> Which ten times faster glides than the sun's beams
> Driving back shadows over louring hills.
> Therefore do nimble-pinioned doves draw love,
> And therefore hath the wind-swift Cupid wings.

After this explanation of how the conventional imagery of love has originated, Juliet indulges her fancy about the nurse's slowness :

> Had she affections and warm youthful blood,
> She would be swift in motion as a ball;
> My words would bandy her to my sweet love,
> And his to me.

When the lovers meet in Friar Lawrence's cell, Romeo feels inadequate to express his feelings and asks Juliet to try:

> Ah, Juliet, if the measure of thy joy
> Be heaped like mine, and that thy skill be more
> To blazon it, then sweeten with thy breath
> This neighbour air, and let rich music's tongue
> Unfold the imagined happiness that both
> Receive in either by this encounter.

Song seems the only language adequate. Juliet answers,

> Conceit, more rich in matter than in words,
> Brags of his substance, not of ornament.
> They are but beggars that can count their worth;
> But my true love is grown to such excess
> I cannot sum up sum of half my wealth.

She answers, I take it, that a conception of love that is full of the thing itself rather than of words, and talks only of that substance, does not use an ornament such as that of music's tongue. They have been bragging of love's substance without ornament. But now she has discovered that she can't say half of what she feels. Both Juliet and Romeo's expression is turgid here to make it apparent that they cannot express their passion, that they are too moved to have any clear mental activity. When she is alone, waiting, and too impatient to do anything, Juliet can use the old jargon:

> Gallop apace, you fiery-footed steeds,
> Towards Phoebus' lodging! Such a waggoner
> As Phaëton would whip you to the west
> And bring in cloudy night immediately.
> Spread thy close curtain, love-performing night,
> That runaways' eyes may wink, and Romeo
> Leap to these arms untalked of and unseen.

She also asks quiet night to come, 'Thou sober-suited matron all in black'. Then she repeats 'Come, night!' and 'Come, Romeo!' It is not good poetry, but it expresses her waiting. She goes on to ridiculous conceits:

> Give me my Romeo; and, when he shall die,
> Take him and cut him out in little stars,
> And he will make the face of heaven so fine
> That all the world will be in love with night
> And pay no worship to the garish sun.
> Oh, I have bought the mansion of a love,
> But not possessed it; and though I am sold,
> Not yet enjoyed. So tedious is this day
> As is the night before some festival
> To an impatient child that hath new robes
> And may not wear them.

Dare I say her tedium expresses itself in tedious poetry? She is filling in time. When she is told of Romeo's banishment she does not express her horror in sonnet-like artifice. She means it when she says her heart will break and she will die with Romeo.

> Is Romeo slaughtered? and is Tybalt dead?

When she knows the truth, she rages against Romeo as a 'fiend angelical'. Then she is horrified that she has doubted him. She bewails his banishment, and she is comforted that the nurse will find him to come and take farewell. This is a turmoil of extreme and conflicting emotion, suggested by Brooke, but much better done by Shakespeare. Nor does Romeo bewail his absence in sonnet talk. Like Juliet he is distraught. At his most coherent he says,

>   Heaven is here
> Where Juliet lives, and every cat and dog
> And little mouse, every unworthy thing,
> Live here in heaven and may look on her,
> But Romeo may not. More validity,
> More honourable state, more courtship, lives
> In carrion flies than Romeo: they may sieze
> On the white wonder of dear Juliet's hand,
> And steal immortal blessing from her lips,
> Who even in pure and vestal modesty
> Still blush, as thinking their own kisses sin;
> This may flies do, when I from this must fly;
> And say'st thou yet that exile is not death?

This states the facts of the case, that cats and dogs and flies may be where Juliet is, but not himself. Romeo ends by throwing himself on the ground in abandoned misery. Brooke is responsible for his frenzy rather than Shakespeare, who tempers the extremes both of his and Juliet's expression. When the nurse comes in, Romeo's one thought is for Juliet :

> Where is she? and how doth she? and what says
> My concealed lady to our cancelled love?

Shakespeare treats the scene where they part as he did the balcony one—dramatically, expressing their love by showing their relationship, not by talk of love. They express their love and their grief by their attitudes. Each is too concerned with the other to be self-reflective. They notice each other, answer each other, want to do as the other wants. It is drama rather than poetry, but drama with the sensitiveness and imagination of poetry : Juliet asks,

> Wilt thou be gone? It is not yet near day.
> It was the nightingale, and not the lark,
> That pierced the fearful hollow of thine ear.

And she keeps it clear that this is no mythical nightingale, for it 'sings on yond pomegranate tree' every night. Romeo replies, 'It was the lark'. The structure of his sentence echoes Juliet's and he uses the lark as a symbol for morning as Juliet does the nightingale for night. But just as the nightingale was an actual bird, so presumably is the lark, 'the herald of the morn', and he immediately points to the actual dawn in the sky.

> Look, love, what envious streaks
> Do lace the severing clouds in yonder east.
> Night's candles are burnt out, and jocund day
> Stands tiptoe on the misty mountain tops.

Embedded in the facts is the endearment, 'love', which gives the quality of his voice. Imagery lights up this language, but it is not sugared speech. We can apply modern criteria in describing it. Thus we can know the precise moment of dawn referred to. It is the very first sign. The sun is not yet at the horizon's rim. There is light only where the overcast sky breaks to leave a gap where the two sides of the cloud are severing. This alone shows the light, except that it gleams in the mist on the mountain tops. That is to say, this is a particular individual image—perhaps of an actual dawn remembered. Night's candles could refer either to stars or to actual candles. In any case the image takes warmth from candles in the lovers' room, now burnt out. 'Jocund day' standing triumphant on the top of the mountains is ready perhaps to dive into the world below, which is still in darkness. This imagery can be tested against fact. Juliet uses prose to express the hardship of parting, 'Thou needst not to be gone', she protests. Romeo relates with her :

> Let me be ta'en, let me be put to death;
> I am content, so thou wilt have it so.
> I'll say yon gray is not the morning's eye,
> 'Tis but the pale reflex of Cynthia's brow;
> Nor that is not the lark whose notes do beat
> The vaulty heaven so high above our heads.
> I have more care to stay than will to go:
> Come, death, and welcome! Juliet wills it so.
> How is't, my soul? Let's talk; it is not day.

He expresses the fullness of his love by agreeing to accept death if she wills it, so his common sense over leaving is entangled in his extravagant love. And Juliet expresses her love by accepting his common sense with urgency :

> It is, it is! Hie hence, be gone, away!
> It is the lark that sings so out of tune,
> Straining harsh discords and unpleasing sharps.
> Some say the lark makes sweet division:
> This doth not so, for she divideth us.
> Some say the lark and loathéd toad changed eyes;
> Oh now I would they had changed voices too,
> Since arm from arm that voice doth us affray,
> Hunting thee hence with hunt's-up to the day.
> Oh now be gone! More light and light it grows.

That the argument is in terms of nightingale and lark carries over the imagery of birds from the balcony scene. This gives the impression of a spiritual quality in their love. It is of the air.

But the birds are real ones of the night and dawn as well. Romeo picks up Juliet's last words :

> More light and light, more dark and dark our woes.

He responds in her terms again when she has a premonition, seeing him at the bottom of a tomb. 'Either my eyesight fails or thou look'st pale', she says, and he replies,

> And trust me, love, in my eye so do you,
> Dry sorrow drinks our blood.

Here as in the balcony scene their closeness is expressed verbally by the relatedness of their talk, by the way each reflects the other, with interchanges that qualify or build up or echo what is said. And there is either no imagery, or imagery related to their situation; it is particular to the situation, and, unrelated with its context, would lose its depth of meaning. So even when traditional imagery is used, it does not create a sugared context. In *Romeo and Juliet* we hear the genuine voice of young love.

One gets some impression of the sort of man Shakespeare must have been from a study of these plays. We can say his humour was not bitter or censorious. We can also say that although he certainly had opinions or points of view, he was not a moralist. Apart from these plays, his delight in Falstaff and Sir Toby shows that he was not. Nor was he a teacher, as comparison with Ben Jonson brings out, for he does not portray vice in order to make us hate it. His comedy has been called 'festive';[53] it releases us from the pressures of anxiety and moral strain, from pretence and insincerity. It is for fun, for genuineness not clouded by cluttering conventions. *Romeo and Juliet* is possibly immature tragedy, that is to say it is tragedy of young love defeated because of the rough world that makes its environment. There is more to Shakespeare's mature tragedy than this. But it shows Shakespeare able to give imaginative expression to genuine feeling. He is an artist; that is to say, a conscious practitioner in the art of expressing feeling. He does not write by chance, nor wholly by intuition, but with deliberate design.

III

THE DARK LADY

We have seen that the literature of chivalric and Platonic love had some reality in its day with a reference outside itself, but that this had largely disappeared by the reigns of Henry VIII and of Elizabeth, which saw the very end of the tradition. These monarchs stand in the doorway of the modern world having only a romantic attachment to the old outlook, as seen in such things as poets, musicians and courtiers honouring Queen Elizabeth as the virgin Queen—so to say a sonnet Queen. It was in her reign that the English love sonnet had its short flowering. Perhaps I should say fruitage rather than flowering since by this time it was over ripe, at the decadent end of its history, with no basis in social reality. Therefore, and since sonnet love was in any case a courtiers' game, it is not surprising that Shakespeare, a man of the people, should have been struck by its unreality and artificiality.

But there was another reason for Shakespeare's attitude. About this time the ideal of poetry as 'sugared', as rhetoric, as beautiful artifact was played out. We can still see it in their books of rhetoric and the art of poetry, but the new poets had grown out of it. Plain speech began to win their approval, and the beginnings of an ideal of truth to nature. This new attitude dates from precisely the sonnet period, the 1590s.[54] I have shown Shakespeare considering the question in *Love's Labours Lost,* and suggested that in *Romeo and Juliet* he plays with both modes of expression, setting one against the other for dramatic purposes, the sugared style as contrast for the plain speech of real love. I have also suggested that he made a considered choice. He began in the old style and moved into the new, although from the first his own finest imaginings, as we see them, tended to be in the new style. Thus *Venus and Adonis* is ornate, but the imagery often shows a modern fidelity to the thing seen, and this we also find in his earliest plays. Indeed this sort of imaginative truth possibly has a place in all great narrative poetry; it is certainly there in both Homer and Chaucer. Nevertheless there are fashions, and about this time a shift occurred from court artifice to truth to nature. That Shakespeare posed the question of ornate or plain speech in the theatre shows that it was not just a scholar's or a poet's problem. *Love's Labours Lost* presupposes cultured young men ready for the new approach, or at least for criticism of the old. There is a climate favouring a new approach to the sonnet.

This is the context in which Shakespeare wrote his sonnet sequence. To us it may seem a strange one, but if it does, this suggests something wrong in our approach. The sonnets have been misread through being studied out of context. Lacking the background that gave them meaning, we had the problem of explaining them, and so have invented such theories as that they were autobiographical, expressions of the poet's relationship with a real man, and if not written to a real woman, were at least about her. Or we may read them as self-contained reflections whose recondite expression reflects depth of experience. But this cannot have been the approach of either Shakespeare or his contemporaries. Shakespeare must have had the cadences, imagery and ideas of his predecessors in his mind as he wrote. He used the same or similar tunes and the same imagery and conceits as the other sonneteers, to pay the same flattering and devoted attention, but to a man, not a woman. Apart from this he differed from them only by beginning his sonnet sequence with a section of seventeen sonnets each coming to an identical and ridiculous climax in the couplet, begging his friend to marry and that for the most fantastic of reasons, and by reserving the more vituperative outpourings of sonnet tradition for a woman. That is to say he reduced the whole thing to the absurd.

Nothing is more difficult than to prove a joke, for the only proof is to be surprised into laughter by it, since unexpected-ness makes one of its essential elements. By a stroke of luck I made a chronological study of the main Elizabethan sonneteers for another purpose, and was surprised into laughter when I arrived at Shakespeare. My difficulty in showing that he wrote his sonnets as a parody is that I cannot recreate this experience for others. It seems I must give the game away first. However, as those on the dark lady already strike many readers as unconvincing taken seriously, they may provide a good opening. They can hardly have been written to a woman in compliment, and unless one approaches them already convinced, it is difficult to believe that they could have been written about a real woman. Indeed, nothing is easier than to show they are parodies. Some can even be shown to have a particular sonnet in view, and in general their meaning is best unlocked with this key.

There can be no mistake about this :

Sonnet 130

> My mistress' eyes are nothing like the sun,
> Coral is far more red, than her lips red,
> If snow be white, why then her breasts are dun:
> If hairs be wires, black wires grow on her head:
> I have seen roses damasked, red and white,
> But no such roses see I in her cheeks,
> And in some perfumes is there more delight,
> Than in the breath that from my mistress reeks.
> I love to hear her speak, yet well I know,
> That music hath a far more pleasing sound:
> I grant I never saw a goddess go,
> My mistress when she walks treads on the ground.
> And yet by heaven I think my love as rare,
> As any she belied with false compare.

This could be nothing other than a parody. Shakespeare assumes a mocking naivety in which he says his lady has none of the wonderful qualities common to the ladies of other poets and yet he thinks her as good as any woman about whom such lies are invented.

An attempt has been made to find a particular sonnet with this dart sticking in it, the favourite being sonnet VII of Watson's *Passionate Centurie of Love:*

Hark you that list to hear what saint I serve :
Her yellow locks exceed the beaten gold;
Her sparkling eyes in heaven a place deserve;
Her forehead high and fair of comely mould;
   Her words are music all of silver sound;
   Her wit so sharp as like can scarce be found;
Each eyebrow hangs like Iris in the skies;
Her eagle's nose is straight of stately frame;
On either cheek a rose and lily lies;
Her breath is sweet perfume, or holly flame;
   Her lips more red than any coral stone;
   Her neck more white, than aged swans yet moan;
Her breast transparent is, like crystal rock;
Her fingers long, fit for Apollo's lute;
Her slipper such as Momus dare not mock;
Her virtues all so great as make me mute :
   What other parts she hath I need not say,
   Whose face alone is cause of my decay.

Although Shakespeare probably has this in mind, the sonnet is not close enough to qualify as the one and only. If we compare Shakespeare's sonnet with it, item by item, we can see that he must have had some other sonnet in mind as well, Watson's saint has not eyes like the sun, although 'Her sparkling eyes in heaven a place deserve'; they could be stars. 'Coral is far more red than her lips' red' seems to point to him. In Watson her 'breasts' are 'transparent' not white, but Shakespeare's 'white' may have come from 'her neck'. His lady's hair is not composed of wires. This certainly is a parody of something not in Watson's sonnet. In Watson her cheeks are lily-like as well as like roses. Shakespeare also seems to remember Watson's 'Her breath is sweet perfume'. It is likely too that he may have remembered that the words she spoke were music. But Watson's love does not walk ('go') like a goddess. Finally there is much more in Watson that could be parodied, and that probably would have been seized on by any poet intending to attack this particular sonnet.

The difficulty about identifying what is not in Watson's sonnet lies in their being too great a choice. Most of the items are sonnet commonplaces. Shakespeare is doing something like he did in *Love's Labours Lost*—make fun of prevailing fashion rather than one particular person. Although we can agree that he has Watson's sonnet in mind, Dover Wilson's somewhat heated claim[55] that he is the only target cannot be substantiated. Wilson seems to have some prejudice against accepting a skit against the sonnet in general. Why for instance does he call Watson, 'a pretentious poetaster'? His denigration suggests some fear. But the point of Shakespeare's sonnet certainly seems to be that his lady is odd in lacking the common characteristics of sonnet ladies. And indeed the many sonnets that have been suggested as the source of this parody is proof that no one is specially aimed at. I shall confine my examples to some of those that, as I hope to show, Shakespeare must certainly have read.

There can be no doubt of Barnabe Barnes' sonnet LXXII, which carries something of the cadence or tune of Shakespeare's, which we might expect in a direct parody. It begins

> My mistress' beauty matched with the graces

And includes

> Love's goddess, in love's graces she surpasseth :

which may have suggested Shakespeare's goddess. In his sonnet immediately preceding, Barnes says that her 'hairs' (in the plural) are of 'angel's gold'. Although the reference is anything but clear, we also find there that Phoebe and Venus have their couches in her cheeks and they are filled with both lilies and roses. In sonnet XLVIII he says he does not ask for jewels from anywhere in the world, but only from his love, and among the diamonds, pearls and rubies he mentions that

> Her hairs no grace of golden wires want.

So here is one very striking and relevant item not in Watson. Sonnet XXXIV has this :

> My mistress' eyes, mine heaven's bright sun.

His next two sonnets follow this up.

I have shown that Shakespeare parodies with not one but several of Barnes' sonnets in mind. Although, as I shall show, he sometimes assaults one particular sonnet, his more general practice is rather to write with one poet in the foreground and others in the background, as he does in this sonnet. Constable's sonnet IX of his first decade for instance may be relevant here:

> My lady's presence makes the roses red,
> Because to see her lips, they blush for shame:
> The lily's leaves (for envy) pale became,
> And her white hands in them this envy bred.
> The marigold the leaves abroad doth spread,
> Because the sun's, and her power is the same;
>
> .   .   .   .   .   .
>
> In brief, all flowers from her their virtue take;
> From her sweet breath, their sweet smells do proceed;
> The living heat which her eye beams doth make,
> Warmeth the ground, and quickeneth the seed.

Barnes was certainly a poetaster and possibly Constable, but the other sonneteers contributing to the background of this sonnet include those that no one need scorn. Among them Daniel in sonnet XVIII indicates that Delia's 'tresses' are 'golden ore', her 'breathing sweet' has 'Arabian odours' and she competes with goddesses. She is told

> To Thetis give the honour of thy feet.

So it may be here that Shakespeare got his goddess's walk. Delia is also told to give her 'sweet voice back unto the spheres'. Spenser, possibly the greatest sonneteer of them all, writes in the commonplaces that Shakespeare mocks. His love's sweet breath in sonnet LXIV, as he discovered when he kissed her lips, smelled like gilly-flowers, her cheeks were like roses, and after listing them all, he says,

> Such fragrant flowers do give most odorous smell,
> But her sweet odour did them all excel.

Shakespeare could hardly have forgotten this, if he had read it as I think he must, yet we cannot pin point it from his sonnet. Nor could he have forgotten sonnet LXXXI, which is relevant and which remains in the memory because it has the most singing quality of them all :

> Fair is my love, when her fair golden hairs
> With the loose wind ye waving chance to mark :
> Fair when the rose in her red cheeks appears,
> Or in her eyes the fire of love does spark.
> Fair when her breast like a rich laden bark,
> With precious merchandise she forth doth lay.

The sun with which Shakespeare opens his sonnet can be said to dominate sonnet literature. I shall give a few examples to show how pervasive its influence, from poems Shakespeare must have read, although we cannot know that just these are responsible for his line. We have already noted Watson's 'sparkling eyes in heaven'. Daniel puts the same image in different words in sonnet XLIX where Delia's eyes are called 'celestial fires'. In his third sonnet Daniel says that lovers are dazzled with their sun. Watson in sonnet LII of his *Tears of Fancie* makes the sun stand for his lady. Her disdain eclipses it; he refers to it as

> My glorious sun in whom all virtue shrouds,
> That light the world but shines to me in cloud.

Wyatt in sonnet XL of Tottel's Miscellany says,

> The lively sparks, that issue from those eyes,
> Against the which there vaileth no defence,
> Have pierced my heart, and done it none offence.

Constable's Diana can compare with any sonnet lady in being like the sun. She even has two suns, one for each eye, in the first sonnet of Decade 7. If we turn back to the first line of Shakespeare's sonnet we find that his mistress' eyes are 'nothing like' the sun. This may imply that there are many sorts of ways by which the sonnet lady's eyes can be said to be like the sun, and he intends the emphasis of 'nothing like' to mean not in any of such ways. On the other hand 'nothing like' might imply no more than a general emphasis, like coral being 'far more red', not necessarily meaning that although its redness is not the most brilliant of reds, as it may be the most beautiful, it is still redder than her lips.

My conclusion is that sonnet 130 has a composite background, perhaps not inconsistent with a *Road to Xanadu*-like composition, and that the greater English sonneteers as well as the lesser must suffer its criticism. If the lesser men had never written, there would remain a large enough bull's-eye for its dart to find a home in. I have not yet proved that Shakespeare had read any of these, but I hope the cumulative evidence of correspondences will carry this conviction, especially as among them are particular instances, by themselves, striking enough to be accepted as proof.

Shakespeare's very first sonnet to the lady (no. 127) is a direct and incontrovertible comment on Sidney's seventh in *Astrophel and Stella*. Black eyes were not the correct sort in sonnet convention, but the real Stella had this, so Sidney poetised them in sonnet VII:

> When nature made her chief work, Stella's eyes,
> In colour black, why wrapped she beams so bright?
> Would she in beamy black like painter wise,
> Frame daintiest lustre mixed with shadows light?
> Or did she else that sober hue devise,
> In object best, to strength and knit our sight:
> Lest if no veil these brave beams did disguise,
> They sun-like would more dazzle than delight.
> Or would she her miraculous power show,
> That whereas black seems beauty's contrary,
> She even in black doth make all beauties flow:
> But so and thus, she minding love should be
> Plaste ever there, gave him his mourning weed:
> To honour all their deaths, who for her bleed.

Sidney asks among other things whether nature made Stella's eyes black so that the beams from this sun should delight and not dazzle, or was it, although black seems the opposite of

beauty, that she wanted to make beauty discernible even in
what is black. Nature gave them this mourning colour to
honour all those who die for the sake of her love.

It has been suggested that Shakespeare also has Fulke
Greville's sonnet LVIII in mind. Caelica wore a golden wig in
her youth, and her own black hair in old age. Here are
relevant lines from the sonnet:

> ... Caelica, when she was young and sweet,
> Adorned her head with golden borrowed hair,
> To hide her own for cold, she thinks it meet
> The head should mourn, that all the rest was fair;
> And now in age when outward things decay,
> In spite of age she throws that hair away.
> Those golden hairs she then used but to tie
> Poor captive souls which she in triumph led,
>   .   .   .   .   .   .
> And now again her own black hair puts on,
> To mourn for thoughts by her worths overthrown.

The fourth line seems to have suggested Shakespeare's
eleventh, but I do not read his sonnet as having any reference
to a wig.

Sonnet 127

> In the old age black was not counted fair,
> Or if it were it bore not beauty's name:
> But now is black beauty's successive heir,
> And beauty slandered with a bastard shame,
> For since each hand hath put on nature's power,
> Fairing the foul with art's false borrowed face,
> Sweet beauty hath no name no holy bower,
> But is profaned, if not lives in disgrace.
> Therefore my mistress' eyes are raven black,
> Her eyes so suited, and they mourners seem,
> At such who not born fair no beauty lack,
> Slandering creation with a false esteem,
> Yet so they mourn becoming of their woe,
> That every tongue says beauty should look so.

I interpret thus: In the old days black was not classed among beautiful things, or if it was, it was not given the name of beauty. But nowadays—that is since Sidney's sonnet—black has inherited beauty's estate or qualities and is what the word beauty implies, so that beauty is slandered as having produced a bastard. Shakespeare then uses the imagery of 'make up'. It is the face that is made up, and there is no reference to hair or wig. Sidney, in calling Stella's black eyes beautiful has falsely made up the ugly to look beautiful, since when, beauty has been profaned, or at least counted as disgraced. Because this is now the fact, the eyes of Shakespeare's mistress are raven black (as black as could be) and like Stella's they mourn. Sidney gave a poetically sensible reason for Stella's eyes mourning. Shakespeare makes nonsense of it. His lady's eyes mourn at those who, since they are not fair do not lack beauty. This is a hit at Greville's fourth line. And to say this, is to slander nature's creation, which was the active agent in Sidney's sonnet, with a false estimate. Yet they mourn so becomingly that everyone says this is what beauty should look like.

'Therefore' was a strong word for Shakespeare to use. It is *because of* this change in fashion, because black has inherited the place of fairness, that Shakespeare's mistress has black eyes. Stella's were in fact black, and Sidney invented a flattering explanation. Shakespeare accepts the explanation, although with distaste, and says because of this new convention, his mistress, who must by definition be beautiful, has black eyes. So this is why, according to Shakespeare's express statement, the lady of his sonnets is dark. This was his first sonnet in the series on the lady. He proceeds to show that she is as black in character as in looks. It introduces not only a group of sonnets with this theme, but the whole series to her. It is clear that if this is the reason she is black, she is not a real woman but a travesty mocking Sidney's lady. Shakespeare, like all artists, must have known that the opening of a work gives it a direction. His plays are constructed so. That he began his sonnets on the woman with this statement should alert his readers to his mocking intention.

This is immediately followed by a direct parody of a sonnet of Constable that survived until recently only in manuscript and therefore is clear proof that Shakespeare had read his sonnets in manuscript.[56]

Constable wrote,

> Not that thy hand is soft is sweet is white
> Thy lips sweet roses, breast sweet lily is
> That love esteems these three the chiefest bliss
> Which nature ever made for lips' delight
> But when these three to show their heavenly might
> Such wonders do, devotion then for this
> Commandeth us, with humble zeal to kiss
> Such things as work miracles in our sight
> A lute of senseless wood by nature dumb
> Touched by thy hand doth speak divinely well
> And from thy lips and breast sweet tunes do come
> To my dead heart the which new life do give
> Of greater wonders heard we never tell
> Than for the dumb to speak the dead to live.

This is Shakespeare's sonnet :

Sonnet 128

> How oft when thou my music music play'st,
> Upon that blesséd wood whose motion sounds
> With thy sweet fingers when thou gently sway'st,
> The wiry concord that mine ear confounds,
> Do I envy those jacks that nimble leap,
> To kiss the tender inward of thy hand,
> Whilst my poor lips which should that harvest reap,
> At the wood's boldness by thee blushing stand.
> To be so tickled they would change their state,
> And situation with those dancing chips,
> O'er whom thy fingers walk with gentle gait,
> Making dead wood more blest than living lips,
> Since saucy jacks so happy are in this,
> Give them their fingers, me thy lips to kiss.

The correspondence is unmistakable. There is both a deliberately intended correspondence and one probably undesigned.
To take the latter first. Bringing to life by kissing or touching
make essential elements in both, but Shakespeare's creative
memory has altered the relationship. Thus

> Making dead wood more blessed than living lips

uses Constable's 'wood' for the instrument, but his was 'sense-less'. Shakespeare has transferred 'dead' from Constable's 'heart'. The wood had been made 'blessed', corresponding with the divine quality given to its sound by Constable. 'More blessed' says Shakespeare than 'living lips'. The 'life' in Constable was given to his dead heart by his lady's lips. In Shakespeare's creating mind lips have been thought of as alive, since in Constable they were life-giving. This is an unconscious mix-up that could not have been deliberately designed. Indeed it is quite difficult to disentangle consciously. It is the sort of memory-work demonstrated in Livingstone Lowes' *The Road to Xanadu,* and makes good evidence that Shakespeare, not Constable, was the 'borrower'.

Shakespeare's conscious mind was after something of its own. Constable's lady by the miraculous touch of her hand on the lute brought senseless wood to speak divinely. Not so Shakespeare's. I take it he has a distinguishing accent on *'thou'*. He begins by exclaiming on how often when 'thou' as distinct from Diana, 'play'st' the wood that you bless with your fingers ... He chooses not a poetic lute, speaking divinely by a miraculous touch, but one of the keyed instruments that went to create the piano, the most unpoetic of them all. Its sound he refers to as

The wiry concord that mine ear confounds.

—a sound beautiful neither in *timbre* nor in clarity. The action in playing it was certainly not poetical or magical in any way. The mechanism by which the sounds were made was far from being miraculous. It was done by little hammers striking the strings, which the player had to keep from jumping out of place by holding one hand over them as she played with the other. The jacks touched the palm of the hand and fell back into place. The comparison can be nothing but parody. There is a pun on 'jacks' too, for a Jack was any Tom, Dick or Harry; 'saucy jacks' many of them, leap up 'to kiss the tender inward' of her hand, one after other in turn. The movement is of nimble dancers. Constable makes his lady's hand the wonder, bringing wood to life. Shakespeare makes the wood kiss the tender hand. If we have any doubts about Shakespeare's intention, they should be resolved by the sonnet that follows, 'The expense of spirit in a waste of shame'. The juxtaposition of this immediately on jacks in action would not be missed by Shakespeare's friends. He begins his series on the lady by establishing his key, which he does with a group of sonnets whose mockery is unmistakable. Sonnet 128 already hints at the looseness of the lady's morality in preparation for 129. The parody consists in the jacks kissing her hand, as much as in the far from miraculous way by which she produces the wiry sound from the instrument. I shall return to sonnet 129 later.

After 'The expense of spirit' comes sonnet 130, which I have already dealt with, then another on the lady's blackness, climaxing in

> In nothing art thou black save in thy deeds.

Sonnet 131

> Thou art as tyrannous, so as thou art,
> As those whose beauties proudly make them cruel;
> For well thou know'st to my dear doting heart
> Thou art the fairest and most precious jewel.
> Yet in good faith some say that thee behold,
> Thy face hath not the power to make love groan;
> To say they err, I dare not be so bold,
> Although I swear it to my self alone.
> And to be sure that is not false I swear
> A thousand groans but thinking on thy face,
> One on another's neck do witness bear
> Thy black is fairest in my judgement's place.
> In nothing art thou black save in thy deeds,
> And thence this slander as I think proceeds.

Here Shakespeare says his lady is as tyrannous as those whose beauty makes them cruel because she knows that his doting heart thinks her a jewel, as all the other sonneteers think their lady. Yet other people say her face has not the power to make love despair, (as it made Watson decay in the sonnet already quoted). But it is indeed true, he suggests, that he groans a thousand times if he thinks of her face—a double-edged statement. He says these groans, one on another's neck, bear witness that her black is fairest to him, but then comes the stab; she is not black in anything but her deeds, and perhaps he means he likes to sin with her. Anyhow it is out of this that the slander about her face has arisen.

This parody has ample justification. All sonnet ladies are tyrants made cruel by their beauty, whose lovers groan. Shakespeare's addition of blackness or ugliness and sinfulness sends the balance down firmly on the absurd, which it was trembling over anyhow. One never doubts that the sonneteers are just playing a game of their ladies being tyrants and of themselves as in despair. Shakespeare's mock is to take it all seriously—a weapon we have seen him use in both *Love's Labours Lost* and in *As you like it*. It is taken so seriously, as I need remind no one, that without the background that explains it, he has convinced many readers of the reality of his man and woman.

The following are examples from Daniel, Barnes and Spenser of ladies made tyrannous and cruel by their beauty and of their lovers in despair. In sonnet VI Daniel begins,

Fair is my love, and cruel as she is fair.

In his second he sends forth his 'wailing verse' to 'Sigh out a story of her cruel deeds'. In sonnet XXI he calls her 'the tyrant' 'whose unkindness kills', and says he sacrifices his youth to her 'and she respects not it'. In the next he is betrayed by hope that promised him relief 'A thousand times'. We may note that Shakespeare has a 'thousand groans' in his context. Even so he hardly outdoes the noise that other sonneteers make. Constable has an 'ever groaning heart' (decade 5, sonnet IV). Perhaps I can conclude with Daniel's sonnet XVII where he says,

                         her pride is so innated,
She yields no place at all for pity's dwelling.

One could illustrate more fully from Daniel. Barnes in sonnet LXXIII asks his lady how nature can have given her body graces

Where neither they, nor pity find a place?

Ah they been handmaids to thy beauty's fury
Making thy face to tyrannise on men.

And Spenser in sonnet XXVII with more gentle manners
asks

Fair proud now tell me why should fair be proud.

He returns to this theme in XXXI. His 'proud one' uses her
beauty 'such poor thralls' to 'embrew' with 'her cruel hands'.
He asks the question in XLIX that Shakespeare answers in his
sonnet :

Fair cruel, why are ye so fierce and cruel?
Is it because your eyes have power to kill?

In sonnet X he is driven to complain,

See how the tyraness doth joy to see
The huge massácres which her eyes do make.

Sonnet 132 returns to Stella's black eyes :

Thine eyes I love, and they as pitying me,
Knowing thy heart torment me with disdain,
Have put on black, and loving mourners be,
Looking with pretty ruth upon my pain.
And truly not the morning sun of heaven
Better becomes the grey cheeks of the east,
Nor that full star that ushers in the even
Doth half that glory to the sober west
As those two morning eyes become thy face:
Oh let it then as well beseem thy heart
To mourn for me since mourning doth thee grace,
And suit thy pity like in every part.
Then will I swear beauty herself is black,
And all they foul that thy complexion lack.

Stella's eyes were black because pity made them mourn. So
with Shakespeare's lady, but they mourn because they know
her heart disdains. He identifies her eyes sonnet-fashion with

the sun, and by punning on mourning/morning says that they become 'her face' as well as the sun the morning sky. He is probably parodying Wyatt's sonnet XLI, for Wyatt hoped that 'one beam of ruth' (Shakespeare's word, too) might be in his lady's 'cloudy look'. Hence 'the grey cheeks of the east'. If her eyes are the sun and have a beam of pitch, then to correspond the heaven must have cheeks. It is easy to become so bemused with sonnet imagery that one's mind loses its freshness and accepts it as natural. But Shakespeare's mind, as we saw from the mockery in his plays, is too alert for this. He does not use imagery mindlessly. The image of eyes being black because they mourn, which he has already made fun of, his identification of the mourning eyes with the morning sun because the sonnet lady's eyes are suns and because of the apt pun, and his giving the mourning/morning sky cheeks, which moreover he robs of what might be the support of their context by calling it 'eastern'—a word with factual associations—all these confirm his intention of parody. This is not something written in the sleep of convention.

By asking the lady to let it 'beseem' or be fitting or becoming for her heart as well as her eye to pity him, and so make pity becoming to her in all her parts, Shakespeare intends impertinence. That his lady's pity has its origin and justification in being becoming is insulting and this underlies the argument. He then proceeds to his next thrust. As a sonnet lady she cannot grant his request without changing her whole character; he can safely swear his final couplet. So Shakespeare has taken the sonnet talk seriously, and by playing with it made it nonsense.

Sonnet 132 ends Shakespeare's first group of sonnets on the lady. It began by mocking Sidney's sonnet on Stella's eyes and closes with it. The series thus has form. All six sonnets can be nothing but parody. That 129 should appear among them shows that this too must be taken as mockery. I shall show later that this is so. It has been taken seriously. But its position here is important and it cannot have got into this place by some unaccountable means. I have already shown that it springs out of the previous sonnet. It is also relevant that its opening puns on 'expense' and 'waste' pick up the imagery of accountancy from sonnet 127 where in the old age black was not 'counted' fair, also a pun. In a similar way the first line of sonnet 133 picks up 'groaning' from sonnet 131 and carries over the lady's cruelty.

This may be the place to stress that Shakespeare's sonnets take meaning from each other. And indeed this is true of the Elizabethan sonnet sequence in general. They were far from being collections of miscellaneous poems. Shakespeare's readers would be accustomed to sonnet series in some such form, and would expect to find groups where each new sonnet said the same thing a little differently, or else carried forward the theme of the previous one. This was sometimes done quite crudely by beginning each new sonnet with the last line of the preceding. Thus Constable's sonnet VI of decade 5 ends

> But being care, thou fliest me as ill fortune,

and this is the first line of sonnet VII. So on he goes repeating the last line of each sonnet in the first line of the next till sonnet IX. Daniel has a similar series beginning with XXXI, although he tends to vary the repetition a little. Thus sonnet XXXIV ends,

> They will remain, and so thou canst not die.

And XXXV opens,

> Thou canst not die whilst any zeal abound.

Making some sort of link between sonnets must have constituted one of the problems of writing a sonnet sequence. Some poets do it more skilfully than others, and as far as I have noticed, none so skilfully as Shakespeare. The danger was monotony, an inability to progress, which we can see in Daniel. But the alternative to linking must have been chaos. Related with this problem was that of making each sonnet a unity in itself. Indeed writing a good sonnet series called for great art. There were contrary tensions, that although they gave scope for variety and life were traps for the lesser men. Thus the sonneteer had to make each sonnet a thing perfect in itself, and in so far as he followed Petrarch he had to balance it in an

D

octave and sestet, each of which had its own unity and yet had to contribute to the total meaning. If he used the Elizabethan (Shakespearean) form he had to sing the same tune in each of the three quartets and therefore repeat in a parallel construction. The difficulty in this form was to integrate the final couplet so that it did not seem just something tacked on. Then besides relating each sonnet with its neighbour and giving it its own perfection, whether in the Petrarchan or the Elizabethan form, the poet had to make his thought progress. A hundred sonnets saying the same thing would be quite intolerable. So there was the problem of each sonnet leading on to its successor. This could play against its internal unity, at worst leading to formlessness.

Shakespeare's close integration of his sonnets, with each taking colour from its predecessors and throwing its tinge on its successors, means that the order in which we find the sonnets should not be tampered with. Not all Shakespearean critics have given him this respect, although his editors do. Among them Dover Wilson suggested that although those to the man are in a planned and coherent order, those to the woman are not. But his object in suggesting a rearrangement was to make them fit his story. So also Brents Stirling states the principle very clearly in his study of the sonnets to the lady:[57]

> The existing text includes combinations so pointed, so unmistakable, that they may imply a Shakespeare who joined sonnets clearly and emphatically or not at all ... [But] its internal authority is limited to 'clear' combinations that cannot be questioned.

By taking advantage of his last sentence he suggests altering the order of the sonnets on the woman. This in my opinion weakens his case. If the order does not fit one's theory, it is the theory and not the order that should be reconsidered. Since it was customary for sonnets to be linked in groups, and since part of the conscious art of the sonneteer consisted in doing this artistically—and no one is more artistic than Shakespeare—we should accept his order as in every case significant. Thus that he begins his series on the lady by establishing a key of mockery and that this includes sonnets 128 and 129, which present love at its lowest, is significant. It is indeed the key of the whole series. Before I examine sonnet 129, it may be a good plan to look at sonnet 141 with this in our minds.

Like 130, sonnet 141 parodies not one particular sonnet, but the convention as a whole, only it approaches from the angle of the poets' experience rather than from that of the ladies' characteristics. Like 130 too, it mocks by simulating naive acceptance of the conventions and expressing surprise at finding the facts so different. Sonnet 130 is light in tone in contrast with its predecessor, which shocks with its extreme denigration of love. Sonnet 141 follows the method of 130, but integrates the offensiveness of 129 with the lighter presentation.

Sonnet 141

> In faith I do not love thee with mine eyes,
> For they in thee a thousand errors note,
> But 'tis my heart that loves what they despise,
> Who in despite of view is pleased to dote.
> Nor are mine ears with thy tongue's tune delighted,
> Nor tender feeling to base touches prone,
> Nor taste, nor smell, desire to be invited
> To any sensual feast with thee alone:
> But my five wits, nor my five senses can
> Dissuade one foolish heart from serving thee,
> Who leaves unswayed the likeness of a man,
> Thy proud heart's slave and vassal wretch to be:
> Only my plague thus far I count my gain,
> That she that makes me sin, awards me pain.

This begins by echoing the last line of sonnet 140, which goes,

> Bear thine eyes straight, though thy proud heart go wide.

The 'proud heart' is Spenserian. It is the poet's eyes and heart that he now writes of not those of the lady as in the previous sonnet. The 'sensual' aspect and her being a 'plague' throw back to sonnet 137, where the lady is referred to as 'the bay where all men ride' and a 'false plague'. That in its turn throws back to sonnet 129 and the 'saucy jacks' in 128 to whom she offers her open palm. 'Slave' and 'vassal' are implied in the tyrant of sonnet 131. The last line anticipates the first of the next sonnet :

> Love is my sin, and thy dear virtue hate.

This sonnet is therefore sunk in a context, which it also helps to maintain, of parody by denigration.

Although no one sonnet is parodied here, there seems a particular reference to Constable. We could say it parodies Constable and those like him. Thus the eye-heart motive is one of the oldest and most general of sonnet themes but Constable runs it. This is true of the other motives. I shall illustrate each in order as they come. Particularly relevant, for instance, at the opening, is Constable's sonnet V in decade 7, which stresses that if his love had 'not been so excellently fair' his muse would not have mourned for her. In the eighth sonnet of decade 4 his fate asks why he judged between his 'eyes and heart'. His eyes have been exiled from Diana's 'bright beams' and yet his heart is 'bound to them with love's dart'. If his eyes had been allowed to rest there, they would have eased his heart. Shakespeare states aggressively that on the contrary he does not love with his eyes, and for the comic reason that his heart loves what they 'despise'. Then with reference to the lady's voice, poets could not go much further than Constable who, when dealing with creation in the first sonnet of decade 7 says to Diana,

> . . . in thy breath, that heavenly music wons
> Which when thou speakest, angels their voices strains.

But again, something of this sort is true of all sonnet ladies, and Shakespeare may possibly have in mind Watson's *Passionate Centurie* which devotes a series of sonnets to the music of his lady's voice. Constable may have suggested the feast of senses too, for *Diana* combines a suggestion for it with the eye-heart motive in decade 5 sonnet IV. There we find that 'mine heart' 'feedeth mine eyes'. But again, there are other poets in like case. Spenser in sonnet XXXV writes,

> My hungry eyes through greedy covetise,

Still to behold the object of their pain :
With no contentment can themselves suffice,
But having pine and having not complain.

Watson in sonnet XVI of the *Passionate Centurie* relates his
ear with this theme as well as his eye :

She feeds mine ear with tunes of rare delight,
Mine eye with loving looks.

Barnes too seems to have contributed something to the parody
in his third sonnet where the prison keys are sight, hearing and
touch. These let his heart out of prison and escape to his lady.
Shakespeare, on the contrary, says that his senses do not desire
to be invited to a feast with his lady.

Shakespeare calls the feast 'sensual', and by doing so relates
it with what was the fundamental human problem in sonnet
love. Constable may be involved in this also for he defends
himself against such an accusation in the first sonnet of decade
5.

Ay me poor wretch, my prayer is turned to sin,
I say I love, my mistress says 'tis lust :
Thus most we lose, where most we seek to win,
Wit will make wicked what is ne'er so just.
And yet I can supplant her false surmise.
Lust is a fire, that for an hour or twain
Giveth a scorching blaze, and then he dies.
Love, a continual furnace doth maintain.

The actual image of the feast may have been suggested by
Spenser's sonnet LXXVII :

Was it a dream, or did I see it plain,
A goodly table of pure ivory :
All spread with junkets, fit to entertain,
The greatest prince with pompous royalty.
'Mongst which there in a silver dish did lie,
Two golden apples of unvalued price :
. . . .
Exceeding sweet, yet void of sinful vice,

> That many sought yet none could ever taste,
> Sweet fruit of pleasure brought from Paradise :
>
> .   .   .   .   .   .
>
> Her breast that table was so richly spread,
> My thoughts the guests, which would thereon have fed.

Although Spenser does not make his feast sensual, there is reason enough for this epithet in some of his other sonnets. No. LXXXIV opens thus :

> Let not one spark of filthy lustful fire
> Break out, that may her sacred peace molest :
> Nor one light glance of sensual desire.

Spenser was not one of the youthful sonneteers who love from a distance, and in this sonnet he says he will control his desires and his modest thoughts will visit her 'chaste bower of rest Accompanied with angelic delights'. Sidney and Greville too found that against all the rules, their love involved desire. Here we see the sonnets decadent, although the chastity of the ladies is never in question. But when it comes to criticising sonnet love or desire as sinful, it must eventually lead to denigration of woman. Chivalric love faced this criticism from the start. Capellanus who invented the Arthurian story with the chivalric code of love, ended his book by criticising love as sinful and woman as the temptress. Both Sidney and Spenser take care not to impugn the chastity of their ladies. But Shakespeare would be aware that love as sin involved woman as sinful. He would know of Bruno's attack on sonnet literature from this angle in Florio's translation. Here is a passage from it as quoted by Frances Yates.[58]

> Good God ! what more vile, what more ignoble spectacle can present itself to a wholesome eye than that of a man who is dreamy, afflicted, tormented, sad, melancholy, now hot, now cold, now fervent, now fearful, now pale, now red, with countenance now perplexed, now resolute, who spends the best part of his time, the best part of his fleeting life distilling the elixir of his brain writing down and publicly recording the perpetual tortures, the heavy torments, the weary

thoughts and speeches, the bitter meditations generated beneath the tyranny of an unworthy, imbecile, infatuated, wanton, filthy wretch of a woman?

In fact a sonneteer whose lady has been blackened! So Shakespeare had a precedent. Indeed we have seen that he thought it a joke to present the sonnet ladies in *Love's Labours Lost* as obsessed with the idea of sex, and Rosaline, whose resemblance with the dark lady of the sonnets, is obvious, dancing suggestively with Boyet as her jack. Because some of the sonneteers are not chaste like their lady, because even when as in general they are, their misery comes from her chaste disdain, indicating that they wished she were not, and because it all seemed unnatural and artificial, 'therefore', if I may use Shakespeare's own key word in his explanation of her darkness, therefore his lady is not chaste. All this lies behind not only sonnets 141, 137, 128 and 129, but also the whole idea of the moral darkness of his lady of the sonnets. Before dealing with sonnet 129, as I am now ready to do, I must return for a moment to Constable for the poetry parodied in the last lines of sonnet 141. In decade 4 sonnet V he tells Diana to

Count it a loss to lose a faithful slave.

Shakespeare says on the contrary that he is his lady's proud heart's slave and vassal wretch, and he counts it a gain that she who makes him sin awards him pain. Constable's first sonnet in the same decade laments that the poet must leave Diana and cannot bear to:

In vain my wit doth tell in verse my woe,

for his heart cannot stop loving her. In the eighth sonnet of decade 1 we find:

All pains if you command, it joy shall prove,
        ... then say but this;

.   .   .   .   .

I do command thee without hope to love.
So, when this thought my sorrow shall augment,

> That mine own folly did procure my pain,
> . . . . . .
> It was your will, and not my want of wit:
> I have the pain, bear you the blame of it.

This Shakespeare turns round the other way, making nonsense in his last line. There may also be some influence from the sixth sonnet in decade 3, which was Sidney's although not printed among his works till 1598 when it makes the first of *Certain Sonnets*. The sonnet opens,

> Since shunning pain, I ease can never find:

says that he yields, 'Oh love, unto thy loathed yoke', and ends,

> Thou art my lord, and I thy vowed slave.

Here again we must notice that this theme is not by any means confined to poems in *Diana*. Daniel also expressed the same attitude in sonnet XIV with,

> So much I please to perish in my woe.

And Spenser expresses it in his best singing style in sonnet XLII.

> The love which me so cruelly tormenteth,
> So pleasing is in my extremest pain:
> That all the more my sorrow it augmenteth,
> The more I love and do embrace my bane.
> Nor do I wish (for wishing were but vain)
> To be acquit from my continual smart:
> But joy her thrall for ever to remain,
> And yield for pledge my poor captivéd heart.

Sonnet 129

> The expense of spirit in a waste of shame
> Is lust in action, and till action, lust

Is perjured, murderous, bloody full of blame,
Savage, extreme, rude, cruel, not to trust,
Enjoyed no sooner but despised straight,
Past reason hunted, and no sooner had
Past reason hated as a swallowed bait,
On purpose laid to make the taker mad.
Made in pursuit and in possession so,
Had, having, and in quest, to have extreme,
A bliss in proof and proved and very woe,
Before a joy proposed behind a dream
All this the world well knows yet none knows well,
To shun the heaven that leads men to this hell.

This seems a tirade against lust by one who has experienced it.
I have not gone into the psychology of lust. It may be that the
qualities which Shakespeare refers to particularly characterise
it, but it strikes me that those listed in lines three and four are
precisely those said by the sonneteers to characterise their
chaste ladies. Indeed it looks as if a *Road to Xanadu*-like
entanglement of memories has coalesced to give Shakespeare
his impression of lust.

Constable's third sonnet of his fifth decade seems to have
determined Shakespeare's theme. He writes,

If ever sorrow spoke from soul that loves,
As speaks a spirit in a man possessed,
In me her spirit speaks.

He then describes himself as 'raging mad'. So Constable writes,
he says, of the madness of a man possessed by the spirit of his
lady. 'Possessed', 'mad' and 'spirit' are the key words. Shakespeare does not follow the rest of the sonnet, but elaborates this
opening mainly by substituting lust for the spirit of Constable's
lady. He gives a double meaning to 'spirit', following Constable in this, although they are not the same meanings. Constable's 'spirit' refers to that of his lady, but it is like the evil
spirit that possesses a madman. The first meaning of Shakespeare's 'spirit' suggests something trailing clouds of glory, if
this is not too anachronistic a way of putting it. But Crutwell[59]
has shown that it could also mean 'the spirit generative', a term

in 'sexual physiology'. He considers that Shakespeare says that this is lost 'in the act of sex'.

Another sonnet parodied is Barnes' no. X, where he complains that his lady keeps his heart by a charter,

> Sealed with wax of steadfast continence,

that holds his heart mercilessly and yet denies him. He asks,

> What skills to wear thy girdle or thy garter,
> When other arms shall thy small waste embrace?
> How great a waste, of mind and body's weal.

Barnes' 'waste of mind' has become Shakespeare's 'expense of spirit'. 'Spirit' is the operative word in Constable, and Shakespeare takes it as his, but the idea and the shape of his phrase is Barnes's. We might note incidentally that Barnes brings together waist/waste, a sort of pun that could have fixed his sonnet in Shakespeare's memory. Shakespeare puns all four nouns in his first line, or gives them double meanings. Thus 'expense' means expending or using as one spends energy, but it also involves the metaphor of spending an extravagant sum of money. Both meanings may have been suggested by Greville's sonnet XLI where we find,

> When honour's audit calls for thy receipt,
> And chargeth on they head much time mispent;
> Nature corrupted by thy vain conceit,
> Thy reason servile, poor, and passion-rent.

Shakespeare's double meaning is here, for time and passion are spent and this is charged in a context where the auditor requires a receipt. Other aspects of Greville's sonnet appear in Shakespeare's also. 'Reason' is servile in Greville, submissive in Shakespeare's hunt, nature is corrupted in both, and it is passion that is spent. These three sonnets, then, have fused in Shakespeare's mind in a tangle fit for Livingston Lowes to describe. All I need for my purpose is to point out the entanglement and its relevance.

I have still to deal with 'waste of shame'. In one sense the phrase means a shameful waste, where 'waste' has the meaning of the second word in Barnes' pun, and is what Greville's auditor complains of. But 'shame' also has a double meaning for the waste is shameful not only because it offends the auditor, but with the moral turpitude that Greville intends. The second meaning of Shakespeare's 'waste' is that of a desolate territory. We could paraphrase, 'The expense of spirit in a desolation of shame'. If we take this meaning and do not let their puns cheapen 'spirit' and 'expense' the line is emotionally charged, every word involving its idea in the superlative. Thus 'spirit' has an unqualifiable value, 'expense' entails the fullest use of it, 'waste' has associations of utter desolation and 'shame' is a complete loss of self-esteem. Shakespeare puns all this and says it is 'lust in action'. He then says that lust 'till action' or before action is what the sonneteers describe in their ladies. Thus he suggests that lust is what the sonneteers write of, and that every way you look at it, they are miseries.

This is writing on two levels. At one the words carry elemental associations, and are felt to have a profound meaning, stirring us to the depth. At the other level they pun, or carry a second meaning inconsistent with their first. It is as if a huge cloud from the empyrean slammed down to kill a flea. If we do not notice the flea we are impressed by the storm in its own right. But if we do, we realise that the sublime words each cloak an instrument well fitted to kill the flea. Shakespeare writes like this frequently in the sonnets. It is one reason for his punning. It is not just that his words have multiple associations, for this is one of his general characteristics, but that the double and opposite senses in which the words are used destroy the meaning rather than enrich it. In such parody poetry is not ridiculed, it is used as an element in a parody of poetic artifice.

Lust, if we identify it with desire, was a sonnet theme, as is evident in some of the sonnets I have aready quoted. Sidney's sonnet on desire was not printed till 1598 in *Certain Sonnets*. Shakespeare might have seen it in manuscript, although we cannot be sure of this : He refers to desire as,

> Thou blind man's mark, thou fool's self chosen snare,
> Fond fancy's scum, and dregs of scattered thought,

Band of all evils, cradle of causeless care,
Thou web of will, whose end is never wrought.
Desire, desire I have too dearly bought,
With prize of mangled mind thy worthless ware,
Too long, too long asleep thou hast me brought,
Who should my mind to higher things prepare.
But yet in vain thou hast my ruin sought,
In vain thou madest me to vain things aspire,
In vain thou kindlest all thy smokey fire.
For virtue hath this better lesson taught,
Within myself to seek my only hire :
Desiring nought but how to kill desire.

Here are similarities with Shakespeare's sonnet, but no direct
pointers to it. And his sonnet can be fully accounted for without it.

Although it seems likely that Constable's sonnet triggered off
Shakespeare's, and that Barnes' and Greville's are closely
associated with it, it explodes a great deal of other material.
Let us run through the sonnet in detail. We may begin by
asking why it was only 'till action' that lust

Is perjured, murderous, bloody full of blame,
Savage, extreme, rude, cruel, not to trust,

the answer presumably being because these are the lady's
characteristics in her chastity, before lust is active. As the items
on the list are not qualified or made specific, they are impossible to identify, although easy to illustrate. As to perjury and
not being 'to trust', Daniel in sonnet XXII, already quoted,
says he can find 'no truth at all' in Delia. Nearly all the sonnet
ladies commit murder—murder by disdain we might call it. I
have already illustrated this. It is related with their cruelty,
which Daniel bewails from sonnet to sonnet. He begins in
sonnet I casting 'the account of all' his care, looking on 'the
dear expenses' of his youth, rather as Shakespeare begins his
sonnet. In the next he sighs out 'a story of her cruel deeds'. She
kills him 'with disdain' in sonnet III, and so on he goes. In
sonnet XXIX he says she has 'murdering eyes'. Constable's
Diana is as criminal. He warns her in decade 2, sonnet IV to

beware 'of murder's guilt', to no purpose apparently, for in the next he says his heart has been found murdered. In decade 7, sonnet IX he asks why she must 'be still unkind and kill me so?' Why should she impose 'Death and disdain' on him? But of all savage ladies, Daniel's is the most savage. In sonnet XVIII, which I have already referred to, we find:

> restore thy fierce and cruel mind,
> To Hyrcan tigers, and to ruthless bears.

Indeed all sonneteers live like Constable in decade 8, sonnet II

> Under the burden of [her] cruel hate.

I need not illustrate that reason is always powerless to deal with the lover, nor that the imagery of the hunt belongs to this tradition. The madness is principally Constable's although that too could be illustrated from other poets. The bait laid to catch the lover is very common.

> Made in pursuit and in possession so

suggests that the mock lust which Shakespeare writes of is made by poets in their verses as they pursue the theme of love. In the second sonnet of *The Passionate Centurie* we find,

> My heart is set him down twixt hope and fears
> Upon the stony bank of high desire,
> To view his own made flood of blubbering tears.

The flood is 'own made' in the course that love runs. The emendation of 'mad' for 'made', which many editors accept, makes sense and stresses the madness and possession, but it is not really called for. This sonnet of Watson's may well be in Shakespeare's mind, for its 'black despair', as the place where

> No sun comes there nor any heavenly saint,

may have contributed to the associations that underlie the end of Shakespeare's sonnet. The double relevance is confirmatory.

> Had, having, and in quest, to have extreme,
> A bliss in proof and proved, and very woe.

is probably misprinted; the reading should almost certainly be,

> A bliss in proof, and proved a very woe.

The lines seem to have been suggested by Spenser's sonnet XXXV quoted above, where Stella's hungry eyes,

> With no contentment can themselves suffice,
> But having pine and having not complain.

Perhaps the ending in a 'dream' comes from no. L of Watson's *Passionate Centurie*, where he 'dies in dreams'. An early example of the hysterical tone of the sonnet can be seen in his *Tears of Fancie,* sonnet XXXIX, which has lists and sudden hysterical contradictions like,

> Here ends my sorrow, no here my sorrow springeth.

But he is by no means the only hysterical lover, buffetted between contrary attitudes.

The sonnet-ending has a rich background. Thus sonnet LVI of *The Tears of Fancie* has,

> Were all the woes of all the world in one,
> Sorrow and death set down in all their pride :
> Yet were they insufficient to bemoan,
> The restless horrors that my heart doth hide.
> Where black despair doth feed on every thought.

In sonnet II of the sixth decade Constable says that to love is

> To live in hell, a heaven to behold,
> To welcome life, to die a living death.

He then gives a list of contrasts that may well have influenced Shakespeare. In his seventh decade, sonnet II we find:

> Excluded heaven, what can remain but hell?

Sidney comes even closer in his second sonnet of *Astrophel and Stella*

> To make myself believe that all is well,
> While with a feeling skill I paint my hell.

and he ends sonnet XXXVI by saying he cannot escape from Stella by 'sense's privilege', and in sonnet LXXXVI,

> No doom shall make one's heaven become his hell.

Perhaps it should just be said, however, that heaven and hell are obvious extremes to contrast, and even that 'hell' is an easy word to rhyme.

Drayton unifies the whole situation of torment and madness and incoherent experience in Amour 43 of the 1594 edition of *Idea's Mirrour*:

> Why do I speak of joy, or write of love,
> When my heart is the very den of horror,
> And in my soul the pains of hell I prove,
> With all his torments and infernal terror
>
> .   .   .   .   .
>
> But still distracted in love's lunacy,
> And Bedlamlike thus raving in my grief,
>
> .   .   .   .   .
>
> Now I deny her, then I do confess her,
> Now I do curse her, then again I bless her.

That Drayton sums up so admirably suggests that he comes after all the other sonneteers and so is well placed to do this. He could conceivably have written *Idea's Mirrour* in 1591 or soon after. Shakespeare could conceivably have read his sonnets before writing his own. But his sonnets do not seem to form part of the brew that boiled up into Shakespeare, *Road to*

Xanadu-wise. Nor are they necessary to supply missing por-
tions of the jig-saw puzzle, if I may change the metaphor.
They have the distinct clarity of this sonnet, which reads like a
conscious summary of the poetry that includes Shakespeare.

To conclude, sonnet 129 is quite as clearly a parody of
Constable's man possessed by his lady's spirit as the sonnets it
appears amongst are demonstrably parodies. But there is also
as clear a background of associated memories, which enrich the
parody.

Sonnets 133 and 134, which open the second group on the
lady, play with the traditional attitude of lovers being identified. Shakespeare makes this absurd by entangling the friend in
the situation; three people are identified. To have two treated
like this, sonnet fashion, is acceptable, but three is too much; it
is ridiculous. Three-foldness is important also in itself and was
felt to have a special value; sonneteers often have things and
qualities in three. Shakespeare makes fun of it for instance in
sonnets 11 and 105. Here, as elsewhere, he suggests that such
an important three must be like the Trinity, and adds a suggestion of the crucifixion by punning 'crossed'; that is he plays on
the identity of three in a crucified situation. He makes sure of
linking the sonnet with its context by carrying on from previous ones the imagery of the groaning heart, the wound, the
torture, the cruelty.

Sonnet 133

> Beshrew that heart that makes my heart to groan
> For that deep wound it gives my friend and me;
> Is't not enough to torture me alone,
> But slave to slavery my sweet'st friend must be.
> Me from myself thy cruel eye hath taken,
> And my next self thou harder hast engrossed,
> Of him, myself, and thee I am forsaken,
> A torment thrice three-fold thus to be crossed:
> Prison my heart in thy steel bosom's ward,
> But then my friend's heart let my poor heart bail,
> Whoe'er keeps me, let my heart be his guard,
> Thou canst not then use rigour in my gaol.
> And yet thou wilt, for I being pent in thee,
> Perforce am thine and all that is in me.

This is to say that Shakespeare, who identifies with both his male and his female friends, is in a sorry situation. He curses her heart that makes his heart groan for the wound she gives him and his friend. It is a common sonnet play that the lady's eye enslaves, captures, takes possession of her lover. This lady's cruel eye has stolen the poet from himself, and worse still has done the same with his friend. So Shakespeare has lost his friend, himself and her. He then makes a ridiculous tangle by weaving a more fantastic story round it. He says in effect, let the situation or story be that she imprisons his heart, but then let his heart bail out his friend's. Whoever is my keeper, he says, let me be his so that she will not be able to be hard in the gaol where he keeps his friend. Yet she will; for since he is imprisoned in her, then everything in him is hers. That is to say there is a complete identity between him and her, and therefore she has his friend to torture. Shakespeare invented this phantasy of a terrible situation with light wit and ingenuity. It is moulded on the sort of phantasy common among sonneteers and brought to a pitch of absurdity in Barnes. In fact this and the following sonnets are unmistakable parodies of Barnes' sonnets II to IX. They begin thus:

> Whiles with strong chains, of hardy-tempered steel,
> I bound my thoughts, still gadding fast and faster:
> When they through time, the differences did feel,
> Betwixt a mistress' service and a master.
> Keeping in bondage jealously enthralled,
> In prisons of neglect, his nature's mildness,
> Him I with solitary studies walled,
> By thraldom cloaking his outrageous wildness.
> On whom my careful thoughts I set to watch,
> Guarding him closely, lest he should out-issue:
> To seek thee (Laya) who still wrought to catch,
> And train my tender boy, that could not miss you:
> So you bewitched him once, when he did kiss you:
> That by such sleights, as never were found out
> To serve your turn he daily went about.

> He when continual vigil moved my watch,
> Some-deal by chance, with careful guard to slumber:

> The prison keys, from them did slowly snatch,
>   Which of the five were only three by number.

I have already referred to them, sight, hearing and touch. These

> Laid open all for his escape : now there,
> The watch-men grinned for his impiety,
> What crosses bred this contrariety :
> That by these keys, my thoughts in chains be left,
> And by these keys, I of mine heart bereft.

This is by no means clear on a first reading. To whom does 'him' refer? From the sonnets following it appears that 'him' refers to Barnes' heart. I take this to mean : first he bound his thoughts, that were gadding, in steel (hence Shakespeare's 'steel bosom's ward'), and they in time learnt to serve him, the master, and found it different from serving a mistress. Then he kept his heart (him) in bondage and walled him in with solitary studies, choking his wildness; and he set his thoughts to guard him. At last when his thoughts were asleep, his heart got the keys of his prison, with the result that Barnes' thoughts were chained up and his heart escaped. The story goes on, however, that Laya gives his heart up for a 'richer prize', and his heart posted amain to Parthenope (sonnet V) and asked her pardon. She grants it and asks the poet to do so too. He, however, wants some surety for his heart, and she gladly agrees. She offers anything he likes for a pawn, and he chooses her love, which she gives, and he 'was content to set at liberty My trembling heart' (sonnet VII). I need not go into the further complications. This is enough to show the sonnet mode that Shakespeare is guying. He follows Barnes' story closely. His lady imprisons his friend's heart in steel and Shakespeare gives his heart as bail to find, as did Barnes, that his plan did not work out to his advantage after all. Here is the sequel to Shakespeare's story.

Sonnet 134

> So now I have confessed that he is thine,
> And I myself am mortgaged to thy will,

Myself I'll forfeit, so that other mine,
Thou wilt restore to be my comfort still:
But thou wilt not, nor he will not be free,
For thou art covetous, and he is kind,
He learned but surety-like to write for me,
Under that bond that him as fast doth bind.
The statute of thy beauty thou wilt take,
Thou usurer that put'st forth all to use,
And sue a friend, came debtor for my sake,
So him I lose through my unkind abuse.
Him have I lost, thou hast both him and me,
He pays the whole, and yet am I not free.

So then Shakespeare is mortgaged or pawned to her will. But he offers to forfeit himself to get his friend released. However, she will not allow this, nor does his friend want to be freed. He wrote his name to the bond as surety for Shakespeare and that binds him. But she uses the law of her beauty and takes all she can from the one who came as his surety. So the poet loses his heart through being unkindly abused, and also his friend and his lady. He therefore pays the whole as he remains in love with the lady, and yet is not freed by settling the debt. All this resembles Barnes' experience down to the bitter end, for when Parthenope was going to set his heart free, it 'straight began to fawn, Upon his mistress' kindly courtesy'. So he is deprived of his heart by her. He remonstrates with her and shows her the mortgage in which she became his heart's bail (sonnet VIII),

But, when the mortgage should have cured the sore:
She passed it off, by deed of gift before.

So she released his heart and robbed him of his heart's treasure (sonnet IX). All he can do is to mourn for this loss of his heart to her. There can be no doubt that Shakespeare is parodying this tale of woe. He makes it ridiculous by having a real friend involved, whereas Barnes is writing a pure phantasy about his heart. His way of guying Barnes is the same as he used to make fun of Lodge's pastoral love in *As you like it*. He turns a fantastic story into a ridiculous metaphor of what he presents as a real story. As a real story it is nonsense.

Although there can be no doubt that Shakespeare aims this

joke at Barnes, he was by no means the first to talk in this ridiculous way. Wyatt (XLVI of Tottel) gives his heart to his lady :

It was once mine, it can no more be so.

There is no comfort for either of them.

And yours the loss, and mine the deadly pain,

which Shakespeare echoes in his last line of sonnet 134. Spenser is another poet who offers himself freely as a slave and pledge. In sonnet XLII he says he rejoices

> her thrall for ever to remain,
> And yield for pledge my poor captivéd heart
> The which that it from her may never start,
> Let her, if please her, bind with adamant chain.

The next two sonnets pun on Shakespeare's name—a custom of sonneteers. Some also pun on their lady's name. Here Shakespeare does it thoroughly; perhaps I should say outdoes it.

Sonnet 135

> Whoever hath her wish, thou hast thy Will,
> And Will to boot, and Will in over-plus,
> More than enough am I that vex thee still,
> To thy sweet will making addition thus.
> Wilt thou whose will is large and spacious,
> Not once vouchsafe to hide my will in thine,
> Shall will in others seem right gracious,
> And in my will no fair acceptance shine:
> The sea all water, yet receives rain still,
> And in abundance addeth to his store,
> So thou being rich in Will add to thy Will,
> One will of mine to make thy large Will more.
> Let no unkind, no fair beseechers kill,
> Think all but one, and me in that one Will.

Sonnet 136

If thy soul check thee that I come so near,
Swear to thy blind soul that I was thy Will,
And will thy soul knows is admitted there,
Thus far for love, my love-suit sweet fulfil.
Will, will fulfil the treasure of thy love,
I fill it full with wills, and my will one,
In things of great receipt with ease we prove,
Among a number one is reckoned none.
Then in the number let me pass untold,
Though in thy store's account I one must be,
For nothing hold me so it please thee hold,
That nothing me, a something sweet to thee.
Make but my name thy love, and love that still,
And then thou lov'st me for my name is Will.

'Will' has three references. It refers to William Shakespeare; it means what one wants or wishes or determines; and it also has the sense common in Shakespeare's time of sex-desire. Where it has a capital letter it refers to William Shakespeare, himself, perhaps exclusively. In the first line of sonnet 135 the meaning of the word is not yet determinable; the sonnet is written to explain it. In the fourth line it probably has the second meaning, in the fifth the third. The poet suggests that since it is 'large and spacious' there should be room for his 'will' in the second and third sense. The 'will' of the next two lines means desire. As the sea has always room for more rain, so she, already rich in all senses of 'will', should go on adding or increasing them all. He brings everything to a climax in the last word.

In the next sonnet Shakespeare says that if her soul or conscience checks her, then since it is blind or not conscious, or perhaps he means blind because in love, she can swear to it that he is her William, and her soul knows that will, meaning love, is admissable. Thus far for that meaning. Then he tells her to fulfil his love suit. 'Will' of the fifth line is a pun on himself and desire. Possibly in the sixth line both 'wills' mean desire. Since she has many loves, one more means nothing. It is all summed up in the couplet.

These sonnets spring out of the two previous, where the lady keeps both men in thrall, and they look forward to sonnet 137, where his love is blind, and where the lady is characterised perhaps most offensively of anywhere in the sonnets as 'the bay where all men ride'.

Sonnet 137

Thou blind fool love, what dost thou to mine eyes,
That they behold and see not what they see:
They know what beauty is, see where it lies,
Yet what the best is, take the worst to be.
If eyes corrupt by over-partial looks,
Be anchored in the bay where all men ride,
Why of eyes' falsehood hast thou forgéd hooks,
Whereto the judgement of my heart is tied?
Why should my heart think that a several plot,
Which my heart knows the wide world's common place?
Or mine eyes seeing this, say this is not
To put fair truth upon so foul a face,
In things right true my heart and eyes have erred,
And to this false plague are they now transferred.

Here Shakespeare asks love, which is blind, how it has blinded him, since although he can distinguish beauty perfectly well he sees what is 'the worst' as if it were 'the best'. In the second quatrain he proceeds from this to ask why since his eyes have been corrupted by his prejudiced vision, love has made hooks of that false vision to catch and hold his heart in the same false judgement as that of his eyes. In the third quatrain he questions both eyes and heart; firstly why does his heart think what everyone knows is the world's common place, is his own particular property, and secondly why should his eyes which see this, call a foul face beautiful. The couplet sums up by saying that both eyes and heart have erred, or gone astray and transferred themselves from the truth to this 'false plague'.

The sonnet parodies Sidney. Stella is chaste and hates his unchaste love, as he tells us in sonnet LXI. So 'With chastened mind' he must relinquish what she hates. In the next sonnet he complains that she is unkind and she replies,

That love she did, but with a love not blind.

. . . . .

And therefore by her love's authority;
Willed me those tempests of vain love to flee :
And anchor fast myself on virtue's shore.

Shakespeare parodies by saying the opposite. Stella's love is not blind, and she asks her love to anchor himself on virtue's shore. Shakespeare makes love blind and it blinds him; his lady is not chaste and is anchored in the bay where all men ride. The parody is inescapable.

Sidney follows up this imagery in LXV. He complains to Cupid,

when naked boy, thou couldst no harbour find

. . . .

I lodged thee in my heart; and being blind
By nature born, I gave to thee my eyes.

This is what happened to the eyes of the poet being parodied; it is how love made him blind. So Shakespeare asks how he was made blind by love. And here also he got the harbour and the heart where his love was lodged. It is all the more disastrous in Shakespeare, who complains that love made him see falsely, and not be able to perceive clearly what happens in the harbour of his heart where his lady is. All the men are riding in that harbour, he suggests.

It was also Sidney who suggested the change in the looking or seeing that involved the falsehood, and whose questioning approach Shakespeare mimics. In sonnet LXXXVI he asks Stella,

Alas whence comes this change of looks? If I
Have changed deserts, let mine own conscience be
A still felt plague to self condemning me.
Let woe grip on my heart, shame load mine eyes.

So also in Shakespeare's sonnet his miserable question reveals that because of his falseness his conscience has indeed become a plague. Woe has gripped his heart, and shame hooded his eyes.

You might say that Shakespeare writes after the event which Sidney denies. His heart and eyes have gone astray and arrived at the false plague of self-condemnation.

If we can allow the sound of a word rather than its meaning to operate in Shakespeare's memory, we can discover why he used 'bay' in recollecting Sidney's 'harbour'. The rhythm requires a monosyllable of course but not necessarily 'bay'. Spenser writes in sonnet XXIX,

> See how the stubborn damsel doth deprave
> My simple meaning with disdainful scorn :
> And by the bay which I unto her gave,
> Accounts myself her captive quite forlorn,
> The bay (quoth she) is of the victors borne
> Yielded them by the vanquished as their meads
>
> . . . . . .
>
> But sith she will the conquest challenge needs,
> Let her accept me as her faithful thrall.

'Bay' here refers to the laurel and not a harbour. But it occurs in a similar context to that of Shakespeare's sonnet. Spenser's 'damsel' 'depraves' the poet's simple meaning. He gives her the 'bay' that acknowledges him her captive. It is giving one's heart that does this. The poet asks her to accept him as 'thrall'. It may be some argument that when I was reading Spenser's sonnets on the alert for influences, this immediately reminded me of Shakespeare's 'bay'. So also did Barnes' sonnet XVI where 'bay' with the meaning of laurel signifying the lady's conquest also occurs. In Barnes there is a closer resemblance to Shakespeare since he refers to his heart, which

> in her body lies imprisoned :
> For (mongst all bay-crowned conquerors) no such
> Can make the slavish captive boast him conquered
> Except Parthenope.

There still remains to account for the 'forged hooks' and the 'several plot' that is the 'wide world's common place'. Hooks and baits are too common to pin on any one poet, but Spenser's sonnet XLVII will illustrate the image :

Trust not the treason of those smiling looks,
Until ye have their guileful trains well tried :
For they are like but unto golden hooks,
That from the foolish fish their baits do hide.

The 'several plot' that turns out 'the wide world's common place' is a *Road to Xanadu*-like conglomerate, not necessarily indicating one poet in particular. In sonnet LXIV Greville complains that

what before was filled by me alone,
I now discern hath room for everyone.

In other words what he thought a 'several plot' has room for everyone. Constable in his second sonnet of decade 4 says that his lady has many 'obedient subjects',

So many eyes die with one look's disdain.

. . . . . .

Thou hast such means to conquer men withal,
As all the world must yield.

He makes no doubt about the nature of this conquest by ending,

For one will sooner yield unto thee then
When he shall meet thee naked all alone.

Here is Shakespeare's 'all the world' in a similar context. Then to return to Greville, in sonnet XXXVIII he says he 'Lodged in the midst of paradise, your heart' but was expelled because his eyes found knowledge :

And glassy honour, tender of disgrace,
Stands seraphin to see I come not there;
While that fine soil, which all these joys did yield,
By broken fence is proved a common field.

We need to note that it is not Greville's love who is the common field, but paradise when its fence is broken. This is precisely Shakespeare's image. The fence separates the several, or individual plot from the common. Greville's 'common field' suggests a 'several plot' as its opposite. Shakespeare calls the common a 'common place' not a 'common field' probably intending a pun on 'commonplace', it being the commonplaces of the sonnets that he parodies.

Sonnet 138

> When my love swears that she is made of truth,
> I do believe her though I know she lies,
> That she might think me some untutored youth,
> Unlearnéd in the world's false subtleties.
> Thus vainly thinking that she thinks me young,
> Although she knows my days are past the best,
> Simply I credit her false speaking tongue,
> On both sides thus is simple truth suppressed:
> But wherefore says she not she is unjust?
> And wherefore say not I that I am old?
> Oh love's best habit is in seeming trust,
> And age in love, loves not to have years told.
> Therefore I lie with her, and she with me,
> And in our faults by lies we flattered be.

The aim of this sonnet is obviously to arrive at the pun on 'lie' in the second last line. It has for background sonneteers claiming that they do not lie when they profess their love, but the truth being that their love is usually just a courteous play with little reality in it, and that their claims are far too extravagant to be credible. Shakespeare turns the situation round into one of incredible prose reality, and says I know my love is a liar but I believe her all the same in order to pretend I am innocent and therefore younger than in fact I am. But she can see for herself how old he is. Why this nonsense? And he answers with his punning couplet. I need hardly say that so far from the sonneteers concealing their age, they protest that they are old beyond their years, worn out by love. I shall illustrate this in the next chapter. Here Shakespeare makes the joke of trying to hide his age in contradistinction from the youthful sonneteer who assumes more years than he has.

Sonnet 139

> Oh call not me to justify the wrong,
> That thy unkindness lays upon my heart,
> Wound me not with thine eye but with thy tongue,
> Use power with power, and slay me not by art,
> Tell me thou lov'st elsewhere; but in my sight,
> Dear heart forbear to glance thine eye aside,
> What need'st thou wound with cunning when thy might
> Is more than my o'erpressed defence can bide?
> Let me excuse thee, ah my love well knows,
> Her pretty looks have been mine enemies,
> And therefore from my face she turns my foes,
> That they elsewhere might dart their injuries:
> Yet do not so, but since I am near slain,
> Kill me outright with looks, and rid my pain.

Shakespeare begs the lady not to ask him to justify the wrong which she herself has caused by her unkindness. All sonnet ladies wound with their eyes. He asks her not to slay him with this art, but with her tongue, to use this powerful weapon with the power she has. It may not be very complimentary to suggest that her tongue is powerful? However, Shakespeare only says that it is enough to tell him she loves elsewhere. If she does this, she can then control her wish to look away from him, for there is no need to use this artful weapon, when the power she has over him because he loves her is more than he can defend himself against. Then in the sestet he changes his tone and excuses. He pretends that it is because she is sorry that her looks are his enemies, that she looks away from him to others, so hurting them, not him. But he asks her nevertheless to look at him, to put him out of his pain by killing him outright since he is nearly dead anyhow.

This is so close to what all the sonneteers say that it could almost be taken seriously as an exercise in the tradition. It has subtle touches, however, pointing at his game. Thus Shakespeare begins by accepting the wrong as something that the lady *expects* him to justify. What the wrong is he leaves vague. Daniel knew. In his third sonnet he talks of judging 'the wrongs that she has done', and he ends sonnet XIX,

Yet let her say that she hath done me wrong,
To use me thus and know I loved so long.

In his third sonnet he makes it clear that what she has done is
to 'kill me with disdain'. 'Use power with power' comes from
Constable. Sonnet IX of decade 7 begins,

Wilt thou be still unkind, and kill me so?

.   .   .   .   .

Suffice the world shall, (for the world can say)
How much thy power hath power.

This is where Shakespeare's lady's power comes from. The
context is the same as Shakespeare's, the lady unkind and
killing him by her unkindness, only Shakespeare has made one
of her powers that of her tongue. No sonneteer but would have
his lady look at him though it hurts, even if it kills him. Nor is
there one who does not make excuses for her. They ask for a
quick death too. Both Constable and Sidney do this, using
terms of affection. Shakespeare's tone is very affectionate, and
not alone because of his 'sweet heart'. His opening 'Oh call me
not to' echoes Sidney's, 'Oh look, oh shine, oh let me die'. But
before I quote it, here is Constable's decade 4, sonnet V:

Dear, if all other favours you shall grudge
Do speedy execution with your eye.

Sidney in sonnet XLVIII has,

Soul's joy, bend not these morning stars from me,

.   .   .   .   .

Oh look, oh shine, oh let me die and see,
For though I oft myself of them bemoan,
That through my heart their beamy darts be gone,
Whose cureless wounds even now most freshly bleed;
Yet since my death's wound is already got,
Dear killer, spare not thy sweet cruel shot,
A kind of grace it is to kill with speed.

There can be no doubt of the satire intended in sonnet
140:

Sonnet 140

> Be wise as thou art cruel, do not press
> My tongue-tied patience with too much disdain:
> Lest sorrow lend me words and words express,
> The manner of my pity wanting pain.
> If I might teach thee wit better it were,
> Though not to love, yet love to tell me so,
> As testy sick men when their deaths be near,
> No news but health from their physicians know.
> For if I should despair I should grow mad,
> And in my madness might speak ill of thee,
> Now this ill wresting world is grown so bad,
> Mad slanderers by mad ears believed be.
> That I may not be so, nor thou be lied,
> Bear thine eyes straight, though thy proud heart go wide.

Considering all he has said, and all that it is expected that sonneteers should say, 'tongue-tied' is hardly the right word. It is a little too late to fear that sorrow might lend him words, and that they might complain of his unpitied ('pity wanting') pain. Indeed considering how the sonneteers obviously enjoy moaning, it seems pointless to ask his lady to pretend she loves. The absurdity comes to a climax in the suggestion that if he should despair he might go mad and speak ill of her; in sonnet after sonnet he has done practically nothing else. And the absurdity takes a further step with the naivety of saying that, the world being so mad, mad slanderers might be believed. He ends suggesting that she keep her 'eyes straight', although her 'proud heart go wide'. There is probably a double meaning in 'proud'. She disdains him, but the word also has a sexual connotation fitting with her heart going wide.

This obstreperous sonnet may parody such plaintive cases as that of Constable in *Diana*, decade 7 sonnet VI, with,

> now, silence, wearily confined
> In tedious dying: and a dumb restraint
> Breaks forth in tears from mine unable mind,
> To ease her passion by a poor complaint.

Possibly he also has Constable's last sonnet in decade 3 in mind. Shakespeare is trying, as he puts it,

If I might teach thee better wit,

and Constable to teach Diana to be 'inconstant to disdain' :

> The wittiest women are to sport inclined
> Honour is pride, and pride is nought but pain.

Shakespeare's sonnet deals in 'wit' and pride. Perhaps also, since Constable is certainly in his mind, his sonnet V of decade 6, where he says,

> Yet as thou turned thy chaste fair eye aside,
> A flame of fire did from thine eyelids go,
> Which burnt my heart,

explains why Shakespeare tells his unchaste lady to,

> Bear thine eyes straight, though thy proud heart go wide.

That is, do not light a fire in your eyes, though your heart does this for everyone. Or it may be a reference to her glancing aside in the previous sonnet.

Sonnet 141 is unambiguous parody, as I have already shown.

In sonnet 142 Shakespeare begins by echoing the last line of 141, and making a bald factual statement of what the situation really is.

Sonnet 142

> Love is my sin, and thy dear virtue hate,
> Hate of my sin, grounded on sinful loving,
> Oh but with mine, compare thou thine own state,
> And thou shalt find it merits not reproving,
> Or if it do, not from those lips of thine,
> That have profaned their scarlet ornaments,
> And sealed false bonds of love as oft as mine,
> Robbed others' beds' revenues of their rents.
> Be it lawful I love thee as thou lov'st those,
> Whom thine eyes woo as mine importune thee,
> Root pity in thy heart that when it grows,

Thy pity may deserve to pitied be.
If thou dost seek to have what thou dost hide,
By self example mayst thou be denied.

This sonnet can be explained best by what it parodies. It not only has its roots in the previous sonnet but is integrated into the context as a parody of some of the sonnets already mocked in no. 137. The first line gives a clue, for in sonnet LXI Sidney says that Stella's 'chaste love, hates this love in me'. This is what Shakespeare parodies. His love is sin and her virtue hate like Stella's, and the hate is like Stella's, grounded in his sinful loving. But, says Shakespeare taking his lady to be as bad as himself, compare it with your own sin and you will see that you of all people have no right to criticise. Sidney's sonnet LII deals with this virtue and sin, beginning,

A strife is grown between virtue and love.

This has given Shakespeare 'thy dear virtue hate'. Sidney's sonnet ends,

Let virtue have that Stella's self, yet thus,
That virtue but that body grant to us.

So there is very good reason why Shakespeare should suggest that the woman Sidney really wants is not a chaste one. But it is not only Sidney that comes in for parody. Constable's sonnet VI of decade I also does. He begins,

Mine eye with all the deadly sins is fraught,

and proceeds to show how his love has lead him to each of the deadly sins in turn till

These sins procured have a goddess' ire.

Constable certainly suggested the scarlet ornaments through which judgement comes. His sixth sonnet of decade 4 has

Your lips (in scarlet clad) my judges be,
Pronouncing sentence of eternal no.

Constable is thinking of the judge clad in scarlet, which he probably got from Sidney's 'scarlet judges' in sonnet LXXIII. Shakespeare has remembered not this, but judgement issuing from scarlet lips. This has suggested scarlet wax sealing as many false bonds of love as his own, and he makes the lady as reprobate as he can by continuing his image of bonds and saying she robs the revenue of other beds of their due. Still using legal imagery that has come from the scarlet ornaments of Constable's sonnet he says that if it is lawful he loves her as much as she loves others. It is interesting to see how the associations of the scarlet-clad judge control Shakespeare's expression although neither the judge nor his cloak is mentioned. The theme of the sonnet is the lady judging, and this comes through her scarlet ornaments; they have also become red wax sealing false bonds, but originally they cloaked a judge whose pronouncements of the truth have a sacred quality. Thus the falsehoods of the lady are appropriately said to profane them. You cannot profane an ornament, but you can the almost divine quality of a judge's verdict. There is indeed such a thing as contempt of court, though not of an ornament. So we see the original image, although it is unexpressed, still influencing the imagery. Lines eleven and twelve imply that when the pity she has implanted grows into love, then she will deserve to be pitied for if one loves one is automatically denied, or at least this is what her behaviour to him suggests, as likewise the experience of all sonneteers. Finally her concealing her own desires may teach others how to deny her.

Sonnet 143 brings complaining to the height of the absurd. The sonneteers behave like babies crying for their lady, weeping continuously for what they cannot get, utterly dependent on her, and complaining like spoilt children. The sonneteer, taken seriously, seems the most undignified of objects. Shakespeare says as much in this sonnet and adds to the fun by making the whole situation undignified. It is so uproarious that critics looking for something serious find it difficult to swallow. But there is no getting away from its being Shakespeare's, and intended to have its place here. It is well integrated with its immediate predecessor in theme, and with the context in general. Here is precisely the same situation as in the previous sonnet, where the lady goes after other men, and leaves Shakespeare without a look, and where he complains of it.

Sonnet 143

> Lo as a careful housewife runs to catch,
> One of her feathered creatures broke away,
> Sets down her babe and makes all swift dispatch
> In pursuit of the thing she would have stay:
> Whilst her neglected child holds her in chase,
> Cries to catch her whose busy care is bent,
> To follow that which flies before her face:
> Not prizing her poor infant's discontent;
> So run'st thou after that which flies from thee,
> Whilst I thy babe chase thee afar behind,
> But if thou catch thy hope turn back to me:
> And play the mother's part kiss me, be kind.
> So will I pray that thou mayst have thy Will,
> If thou turn back and my loud crying still.

Needless to say Shakespeare did not find the image of the henwife in any other sonnet. There might be suggestions for the child. Daniel makes his verse a crying child. He begins his second sonnet :

> Go wailing verse, the infants of my love.

The 'infants' are offspring of his love, not necessarily children, but he does tell them to,

> Waken her sleeping pity with your crying.

And in sonnet XLIX he says he will be content

> that her frowns should be
> To my infant style the cradle, and the grave.

Cupid of course was a baby, and it is just possible that Sidney's confrontation of him might have suggested Shakespeare's sonnet. Since the situation is, so to say, an exact metaphor of that in 142, and since almost any sonneteer deserves this

E

picture of his wailing, I do not think we need look further. Here are relevant cuttings from Sidney. In sonnet XVII he makes Cupid's mother shove him from her lap, and when at length he is satisfied with his play,

> Oh how for joy he leaps, oh how he crows.

In sonnet XI also, Love behaves like a child. But this is Cupid. However, Sidney tells ambitious poets in sonnet XV :

> if both for your love and skill . . .
> You seek to nurse at fullest breast of fame,
> Stella behold and then begin to write.

In the next sonnet he comes even nearer to Shakespeare where he says that until he saw Stella and understood, wherever he heard lovers complaining,

> I thought those babes of some pin's hurt did whine.

Sonnet 143 makes a devasting comment on the relationship of the sonnet poet to his lady. It is undignified ridicule, and seems a final blow. After it we have to pick up the threads as if anew, and this gives a sense of starting on the final lap.

Shakespeare has now written more than his century on his two loves, and in sonnet 144 he, as it were, sums up, generalises, adds a postcript. He looks back on the situation of his two loves, to say precisely what is the truth of it. From its very beginning Platonic love was divided against itself, for it had two dynamisms, one leading to spiritual development, and the other tending to degrade. Plato advocated the spiritual that reached its highest in love between men where it had not a physical expression. When Dante, and more to our point Petrarch, transferred the Platonic ideal of a purely spiritual love to that for a woman, conflict inevitably resulted. David Kalstone[60] emphasises this. Laura, he notes, both wounds and heals. Although she is the heavenly vision who enriches the imagination, separation from her leads to frustration and exhaustion. Both these attitudes colour the sonnet tradition, and this duality is very apparent in the English sonneteers.

Some of them seem almost to hate as much as they love; at
least their lady is hateful as much as adorable. As a rule these
sides are kept apart. The lady appears the incarnation of all
goodness and loveliness in one sonnet, a fiend in another. But
the poets also have moments when they are aware of being
ambivalent. We can see this right from the start. No. CCCI of
the Songs added to the second edition of Tottel's Miscellany[61]
has :

> Holding my peace alas how loud I cry,
> Presséd with hope and dread even both at once,
> Strainéd with death, and yet I cannot die.

And Watson in sonnet LXIII of his *Passionate Centurie* says
that

> Love hath two shafts, the one of beaten gold,
>
> .   .   .   .   .   .
>
> The other is of lumpish leaden mould,
> And worketh none effect, but what is nought.

I need not illustrate further, for this ambivalence is there in
sonnets from which I have already quoted. Shakespeare
brought this duality to a climax by splitting the two sides
asunder and giving all the good to one and all the bad to the
other, the spiritual to the man, the physical to the woman. I
take this to be the origin not only of his dark lady, but of the
friend with whom his relationship is that of ideal love. No one
can doubt that his lady reflects only the dark side of sonnet
love. His sonnets to the man tend to reflect only the light, or
good side. This situation is more ridiculous than it would have
been if Shakespeare had split the contradiction between two
women. That would not have been a comic situation. So
Shakespeare parodies by investing a man with every virtue of a
sonnet lady and by representing his relationship with him as
exactly like that of the happier sonnet relationship, and by
giving to his lady all the 'bad' qualities of the sonnet tradition.
Moreover he complicates the situation by making the lady and
the man-friend fall in love with each other. He describes his
intention in sonnet 144, where he says who or what his friends

are and what the situation. It is presented as a naïve statement of facts. And it brings the whole sonnet situation to a focus, summing up and explaining. In its way it is quite as outrageous a situation as that in sonnet 143.

Sonnet 144

> Two loves I have of comfort and despair,
> Which like two spirits do suggest me still,
> The better angel is a man right fair:
> The worser spirit a woman coloured ill.
> To win me soon to hell my female evil,
> Tempteth my better angel from my sight,
> And would corrupt my saint to be a devil:
> Wooing his purity with her foul pride.
> And whether that my angel be turned fiend,
> Suspect I may, yet not directly tell,
> But being both from me both to each friend,
> I guess one angel in another's hell.
> Yet this shall I ne'er know but live in doubt,
> Till my bad angel fire my good one out.

I need not paraphrase. The meaning is obvious unless sex-punning is intended, which would fit the context. Shakespeare begins by stating a plain fact for our information. But he then gives so much emphasis to the imagery of spirits, angels and devils, that they appear more real than the two human beings. And this represents the truth, for the sonnet man and woman are merely figures invented to carry this contrast—the two loves, a good and a bad yoked together as Plato has it. Although the situation is Platonic, the imagery is Christian with its angels, saints, devils, temptation and hell. And this again fits the climate of Shakespeare's day.

After this sonnet, comes one of those silly little songs characteristic of the Elizabethan age. They were felt to fit a sonnet context. Even Spenser's *Amoretti* ends with pretty stanzas on Cupid, and indeed Shakespeare's own sonnets end with a fairy tale about Cupid.

Sonnet 145

> Those lips that love's own hand did make,
> Breathed forth the sound that said I hate,

To me that languished for her sake:
But when she saw my woeful state,
Straight in her heart did mercy come,
Chiding that tongue that ever sweet,
Was used in giving gentle doom:
And taught it thus anew to greet:
I hate she altered with an end,
That followed it as gentle day,
Doth follow night who like a fiend
From heaven to hell is flown away.
I hate, from hate away she threw,
And saved my life saying not you.

We can be sure this was not included by some oversight since it is integrated into the context of heaven and hell, fiend, hate and love. The point lies in deliberately making a silly irrelevance between the related sonnets 144 and 146.

Sonnet 146

Poor soul the centre of my sinful earth,
My sinful earth these rebel powers that thee array,
Why dost thou pine within and suffer dearth
Painting thy outward walls so costly gay?
Why so large cost having so short a lease,
Dost thou upon thy fading mansion spend?
Shall worms inheritors of this excess
Eat up thy charge? Is this thy body's end?
Then soul live thou upon thy servant's loss,
And let that pine to aggravate thy store;
Buy terms divine in selling hours of dross;
Within be fed, without be rich no more,
So shall thou feed on death, that feeds on men,
And death once dead, there's no more dying then.

This like sonnet 144 expresses Christianised Platonism. The soul is a prisoner in its material 'mansion' of 'earth' (clay or flesh). This earthly mansion is by definition sinful, worthless. It makes a serious comment on spending one's life in worthless joys of the flesh and comes quite as unexpectedly as the triviality of sonnet 145 was unexpected. It originated from Daniel's sonnet XXIV, which also partly accounts for Shakespeare's sonnet 151. Both Shakespeare's sonnets have as their theme the contrast of Plato's two loves, or the contrast between the spiritual and the material, or in this context, the flesh. This is clearer in sonnet 151.

Sonnet 151

> Love is too young to know what conscience is,
> Yet who knows not conscience is born of love,
> Then gentle cheater urge not my amiss,
> Lest guilty of my faults thy sweet self prove.
> For thou betraying me, I do betray
> My nobler part to my gross body's treason,
> My soul doth tell my body that he may,
> Triumph in love, flesh stays no farther reason,
> But rising at thy name doth point out thee,
> As his triumphant prize, proud of this pride,
> He is contented thy poor drudge to be
> To stand in thy affairs, fall by thy side.
> No want of conscience hold it that I call,
> Her love, for whose dear love I rise and fall.

Daniel's sonnet runs thus:

> Oft in vain my rebel thoughts have ventured,
> To stop the passage of my vanquished heart:
> And shut those ways my friendly foe first entered,
> Hoping thereby to free my better part.
> And whilst I guard these windows of this fort,
> Where my heart thief to vex me made her choice:
> And thither all my forces do transport,
> Another passage opens at her voice.
> Her voice betrays me to her hand and eye:
> My freedom's tyrants conquering all by art:
> But ah, what glory can she get thereby,
> With three such powers to plague one silly heart.
> Yet my soul's sovereign, since I must resign;
> Reign in my thoughts, my love and life are thine.

On a first reading the thought here is not very clear. The 'rebel thoughts' are on the side of the poet's 'better part', but his 'vanquished heart' is his 'friendly foe', what he really wants. The implied imagery is that of a besieged castle, and his thoughts have blocked the passage by which his heart first entered. He guards the windows of the fort against his heart, but Delia's voice opens another passage and betrays him to her hand and eye, and so she takes the castle. He has therefore to resign to her. She becomes his sovereign who now rules his thoughts and possesses his love and life. She is his 'soul's sovereign'. Shakespeare has taken the beleaguered castle and the rebels arrayed against his soul in sonnet 146 from Daniel, but the building is a 'mansion' in which the soul lives rather than a fort that defends it, or that it must take. He develops the situation. Its inhabitants, who represent the soul, are starving because of the submerged image of the siege, although its walls are painted 'costly gay'. This is the point taken up in the second quatrain, where the image changes. It is foolish of the soul to go to the expense of painting the mansion as the lease is so short, and particularly when after the lease is finished, the heirs will be worms. A third image is added in the next quatrain, that of the body as servant of the soul; it should be left to starve, to enrich its master. Get spiritual wealth by selling 'hours of dross'; that is, cease wasting time on what has no value, and spend it on the soul. Be fed within the mansion and have a rich exterior no longer. Then the soul will inherit eternal life and profit from death, which feeds on the body.

Sonnet 151 takes from Daniel's sonnet not the imagery of the beleaguered castle, but the idea of betrayal. It has the same theme as that of 146 in so far as it deals with two sorts of love. One sort is what one can do with a good conscience, and this love indeed awakens conscience. He is discussing his mistress's condemnation of him in sonnet 150, and urges her to stop since if he is at fault, so is she. She cheated him into betraying his nobler part to his body, as Daniel's 'better part' is betrayed. Then, looking at the other sort of love he has been betrayed into, he says that when the soul tells him he may triumph in love, as Daniel's love triumphed, his body interprets it in its own physical terms and acts accordingly. But he ends, this is not for lack of conscience since it is for love that he does so. His imagery is sexually suggestive.

All three sonnets have the soul as their main concern, and

here their main relationship with each other lies. Daniel's soul's sovereign is his lady, which implies an ideal and spiritual love. Shakespeare takes the soul to be the immortal element in man, the spiritual which exists as something distinct from the body. He begins sonnet 151 on the plane of betrayal by his 'gentle cheater' to fulfilment in blatant and unashamed sex. I should guess that there should be no comma after 'call' in the second last line, and that Shakespeare intends to say that it is not lack of conscience that makes him call the lady love, for whose sake he has arrived at this conclusion. The irony of sonnet 151 is very nearly bitter. We must look at it not in a modern way where we no longer think of the spiritual and the physical as being distinct, for we are neither Platonic nor Christian in this. Shakespeare is protesting against neoplatonism which suggests that one can choose a spiritual love as against a physical. The view implied by sonnets 146 and 151 is that Daniel's sonnet with his lady as his 'soul's sovereign' is poetry of empty artifice. Sonnet 151 parodies it. Daniel begins with betrayal and ends by accepting it. Shakespeare begins with love leading to conscience and ends by accepting this betrayal of conscience ending in physical love.

We cannot in the same way say that sonnet 146 is a parody. It has a more directly moral tone, and says what it does without sarcasm, which is surprising for it makes a dignified comment on a situation which Shakespeare has been treating grossly and without dignity. It is like death entering at the end of *Love's Labours Lost* to make the final test of truth. In approaching the end of his sonnet sequence Shakespeare becomes serious. The soul has been treated badly, and it is time to make amends. This sonnet gives a new and unexpected depth to the situation. There is more to be said, however. Memory depends on the strength of the original imprint. That this sonnet of Daniel's should form the basis of the imagery of two sonnets, both treating the subject of spiritual and physical love, must mean that Shakespeare considered Daniel's statement about the soul seriously. It suggests that his criticism here is not just light-hearted fun, although it is this also. He at least took the position seriously enough to give it a considered statement within his fun-making. And he says that the soul and the body are distinct and have opposite aims, which makes good Christianity. No woman can be the soul's sovereign. The soul wins eternity only by treating its servant the body badly. Incidentally today Shakespeare could not have used imagery of the master starving his servants to contribute to his wealth; it would arouse a negative social reaction, where he intended a positive. A poet's imagination must function within his social environment even if he is Shakespeare.

Sonnet 147 begins a new theme. It parodies the conventional sonnet situation of love as a madness and fever. Reason, as all sonnet readers know is powerless against it. The madness of love goes back to Plato. Petrarch introduced it to the sonnet tradition as a disease of love. But to take two examples closer to Shakespeare, Barnes in sonnet XXII complains that he can find no physic to cure 'a burning fever' which oppresses him, and Spenser says in sonnet L,

> Long languishing in double malady,
> Of my heart's wound and of my body's grief :
> There came to me a leach that would apply
> Fit medicines for my body's best relief.
> Vain man (quoth I) that hast but little prief :
> In deep discovery of the mind's disease,
> Is not the heart of all the body chief ?
> And rules the members as itself doth please.
> Then with some cordials seek first to appease,
> The inward languor of my wounded heart,
> And then my body shall have shortly ease :
> But such sweet cordials pass physician's art.
> Then my life's leach do you your skill reveal,
> And with one salve both heart and body heal.

Here is Shakespeare on it :

Sonnet 147

> My love is as a fever longing still,
> For that which longer nurseth the disease,
> Feeding on that which doth preserve the ill,
> The uncertain sickly appetite to please:
> My reason the physician to my love,
> Angry that his prescriptions are not kept

> Hath left me, and I desperate now approve,
> Desire is death, which physic did except.
> Past cure I am, now reason is past care,
> And frantic mad with evermore unrest,
> My thoughts and my discourse as mad men's are,
> At random from the truth vainly expressed.
> For I have sworn thee fair, and thought thee bright,
> Who art as black as hell, as dark as night.

This makes one of the stories that abound in the sonnets. Shakespeare brings it to a ridiculous climax, giving as proof of his frantic madness, his having sworn that his lady is fair and bright when she is 'black as hell' and 'dark as night', which returns to the theme of his opening sonnet in the series to his lady, that dominates them all.

Sonnet 148

> Oh me! What eyes hath love put in my head,
> Which have no correspondence with true sight,
> Or if they have, where is my judgment fled,
> That censures falsely what they see aright?
> If that be fair whereon my false eyes dote,
> What means the world to say it is not so?
> If it be not, then love doth well denote,
> Love's eye is not so true as all men's: no,
> How can it? Oh how can love's eye be true,
> That is so vexed with watching and with tears?
> No marvel then though I mistake my view,
> The sun itself sees not, till heaven clears.
> Oh cunning love, with tears thou keep'st me blind,
> Lest eyes well seeing thy foul faults should find.

This comments on the previous sonnet, analysing in simulated anxiety to see what can be the truth. It parodies Daniel whose sonnet IX drips with misery, and from which Shakespeare has taken his questioning tune: 'Oh if they have... If that be fair... If it be not... Oh how can. . . ." He parodies the tune itself in lines 8 and 9 where he suddenly drops from his musical plaint to 'no, How can it?' His opening, 'Oh me,' may have this colloquial intention.

Here is Daniel's sonnet:

> If this be love, to draw a weary breath,
> Paint on floods, till the shore, cry to the air:
> With downward looks, still reading on the earth;
> The sad memorials of my love's despair.
> If this be love, to war against my soul,
> Lie down to wail, rise up to sigh and grieve me:
> The never-resting stone of care to roll,
> Still to complain my griefs, and none relieve me,
> If this be love, to clothe me with dark thoughts,
> Haunting untrodden paths to wail apart;
> My pleasures horror, music tragic notes,
> Tears in my eyes, and sorrow at my heart.
> If this be love, to live a living death;
> Oh then love I, and draw a weary breath.

Shakespeare accepts that this is love and justifies him. 'How can love's eyes be true, That is so vexed with watching and with tears?' He echoes his other sonnets too. Daniel's seventh begins like Shakespeare's,

> Oh had she not been fair and thus unkind,
> Then had no finger pointed at my lightness:
> The world had never known what I do find,
> And clouds obscure had shaded still her brightness.

Shakespeare asks, 'If that be fair' whereon his false eyes dote, why does 'the world', (which in Daniel would not have known, but in Shakespeare is not so naïve) why does it contradict him. Shakespeare probably got the heavens having to clear before the sun sees from this verse. Daniel's third sonnet is relevant. 'Clear-sighted you, soon note what is awry,' he says of those not in love, then points to those who are:

> You blinded souls whom youth and errors lead,
> .   .   .   .   .
> Ah you, and none but you my sorrows read.

With this in mind Shakespeare comes to the end of his sonnet.

Although Daniel is certainly Shakespeare's target, he is no more miserable than other sonneteers. Of these perhaps Spenser may be in Shakespeare's memory, where in sonnet XLV he says that if his lady's perfect image were not 'with sorrow dimmed and deformed' her beauty would appear. Shakespeare's joke is to say that sorrow hides his love's ugliness. This is what his eyes blinded by love cannot see.

Shakespeare brought sonnet commonplaces to an insulting final couplet in both sonnets 147 and 148. He opens 149 defending himself. He still has Daniel's tune. How can you, he asks, say I do not love you when I always side with you against myself. If his lady had been real, she would no doubt have had a ready answer with ample evidence for it. Shakespeare presumably meant us to notice the weakness in his defence.

Sonnet 149

> Canst thou Oh cruel, say I love thee not,
> When I against myself with thee partake:
> Do I not think on thee when I forgot
> Am of myself, all tyrant for thy sake?
> Who hateth thee that I do call my friend,
> On whom frown'st thou that I do fawn upon,
> Nay if thou lour'st on me do I not spend
> Revenge upon myself with present moan?
> What merit do I in myself respect,
> That is so proud thy service to despise,
> When all my best doth worship thy defect,
> Commanded by the motion of thine eyes.
> But love hate on for now I know thy mind,
> Those that can see thou lov'st, and I am blind.

Spenser in sonnet XLIV takes part against himself. He refers to

> this continual cruel civil war,
> The which myself against myself do make.

But it is Daniel whom Shakespeare chiefly mocks. In sonnet XII he writes,

My ambitious thoughts confined in her face,
Affect no honour, but what she can give me :
My hopes do rest in limits of her grace,
I weigh no comfort unless she relieve me.

His 'ambitious thought confined in her face' and his assumption of no honour but what she gives, are taken over by Shakespeare, who asks what merit does he respect in himself that despises service to her. The hopes of both poets are centred in their lady. Daniel says so in a general statement and Shakepeare illustrates it with detailed examples. Here also is the explanation of the puzzling reference to 'the motion of these eyes'. Daniel writes,

My fortune's wheel, the circle of her eyes,
Whose rolling grace deign once a turn of bliss.
All my life's sweet consists in her alone,
So much I love the most unloving one.

'All my life's sweet' parallels Shakespeare's 'all my best'. Both consist in loving and worshipping one who is 'unloving' or has defects. And what commands this is 'the motion of her eyes', which is that of fortune's wheel, as Daniel has it. Shakespeare ends with his lady loving only those who can see, whereas like all conventional lovers the poet is blinded by love.

Sonnet 150 begins by asking where the lady gets all this power to sway her lover's heart for insufficient reasons, thus giving the lie to his true sight. The question is the motive of the whole sonnet. The tone of voice is that of the unhappy lover, but we are asked what is the sense of it, is there any ?

Sonnet 150

Oh from what power hast thou this powerful might,
With insufficiency my heart to sway,
To make me give the lie to my true sight,
And swear that brightness doth not grace the day?
Whence hast thou this becoming of things ill,
That in the very refuse of thy deeds,
There is such strength and warrantise of skill,
That in my mind thy worst all best exceeds?

Who taught thee how to make me love thee more,
The more I hear and see just cause of hate,
Oh though I love what others do abhor,
With others thou shouldst not abhor my state.
If thy unworthiness raised love in me,
More worthy I to be beloved of thee.

Perhaps the second quatrain should be clarified. Shakespeare asks where do you get the power to make bad things becoming, so that the refuse or rubbish, or what is fit only to be thrown away and rejected, is such a good warrant or justification of your power that it exceeds the best of everything. He may have in mind a sonnet he has already parodied—Constable's sonnet IX of decade 7, which refers to his mistress's cruelty and inhumanity, although he loves her, and where he says,

Suffice the world shall, (for the world can say)
How much thy power hath power.

So Shakespeare asks where the lady gets this power that makes him love her more, the more there is cause to hate.

Sonnets 151 and 152 return to sex imagery and the lady's unfaithfulness. I have already dealt with 151. Sonnet 152 carries over its theme.

Sonnet 152

In loving thee thou know'st I am forsworn,
But thou art twice forsworn to me love swearing,
In act thy bed-vow broke and new faith torn,
In vowing new hate after new love bearing:
But why of two oaths' breach do I accuse thee,
When I break twenty: I am perjured most,
For all my vows are oaths but to misuse thee:
And all my honest faith in thee is lost.
For I have sworn deep oaths of thy deep kindness:
Oaths of thy love, thy truth, thy constancy,
And to enlighten thee gave eyes to blindness,
Or made them swear against the thing they see.
For I have sworn thee fair: more perjured eye,
To swear against the truth so foul a lie.

The lady is not only a traitor, like the poet, but twice forsworn since she is not faithful to him. But how can he complain, he asks, since all his oaths are to 'misuse' her, and he loses all his honesty in her. This sounds very moral, but in the sestet Shakespeare gives it a twist. He has sworn that she has virtues, and worst of all, as a climax he has sworn that she is fair. This perjury, he says, is obviously worse than hers—'To swear against the truth so foul a lie'. This repeats his ending of sonnet 147, where it proved his madness. He is not going to give up the joke he has led us to expect. But wait.

In his sonnets on the lady, Shakespeare has been writing in plain speech of ugly prose facts, treating the whole thing with mock seriousness as a man dealing with facts must, and simulated it so well that many of his readers, even although he has surprised them, have taken it all for truth. But he ends with two sonnets of sugared myth, which sound quite unreal and artificial after his common-sensical down to hell treatment of the sonnet tradition.

Sonnet 153

> Cupid laid by his brand and fell asleep,
> A maid of Dian's this advantage found,
> And his love-kindling fire did quickly steep
> In a cold valley-fountain of that ground:
> Which borrowed from this holy fire of love,
> A dateless lively heat still to endure,
> And grew a seething bath which yet men prove,
> Against strange madadies a sovereign cure:
> But at my mistress' eye love's brand new fired,
> The boy for trial needs would touch my breast,
> I sick withal the help of bath desired,
> And thither hied a sad distempered guest.
> But found no cure, the bath for my help lies,
> Where Cupid got new fire; my mistress's eye.

Sonnet 154

> The little love-god lying once asleep,
> Laid by his side his heart inflaming brand,
> Whilst many nymphs that vowed chaste life to keep,

Came tripping by, but in her maiden hand,
The fairest votary took up that fire,
Which many legions of true hearts had warmed,
And so the general of hot desire,
Was sleeping by a virgin hand disarmed.
This brand she quenched in a cool well by,
Which from love's fire took heat perpetual,
Growing a bath and healthful remedy,
For men diseased, but I may mistress' thrall,
Came there for cure and this by that I prove,
Love's fire heats water, water cools not love.

Although mythological and unrelated in style with the other sonnets, these have an obvious relevance to the aspect of love Shakespeare has been treating. In fact they imply a similar situation, but make it pretty. This must have been designed, for the sonnets to the man friend end (sonnet 126) with a similar contrast. It is in couplets with a traditional flavour, while at the same time carrying on the argument. Coming at the end like this, and unrelated stylistically, these throw up the contrast between the honest kersey of his own style and the artificiality of the conventional. It is as if he meant to say, 'sugar is very well, but not the stuff to make real love out of'. He leaves us to draw the deduction, trusting that he has made his point, and that we shall now think them funny.

To sum up: Shakespeare began the sonnets on the dark lady with a parody on Sidney's sonnet. Because Sidney has changed beauty from fair to dark, 'therefore' his lady will be dark also, and not only dark in looks, but in her moral character. In this way he leads skilfully into other parodies of the dark aspect of sonnet love, with the lady cruel, tyrannous, a murderer. From the darkness comes the joke of her impurity also, in which he parodies chiefly Greville and Sidney, but not them alone. Thus he created a travesty of the sonnet lady, which highlights the artificiality of the sonneteers when they rave against their mistresses.

We now have sufficient evidence to be sure that Shakespeare has read the sonnets I have examined, not only from cumulative evidence, but because of correspondences that put beyond doubt the influence of one poet on another. And we can be

sure that it is Shakespeare who 'borrows', since the relationship
is that of parody. Even apart from this, I have shown Shakespeare's mind at work on his material, both consciously and
through unconscious associations in what I have called *Road to
Xanadu*-like entanglements. I have suggested that a comparison with Drayton's 1594 sonnets clarifies the difference. I have
also suggested that Shakespeare's memory has a musical
element, evident in his use of the cadences of other poets in his
parodies. The parodying of Daniel in his last sonnets relies very
clearly on this. I have also suggested that it is likely that a
Livingston Lowes type of analysis might reveal memory of
sounds of words as a linking-factor in his creativeness, although
this needs to be investigated. If it were accepted that Shakespeare had read these sonneteers and other material that his
parody in the sonnets to the man throws up, there would be
enough background for such an investigation. And his *Sonnets*
are a limited area like *The Ancient Mariner* that could be dealt
with thoroughly.

I have not pointed out borrowings by one sonneteer from
another, as this is irrelevant to my theme. Where we can be
clear which influenced Shakespeare I have said so, but the
general inference is that both may be in his mind, if not consciously, at least in his latent memory.

IV

THE MAN FRIEND

It was shocking of Shakespeare to begin his sonnet sequence by trying to persuade his friend to marry. In the flabby end of the sonnet tradition in England, the sonneteer could plead with his lady to marry him and even end by adding an *Epithalamion* but this was a different matter, for he worshipped her with the irrationality and passion of romantic love. Shakespeare writes to a man, and he advocates the contractual bond that courtly lovers held in contempt. The motive he suggests is that of self-propagation and for the extraordinary purpose of handing on his beauty to succeeding generations. This must have startled his contemporaries. His private friends are also likely to have noticed that the first sonnets in their sweet, ornate tones, use arguments from a very lengthy, learned and earnest 'Epistle to persuade a young gentleman to marriage', which was written by Erasmus and had appeared in Thomas Wilson's *The Arte of Rhetorique* in 1553. This was a sort of text book, the sort of book that might have been recommended reading in English departments of our universities, if they had existed then. All prospective poets or young men interested in literature could be presumed to have read it. That Shakespeare did, we can see from its reflection in his first seventeen sonnets. A young man educating himself, or being educated in a culture where the sonnets flourished, would be familiar with it. We can be sure that the private friends among whom Shakespeare's sonnets circulated must have been so. It will be remembered that Holofernes' last words in *Love's Labours Lost* were, 'This is not generous, not gentle, not humble', which have the very cadence of Erasmus when he says that it will be 'much more honest, more profitable, and also more pleasant for you, to marry'. Indeed it is just possible that Erasmus's treatise may have been used in the schools where they trained boys and young men to discuss such topics in Latin debate to practice rhetoric, or the art of persuasion; in *The Arte of Rhetorique* it stands as a model for writing. We have already seen that the question of courtly love as against a view of women as jades was used for a somewhat similar purpose in language study. These debates sometimes stimulated work outside the schools, showing that they had a formative influence and must have been memorable. Thus Milton's *L'Allegro* and *Il Penseroso* originated in just such a Latin debate. That Sidney treated Erasmus's theme of marriage in his *Arcadia,* and used some of his arguments suggests that it made one of these debate-provoking themes. The *Arcadia* itself was of course well known. At the end of the first book Geron an old man, invites Histor to a poetic exchange on marriage. The old man says

> there is no greater bliss,
> Than is the quiet joy of loving wife;

and the young man retorts, yes if the woman is rich, but as it is most wives make home a pain with

> Either dull silence, or eternal chat;
>
> .   .   .   .
>
> If he do praise the dog, she likes the cat.
>
> .   .   .   .

Geron answers that there are always instances of bad luck but

> Nature above all things requireth this,
> That we our kind do labour to maintain;
>
> .   .   .   .
>
> Thy father justly may of thee complain,
> If thou do not repay his deeds for thee,
> In granting unto him a grandsire's gain.

A man should not 'murder [his] posterity'.

Riches of children pass a prince's throne;
Which touch the father's heart with secret joy,
When without shame he saith, these be mine own.

The joke Sidney makes is against the shrew, and this is much livelier than the old man's commendations, some of which Shakespeare echoes in his sonnets.

Erasmus's epistle is a solemn treatise,[62] beginning with Adam and tracing the esteem in which marriage was held down the ages. Jesus is said to have approved it; the Romans and the Greeks did. Erasmus notes that the Persians and the Hebrews showed a very particular respect for it by having more than one wife. He conceivably may not have meant this as a joke; on the other hand, must not all young men have received it so? And Erasmus was certainly human enough to include among the joys of marriage, 'a pretty little boy, running up and down your house, such a one as shall express your look' and 'call you dad'. Your children, he says, will comfort you 'in your latter days', bury you at last, and inherit your property. In old age the married man will see 'his own countenance which he had being a child, to appear lively in his son'. 'Death is ordained for all mankind, and yet by this means only, nature' gives 'us a certain immortality' as a 'young graft buddeth out, when the old tree is cut down'. The humanist in Erasmus comes out in his stress on marriage as natural, and what is natural being virtuous. 'To live single' is 'barren' and not 'agreeing with the state of man's nature'. He thinks it is despicable to live only to oneself. He notes that if no one married, in the span of a generation there would be no human beings on earth. Tilling the ground makes a memorable analogy:

Even as all grounds though they be very fruitful, are not therefore turned into tillage for man's use and commodity, but part lyeth fallow, and is never manured, part is kept and cherished . . . for man's pleasure : and yet in all this plenty of things, where so great store of land is, nature suffereth very little to wear barren : But now if none should be tilled, and ploughmen went to play, who seeth not but that we should all starve, and be fain shortly to eat acorns.

Or again :

> it is for the commonweal's behoof, that every man should
> well and truly husband his own. If that man be punished,
> who little heedeth the maintenance of his tillage ... what
> punishment is he worthy to suffer, that refuseth to plough
> that land, which being tilled, yieldeth children?

A man, he says, who has no mind to marry is no man. Rather
he is a stone, an enemy to nature, a rebel to God himself,
seeking through his own folly, his last end and destruction. If
you do not marry you are a 'murderer of your stock'. A
ploughman gives God a tithe, but if you do not marry, nothing
is left of yourself. This is not an academic question for
Erasmus. He is thinking of the celibate clergy, who do not
much appeal to him. Or at least he thinks a young man of
ancient family with great lands should have regard to his 'posterity', and not perish without issue. To marry is 'better for the
common weal'. And all especially if there is a very eligible
maid ready for him.

Shakespeare's opening sonnets parody this, using all these
arguments. Dover Wilson, who takes them very seriously, con-
jectures that Shakespeare may have been invited to Wilton for
William Herbert's seventeenth birthday (hence the seventeen
sonnets) and asked to write them to persuade the young man
to marry someone he had refused to consider. But he is more
likely to have done it as a joke. The youth he addresses has not
great estates, or family responsibilities. His one distinction lies
in his good looks. Beauty is his inheritance and he is urged to
marry to preserve this for the world, to make his beauty
immortal. In fact he is like the sonnet lady with whose immortality her poet is concerned. The only question can be
whether Shakespeare used the sonnets to point the Erasmus
parody, or Erasmus to parody the sonnets, or whether, most
likely, he intended an equal emphasis. All seventeen sonnets
are structured to climb wittily to their inevitable end in an
identical laughable climax which parodies equally Erasmus
and the sonneteers. Although they give us a sophisticated
pleasure with their flawless progress to absurdity and their
'honey-tongued' and 'fine-filed' phrase, the type of joke is

quite common. It was the main ingredient in the Tommy Handley personalities of the last war, where one watched for each comic to reveal precisely the facet of himself one expected. A pantomime joke of my very early childhood depended on the same psychology, for unwanted and embarrassing things were all put in the stew; the most unlikely objects came to this inevitable end. And besides with this perennial joke done with supreme art, the sonnets must have appealed to young men brought up in this culture, by parodying both a stock theme of their serious education and a literary game of the moment. Indeed here is the theme of *Love's Labours Lost,* only scored as chamber music, not for a large orchestra.

Sonnet 1

> From fairest creatures we desire increase,
> That thereby beauty's rose might never die,
> But as the riper should by time decease,
> His tender heir might bear his memory:
> But thou contracted to thine own bright eyes,
> Feed'st thy light's flame with self substantial fuel,
> Making a famine where abundance lies,
> Thyself thy foe, to thy sweet self too cruel:
> Thou that art now the world's fresh ornament,
> And only herald to the gaudy spring,
> Within thine own bud buriest thy content,
> And tender churl mak'st waste in niggarding:
> Pity the world, or else this glutton be,
> To eat the world's due, by the grave and thee.

This sonnet introduces the imagery Shakespeare will use in his opening section of six sonnets. We can see both Erasmus and the sonneteers in it. The sonneteers were concerned with the immortality of their ladies. Shakespeare parodies by writing about this to a man with a sonnet lady's quality, and he uses Erasmus's arguments. He begins by making sure that his readers, or listeners if he read his sonnets to his friends, cannot miss Erasmus. The increase from fair creatures, the heir like his father, the man without heir being 'self substantial', the famine, burying in the bud, the waste—all come from him. The sonnet ends with the choice: pity the world, or eat what is the world's due by letting your beauty be buried with you. We can see the tone of parody in inflated expression; all is superlative. Beauty is the fairest of its sort, not just 'fairest creatures' but 'beauty's rose', which suggests the eternal core of all loveliness. A famine and abundance might be relevant considerations for the heir of a great realm; they are ridiculous related to the fate of the poet's friend. But Shakespeare goes even further than this; he asks him to 'pity the world', the alternative being to eat what is due to it. The youth's beauty makes him 'the only herald' of spring, 'the world's fresh ornament'. By not marrying he risks burying all the promise that is only beginning to bud. The argument is a thing of the imagination, and it glows with a flawless polish, but is no less bombast.

If we now turn from the Erasmus background to that of the sonneteers, we notice at once the singing sonnet tune, possibly that of Daniel where he laments the mortality of his lady and promises to give her immortality by his verse. It cannot be doubted that Daniel was in his mind as he wrote the opening sonnets. But the theme of not wasting beauty is much older than that of the sonnets. Among the English sonneteers we find it right at the beginning in Surrey, who in sonnet XIV of Tottel refers to 'The golden gift that nature' gave his love,

> Where beauty so her perfect seed hath sown.

He pleads with her not to 'deface' her gifts,

> But mercy him thy friend, that doth thee serve,
> Who seeks always thine honour to preserve.

Daniel in sonnet XXXI has the rose, the spring, the 'waste', the 'sweet beauty':

> Look Delia how we esteem the half-blown rose,
> The image of thy blush and summer's honour:
> Whilst in her tender green she doth enclose
> That pure sweet beauty, time bestows upon her.

It ends,

> Oh let not then such riches waste in vain;
> But love whilst that thou mayst be loved again.

The detail of the friend being 'the world's fresh ornament' comes from Spenser, whose lady was, as he says in sonnet LIII, 'made for to be the world's most ornament', adding that 'mercy doth with beauty best agree'. Shakespeare's friend is asked to show his mercy by marrying.

Sonnet 2

> When forty winters shall besiege thy brow,
> And dig deep trenches in thy beauty's field,
> Thy youth's proud livery so gazed on now,
> Will be a tottered weed of small worth held:
> Then being asked, where all thy beauty lies,
> Where all the treasure of thy lusty days;
> To say within thine own deep sunken eyes,
> Were an all-eating shame, and thriftless praise.
> How much more praise deserved thy beauty's use,
> If thou couldst answer this fair child of mine
> Shall sum my count, and make my old excuse
> Proving his beauty by succession thine.
> This were to be new made when thou art old,
> And see thy blood warm when thou feel'st it cold.

This is pure Erasmus but from the personal rather than the community angle. The dearth and the winter concern the man not nature. It is also a sonnet theme, winter digging trenches in beauty's brow being a commonplace, perhaps originating from Virgil, Horace and Ovid.[63] But Shakespeare's echo may come from not further away than *Delia*, where Daniel says of himself in sonnet IV,

> all the world may view
> Best in my face, how cares have tilled deep furrows.

Shakespeare's sonnet culminates in the fatuous old man showing his child, and claiming that it has the beauty of his own youth, here taking the pose of Erasmus. Perhaps I should say that 'tottered' is a variant of 'tattered'.

Sonnet 3

> Look in thy glass and tell the face thou viewest,
> Now is the time that face should form another,

Whose fresh repair if now thou not renewest,
Thou dost beguile the world, unbless some mother.
For where is she so fair whose uneared womb
Disdains the tillage of thy husbandry?
Or who is he so fond will be the tomb,
Of his self love to stop posterity?
Thou art thy mother's glass and she in thee
Calls back the lovely April of her prime,
So thou through windows of thine age shalt see,
Despite of wrinkles this thy golden time.
But if thou live remembered not to be,
Die single and thine image dies with thee.

Here again is an amalgam of Erasmus and the sonneteers.
Erasmus suggests the imagery of tillage, 'the uneared womb',
the husbandry, the accusation of self-love stopping posterity,
and the child perpetuating one's image. Sonneteers delight in
imagining their lady looking at herself in her mirror. Daniel in
sonnet XXXIII says to his lady,

When men shall find thy flower, thy glory pass,
And thou with careful brow sitting alone:
Received hast this message from thy glass,
That tells thee truth, and says that all is gone.

then

Thou mayst repent, that thou hast scorned my tears,
When winter snows upon thy golden hairs.

Barnes begins his sonnet series,

Mistress behold in this true-speaking glass,
Thy beauty's graces of all women rarest.

It is not so natural, however, when Shakespeare begins by
catching his man friend in this attitude, thinking of 'fresh
repair'.

Sonnet 4

> Unthrifty loveliness why dost thou spend,
> Upon thyself thy beauty's legacy?
> Nature's bequest gives nothing but doth lend,
> And being frank she lends to those are free:
> Then beauteous niggard why dost thou abuse,
> The bounteous largess given thee to give?
> Profitless usurer why dost thou use
> So great a sum of sums yet canst not live?
> For having traffic with thy self alone,
> Thou of thy self thy sweet self dost deceive,
> Then how when nature calls thee to be gone,
> What acceptable audit canst thou leave?
> Thy unused beauty must be tombed with thee,
> Which used lives the executor to be.

This carries over the imagery of 'unthrifty loveliness', of beauty as a legacy, a large fortune which he does not use; her audit will not be acceptable at his death, for all his wealth will be entombed with him, and he will have no heir or executor. The sonnet is in terms suitable in Erasmus's argument, but the legacy of Shakespeare's friend is that of beauty. This is what nature bequeathed, or rather lent him. He is a 'beauteous niggard', deceiving his 'sweet self', as we find repeated in sonnet 5.

Sonnet 5

> Those hours that with gentle work did frame
> The lovely gaze where every eye doth dwell
> Will play the tyrants to the very same,
> And that unfair which fairly doth excel:
> For never resting time leads summer on,
> To hideous winter and confounds him there,
> Sap checked with frost and lusty leaves quite gone,
> Beauty o'er-snowed and bareness everywhere,
> Then were not summer's distillation left
> A liquid prisoner pent in walls of glass,
> Beauty's effect with beauty were bereft,
> Nor it nor no remembrance what it was.
> But flowers distilled though they with winter meet,
> Lose but their show, their substance still lives sweet.

After repeating the arguments and imagery he has already used, in the octave, Shakespeare introduces the metaphor of distilling in the sestet. He unites them in the couplet to complete one of his loveliest sonnets—tuneful and richly loaded. No doubt Meres had this sort of sonnet in mind when he called them 'sugared'. This is not a good term for such poetry. Perhaps Meres had bad taste? But he chose Shakespeare out of all his contemporaries as the English Ovid. One also asks if he realised they were parodies. But if he was among Shakespeare's friends he could hardly have failed to. Perhaps they referred to the sonnets as 'Shakespeare's sugared sonnets', meaning those in which he parodied the sugared verse of sonneteers. Shakespeare himself might have presented them as such. Otherwise one would have expected Meres in this context to refer to them as Shakespeare's sonnets without the epithet. It is in this sense that I have used the phrase in my title, although we cannot really know why Meres did.

The theme of this sonnet is a commonplace, found among the earliest English sonneteers. Surrey in sonnet IX laments,

> Thou farest as fruit that with frost is taken,
> Today ready ripe, tomorrow all to shaken.

But I shall show later that the octave is Ovid sonnetised, to which the sestet is offered in answer.

The next sonnet gathers up the image of distilling, unites it with images from sonnet 4 and gives a comic twist by granting him ten children. 'Living in posterity' is a common idea in the poets that Shakespeare parodies. Daniel has it in sonnet XXXIV, which may well be in Shakespeare's mind as he wrote sonnets 5 and 6:

> When winter snows upon thy golden hairs,
> And frost of age hath nipped thy flowers near :
> When dark shall seem thy day that never clears,
> And all lies withered that was held so dear.
> Then take this picture which I here present thee,
>   .   .   .   .   .   .
> Here see the gifts that God and nature lent thee;
>   .   .   .   .   .   .
> This may remain thy lasting monument,

Which happily posterity may cherish :
These colours with thy fading are not spent;
These may remain, when thou and I shall perish.
If they remain, then thou shalt live thereby;
They will remain, and so thou canst not die.

Sonnet 6

Then let not winter's ragged hand deface,
In thee thy summer ere thou be distilled:
Make sweet some vial; treasure thou some place,
With beauty's treasure ere it be self killed:
That use is not forbidden usury,
Which happies those that pay the willing loan;
That's for thyself to breed another thee,
Or ten times happier be it ten for one,
Ten times thy self were happier than thou art,
If ten of thine ten times refigured thee,
Then what could death do if thou shouldst depart,
Leaving thee living in posterity?
Be not self-willed for thou art much too fair,
To be death's conquest and make worms thine heir.

This ends the first group in this section. The following sonnets have different themes, and part of the interest lies in seeing how the poet manages to bring them to the same conclusion.

Sonnet 7

Lo in the orient when the gracious light,
Lifts up his burning head, each under eye
Doth homage to his new appearing sight,
Serving with looks his sacred majesty,
And having climbed the steep up heavenly hill,
Resembling strong youth in his middle age,
Yet mortal looks adore his beauty still,
Attending on his golden pilgrimage:
But when from highmost pitch with weary car,
Like feeble age he reeleth from the day,
The eyes (fore duteous) now converted are
From his low tract and look another way:
So thou, thyself out-going in thy noon:
Unlooked on diest unless thou get a son.

The rising sun is like a wave gathering strength to reach its
height at noon, and pitching on the beach in the last quatrain
to ebb away at 'diest'. The clause that follows stands out from
this great movement, appearing something left over or tacked
on, but receiving emphasis from its isolation, which therefore
throws its irrelevance and bathos into relief. The sonnet
parodies Daniel no. XXVIII:

> Raising my hopes on hills of high desire,
> Thinking to scale the heaven of her heart:

he is thrown down by her disdain and protests,

> Yet I protest my high aspiring will,
> Was not to dispossess her of her right:
> Her Sovereignty should have remained still,
> I only sought the bliss to have her sight.

Shakespeare's sun takes the place of Daniel's hope and of his
lady's 'sovereignty'. He 'Doth homage' to its 'sight', 'Serving
with looks his sacred majesty'. This contrasts with Daniel desiring only to 'have her sight'. While Daniel scales 'The hills of
high desire', 'the heaven of her heart', Shakespeare's sun
climbs 'the steep-up heavenly hill', and falls from its 'high
most' point, which compares with Daniel's 'high desire'. Daniel
also 'presumed too high a part', so her desire threw him down.
'Steep up' is used as an adjective; this sort of grammar seemed
less violent in Shakespeare's day than it does in ours. 'Steep up
heavenly hill' has the cadence of Daniel's 'high aspiring will',
but 'steep up' might be an aural memory from a sonnet of
Sidney's in the third book of *Arcadia*, where he has,

> Do not disdain, oh straight up raiséd pine.

Sidney's usage is normal; 'up raised' is a verb (past participle)
and 'straight' an adverb. The 'up' is linked with 'raised' not
'straight'. In 'steep up' the preposition is linked with the *preceding* adjective, but retains its adverbial implication of climbing. If Shakespeare's latent memory retained Sidney's line to

contribute 'steep up', it makes evidence for the musical element in his creativeness, which I have already suggested.

Sonnet 8

> Music to hear, why hear'st thou music sadly,
> Sweets with sweets war not, joy delights in joy:
> Why lov'st thou that which thou receiv'st not gladly,
> Or else receiv'st with pleasure thine annoy?
> If the true concorde of well tuned sounds,
> By unions married do offend thine ear,
> They do but sweetly chide thee, who confounds
> In singleness the parts that thou shouldst bear:
> Mark how one string sweet husband to another,
> Strikes each in each by mutual ordering;
> Resembling sire, and child, and happy mother,
> Who all in one, one pleasing note do sing:
> Whose speechless song being many, seeming one,
> Sings this to thee thou single wilt prove none.

The meaning of this is problematic. What it means musically is difficult, and possibly cannot be clarified without presuming a misprint. I take it to refer to instrumental music, string music, a 'speechless song'. I also take it as referring to harmonic music, not polyphonic. It is clearly music with a chordal progression, hence father, wife and child in line 11, making the three notes of the chord or concord, that by a union form one harmony. The theme is 'Music to hear'. A chord is in fact heard by the undiscriminating ear as one note, which receives a colouring from the harmony or concord made by the amalgam of the three notes. This seems to be what Shakespeare is referring to in lines 7 and 8, if we can take 'bear' in the eighth line as a misprint for 'hear', which also makes a better rhyme with 'ear'. There is certainly a misprint in the line. If 'bear' is right then 'parts' should be singular, since the player could 'bear' only his own single part. To confound in singleness the parts one hears is to hear only the melody, the top notes of the chords, and be unable to distinguish the three notes that the strings play at once, or all in one, combining to make one pleasing melody or song, that says if you do not marry you will be nothing.

The opening quatrain is not much clearer. I do not take it to mean just that the friend is 'never merry when he hears sweet music', for that does not fit the context. I take music and marriage to be identified from the first word. Marriage is the reference and music the analogy. The friend is presumed throughout to like music but not marriage. This is the inconsistency. The friend is asked, why do you hear music sadly—this marriage-music. In the music you hear, sweet note does not war with sweet note, and in marriage joy delights in joy. Why love musical sound but not receive marriage gladly; or he may mean why receive the sounds with pleasure when their marriage annoys you. If the married unions of the harmony which you hear offend your ear they scold you, who hears as a single melody the parts you should hear as three. Look how one string strikes like a sweet husband with another in such a way that each contributes to the sound of the other—as in fact happens when more than one note is played at once. These separate notes forming the one chord are like father, child and mother who, all played together at once, give the impression of one solid harmony. This melody or song you hear, made of three separate parts, but seeming like one, says to you, if you do not combine in marriage you will end by being nothing.

Shakespeare got his theme from Daniel's sonnet XLVII, which has imagery from lute playing :

> Like as the lute that joys or else dislikes,
> As is his art that plays upon the same :
> So sounds my muse according as she strikes,
> On my heart strings high tuned unto her fame.
> Her touch doth cause the warble of the sound,
> Which here I yield in lamentable wise,
> A wailing descant on the sweetest ground,
> Whose due reports give honour to her eyes.
> Else harsh my style, untunable my muse,
> Hoarse sounds the voice that praiseth not her name :
> If any pleasing relish here I use,
> Then judge the world her beauty gives the same.
> Oh happy ground that makes the music such,
> And blessed hand that gives so sweet a touch.

The conceit is worked out in elaborate detail. Daniel's muse is the lutenist who sings harshly except when praising Delia's name, and accompanies herself by playing on his heart strings. He is the descant and Delia the ground. The descant wails, as indeed do most of Daniel's sonnets. The 'sweetest ground' is a figured bass for it 'makes the music such'; that is to say the bass or ground is written out, the chords being indicated by figures above each note; it is correct to say that the ground determines the harmony. Shakespeare parodies Daniel's imagery of his love, as a lute accompaniment, where he and Delia are each parts, by identifying marriage with music, each part of which is one person in the relationship. He follows it out in detail and makes such a close association that it is, as we have seen, quite difficult to be sure when he is talking of marriage and when of music. Unlike Daniel who uses the lutenist as a simile, Shakespeare purports to be writing of two equal realities. It is as if he had learnt from Daniel that there is no distinction between music and love, which he alters to marriage.

There can be equally little doubt about the mocking tone of the next sonnet:

Sonnet 9

> Is it for fear to wet a widow's eye,
> That thou consum'st thyself in single life?
> Ah, if thou issueless shalt hap to die,
> The world will wail thee like a makeless wife,
> The world will be thy widow and still weep,
> That thou no form of thee hast left behind,
> When every private widow well may keep,
> By children's eyes, her husband's shape in mind:
> Look what an unthrift in the world doth spend
> Shifts but his place, for still the world enjoys it
> But beauty's waste hath in the world an end,
> And kept unused the user so destroys it:
> No love toward others in that bosom sits
> That on himself such murd'rous shame commits.

A twentieth century reader of Erasmus is likely to notice that the woman appears only as she contributes to her husband's happiness and well being. Thus he says:

If you live in prosperity your joy is doubled; if the world go not with you, you have a wife to put you in good comfort.

In adversity he says that although one's best friend may desert one, one's wife remains; there is no pleasure to compare with such a fellowship. What the wife feels about all this Erasmus does not consider. Since Shakespeare's treatment of women in his plays suggests that he appreciated them as persons in their own right, it may be that he noticed the omission. It would then give force to his opening sarcasm. In any case fearing to 'wet a widow's eye' can hardly be an argument against marriage. With Erasmus in the background it is doubly absurd.

This is a fresh theme, but it is linked with the previous sonnet in the second line by 'single' life. The second quatrain throws back to sonnet 3 by considering that he has left no form of himself, and the third with 'unthrift' and 'waste' to the theme introduced in 1. It says that the man unthrifty in his use of 'the world' does not destroy what he loses, for if he squanders his property it merely changes hands and so is still enjoyed by the world. But beauty is not transferable. If it is not used, in the end it perishes. One does not love one's neighbour if one murders one's own quality. It will be remembered that Erasmus said that a man who does not marry is like a murderer. Shakespeare now takes up this theme, which he continues in the next sonnet, making a contrasting pair with this. In this he stresses the altruistic motive, the fear to wet a widow's eye, and especially to hurt 'the world'; he uses the word five times so that we cannot escape from the incongruity. In the next sonnet he scoffs at this altruism.

Shakespeare's sonnet background for no. 9 is the same as for sonnet 1, namely Daniel's sonnet XXXI, which also forms the background for sonnet 12. I need not quote again. In sonnet 12 he says that 'summer's green' ends on the bier, and his friend goes 'among the wastes of time'.

Sonnet 10

> For shame deny that thou bear'st love to any
> Who for thyself art so unprovident
> Grant if thou wilt, thou art beloved of many,

F

But that thou none lov'st is most evident:
For thou art so possessed with murd'rous hate,
That 'gainst thyself thou stick'st not to conspire,
Seeking that beauteous roof to ruinate
Which to repair should be thy chief desire:
Oh change thy thought, that I may change my mind,
Shall hate be fairer lodged than gentle love?
Be as thy presence is gracious and kind,
Or to thyself at least kind hearted prove,
Make thee another self for love of me,
That beauty still may live in thine or thee.

Besides making a link with the previous sonnet by scoffing at its
sham love, and repeating 'shame' from the last line, Shakespeare also reflects its 'murderous' shame in 'murderous hate'.
Although you may be loved by many, he says, you certainly
love no one. This theme—that being improvident for oneself in
not marrying is a sign of lack of love for one's neighbours, and
indeed of being murderous—is pure Erasmus. His friend is so
murderous, says Shakespeare, that he even plans a crime
against himself. A new image is then introduced, that of repair-
ing a roof, the symbol of the permanence of the family, and so
the permanence of his beauty. Finally Shakespeare suggests a
change of attitude so that he himself can change his opinion of
his friend. Shall the hate of himself evident by his not marrying
be lodged in a fairer house than love? Since he is in fact kind,
he should, says Shakespeare, be kind to himself and marry. In
the couplet a completely new motive is suggested. The poet has
pleaded with his friend to marry for his own sake, for the sake
of others, for the world's sake. Now he asks him to marry for
his sake, 'for love of me'. This has neither been led up to, nor is
it followed up. But it is the obsession of the sonneteers.

'Ruinate' may have a latent history. Spenser's 'proud and
pitiless' fair, in sonnet LVI,

> Finding a tree alone all comfortless,
> Beats on it strongly it to ruinate.

Delia's eyes, in sonnet XXIX, cause a storm :

> The broken tops of lofty trees declare,
> The fury of a mercy wanting storm.

Shakespeare's friend is said by keeping his beauty unshared, that is to say by keeping to himself and not showing mercy, to ruinate a roof, a situation usually brought about by both neglect and storms; its situation is that of Spenser's and Daniel's trees. But the word 'ruinate' seems more applicable to Shakespeare's roof, and hence may have suggested that. The linking of the two trees gives what ruinates a roof.

Sonnet 11

> As fast as thou shalt wane so fast thou grow'st,
> In one of thine, from that which thou departest,
> And that fresh blood which youngly thou bestow'st,
> Thou mayst call thine, when thou from youth convertest,
> Herein lives wisdom, beauty, and increase,
> Without this folly, age, and cold decay,
> If all were minded so, the times should cease,
> And threescore year would make the world away:
> Let those whom nature hath not made for store,
> Harsh, featureless, and rude, barrenly perish,
> Look whom she best endowed, she gave thee more;
> Which bounteous gift thou shouldst in bounty cherish,
> She carved thee for her seal, and meant thereby,
> Thou shouldst print more, not let that copy die.

This carries on directly from sonnet 10. Shakespeare refers to the child growing to maturity as the father wanes. He uses Erasmus's argument that 'If all were minded' not to marry, in a generation mankind would cease to exist. Shakespeare has calculated the exact time of the life of one man, seventy years. Daniel gave him the opening image in sonnet XXXIII :

> My faith shall wax, when thou art in thy waning.
> The world shall find this miracle in me,
> That fire can burn, when all the matter's spent.

So Shakespeare's child will wax. This is the miracle that could occur when the father is growing old. The sonnet is an example of thinking in threes, 'wisdom, beauty, and increase' being contrasted with 'harsh, featureless, and rude'. The couplet has little to do with what precedes except that it is nature that 'carved'. That it is a seal that she carves, whose purpose is to print, is the more striking for being unprepared for and this gives emphasis to the last words, 'Thou shouldst not let that copy die.'

The last six sonnets of this series take on a deeper, more resonant tone. Sonnet 12 gives this by solemnly phrased parallel clauses beginning 'When'; each comes like a great clock striking. 'Then', introducing the sestet, gives the antithesis to the temporal parallels.

Sonnet 12

> When I do count the clock that tells the time,
> And see the brave day sunk in hideous night,
> When I behold the violet past prime,
> And sable curls or silvered o'er with white:
> When lofty trees I see barren of leaves,
> Which erst from heat did canopy the herd
> And summer's green all girded up in sheaves
> Borne on the bier with white and bristly beard:
> Then of thy beauty do I question make
> That thou among the wastes of time must go,
> Since sweets and beauties do themselves forsake,
> And die as fast as they see others grow,
> And nothing 'gainst time's scythe can make defence
> Save breed to brave him, when he takes thee hence.

This moves with great dignity—not 'When I count' but 'When I do count', not 'When I see', but 'When I behold', and the barren trees are 'lofty'. Being borne on a bier implies the most solemn of processions. 'The wastes of time' must be vast indeed. And the climax of time's scythe is the end of all. This grand music sweeps us off beyond our depth, since it is a bombast we 'take', not questioning such details as whether we 'behold' a fading violet, until its solemn pageantry brings us to the defence against time in the last line. Then we receive a shock. 'Breed' has no lofty associations, and the other words are homely enough for a child to be carried off to bed.

The imagery of the sonnet was suggested by Ovid, as I shall show later. Incidentally, 'or' in line 4 is almost certainly a misprint for 'all'.

Sonnet 13

> Oh that you were yourself, but love you are
> No longer yours, than you yourself here live,
> Against this coming end you should prepare,
> And your sweet semblance to some other give.
> So should that beauty which you hold in lease
> Find no determination, then you were
> Yourself again after your self's decrease,
> When your sweet issue your sweet form should bear.
> Who lets so fair a house fall to decay,
> Which husbandry in honour might uphold,
> Against the stormy gusts of winter's day
> And barren rage of death's eternal cold?
> Oh none but unthrifts, dear my love you know,
> You had a father, let your son say so.

This sonnet also has the exaggerated cadence of parody. The key is presented in the first words, 'Oh that you were yourself', which is emotional and has the tune of affectionate persuasion, making an Erasmus-like argument in sugar. The sonnet con- is over-stressed, with its 'love', 'dear my love', 'your sweet semblance' 'your sweet issue' 'your sweet form'. And all it prepares for is the fatuity,

> dear my love you know,
> You had a father, let your son say so,

~~making an Erasmus-like argument in sugar~~. The sonnet con-denses previous arguments. Holding beauty in lease is the theme of sonnet 4. It is now suggested, still in legal terms, that it should 'Find no determination', or not come to an end. Issue bearing his friend's form comes from sonnet 9, letting the fair house decay from sonnet 10, the winter's storm sonnet 5, while death belongs to the present context.

Sonnet 14 reflects Sidney in XXVI, where referring to astrology, he says,

> For me I nature every deal do know,
> And know great causes, great effects procure,
> And know those bodies high, reign on the low.

And if these rules did fall, proof makes me sure,
Who oft bewrays my after following case,
By only those two stars in Stella's face.

Shakespeare comments, using a similar argument:

Sonnet 14

Not from the stars do I my judgement pluck,
And yet methinks I have astronomy,
But not to tell of good, or evil luck,
Of plagues, of dearths, or seasons' quality,
Nor can I fortune to brief minutes tell;
Pointing to each his thunder, rain and wind,
Or say with princes if it shall go well
By oft predict that I in heaven find.
But from thine eyes my knowledge I derive,
And constant stars in them I read such art
As truth and beauty shall together thrive
If from thyself, to store thou wouldst convert:
Or else of thee this I prognosticate,
Thy end is truth's and beauty's doom and date.

In contrast with Sidney, Shakespeare says his 'astronomy' does not tell him of 'great causes' or how the 'bodies high, reign on the low', whether in great catastrophes like plagues and famines or in matters of 'brief moment', nor does it tell him about politics. Yet just as Sidney's stars are Stella's eyes, from which he learns his fate, so Shakespeare's are his friend's. He learns from them what he has been saying, ever since he began his sonnets, that if his friend marries, his truth and beauty will be stored in his offspring and if he does not, the prophecy is one of doom. His friend's decision on this is the cardinal point of the world's fate no less than of his own.

Sidney's hyperbole is not ridiculous, for his fate does depend on Stella, although any hyperbole is on the razor edge of absurdity. Shakespeare's is ridiculous since he uses it to give great emphasis not only to what we expect him to say, (and which is a near platitude anyhow) but also to a prosaic expression of it. Great things like 'truth and beauty' will result if he converts 'to store' from himself. This sudden collapse in style

cannot be accidenal, particularly as it is paralleled in the last
line of sonnet 12, where 'time's scythe' and going 'among the
wastes of time' are prevented if he 'breed'.

Sonnet 15

> When I consider every thing that grows
> Holds in perfection but a little moment.
> That this huge stage presenteth nought but shows
> Whereon the stars in secret influence comment.
> When I perceive that men as plants increase,
> Cheered and checked even by the self-same sky:
> Vaunt in their youthful sap, at height decrease,
> And wear their brave state out of memory.
> Then the conceit of this inconstant stay,
> Sets you most rich in youth before my sight,
> Where wasteful time debateth with decay
> To change your day of youth to sullied night,
> And all in war with time for love of you
> As he takes from you, I engraft you new.

In sonnet 14 the most momentous decision in the universe was
said to lie in the choice of his friend to marry or not. Here the
'little moment' determined by the 'secret influence' of the stars
is held to be that when his beauty reaches perfection. And
Shakespeare stresses its shortness, and the power of fate that
brings it down. His friend is at this moment now, rich in youth
when waste or death wars with time to bring him to 'sullied
night'. In this moment, however, and for the first time, Shakespeare does not ask his friend to marry, but still using an
Erasmus image—that of engrafting—he writes as a sonneteer
who promises immortal life in his verse. Thus he makes an
almost imperceptible shift from Erasmus's theme of marriage
as the solution of death's threat to that of the sonneteers. That
is, he forecasts the theme he is about to make nonsense of—the
theme of *Love's Labours Lost*. But the sonnet is also designed
to return to the theme of marriage in sonnet 16, which begins
by suggesting that his friend finds a mightier way to

> Make war upon that bloody tyrant time,

namely by marrying.

The magnificent singing tune that Shakespeare uses to
inflate the argument of these sonnets comes from Constable.
Here it is as we find it in decade 7, sonnet V and decade 6,
sonnets V and VI.

> Had she not been so excellently fair,
> My muse had never mourned in lines of woe,
> But I did too inestimable weigh her,
> And that's the cause I now lament me so.
> Yet not for her contempt do I complain me,
> (Complaints may ease the mind, but that is all,)
> Therefore though she too constantly disdain me
> I can but sigh and grieve, and so I shall :
> Yet grieve I not, because I must grieve ever,
> And yet (alas) waste tears away in vain.
> I am resolved, truly to persevere,
> Though she persisteth in her old disdain.
> But that which grieves me most, is that I see,
> Those which most fair, the most unkindest be.
>
> Weary of love, my thoughts of love complained,
> Till reason told them there was no such power,
> And bade me view fair beauty's richest flower,
> To see if there a naked boy remained.
> Dear to thine eyes, eyes that my soul hath pained,
> Thoughts turned them back in that unhappy hour
> To see if love kept there his royal bower,
> For if not there, then no place him contained.
> There was he not, nor boy, nor golden bow,
> Yet as thou turned thy chaste fair eye aside,
> A flame of fire did from thy eyelids go,
> Which burnt my heart through my sore wounded side.
> Then with a sigh, reason made thoughts to cry,
> There is no god of love, save that thine eye.
>
> Forgive me dear, for thundering on thy name,
> Sith 'tis thyself that shows my love distressed,
> For fire exhaled, in freezing clouds possessed,
> Warring for way, makes all the heavens exclaim.
> Thy beauty so, the brightest living flame,

Wrapped in my cloudy heart by winter pressed,
Scorning to dwell within so base a nest,
Thunders in me thine everlasting fame.
Oh that my heart might still contain that fire,
Or that the fire would always light my heart,
Then shouldst thou not disdain my true desire,
Or think I wronged thee, to reveal my smart.
For as the fire through freezing clouds doth break,
So, not myself, but thou in me would'st speak.

This is Shakespeare's solemn, dignified, measured tread. Somewhat similar pompous, general and abstract terms, parallel clauses, affectionate phrases or epithets, contribute to both poets' full emotional tone. Shakespeare fills the tune with majestic language to match, and Constable has often heavy-footed bathos, but it is the same tune. This is important in parody. If Shakespeare read his sonnets aloud to his friends—and he was an actor—tones and tunes of the voice meant to reflect the poet being pilloried, would be exactly copied. Even just talking in the tones of another can be parody. Shakespeare constantly uses this tune of Constable's. Besides in this context, we hear it in the sonnets beginning 'When in disgrace with fortune', 'When to the sessions of sweet silent thought', 'Heavy with toil, I haste me to my bed', 'Being your slave'. It is one of his commonest tunes, and as is apparent, it is used as a sonnet melody not intending just to mimic Constable, but in other contexts to lead onward in beauty and dignity, to sudden bathos in the final couplet. Sonnet 15 ends with the pitiful pose of the poet setting his verse up against the whole course of nature.

Sonnet 16 couples very closely with 15, the sense running on without a break into

But wherefore do not you a mightier way
Make war upon this bloody tyrant time?
And fortify yourself in your decay
With means more blessed than my barren rhyme?
Now stand you on the top of happy hours,
And many maidens gardens yet unset,
With virtuous wish would bear your living flowers,

Much liker than your painted counterfeit:
So should the lines of life that life repair
Which this (time's pencil or my pupil pen)
Neither in inward worth nor outward fair
Can make you live yourself in eyes of men.
To give away yourself, keeps yourself still,
And you must live drawn by your own sweet skill.

(Sonnet 16)

Shakespeare seems to be particularising sonnet XXX of Daniel in this parody:

Then beauty, now the burden of my song.
.   .   .   .   .   .

Must yield up all to tyrant time's desire:
Then fade those flowers which decked her pride so long.
.   .   .   .   .   .

Go you my verse, go tell her what she was.

Daniel writes of beauty yielding to 'tyrant time', where the 'flowers' of her beauty will fade, and offers his verse to perpetuate her memory. Shakespeare says there is a mightier way to war for beauty against 'tyrant time' using Daniel's exact words, than his barren rhyme, 'in living flowers' as distinct from faded. In fact he is saying it would be more sensible to marry.

Sonnet 17

Who will believe my verse in time to come
If it were filled with your most high deserts?
Though yet heaven knows it is but as a tomb
Which hides your life, and shows not half your parts:
If I could write the beauty of your eyes,
And in fresh numbers number all your graces,
The age to come would say this poet lies,
Such heavenly touches ne'er touched earthly faces.
So should my papers (yellowed with their age)
Be scorned, like old men of less truth than tongue,

And your true rights be termed a poet's rage,
And stretched metre of an antique song.
But were some child of yours alive that time,
You should live twice in it, and in my rhyme.

This sonnet brings the series on Erasmus's theme to an end and combines it with the next theme of the poet perpetuating his love in his verse. The last line has both, with the friend living twice, once in his child, and secondly in verse.

Several of Daniel's sonnets provide targets for this. Here is sonnet XLVI:

Let others sing of knights and paladins,
In aged accents, and untimely words:
Paint shadows in imaginary lines,
Which well the reach of their high wits records;
But I must sing of thee and those fair eyes,
Authentic shall my verse in time to come,
When yet the unborne shall say, lo where she lies,
Whose beauty made him speak that else was dumb.
These are the arks the trophies I erect,
That fortify thy name against old age,
And these thy sacred virtues must protect,
Against the dark and time's consuming rage.
Though the error of my youth they shall discover,
Suffice they show I lived and was thy lover.

Both poets are concerned with their verses on their loved one 'in time to come'; the phrase is identical in both. Daniel begins, 'Let others sing of knights and paladins' which showed the extent of 'their high wits'. Shakespeare considers that in the future his verse monument may be scorned as 'an antique song' when he writes of his friend's 'high deserts'. Daniel erects arks and trophies to fortify Delia's name against 'old age' and protect her virtues against 'time's ... range'. Shakespeare anticipates he may be scorned like 'old men' and what he says be 'termed a poet's rage'. Daniel 'must sing' of Delia's 'fair eyes' to authenticate his verse when people say, 'lo where she lies', and Shakespeare considers that if he 'could write the beauty of your eyes', even if his verse is 'but as a tomb' that does not show half his 'parts', future ages would say, 'this poet lies', which may be an aural memory. He parodies by saying that if he did as Daniel does, he would not be believed. Daniel's sonnet obviously sings in Shakespeare's mind as he writes, but the parody does not so much seem consciously designed, as an imprecisely remembered piece of music. Constable may have copied Daniel in decade 8, sonnet IV and Shakespeare may have him in mind too :

> When re-entombing from oblivious ages
> In better stanzas her surviving wonder,
> I may opposed against the monster-rages
> That part desert, and excellence asunder.

The theme of all three poets is perpetuating the beloved in a new age. Constable probably gave Shakespeare 'the tomb' which 're-entombs' in an effort to preserve his friend. There are also recollected sounds in 'rage', 'part', 'desert', all of which Shakespeare uses, 'deserts', 'parts' and 'tomb' all occurring in his first quatrain. The poet being suspected of flattery is a very common theme, but Spenser's sonnet LXXXV may be in Shakespeare's mind here :

> The world that cannot deem of worthy things,
> When I do praise her, say I do but flatter:
> .   .   .   .   .
> But they that skill not of such heavenly matter,
> All that they know not, envy or admire,
> Rather than envy let them wonder at her,
> But not to deem of her desert aspire.

'Heavenly matter' may have suggested Shakespeare's 'heavenly touches' and 'aspire' to her 'deserts' his 'high deserts'.

Sonnet 18

> Shall I compare thee to a summer's day?
> Thou art more lovely and more temperate:
> Rough winds do shake the darling buds of May,
> And summer's lease hath all too short a date:

Sometime too hot the eye of heaven shines,
And often is his gold complexion dimmed,
And every fair from fair sometime declines,
By chance, or nature's changing course untrimmed:
But thy eternal summer shall not fade,
Nor lose possession of that fair thou owest,
Nor shall death brag thou wanderest in his shade,
When in eternal lines to time thou growest,
So long as men can breathe or eyes can see,
So long lives this, and this gives life to thee.

Sonnet 18 begins the new section that lasts till sonnet 32. It
was skilfully prepared for by stepping up the power of time,
and then introducing the poet's verse as a defence. In sonnet
17 Shakespeare said he would preserve his friend in rhyme,
and here he considers what he should say about him. The
sonnet springs very obviously out of his reading of Spenser who
wrote in sonnet IX,

Long-while I sought to what I might compare
Those powerful eyes, which lighté my dark sprite,
Yet find I nought on earth to which I dare
Resemble the image of their goodly light.
Not to the sun : for they do shine by night.

So on he goes, 'Not to the moon . . ., giving a line to each of
his eight suggestions. He also aims to 'eternise' her virtues in
sonnet LXXV. It is just possible that Spenser's sonnet XXVII,
where he says his love 'Shall doff her flesh's borrowed fair
attire' may have suggested Shakespeare's 'lose possession of
that fair thou owest'. Leishman[64] quotes Ronsard for comparison with the ending,

L'esprit vivra toujours qui vous doit fair vivre,
Au moins tant que vivront les plumes et le livre.

But we cannot be sure that Shakespeare had read this to
parody it with breath and eyes.

Sonnet 19 has the same theme as that of the sestet of 18.

Sonnet 19

> Devouring time blunt thou the lion's paws,
> And make the earth devour her own sweet brood,
> Pluck the keen teeth from the fierce tiger's jaws,
> And burn the long lived phœnix in her blood,
> Make glad and sorry seasons as thou fleetest,
> And do whate'er thou wilt swift-footed time
> To the wide world and all her fading sweets:
> But I forbid thee one most heinous crime,
> Oh carve not with thy hours my love's fair brow,
> Nor draw no lines there with thine antique pen,
> Him in thy course untainted do allow,
> For beauty's pattern to succeeding men.
> Yet do thy worst old time despite thy wrong,
> My love shall in my verse ever live young.

The octave is a direct reference to Ovid. It begins with a translation of *Tempus edax rerum* from the last book of his *Metamorphoses*. But Shakespeare probably got his opening words from Spenser's sonnet LVIII, where he refers to

> Devouring time and changeful chance.

Ovid traced the changes and metamorphoses that time has caused from the golden age onwards. When the vegetarian golden age became carnivorous in the iron age,

> The nature of the beast that doth delight in bloody food,
> Is cruel and unmerciful.[65]

And among these beasts he mentions lions and tigers. This is an association that the sonneteers have noticed, for their ladies are compared with lions and tigers because they deserve Ovid's two damning epithets. There is one exception to the changes caused by time says Ovid. Whereas all birds change from being eggs, the phoenix alone does 'Beget itself continually'.[66] Shakespeare with all this in mind, tells time who gave all, to blunt the lion's claws, pluck teeth from the tiger and to burn the phoenix on the pyre that should regenerate it, but he will not permit it to carve wrinkles on his friend's brow, an activity

Ovid also attributes to time. He ends the poet's claim that his verse will defeat time by saying, do your worst, 'old time'; his friend will remain for ever young in his verse.

The world of Ovid makes part of the sonneteers' world. Shakespeare does not accept it. He lives in the actual world, where the sensible way of perpetuating oneself is to marry and have children. In this sonnet he makes his first direct attack. But he has been creating this world, preparing for this attack from the first sonnets, for sonnet 2 has an unmistakable reference to it. Golding's translation[67] of *Tempus edax rerum* is 'Thou time, the eater up of things'. In sonnet 2 Shakespeare calls shame 'all-eating'. This is an almost incomprehensible epithet for 'shame', if one is not reminded by it of Ovid. It is all-eating because it is the shame of what time does. So the sonnets begin with the beautiful young man being recommended to marry to defeat this threat in the sonneteers world, Ovid's world. If we need proof that Shakespeare was referring to Ovid, we have it in other recollections in the sonnet. As already noted, Ovid attributes wrinkles to time. In the same context he likens man's growth to that of the seasons. Shakespeare has this comparison in mind too, and refers to the treasure of 'their lusty days', just as Golding[68] refers to summer becoming 'like a lusty youth'. In sonnet 5 also, Ovid gives its character to the description of time for ever changing things. Never-resting time leads summer to 'hideous winter' with 'lusty leaves quite gone' and 'beauty o'er-snowed'. Golding has, 'Then ugly winter last Like age steals on ... all bald ... with ... hair as white as snow'. Sonnet 12 seems to have this background too, where spring is described as passing into autumn and winter. Night is 'hideous' like Ovid's winter, 'sable curls' are 'silvered o'er with white' and 'summer's green' is 'girded up in sheaves'. Golding refers to the spring as 'green', to which the epithet is more applicable than to summer, and following summer, he says, comes 'harvest when the heat of youth grows somewhat cold'. In Shakespeare the trees grow 'barren of leaves', 'which erst from heat did canopy the herd'. We are not aware of parody in these early sonnets, however, though the contemporary reader might notice a reference to Ovid. Nevertheless this would be the world of poetry he was familiar with. If a sense of its being included in the parody was intended, it is very gently insinuated. Only in sonnet 19 comes open laughter. 'Old time' is disrespectfully treated, told to do his worst, but forbidden to go too far.

Sonnet 20 has been taken by those historians who consider the friend to be a real man as crucial.

Sonnet 20

> A woman's face with nature's own hand painted,
> Hast thou the master mistress of my passion,
> A woman's gentle heart but not acquainted
> With shifting change as is false women's fashion,
> An eye more bright than theirs, less false in rolling:
> Gilding the object whereupon it gazeth,
> A man in hue all hues in his controlling,
> Which steals men's eyes and women's souls amazeth.
> And for a woman wert thou first created,
> Till nature as she wrought thee fell a-doting,
> And by addition me of thee defeated,
> By adding one thing to my purpose nothing.
> But since she pricked thee out for women's pleasure,
> Mine be thy love and thy love's use their treasure.

The grammatical structure of 'master mistress' suggests reference to a woman since 'mistress' is the noun, and 'master' only the epithet. I verified this as the obvious reading by asking an intelligent friend out of the blue if she heard someone referred to thus, what sex she would think implied. The other interpretation is of course permissible. But which is right is not a foregone conclusion. I take this sonnet as comparable with 'Two loves I have of comfort and despair'—a statement by Shakespeare of what he is doing. The person he is writing to has a woman's face, a woman's heart without her fickleness, a brighter eye but a less false; that is to say it is a sonnet woman but without her faults. He has made this sonnet mistress a man, and so refers to him as the 'master mistress' of his passion. If this is the correct interpretation, then he was indeed 'for a woman ... first created'. And Shakespeare confirms this by saying he is not interested in his sex as a man; that is nothing to his purpose.

Sonnet 21 is direct parody of the same sort as 'My mistress' eyes are nothing like the sun' (130).

Sonnet 21

> So is it not with me as with that muse,
> Stirred by a painted beauty to his verse,
> Who heaven itself for ornament doth use,
> And every fair with his fair doth rehearse,
> Making a couplement of proud compare
> With sun and moon, with earth and sea's rich gems:
> With April's first-born flowers and all things rare,
> That heaven's air in this huge rondure hems.
> Oh let me true in love but truly write,
> And then believe me, my love is as fair,
> As any mother's child, though not so bright
> As those gold candles fixed in heaven's air:
> Let them say more that like of hearsay well,
> I will not praise that purpose not to sell.

This is bound in with the context by reflecting 'a woman's face' and 'painted' from the first line of the previous sonnet. But its real relevance lies in belonging to the theme first commented on in 18, when Shakespeare asked how he should describe his friend. At this late stage in our study, it is unnecessary to illustrate the obvious by giving examples of the writing this refers to.

Shakespeare writes sonnet 22 as an interlude on the presumed identification of poet and friend, before returning to his theme of verse-making about him, but he keeps a link with previous sonnets in his imagery of the glass and time's furrows.

Sonnet 22

> My glass shall not persuade me I am old,
> So long as youth and thou are of one date,
> But when in thee time's furrows I behold,
> Then look I death my days should expiate.
> For all that beauty that doth cover thee,
> Is but the seemly raiment of my heart,
> Which in thy breast doth live, as thine in me,

How can I then be elder than thou art?
Oh therefore love be of thyself so wary,
As I not for myself, but for thee will,
Bearing thy heart which I will keep so chary
As tender nurse her babe from faring ill,
Presume not on thy heart when mine is slain,
Thou gavest me thine not to give back again.

The sonneteer's affectation that he is age-worn from despair begins in Petrarch. Sir Sidney Lee[69] calculated that Daniel was twenty-nine years old when he so described himself, and Drayton thirty-one. Shakespeare on my dating was twenty-eight. In order to illustrate his identity with his friend Shakespeare starts by looking at himself in a glass. As long as his friend is young, the wrinkles he sees will not persuade him he is old; there is a transcending truth, as he might say in our terms. When he sees wrinkles in his friend, then he will think his days should expiate his death, make amends for it so that he can meet it perhaps; or death may be the subject, and it should expiate his life; or he may have a less sensible meaning such as that it will be time he justified his life by writing what will not die. In the second quatrain he explains. All the beauty his friend has covers Shakespeare's heart and makes suitable clothing. The heart's clothing is of course the body. Since his heart lives in his friend's breast and his friend's in his, then they must have the same body, and be the same age. This expresses the sonnet attitude of lovers being one, identified, which we saw exploited in sonnets 133 and 134 and made ridiculous. The logic here also makes it absurd. He carries on the fantasy by saying they must each be very careful of themselves since what befalls one will befall the other. Then he assures his friend that he will carry him as carefully as if he were his nurse carrying a baby. He caps the nonsense by saying that when he is slain, his friend will not be able to presume he has a heart, since he gave it not to be returned. As the way a sonneteer is slain is always by his love, we may presume that when Shakespeare is slain, it will be by his friend. So this is an elaborate way of saying that if his friend rejected him he would be heartless. It makes characteristic sonnet nonsense.

Sonnet 23

> As an unperfect actor on the stage,
> Who with his fear is put beside his part,
> Or some fierce thing replete with too much rage,
> Whose strength's abundance weakens his own heart;
> So I for fear of trust, forget to say,
> The perfect ceremony of love's rite,
> And in mine own love's strength seem to decay,
> O'ercharged with burden of mine own love's might:
> Oh let my books be then the eloquence,
> And dumb presagers of my speaking breast,
> Who plead for love, and look for recompense,
> More than that tongue that more hath more expressed.
> Oh learn to read what silent love hath writ,
> To hear with eyes belongs to love's fine wit.

The reference to an actor may suggest a personal experience, whatever else in the sonnets does not. But Spenser's sonnet LIV gives a precedent for a somewhat similar image of the poet as actor. The theme of the lover so replete with passion that he is dumb makes part of the ancient tradition that Petrarch built on. Sonneteers consequently plead that their love may be spoken by their eyes, and seen by their lady's eyes. 'Dumb presagers of my speaking breast' echoes Daniel's sonnet VIII :

> And you mine eyes the agents of my heart,
> Told the dumb message of my hidden grief.

In parody Shakespeare substitutes for communication by eyes, what in fact sonneteers do use, communication by the written word. When he cannot say the right things, or perform the ceremony of love because he cannot take his friend's acceptance on trust and so lacks confidence, he can, he says, at least write it. He uses the actor to represent the master in the ritual of words. Since he is like an actor who cannot say his part from nervousness, or like one overcome by passionate feeling who cannot express himself since his strength is undermined by his feeling, then, he says, let him say it in his books. These are his dumb presagers of his speaking breast. It is much more sensible, he suggests, to read what silent love has written than 'To hear with eyes'. He says with sarcasm that this 'belongs to love's fine wit'; in other words it is what sonneteers do. The joke is both indicated and missed by those who would take 'books' as a misprint for 'looks'.

So much for making his friend immortal in words. In sonnet 24 Shakespeare parodies another way of doing this.

Sonnet 24

> Mine eye hath played the painter and hath stelled,
> Thy beauty's form in table of my heart,
> My body is the frame wherein 'tis held,
> And perspective it is best painter's art.
> For through the painter must you see his skill,
> To find where your true image pictured lies,
> Which in my bosom's shop is hanging still,
> That hath his windows glazed with thine eyes:
> Now see what good turns eyes for eyes have done,
> Mine eyes have drawn thy shape, and thine for me
> Are windows to my breast, where-through the sun
> Delights to peep, to gaze therein on thee
> Yet eyes this cunning want to grace their art
> They draw but what they see, know not the heart.

This parodies a favourite sonnet conceit that has been traced back to Plato, who in the *Phaedrus*, as I have already noted, says that the lover sees himself in his love as in a mirror. It is reflected by sonneteers since Petrarch onwards. Daniel in sonnet XIII says,

> For hapless lo even with mine own desires,
> I figured on the table of my heart :
> The fairest form, the world's eye admires,
> And so did perish by my proper art.

But the framed picture comes from Watson's *Tears of Francie,* sonnet XLV :

> When neither sighs nor sorrows were of force
> I let my mistress see my naked breast :

Where view of wounded heart might work remorse,

. . . . . .

With steadfast eye she gazéd on my heart,
Wherein she saw the picture of her beauty.

He continues in the next sonnet,

My mistress seeing her fair counterfeit
So sweetly framéd in my bleeding breast :

asks for it, 'But it so fast was fixéd' to his heart that he could
not get it off;

Here take my heart quoth I, with it the picture.

Sidney in sonnet **XXXII** makes Morpheus steal Stella's image
from his heart and Spenser tells his lady in sonnet **XLV** not to
look in her glass, but

in myself, my inward self I mean,
Most lively like behold your semblance true.

If it were not that her cruelty has 'dimmed' and 'deformed'
it,

The goodly image of your visnomy,
Clearer than crystal would therein appear.

Constable is perhaps responsible for the glazing of the window
with his eyes. In decade 1, sonnet V he has,

Thine eye, the glass where I behold my heart,
Mine eye the window through the which thine eye
May see my heart, and there thyself espy
In bloody colours how thou painted art.

After the parody in the octave, made by adding one poet to
another, Shakespeare gives the laughing comment :

Now see what good-turns eyes for eyes have done.

One poet draws her shape and another provides the window.
Perhaps the sun gazing in was suggested by Watson's sonnet
XXIII of the *Passionate Centurie*. He writes of his mistress as
she looks in her glass,

> Thou glass, wherein that sun delights to see
> Her own aspect, . . .
> Would God I might possess like state with thee,
> Thou gazeth on her face, and she on thine.

Shakespeare ends with direct criticism. These eyes which provide all this, lack real knowledge of the heart.

Sonnet 25

> Let those who are in favour with their stars,
> Of public honour and proud titles boast,
> Whilst I whom fortune of such triumph bars
> Unlooked for joy in that I honour most;
> Great princes' favourites their fair leaves spread,
> But as the marigold at the sun's eye,
> And in themselves their pride lies buried,
> For at a frown they in their glory die.
> The painful warrior famouséd for worth,
> After a thousand victories once foiled,
> Is from the book of honour razed quite,
> And all the rest forgot for which he toiled:
> Then happy I that love and am beloved
> Where I may not remove, nor be removed.

The meaning is straightforward. Shakespeare pits his lowly
fortune against that of others who are lucky, who have public
honours and titles, who are favourites of the great, or famous
warriors, and he sees their good fortune as vulnerable. But he
loves and is loved, and this will never change. This does not
read like a parody until in the very next sonnet the situation is
presented not as two people far removed from public fame
loving each other, but himself in a relationship with his friend
that suggests quite another situation.

   The marigold is a sonneteer's flower. Watson introduced it
in a prose note to his ninth poem of *The Passionate Centurie*.

He says a nymph aspired to be the love of the sun, but was rejected. Pitying her misery, the gods turned her into a marigold, or heliotropium, and 'she still observeth the rising and going down' of the sun. In his poem he says that he follows his 'she sun' in the same way. It was from Constable, however, that Shakespeare got his image, who in decade 1, sonnet IX shows that his lady's presence gives all the flowers their quality, among them,

> The marigold the leaves abroad doth spread,
> Because the sun's, and her power is the same.

Sonnet 26 gives a very obvious twist to Surrey's sonnet VI, which runs thus:

> Love, that liveth, and reigneth in my thought
> That built his seat within my captive breast,
> Clad in the arms, wherein with me he fought,
> Oft in my face he doth his banner rest.
> She, that me taught to love, and suffer pain,
> My doubtful hope, and eke my hot desire,
> With shamefast cloak to shadow, and refrain,
> Her smiling grace converteth straight to ire.
> And coward love then to the heart apace
> Taketh his flight, whereas he lurks, and plains
> His purpose lost, and dare not show his face.
> For my lord's guilt thus faultless bide I pains.
> Yet from my lord shall not my foot remove.
> Sweet is his death, that takes his end by love.

This is to say that love is his lord, who reigns in his heart, whose castle he has taken and made his residence. She who taught him to love changed to anger in order to put a modest (shamefast) cloak on his 'hot desire'. Her anger made cowardly love run to his heart where he hides and 'dare not show his face'. Although he suffers undeservedly from his lord's guilt, he will not 'remove' his foot, or allegiance. Shakespeare parodies the duty owed to the lord, the lady putting a cloak on his desire, which of course would be naked otherwise, and love hiding because he is afraid. There is a link with previous sonnets since he discusses how the stars determine his relationship with his friend. This relationship is his overt theme, that unites the other. He makes it anything but romantic.

Sonnet 26

> Lord of my love, to whom in vassalage
> Thy merit hath my duty strongly knit;
> To thee I send this written embassage
> To witness duty, not to show my wit.
> Duty so great, which wit so poor as mine
> May make seem bare, in wanting words to show it;
> But that I hope some good conceit of thine
> In thy soul's thought (all naked) will bestow it:
> Till whatsoever star that guides my moving,
> Points on me graciously with fair aspect,
> And puts apparel on my tottered loving,
> To show me worthy of thy sweet respect,
> Then may I dare to boast how I do love thee,
> Till then, not show my head where thou mayst prove me.

The lord of love is Shakespeare's friend, whom he treats with great respect, sending a written embassage to him 'To witness duty'. We saw in sonnet 23 that this can indicate a certain nervousness about speaking to him. The reason soon becomes apparent. Like Surrey's, his love is 'bare', which he amplifies as 'wanting words', his fault is sonnet 23. His duty is bare because not expressed in words, that is, not properly expressed, as Surrey's love was not properly expressed. Presumably his friend's thought is 'all naked' because his love is not expressed at all. All this stressing of nakedness, and the hope for 'some good conceit' is a reference to the inspiration of Surrey's lady in putting a cloak over his desire, with also the second meaning of a 'good conceit' as an ingenious figure of speech. In the sestet we discover what Shakespeare's trouble is. It is being out of 'favour with his stars'. In misfortune his friend will not recognise him. Only when whatever star is responsible points to him 'with fair aspect' will he do so. This would put 'apparel' on his loving, as Surrey's lady did with modesty and made him respectable as we might say today. Surrey is made respectable by having his desire cloaked, Shakespeare by being favoured by fortune, not as used in this sonnet, a romantic reason. He cannot approach his friend for fear until he is accepted as respectable enough to speak to him. Only when his stars favour him again will he be able to clothe his loving, his duty in words and so express it acceptably. When fortune will make him worthy of his friend's 'sweet respect' he will be like Surrey's love when he became worthy of his lady's sweet respect. Then, Shakespeare says, he need no longer hide away like Surrey. As Surrey can then 'show his face', Shakespeare may even 'dare to boast' how he loves his friend and 'show his head', in fact go one better than Surrey. Finally just as in adversity Surrey did not 'remove' his foot or leave his lord, so Shakespeare's duty remained constant. This parody follows Surrey so closely that we cannot doubt it. If there were no other evidence, it alone would prove that Shakespeare had Surrey in his background.

Although Surrey was chiefly in mind when Shakespeare wrote this sonnet, the servile attitude parodied is general in the sonnet tradition. It seems less degraded to a mistress than to a lord. A sonnet of Sidney's and also one of Spenser's may have contributed to this aspect of Shakespeare's sonnet. Sidney in sonnet XLVII complains that he gets from Stella 'no alms, but scorn of beggary', and Spenser in LXI asks,

> What reason is it then but she should scorn,
> Base things that to her love too bold aspire?
> Such heavenly forms ought rather worshipped be,
> Than dare be loved by men of mean degree.

This is Shakespeare's situation. Until fortune favours him he is a man of mean degree, scorned like a beggar improperly clothed, not daring to speak to his lordly friend.

The next two sonnets deal with another commonplace, the absent lover who cannot sleep, or if he sleeps, dreams of his love. He can find no rest or happiness apart from his mistress whether awake or asleep.

Petrarch writes on this theme, and it is there in the English sonnets in Surrey and Wyatt.

Sonnet 27

> Weary with toil, I haste me to my bed,
> The dear repose for limbs with travel tired,

But then begins a journey in my head
To work my mind, when body's work's expired.
For then my thoughts (from far where I abide)
Intend a zealous pilgrimage to thee,
And keep my drooping eyelids open wide,
Looking on darkness which the blind do see.
Save that my soul's imaginary sight
Presents their shadow to my sightless view,
Which like a jewel (hung in ghastly night)
Makes black night beauteous, and her old face new.
Lo thus by day my limbs, by night my mind,
For thee, and for myself, no quiet find.

Sonnet 28

How can I then return in happy plight
That am debarred the benefit of rest?
When day's oppression is not eased by night,
But day by night and night by day oppressed.
And each (though enemies to either's reign)
Do in consent shake hands to torture me,
The one by toil, the other to complain
How far I toil, still farther off from thee.
I tell the day to please him thou art bright,
And dost him grace when clouds do blot the heaven:
So flatter I the swart-complexioned night,
When sparkling stars twire not thou gild'st the even.
But day doth daily draw my sorrows longer,
And night doth nightly make grief's length seem stronger.

Sidney has a not dissimilar pair of sonnets expressing the pain of absence. Here is the sestet of LXXXVIII:

When absence with her mists obscures her light,
My orphan sense slides to the inward sight:
Where memory feeds forth the beams of love,
That where before heart loved and eyes did see,
In heart my sight and love both coupled be,
United powers make each the stronger prove.

This is followed by :

> Now that of absence the most irksome night,
> With darkest shade doth overcome the day :
> Since Stella's eyes that wont give me my day,
> Leaving my hemisphere o'ercast with night,
> Each day seems long, and longs for long stayed night:
> The night as tedious, woos the approach of day:
> Toiled with dusty toils of busy day,
> Languished with horrors of the silent night,
> While no night is more dark than is my day,
> Nor no day hath less quiet than my night :
> With such bad mixture of my night and day,
> That living thus in blackest winter night,
> I feel the gleams of hottest summer's day.

Let us look at some of the correspondences. In sonnet 27 Shakespeare writes of absence when he is tired with travel and 'weary with toil'. In sonnet LXXXIX Sidney says that he was 'Toiled with dusty toils of busy day'. In the former sonnet Sidney says that when frustrated by absence he 'slides to the inward sight'. Shakespeare in 27 says that when he is tired in body 'then begins a journey in my head'. He ends that sonnet saying that neither his limbs by day nor his mind at night can find any rest. This is Sidney's theme in the second sonnet. The parallel between it and Shakespeare's sonnet 28 is close. Shakespeare's day's oppression is not eased by night, nor vice versa; each oppresses the other. Sidney does not make one oppress the other; he compares them and finds both equally insufferable. But he ends sonnet LXXXVIII saying that the united powers of love and sight 'make each the stronger prove' and Shakespeare similarly ends sonnet 28 by saying that day lengthens his sorrow and night makes his grief 'stronger'. Spenser also in sonnet LXXXVII on the same theme says,

> For when as day the heaven doth adorn,
> I wish that night the noyous day would end :
> And when as night hath us of light forlorn,
> I wish that day would shortly reascend.

Daniel ends sonnet XLV which has this theme :

> Still let me sleep, embracing clouds in vain;
> And never wake, to feel the day's disdain.

This compares with Shakespeare's

> I tell the day to please him thou art bright,
> And dost him grace when clouds do blot the heaven.

'Looking on darkness which the blind do see' is an unexpected phrase, and worth comment as it is characteristic of Shakespeare. It may be an echo from Sidney's sonnet XXXII where Morpheus gives him dreams of Stella.

> Teaching blind eyes both how to smile and weep.

If this influenced Shakespeare it would be by one of those shifts in the unconscious that occur in creation. Sidney's eyes, blind to reality in sleep, see in dream, although he does not actually say this. To say that blind eyes see is imprecise. A noticeable aspect of Shakespeare's imagination is its retention of the reality situation. His eyes are open in the dark and see what the blind man sees, namely darkness. It is his 'soul's imaginary sight' that gives him the vision. He describes the fact with psychological accuracy, with the same sort of precision, curiously enough, that one finds in Wordsworth; it has been called prosaic.

Sonnet 29

> When in disgrace with fortune and men's eyes,
> I all alone beweep my outcast state,
> And trouble deaf heaven with my bootless cries,
> And look upon myself and curse my fate.
> Wishing me like to one more rich in hope,
> Featured like him, like him with friends possessed,
> Desiring this man's art, and that man's scope,
> With what I most enjoy contented least,
> Yet in these thoughts myself almost despising,
> Haply I think on thee, and then my state,

(Like to the lark at break of day arising)
From sullen earth sings hymns at heaven's gate,
For thy sweet love remembered such wealth brings,
That then I scorn to change my state with kings.

That this is parody we could not doubt. To be in disgrace with fortune in sonnet language is to be out of favour with one's lady, and to be this is to be in disgrace with her eyes. The two statements mean the same thing. Shakespeare's substituting 'men's eyes' for 'lady's eyes' could be only parody. Having dealt with this situation translated into social terms in his last sonnet, Shakespeare treats it over-emotionally in this, or in other words he behaves as the lover does in his situation. He cries to heaven, he curses his fate, he wishes he had every good fortune, and he makes sure we take it as good fortune in the world, not in the usual sonnet sense. When 'almost despising' himself (why 'almost'?) he just happens ('haply') to think of his friend, and suddenly, instead of praying in despair, he is like a lark singing at 'heaven's gate'.

All this is hysterical, but it is not difficult to find passages to justify the parody, and from many poets. The fortune, the stars, the disgrace, the lady's eyes—all have their antecedents. And the way these are combined in the same sonnets, and seem to belong together is impressive. Sidney in sonnet LXIV writes,

> Let fortune lay on me her worst disgrace.
> Let folk o'ercharged with brain against me cry,
> Let clouds be dim, my fate bereaves mine eyes,
> Let me no steps but of lost labour try,
> Let all the earth in scorn recount my race.

He asks nothing at all

> But that which once may win thy cruel heart,
> Thou art my wit; and thou my virtue art.

And in LXVI he says that in spite of all, there is one hope,

> Stella's eyes sent to me the beams of bliss.

Constable complains of his disgrace in decade 5, sonnet II;

> I do not now complain of my disgrace,
> Oh cruel fair one, fair with cruel crossed:
> Nor of the hour, season, time nor place.

And Daniel in sonnet XX says,

> This is her laurel and her triumph's prize,
> To tread me down with foot of her disgrace:
> Whilst I did build my fortune in her eyes.

Sonnet 30, as already suggested, mocks by singing Constable's tune. Here are grand abstract nouns—'sessions of sweet, silent thought', 'remembrance of things past'. His precious friends are hid in 'death's dateless night'. All the sorrows of the past combine with 'time's waste' in the present and lead to the poet grieving at 'grievances foregone' and 'heavily' telling over 'The sad account of fore-bemoaned moan.' After this full and mournful dignity, comes the familiar speech, dear friend of every day. When Shakespeare thinks of him 'all losses are restored', 'death's dateless night' quite forgot, all 'sorrows end'. We have come to expect this sudden bathos in the couplet, and if I may say so, putting everything in the stew.

Sonnet 30

> When to the sessions of sweet silent thought,
> I summon up remembrance of things past,
> I sigh the lack of many a thing I sought,
> And with old woes new wail my dear time's waste:
> Then can I drown an eye (unused to flow)
> For precious friends hid in death's dateless night,
> And weep afresh love's long since cancelled woe,
> And moan the expense of many a vanished sight.
> Then can I grieve at grievances foregone,
> And heavily from woe to woe tell o'er
> The sad account of fore-bemoaned moan,
> Which I new pay as if not paid before.
> But if the while I think on thee (dear friend)
> All losses are restored, and sorrows end.

The punning has been pointed out by Professor Mahood.[70]
The play on 'dear', 'precious', 'cancelled', 'expense', 'tell',
'account', 'pay', 'paid', 'dear', 'foregone' meaning 'repudiated
and forgotten' as well as just having happened—these give
comic glints in the richly toned verse.

Daniel's sonnet XXV, it should be noted, provides phrases
for sonnets 29, 30 and 31.
It begins,

> Reign in my thoughts fair hand, sweet eye, rare voice.

He calls them his 'heart's triumvirate' and says that

> Whilst they strive which shall be lord of all,
> All my poor life by them is trodden down :
> They all erect their trophies on my fall.
>
> .   .   .   .   .   .
>
> When back I look, I sigh my freedom past,
> And wail the state wherein I present stand.

These lines are echoed in sonnet 31 by 'there reigns love', 'all
love's loving parts', 'the trophies of my lovers gone'. Incidentally, in sonnet X Daniel says that he 'serves a trophy to her
conquering eyes'. The last two lines of my quotation give the
theme of 30, which indeed elaborates it. 'Wail the state' is
echoed in the second line of 29 in 'beweep my outcast state'.

What sonnet 30 does with emotion, 31 does with an ingenious play of mind.

Sonnet 31

> Thy bosom is endeared with all hearts,
> Which I by lacking have supposed dead,
> And there reigns love and all love's loving parts,
> And all those friends which I thought buriéd.
> How many a holy and obsequious tear
> Hath dear religious love stolen from mine eye,
> As interest of the dead, which now appear,
> But things removed that hidden in there lie.
> Thou art the grave where buried love doth live,
> Hung with the trophies of my lovers gone,

Who all their parts of me to thee did give,
That due of many, now is thine alone.
Their images I loved, I view in thee,
And thou (all they) hast all the all of me.

The meaning is tortuous. I take it Shakespeare says that his friend is loved by everyone, so they all give him their heart. Since all Shakespeare's friends are in his friend's heart, he no longer sees them and supposes them dead. But in his friend's heart love reigns, and there are all love's parts, consequently all those friends. Shakespeare has wept for them, even paid his emotional respects in the rituals of death. All these he calls stolen because he paid these respects as interest due to the dead, who he now discovers are not dead at all, but hidden in his friend's heart. [It really was too bad.] His friend is the grave where the loved ones he thought buried live, and where their trophies are hung. They gave all their parts of him (his love for them) to his friend. What was due to many is now his alone. That is to say what he loved in them, he sees in his friend, and his friend (now all of them) has 'all the all' of Shakespeare. In this way a sonnet conceit is treated with logical absurdity. Here also is the play of statements in terms of money that peppered sonnet 30. In fact it is typical sonnet writing a fraction overdone. But just as we can translate sonnet nonsense into some sort of plain sense, so we can with this sonnet. It says that the poet sees all the good qualities of his friends in this particular friend who has all love, who is ideal love in the Platonic sense, giving its form to all separate loves. If you believe in Plato, he seems to say, look what you may be in for.

There can be no doubt, that although rationalised in Platonic terms this is a direct parody of a sonnet of Constable's in the Todd manuscript, where he by no means confines his addresses to one Diana. Here is his introductory, and perhaps presentation sonnet :

Grace full of grace though in these verses here
My love complains of others than of thee
Yet thee alone I loved and they by me
(Though yet unknown) only mistaken were

Like him which feels a heat now here now there
Blames now this cause now that until he see
The fire indeed from whence they caused be
Which fire I now do know is you my dear
Thus divers love's dispersed in my verse
In thee alone for ever I unite
But folly unto thee more to rehearse
To him I fly for grace that rules above
That by my grace I may live in delight
Or by his grace I never more may love.

Constable's is an ingenious conceit to explain his compliments to other than the one lady. Shakespeare starts with the presumption of the conceit that all his loves have disappeared into the one.

In sonnet 31 Shakespeare plays with the idea that the love of his friends has disappeared into his one friend, and so he supposed them dead. In the next he considers the consequence of being dead himself.

Sonnet 32

If thou survive my well contented day,
When that churl death my bones with dust shall cover
And shalt by fortune once more re-survey:
These poor rude lines of thy deceased lover:
Compare them with the bettering of the time,
And though they be outstripped by every pen,
Reserve them for my love, not for their rhyme,
Exceeded by the height of happier men.
Oh then vouchsafe me but this loving thought,
Had my friend's muse grown with this growing age,
A dearer birth than this his love had brought
To march in ranks of better equipage:
But since he died and poets better prove,
Theirs for their style I'll read, his for his love.

This is the last sonnet in the section where Shakespeare writes to immortalise his friend or pay his respects. His friend is asked when he re-reads these verses after his death, and compares them with the much finer literature of that new day, to keep

G

them because Shakespeare's love for him was greater than that of the living poets who by then will have outstripped him. He asks his friend to defend him and say that if he were still alive his poetry would have evolved to match the times. Read it then, he ends, not for its virtue as poetry, but for the love it expresses. Shakespeare has been saying his sonnets will make his friend immortal, and he has been writing of his friend with this in view, but he ends by asking him to keep his verses because they express his love even when he eventually realises they are not worth preserving for their own sake—a sad truth to arrive at. He is saying in fact that they are love's labours lost.

Just as Shakespeare moved from his first theme of persuading his friend to marry by sliding almost imperceptibly into the second theme of immortalising him in verse, so he slides almost imperceptibly from that into excusing his friend's unkindnesses, faults, misdeeds, and accepting them all in love. This third section is more loosely knit than the others, and includes what might appear quite different themes.

Sonnet 33 begins the series with an air of freshness. The final couplet, however, does not change, but only varies, throughout the sequence. This sonnet links closely with 34, and throws back to previous sonnets by using imagery we are familiar with.

Sonnet 33

> Full many a glorious morning have I seen,
> Flatter the mountain tops with sovereign eye,
> Kissing with golden face the meadows green;
> Gilding pale streams with heavenly alchemy:
> Anon permit the basest clouds to ride,
> With ugly rack on his celestial face,
> And from the forlorn world his visage hide
> Stealing unseen to west with this disgrace:
> Even so my sun one early morn did shine,
> With all triumphant splendour on my brow,
> But out alack, he was but one hour mine,
> The region cloud hath masked him from me now.
> Yet him for this, my love no whit disdaineth,
> Suns of the world may stain, when heaven's sun staineth.

This imagery is so common that we cannot credit it to any one sonneteer. They all feel that to be smiled on by their lady is like enjoying the sun and that her frowns are clouds. Watson begins no. LXXVIII of his *Passionate Centurie:*

> What scowling clouds have overcast the sky,
> That these mine eyes cannot, as wont they were,
> Behold their second sun.

Greville in sonnet XVII asks his lady,

> Why cast you clouds on your sweet looking eyes?

Daniel in sonnet XIX writes,

> If beauty thus be clouded with a frown.

These make a few samples from many.

Sonnet 34

> Why didst thou promise such a beauteous day,
> And make me travel forth without my cloak,
> To let base clouds o'ertake me in my way,
> Hiding thy bravery in their rotten smoke.
> 'Tis not enough that through the cloud thou break,
> To dry the rain on my storm-beaten face,
> For no man well of such a salve can speak,
> That heals the wound, and cures not the disgrace:
> Nor can thy shame give physic to my grief,
> Though thou repent, yet I have still the loss,
> The offender's sorrow lends but weak relief
> To him that bears the strong offence's loss.
> Ah but those tears are pearl which thy love sheds,
> And they are rich, and ransom all ill deeds.

Sonnet 33 stated the fact. Sonnet 34 asks why. It is a direct parody of Spenser's sonnet XL, with the imagery less dignified. When his lady smiles, says Spenser,

Likest it seemeth in my simple wit
Unto the fair sunshine in summer's day:
That when a dreadful storm away is flit,
Through the broad world doth spread his goodly ray

. . . . .

So my storm beaten heart likewise is cheered,
With that sunshine when cloudy looks are cleared.

Shakespeare reverses the situation from Spenser's poetic, sentimental one of rejoicing in his lady's smile that spreads its
sunlight over all the land. His love smiled on him only a short
time, and then broke on him in storm. There is nothing poetic
in his imagery. The nuisance of a storm in this situation is that
one has gone out without one's cloak, or mac as we should say
today. The clouds are filled with 'rotten smoke' in the days of
smokey cities. Spenser's heart was 'storm beaten'. But it is not
one's heart that a storm beats. It is Shakespeare's face that is
storm beaten. And afterwards when his friend apolgises, there
is no sunshine. He bears the loss, and his friend's apology is a
weak relief. Shakespeare builds up the irreparable hurt that his
friend has caused in order to give weight to the joke in his
couplet, when he suddenly remembers, it seems, that to the
sonneteer tears are pearls. Sidney's line in sonnet LXXXVII
about Stella's tears is one of many examples:

I weep to see pearls scattered so.

If Stella's tears are pearls, Shakespeare's friend's must be.
Pearls are expensive things, 'rich'. They are a ransom for 'all ill
deeds'. In this way Shakespeare shakes the salt of common
sense over a sonnet fancy.

The excusing of the friend is carried to an extreme in sonnets
35 and 36, which have been taken seriously as showing that
Shakespeare and his friend have involved themselves in dis-
reputable actions, perhaps in a homosexual relationship. But
this is quite ridiculous. The sonnets are obvious parodies of
traditional attitudes. Sonneteers accuse their ladies at great
length and with intense feeling, of heinous faults, but endure
and forgive all. Shakespeare parodies by carrying this complai-

ning and forgiving to an extreme. He magnifies the situation so that we cannot miss seeing the absurdity.

Sonnet 35

> No more be grieved at that which thou hast done,
> Roses have thorns, and silver fountains mud,
> Clouds and eclipses stain both moon and sun,
> And loathsome canker lives in sweetest bud.
> All men make faults, and even I in this,
> Authorizing thy trespass with compare,
> Myself corrupting salving thy amiss,
> Excusing thy sins more than their sins are:
> For to thy sensual fault I bring in sense,
> Thy adverse party is thy advocate,
> And 'gainst myself a lawful plea commence,
> Such civil war is in my love and hate,
> That I an accessary needs must be,
> To that sweet thief which sourly robs from me.

This parodies Watson's no. XVIII of the *Passionate Centurie* where he says,

> Love is a sour delight; . . .
> A breach of reason's law; a secret thief.

But he forgives his lady:

> Yet hurt her not, lest I sustain the smart,
> Which am content to lodge her in my heart.

So Shakespeare protects his friend from suffering for the harm he has done him. He excuses him on the score that 'All men make faults' and even he corrupts himself by condoning his friend's faults, excusing them as more than the fault of others. He aims the sonnet at Watson in the sestet. Watson says that love breaks reason's law. Shakespeare mocks by saying he brings reason to plead for his friend—no not reason, but 'sense'. And 'sense' has a double meaning, the second one being sensual. So his friend's 'adverse party' is also his 'advocate'. Watson would suffer any hurt that his lady might feel, and is 'content to lodge her' in his heart. Shakespeare comments on the civil war between his two attitudes. He is an accessory to the 'sweet thief', to parallel Watson's 'secret thief', who 'sourly' robs from him to compare with Watson's 'sour delight'. Incidentally 'sweet thief' appears an aural memory of 'secret thief'.

Sonnet 36

> Let me confess that we two must be twain,
> Although our undivided loves are one:
> So shall those blots that do with me remain,
> Without thy help, by me be borne alone.
> In our two loves there is but one respect,
> Though in our lives a separable spite,
> Which though it alter not love's sole effect,
> Yet doth it steal sweet hours from love's delight.
> I may not evermore acknowledge thee,
> Lest my bewailed guilt should do thee shame,
> Nor thou with public kindness honour me,
> Unless thou take that honour from thy name:
> But do not so, I love thee in such sort,
> As thou being mine, mine is thy good report.

In the previous sonnet Shakespeare identified with his friend, so made himself his accessory, and began 'a lawful plea' against himself. In 36 he pleads guilty. In fact this is his confession. He confesses that he and his friend are not identical as lovers ought to be; although their undivided love is one, they are different people. Therefore the blots, which were originally his friend's but which he took over, are now his. Shakespeare has taken them on himself and must bear the sole guilt. He goes even further than that. Since he is guilty, and his friend innocent and much respected, he cannot acknowledge him for fear of bringing shame on him, nor can his friend honour him in public. And he asks his friend not to acknowledge him, since he loves him so that his good reputation is Shakespeare's good reputation. By following out the social implications that would arise if he could indeed take over his friend's guilt in this way Shakespeare makes it ridiculous. This is his common device of treating seriously what was never meant to be more than an artifice. But to take these two sonnets as actually damaging evidence of a homosexual relationship between Shakespeare and his friend, as has been done, is to carry the joke further than was intended.

Sonnet 37

> As a decrepit father takes delight,
> To see his active child do deeds of youth,
> So I, made lame by fortune's dearest spite
> Take all my comfort of thy worth and truth.
> For whether beauty, birth, or wealth, or wit,
> Or any of these all, or all, or more
> Entitled in thy parts, do crownéd sit,
> I make my love engrafted to this store:
> So then I am not lame, poor, nor despised,
> Whilst that this shadow doth such substance give,
> That I in thy abundance am sufficed,
> And by a part of all thy glory live:
> Look what is best, that best I wish in thee,
> This wish I have, then ten times happy me.

Historians searching in the sonnets for facts in Shakespeare's life have seized on references to himself as lame. We must not forget, however, what a disadvantage, not to say complete disqualification this would make in an actor. I have not found any other sonneteer suffering from this disability, but Cupid, when Greville asked him to come home in sonnet XXXV, replied,

> Alas, I cannot Sir; I am made lame;
> I light no sooner in sweet Myra's eyes,
> Whence I thought joy and pleasure took their name,
> But my right wing of wanton passion dies.

And Sidney in sonnet XXI says that his

> own writings like bad servants show
> My wits, quick in vain thoughts, in virtue lame.

Shakespeare, then, has authority for using the word metaphorically of what fortune has brought him from love. In any case his disability disappears in the sestet along with his poverty and disgrace. So it was a butterfly limp.

Shakespeare harks back to his opening sonnets here. He is like the father become decrepit, that his friend could have been if he had married, enjoying his 'active child do deeds of youth'. So when fortune, which as we have seen used him with spite, made him lame, he finds all his happiness in the good fortune of his friend. This was the situation he had arrived at by the end of sonnet 36. Still thinking of himself as like the father of the opening sonnets who was to engraft himself, he says he has engrafted his love to the store of good things his friend has. He gives quite a choice of these—beauty, birth, wealth or wit, or any or all or more. This is to mock; it is like a lawyer catering for all eventualities, and does not suggest reference to some actual person, whose qualities he could have stated more precisely. George Wyndham[71] pointed out that 'parts' is 'the technical term for the places on a shield', which would represent entitlement to it. To sit crowned with such gifts of nature would mean that he had inherited them. Shakespeare says that since he does this, 'So then' he is not lame; he mentions this as a natural consequence, a fact that follows. He has all these visible instances of the reality of his friend's abundance, for as a shadow of his friend he has the abundance of his substance, and is made sufficient by it, as Plato's substantial 'idea' gave its quality to its shadows. Consequently, by punning on 'part' as title and portion of, he can say he lives by a part of his friend's glory, his natural inheritance. Then he wishes his friend the best; when he has this wish, he too is best and is therefore ten times happy, thinking no doubt of the ten children he promised his friend.

Sonnet 38 carries this a step further. His friend inspires his muse, and since he has all these desirable qualities,

> How can my muse want subject to invent
> While thou dost breathe that pour'st into my verse,
> Thine own sweet argument, too excellent,
> For every vulgar paper to rehearse:
> Oh give thyself the thanks if aught in me,
> Worthy perusal stand against thy sight,

For who's so dumb that cannot write to thee,
When thou thyself dost give invention light?
Be thou the tenth muse, ten times more in worth
Than those old nine which rhymers invocate,
And he that calls on thee, let him bring forth
Eternal numbers to outlive long date.
If my slight muse do please these curious days,
The pain be mine, but thine shall be the praise.

(Sonnet 38)

Drayton in Amour VIII of his 1594 edition of *Idea's Mirrour*, says there are nine orders of angels, nine muses and nine worthies. His lady is his muse, his worthy and his angel, and therefore

My muse, my worthy, and my angel then,
Makes every one of these three nines a ten.

One asks how one can be sure that Drayton is borrowing from Shakespeare as I agree he is, and not vice versa. The answer is that it is easy to show that Shakespeare's idea of a tenth muse arose naturally in his own context, provided he had a sonnet of Sidney's in mind. Shakespeare begins by saying that his muse can never lack a theme while his friend is there; any credit due to him must go to his friend, who has inspired him. Sidney in his third sonnet says that while other poets are inspired by the nine muses, he has only one muse, who is Stella. It was like Shakespeare to do the implied addition and make the number of the muses ten. Sidney certainly had no such arithmetic in mind. But this is the sort of inconsequent observation that the parodist delights in. He has accepted Sidney's denigration of the other muses that poets use, referring to them as 'those old nine which rhymers invocate'. It seems obvious that he had Sidney's idea in his mind, of himself having a new and superior muse. So he tells his friend to be his tenth muse. But the father with ten children was 'ten times happy'. So, as his muse is 'more in worth', it was natural to stress the same arithmetical evaluation, 'ten times more in worth'. There is no room for any reference to Drayton; the joke is complete without him. And on the other hand, Drayton has noticed that Shakespeare was ten times happy and his muse ten times more in worth because of his friend. He has added only angels to the muses and the ten-fold worth. This was an idea ready for him to take from Shakespeare, that he expresses neatly and with wit, making it his own.

To conclude my comments on Shakespeare's sonnet : he says the verses inspired by his friend bring 'Eternal numbers', probably recollecting Horace and especially Ovid. Then with sonnet illogic but common sense, he immediately refers to his own 'slight muse'. If it pleases 'these curious days,' he says, perhaps intending criticism, 'the pain be mine'. But there seems no point in referring to pain, except as a skit on the correct ending for a sonnet.

> The pain be mine, but thine shall be the praise,

reads almost like a nonsense refrain.

Sonnets 39 and 40 return to the identity of the lovers exploited in sonnets 35 and 36, and lead to further complications.

Sonnet 39

> Oh how thy worth with manners may I sing,
> When thou art all the better part of me?
> What can mine own praise to mine own self bring;
> And what is't but mine own when I praise thee?
> Even for this, let us divided live,
> And our dear love lose name of single one,
> That by this separation I may give:
> That due to thee which thou deserv'st alone:
> Oh absence what a torment wouldst thou prove,
> Were it not thy sour leisure gave sweet leave,
> To entertain the time with thoughts of love,
> Which time and thoughts so sweetly doth deceive.
> And that thou teachest how to make one twain,
> By praising him here who doth hence remain.

Shakespeare makes fun of the theory of lovers being one, by exploring a difficulty involved. Its not being good manners to praise oneself makes it very difficult, he says, for a sonneteer to praise his love. Shakespeare's friend is the better half of him, so he cannot praise him without praising himself. But this is quite intolerable. To get over it he suggests 'let us divided be' and no longer one with each other. Then he will be able to give what is due to his friend. He calls this separation absence, and says it would be a torment but that, although sour, it allows him to have thoughts of love which make the time of his absence seem sweet with the presence of his friend. Absence teaches him how to make one into two since here, where the poet is, he praises his friend who remains away. The joke consists in making all this difficulty over an identity that is only a fancy with no reality at all, and creating an absence equally unreal, which he then treats as if it were real.

The series which this sonnet begins, where the identity of lovers is played with, deals not only with its negation, absence. During it emphasis is laid on thought which can do surprising things, as well as many other sonnet peculiarities.

Sonnet 40

> Take all my loves, my love, yea take them all,
> What hast thou then more than thou hadst before?
> No love, my love, that thou mayst true love call,
> All mine was thine, before thou hadst this more:
> Then if for my love, thou my love receivest,
> I cannot blame thee, for my love thou usest,
> But yet be blamed, if thou this self deceivest
> By wilful taste of what thy self refusest.
> I do forgive thy robbery gentle thief
> Although thou steal thee all my poverty:
> And yet love knows it is a greater grief
> To bear love's wrong, than hate's known injury.
> Lascivious grace, in whom all ill well shows,
> Kill me with spites yet we must not be foes.

This follows up the situation of 39. The poet at the beginning is separate from his friend and so able to give. And he gives all. The situation resembles that in sonnet 31 when all his own friends were lost in his friend's heart. Here he says that when he gives his friend everything, he has no more than he had before, since all that was Shakespeare's was his friend's already. He adds, if I give you my love and you use it for yourself, I cannot blame you. But he does blame him if he considers the love has a bad taste, and so is deceived about it; that is to say if he does not want his love and refuses it. Shakespeare forgives his friend who steals all his poverty, for poverty is all he has, just as Watson forgave his lady thief. Yet love knows it is more painful to bear the wrongs one suffers from one's friends than the pain caused by one who hates us. Love's wrongs, since they concern love, can be called 'lascivious', but in his friend everything, even evil, shows well. So Shakespeare ends,

> Kill me with spites yet we must not be foes.

If we could have any doubt that all this over-subtle play was parody, we could be sure of it because of the last line. The only thing the sonneteer and his love cannot by definition be is 'foes', yet he is always complaining that his mistress kills him with spite, but whatever else happens they cannot be foes. Shakespeare also makes sure of the absurdity by giving his friend 'all his loves', 'yea take them all'. As an example of forgiving all wrongs being good sonnet form, we could take Daniel, who in sonnet XXVII complains,

> The star of my mishap imposed this paining,
> To spend the April of my years in wailing,
> That never found my fortune but in waning,
> With still fresh cares my present woes assailing.
> Yet her I blame not.

But all sonneteers suffer from being killed by spite, and yet not being able to break with their love.

This sonnet seems insubstantial evidence, although it has been used so, that Shakespeare had a real friend who went off with a real mistress, but whom he so loved that he acquiesced in the robbery. In fact he has not said this. He says that he himself gave his friend all his loves—too many to be convincing. He then calls him a thief because he accepted them, and lascivious presumably since he has so many—all of them. In sonnet 41 he starts from this situation and develops it. It also has been taken to prove the treachery of a real friend, and Shakespeare's saint-like forgiveness. Here is his forgiveness:

Those pretty wrongs that liberty commits,
When I am sometime absent from thy heart,
Thy beauty, and thy years full well befits,
For still temptation follows where thou art.
Gentle thou art, and therefore to be won,
Beauteous thou art, therefore to be assailed.
And when a woman woos, what woman's son,
Will sourly leave her till he have prevailed.
Ay me but yet thou mightst my seat forbear,
And chide thy beauty, and thy straying youth,
Who lead thee in their riot even there
Where thou art forced to break a twofold truth:
Hers by thy beauty tempting her to thee,
Thine by thy beauty being false to me.

(Sonnet 41)

As his friend is like a sonnet lady, Shakespeare says he commits
'pretty wrongs' and his beauty and youth naturally open him
to temptation. Like the lady, he is gentle and beautiful, and
like a woman is to be won and assailed. Then Shakespeare
shifts his angle. It is the postulated real woman who woos, and
he says that no man will leave a woman who woos him till he
has prevailed. But, he adds, his friend should have forborn to
give in to her when it was his seat that was assailed. There may
be a composite background for 'seat'. We have already quoted
from Surrey's sonnet VI

Love, that liveth, and reigneth in my thought,
That built his seat within my captive heart.

Wyatt opens sonnet XXXVII of Tottel,

The longé love, that in my thought I harbour,
And in my heart doth keep his residence.

Shakespeare has in mind this imagery of his love living with
him in his heart, and the 'gentle thief' of the sonnet robbing
this residence. Incidentally, both these quotations from Tottel
make love reign or live in the poet's thought. Real love, of
course, is not something one thinks. This may have played a
part in forming the associations behind sonnet 44, where
Shakespeare considers the result 'If the dull substance of my

flesh were thought'. That the same sonnets from Tottel should illuminate two of Shakespeare's sonnets that are near to each other is by no means unique. Indeed it is already obvious how often successive sonnets have a background of the same sonneteer. Here it is of different sonneteers, but printed in the same book. Sonnet 41 ends by introducing a very complicated situation that is developed in the next one. Shakespeare calls his friend doubly false; his beauty has tempted both the lady and Shakespeare himself to love him. By sonnet logic to be loved is to be false to the lover. Barnes states the crime of the beloved very clearly in sonnet IX. He says that Parthenope

> did . . . rob me of mine heart's rich treasure.

In sonnet 40 Shakespeare made his beloved steal a person. There his 'gentle thief' robs him of 'all' his 'poverty', and he lets him have all his loves. Here in 41 the safety-in-numbers factor disappears and it is one particular lady-love of Shakespeare's who has been tempted by the youth's beauty and woos him. If the origin of the theft can be identified in Barnes, the excuses are Daniel's, who in sonnet XLIII says,

> I must not grieve my love, whose eyes would read,
> Lines of delight, whereon her youth might smile :
> Flowers have a time before they come to seed,
> And she is young and now must sport the while.

Shakespeare treats his young sportive friend with this forbearance.

Sonnet 42

> That thou hast her it is not all my grief,
> And yet it may be said I loved her dearly,
> That she hath thee is of my wailing chief,
> A loss in love that touches me more nearly.
> Loving offenders thus I will excuse ye,
> Thou dost love her, because thou knowest I love her,
> And for my sake even so doth she abuse me,
> Suffering my friend for my sake to approve her,

If I lose thee, my loss is my love's gain,
And losing her, my friend hath found that loss,
Both find each other, and I lose both twain,
And both for my sake lay on me this cross,
But here's the joy, my friend and I are one,
Sweet flattery, then she loves but me alone.

This develops the situation already introduced. The first point made is simple. Shakespeare is hurt that the lady has his friend, not that the friend has her. But as, through being a sonneteer, he must excuse those he loves, he proceeds to do so. And a complicated business he makes of it. His friend loves her because he knows Shakespeare does; and it is for Shakespeare's sake also that she abuses him, since it is for his sake that she accepts his friend's approbation. If he loses his friend, it is his love's gain, and by his losing her, his friend gains. They find each other, and he loses both; and they lay this cross on him for his own sake. But here's the fun of it all : he and his friend are one. Then by self-flattery or deception Shakespeare concludes that she loves only him. This is wit, an ingenious play of mind; and it is nonsense. If it were not that some readers have in fact taken it solemnly as part of his real reaction to a very distressing affair in his own life, I should say it is such nonsense that it could not be taken seriously.

Sonnet 43 returns to the theme of sonnets 27 and 28, and perhaps to the substance-shadow theme of sonnet 37.

Sonnet 43

When most I wink then do mine eyes best see,
For all the day they view things unrespected,
But when I sleep, in dreams they look on thee,
And darkly bright, are bright in dark directed.
Then thou whose shadow shadows doth make bright,
How would thy shadow's form, form happy show,
To the clear day with thy much clearer light,
When to unseeing eyes thy shade shines so!
How would (I say) mine eyes be blessed made,
By looking on thee in the living day?
When in dead night thy fair imperfect shade,
Through heavy sleep on sightless eyes doth stay?

> All days are nights to see till I see thee,
> And nights bright days when dreams do show thee me.

In the first quatrain Shakespeare says he sees best in dreams as
he does not pay attention to what he sees during the day, and
when he dreams of his friend his eyes are directed brightly on
him in the dark. In the second quatrain he says that since his
friend's dream image (or shadow of himself) makes dreams
(shadows) bright, the real form (reflected as a shadow in
dreams) would make an even happier sight in clear day. How
blessed then would Shakespeare's eyes be to see his friend in
living day when in dead night his shadow, only an imperfect
reflection of his real form, makes such an impression on eyes
which see nothing in heavy sleep. We have had many instances
of Shakespeare's substance-shadow statements from Plato's
theory of the real substance being reflected by its separate
shadows on earth. There is not much Plato here however,
unless we take it that his 'shadow's form', his friend's body, is
the 'shadow' of his spirit or ideal being, and the 'form' the
shape of this shadow or body. To sum up the argument, Shakespeare says all days are like night till he sees his friend, and all
nights like day when dreams reveal him.

Sonnets 44 and 45 might be an answer to Watson, who
prefaces no. III of his *Passionate Centurie* with a prose note
explaining that

> the author talketh with his own heart, being now through
> the commandment and force of love separated from his
> body miraculously, and against nature, to follow his
> mistress.

Watson did not bring this fancy into English poetry. Wyatt in
no. XLI of Tottel says that after his love 'my heart would fain
be gone'. Shakespeare comments how easy it would be if it
were just a matter of thought, but unfortunately the body is
not so volatile.

Sonnet 44

> If the dull substance of my flesh were thought,
> Injurious distance should not stop my way,

For then despite of space I would be brought,
From limits far remote, where thou dost stay,
No matter then although my foot did stand
Upon the farthest earth removed from thee,
For nimble thought can jump both sea and land,
As soon as think the place where he would be.
But ah, thought kills me that I am not thought
To leap large lengths of miles when thou art gone,
But that so much of earth and water wrought,
I must attend, time's leisure with my moan.
Receiving nought by elements so slow,
But heavy tears, badges of either's woe.

Shakespeare gives serious consideration to the sonneteers' fancy
that (as he puts it disrespectfully), 'nimble thought can jump
both sea and land'. He considers that the important thing
would be if his body, 'the dull substance' of his flesh, could be
thought. But 'earth and water' make two of the four elements
that compose this flesh and they are slow. This prepares for the
satiric fancy of the next sonnet.

Sonnet 45

The other two, slight air, and purging fire,
Are both with thee, wherever I abide,
The first my thought, the other my desire,
These present absent with swift motion slide.
For when these quicker elements are gone
In tender embassy of love to thee,
My life being made of four, with two alone,
Sinks down to death, oppressed with melancholy.
Until life's composition be recured,
By those swift messengers returned from thee,
Who even but now come back again assured,
Of thy fair health, recounting it to me.
This told, I joy, but then no longer glad,
I send them back again and straight grow sad.

In medieval theory, health consisted in a good balance of the
four elements that composed the body. So when air and fire, in
their 'absent present' shuttling to and fro between his friend
and himself, are absent, he sinks down with the melancholy

caused by an overbalance of water and earth until, he explains, the missing elements return and he has them all in their right proportions. Suddenly what he is saying is interrupted by their return—'even now', this very minute, here they are, come safely back to report on his friend's health. He rejoices but begins to worry about him and sends them off again for another report. And immediately he becomes sad. This is to make fun not only of the idea of thought skipping about, but of Ovid's idea of the elements. As part of his theory of metamorphosis Ovid draws a picture of the elements that suggests Shakespeare's mockery. Of the four elements he says as Golding translates,[72]

> The earth and water for their mass and weight are sunken
> lower.
> The other couple air and fire the purer of the twain
> Mount up, and nought can keep them down.

He describes the change of water into air in vaporisation when the air

> springeth up aloft, and there becometh fire.
> From thence in order contrary they back again retire.
> Fire thickening passeth into air, and air waxing gross
> Returns to water.

This is remarkably like the way that thought and desire, identified with air and fire, behave in the sonnet. Air and fire, thought and desire, 'present absent with swift motion slide'; it is Ovid played in quick motion. When they are gone leaving only water and earth, these sink down as Ovid's elements sink lower. Ovid's elements of air and fire 'back again retire', as so do Shakespeare's.

Sonnets 46 and 47 deal with the ancient theme of the dialogue between heart and eyes. It is there in Petrarch and the Italian sonneteers and was carried on by Ronsard and the French. For Shakespeare's models we cannot doubt that he had Watson and Constable in mind. Here is sonnet XX of *The Tears of Fancie*:

My heart accused mine eyes and was offended,
Vowing the cause was in mine eyes' aspiring:
Mine eyes affirmed my heart might well amend it,
If he at first had banished love's desiring.
Heart said that love did enter at the eyes,
And from the eyes descended to the heart
Eyes said that in the heart did sparks arise,
Which kindled flame that wrought the inward smart,
Heart said eyes' tears might soon have quenched that flame,
Eyes said heart's sighs at first might love exile
So heart and eyes and eyes and heart did blame,
Whilst both did pine for both the pain did feel.
Heart sighed and bled, eyes wept and gazed too much,
Yet must I gaze because I see none such.

Here is the war as Constable reported it in sonnet VII of decade 6 :

My heart, mine eye accuseth of his death,
Saying, his wanton sight bred his unrest:
Mine eye affirms, my heart's unconstant faith
Hath been his bane, and all his joys repressed.
My heart avows mine eye let in the fire,
Which burns him with an everlasting light,
Mine eye replies, my greedy heart's desire,
Let in those floods which drown him day and night.
Thus wars my heart, which reason doth maintain,
And calls mine eye to combat if he dare.
The whilst my soul, impatient of disdain,
Wrings from his bondage unto death more near;
Save that my love, still holdeth him in hand,
'A kingdom thus divided cannot stand'.

Constable gives a judgement between them in decade 4 sonnet VIII, 'the one to live exiled', and the other to pine 'imprisoned without date'. Here is Shakespeare :

Sonnet 46

Mine eye and heart are at a mortal war,
How to divide the conquest of thy sight,

Mine eye, my heart their picture's sight would bar,
My heart, mine eye the freedom of that right,
My heart doth plead that thou in him dost lie,
(A closet never pierced with crystal eyes)
But the defendant doth that plea deny,
And says in him thy fair appearance lies.
To side this title is impanelled
A quest of thoughts, all tenants to the heart,
And by their verdict is determined
The clear eye's moiety, and the dear heart's part.
As thus, mine eye's due is thy outward part,
And my heart's right, their inward love of heart.

Shakespeare begins by referring to the mortal 'war' of Constable. It is a legal one. He presumes the parties quarrelling over the spoils of love. Professor Mahood[73] lists the legal terms. She notes that 'conquest' can mean 'the personal acquisition of real property otherwise than by inheritance'. 'Side' she says means 'assign to one of two sides or parties', and a 'quest' an 'inquiry upon the oaths of an empanelled jury'. Shakespeare says his eye wants to debar his heart from looking at their picture; his heart says he has a right to see it, is free to do so since his friend lies in his heart. This is how it was with Watson in sonnet XLV (*Tears of Fancie*) where the picture of his mistress was in his heart. Shakespeare says his friend's picture is shut in a strong room that has never been pierced with crystal eyes. This reads like a recollection of Wyatt's sonnet XL in Tottel:

The lively sparks, that issue from those eyes,

.   .   .   .   .   .

Have pierced my heart.

Shakespeare's eye denies that he is in this strong room, saying his friend's appearance is in it, not in his heart. Shakespeare's thoughts are empanelled as jury. That they are tenants of his heart is a humorous reminder of Barnes who said in sonnet **XX,**

Those eyes thy beauty's tenants, pay due tears
For occupation of mine heart thy freehold:
In tenor of love's service (if thou behold)

With what exaction it is held through fears,
And yet thy rents extorted, daily bears.

Shakespeare's tenants decide that each has its rights. The 'outward part' is his eyes' 'due', the say using Barnes' word, and the heart has a right to their inward love, which is a matter of the heart. This is all very satisfactory, and in the next sonnet they make a pact to help each other.

Sonnet 47

> Betwixt mine eye and heart a league is took,
> And each doth good turns now unto the other,
> When that mine eye is famished for a look,
> Or heart in love with sighs himself doth smother;
> With my love's picture then my eye doth feast,
> And to the painted banquet bids my heart:
> Another time mine eye is my heart's guest,
> And in his thoughts of love doth share a part.
> So either by thy picture or my love,
> Thyself away, art present still with me,
> For thou not farther than my thoughts canst move,
> And I am still with them, and they with thee.
> Or if they sleep, thy picture in my sight
> Awakes my heart, to heart's and eye's delight.

This has humour in itself, but it also includes a direct parody of Spenser, who refers in sonnet XXXV to 'My hungry eyes', who cannot be sufficed, or sustain life without the sight of his love, and yet when they see her, gaze on her 'the more',

> In their amazement like Narcissus vain
> Whose eyes him starved.

Shakespeare therefore makes the sight of his friend a feast, but it is still the picture quarrelled over in the last sonnet. He combines them : 'a painted banquet'! In the sestet he deduces that either by his picture which the eye sees, or his love which the heart feels, his absent friend is present in his thoughts and cannot be separated from them. Or if his thoughts sleep, his picture wakens his heart to the delight of both parties—a pretty story.

Sonnet 48

> How careful was I when I took my way,
> Each trifle under truest bars to thrust,
> That to my use it might unused stay
> From hands of falsehood, in sure wards of trust?
> But thou, to whom my jewels trifles are,
> Most worthy comfort, now my greatest grief,
> Thou best of dearest, and mine only care,
> Are left the prey of every vulgar thief.
> Thee have I not locked up in any chest,
> Save where thou art not though I feel thou art,
> Within the gentle closure of my breast,
> From whence at pleasure thou mayst come and part,
> And even thence thou wilt be stolen I fear,
> For truth proves thievish for a prize so dear.

Here Shakespeare makes yet another pretty story. He uses his wit on the 'closet never pierced with crystal eyes' in sonnet 46, where his heart kept his friend safe. He says that when he went away he shut every trifle up in locks that could be trusted, but his friend, compared with whom his jewels are trifles, was not locked up but left a prey to every thief since he comes and goes as he pleases 'Within the gentle closure' of his heart. No wonder he fears he will be stolen, since anyone who knows the truth about him will want to steal such a prize.

Sonnet 49

> Against that time (if ever that time come)
> When I shall see thee frown on my defects,
> When as thy love hath cast his utmost sum,
> Called to that audit by advised respects,
> Against that time when thou shalt strangely pass,
> And scarcely greet me with that sun thine eye,
> When love converted from the thing it was
> Shall reasons find of settled gravity.
> Against that time do I ensconce me here
> Within the knowledge of mine own desert,
> And this my hand, against myself uprear,
> To guard the lawful reasons on thy part,
> To leave poor me, thou hast the strength of laws,
> Since why to love, I can allege no cause.

The play here is with the imagery from money that sonneteers often use, and it is sung inappropriately in Constable's parallel-claused, emotionally toned cadence. 'Against that time' when his friend audits the accounts of their love, 'against that time' when his friend finds serious discrepancies, 'against that time' he can defend himself. The couplet, which reads like a *non sequitur*, is also strongly worded, for words as well as cadence spell dignity from the very opening : 'Against that time' is as solemn as can be. 'Utmost sum' sounds emotional, although in terms of money it only means the total. 'Advised respects' suggests some legal reference, and may do so. To audit because of respects that are advisable sounds even threatening. 'Strangely pass' makes quite a mysterious phrase for 'cut'. 'That sun thine eye' has a most formal courtesy, and 'settled gravity' almost a solemn majesty. In answer Shakespeare makes himself as abstract, ensconsing himself in 'the knowledge of mine own desert'. It is a mock heroic gesture indeed to uprear his hand. But all this pompous righteousness collapses in the couplet.

In sonnets 50 and 51 Shakespeare imagines he is travelling away from his love. He treats it as an actual absence in the physical world, but it began as an abstraction, just as his friend and his lady did. Both sonnets parody Sidney's sonnet XLIX. This is Sidney's :

I on my horse, and love on me doth try
Our horsemanship, while two strong works I prove,
A horseman to my horse, a horse to love;
And now man's wrongs in me poor beast descry.
The reins wherewith the rider doth me tie
Are reverent thoughts, which bit of reverence move,
Curbed in with fear, but with gilt boss above
Of hope, which makes it seem fair to the eye :
The wand is will, thou fancy saddle art,
Girt fast by memory; and while I spur
My horse, he spurs with sharp desires my heart,
He sits me fast however I do stir,
And now hath made me to his hand so right,
That in the manage I myself delight.

Shakespeare writes:

Sonnet 50

> How heavy do I journey on the way,
> When what I seek (my weary travel's end)
> Doth teach that ease and that repose to say
> Thus far the miles are measured from thy friend.
> The beast that bears me, tired with my woe,
> Plods dully on, to bear that weight in me,
> As if by some instinct the wretch did know
> His rider loved not speed being made from thee:
> The bloody spur cannot provoke him on,
> That sometimes anger thrusts into his hide,
> Which heavily he answers with a groan,
> More sharp to me than spurring to his side,
> For that same groan doth put this in my mind,
> My grief lies onward and my joy behind.

Sonnet 51

> Thus can my love excuse the slow offence,
> Of my dull bearer, when from thee I speed,
> From where thou art, why should I haste me thence,
> Till I return of posting is no need.
> Oh what excuse will my poor beast then find,
> When swift extremity can seem but slow,
> Then should I spur though mounted on the wind,
> In winged speed no motion shall I know,
> Then can no horse with my desire keep pace,
> Therefore desire (of perfect'st love being made)
> Shall neigh no dull flesh in his fiery race,
> But love, for love, thus shall excuse my jade,
> Since from thee going, he went wilful slow,
> Towards thee I'll run, and give him leave to go.

As is his way, Shakespeare has transferred what was emphasis on an allegoric parallel into a fact in the real world. He says he travels from his love, and his horse goes slowly. It feels the lack of any urgent desire in him and 'Plods dully on'. If he spurs, it responds with a groan. Shakespeare's 'poor beast' is his horse. Sidney is the 'poor beast' of his own sonnet. He bears man's wrongs. While he spurs his horse, love spurs him 'with sharp

desires', and controls him firmly with its reins. Whereas Sidney
is not interested in his horse except as providing him with a
metaphor for his own situation, Shakespeare's emphasis is on
the horse. He gives, as it were, a horse's-eye view. He introduces the joke gradually. The opening seems merely to represent facts. His horse feels its rider's heavy mood, as horses can
catch the mood of their rider. We do not see the mocking
intention till we are told that its groan, when he spurs it,
reminds Shakespeare of his grief at going away from his love
—an odd remark indeed for a sonneteer; it comes in the
couplet too, where we have been led to expect the axe to fall.
In the next sonnet Shakespeare begins by excusing his horse.
Sonneteers are adept at excusing; it is a habitual attitude. It
leads naturally to wondering what the horse thinks. Here the
real fun emerges. The horse is finding excuses for its rider—
and very good ones. It considers how no horse could keep pace
with its rider's desire. Desire to the horse is made of perfect
love, quite contrary to Sidney's attitude, where he makes the
poet need a firm rein. The horse thinks how desire neighs in his
rider, that this is more than just dull flesh, and is love neighing
for love, which as we can see in *Venus and Adonis* any horse of
Shakespeare's knows all about. 'Thus', says Shakespeare, his
horse excuses him. And it is a friendly beast for it ends by
saying that since his rider went away from his love slowly, it
will run now, and allow him to get to his friend.

Sonnet 52

> So am I as the rich whose blessed key,
> Can bring him to his sweet up-locked treasure,
> The which he will not every hour survey,
> For blunting the fine point of seldom pleasure.
> Therefore are feasts so solemn and so rare,
> Since seldom coming in the long year set,
> Like stones of worth they thinly placed are,
> Or captain jewels in the carcanet.
> So is the time that keeps you as my chest,
> Or as the wardrobe which the robe doth hide,
> To make some special instant special blest,
> By new unfolding his imprisoned pride.
> Blessed are you whose worthiness gives scope,
> Being had to triumph, being lacked to hope.

This has the sonnet theme of hope. Shakespeare imagines himself still absent, and although in the sonneteer's despair, he yet hopes. So he says he is rich. He uses imagery he has already filled our minds with; in the first quatrain we find the image of 'sweet locked up treasure', which brings associations from sonnet 48, and also from sonnet 46, where his friend was kept close in his heart. The second quatrain has associations from sonnet 47, where his heart held a banquet. It ends with the feast like a large jewel surrounded by smaller ones in a gold collar worn at great ceremonies.[74] So then, Shakespeare concludes in the sestet, time is like a chest or wardrobe keeping his friend as a robe for a special occasion, when his magnificence will be unfolded. The couplet sums up that his friend is blessed since his virtues make his presence a triumphal occasion in which one puts on one's best dress, and his absence preserves him for this. I do not know that there is anything very laughter-provoking here unless one thinks concretely of the friend as a gown in a wardrobe. But it seems that Shakespeare does think concretely, and if one does, the imagery is comic.

Sonnet 53

> What is your substance, whereof are you made,
> That millions of strange shadows on you tend?
> Since everyone, hath every one, one shade,
> And you but one, can every shadow lend:
> Describe Adonis and the counterfeit,
> Is poorly imitated after you,
> On Helen's cheek all art of beauty set,
> And you in Grecian tires are painted new:
> Speak of the spring, and foison of the year,
> The one doth shadow of your beauty show,
> The other as your bounty doth appear,
> And you in every blessed shape we know.
> In all external grace you have some part,
> But you like none, none you for constant heart.

Here is a new theme. It is obvious parody. Like sonnet 52 it brings associations from previous sonnets by beginning with his friend as the Platonic substance that has millions of shadows. But there is a difficulty. A substance, no matter what sub-

stance, everyone, has only one shadow. But his friend, who is
one person or substance, has shadows of quite different kinds.
In fact, he says, his friend is 'in every blessed shape we know'.
And besides, he is better than any of them, for none of these
shadows has his constant heart. The fun lies in making his
friend like a sonnet lady, who is compared with goddesses, the
spring, indeed with every blessed thing we know, and all to
their disadvantage. The only thing in which he differs is that
none of these has his constant heart. So Shakespeare asks what
can he possibly be made of. He illustrates the difficulty,
parodying as he does so. Since the ladies of the sonneteers are
commonly likened to divine or semi-divine beings, he follows
suit. And he chooses the beautiful Adonis and the beautiful
Helen. His friend has feminine as well as male beauty.

We can find examples of such 'strange shadows' reflecting
the sonnet lady in any sonnet series. Barnes compares his lady
with a wonderful array of gods. In sonnet LXIV she has
'Pallas' eye', 'Venus rosy cheek', 'Phoebe's forehead'; in sonnet
XIX she is compared with Mercury, Minerva, Bacchus, Venus
and Diana; in sonnet LXXVIII he says Saturn is enthroned
on her frown, Jove has her majesty, Mars her courage, Venus
sits on her lips and chin, Hermes has enriched her wits, Phoebe
won her heart. Daniel crowds gold, Cupid, stars, pearls, ivory,
Arabian odours, Aurora, Thetis, Venus, the spheres, tigers,
bears and marble all into one sonnet, no. XVIII. Spenser
comes nearer to Shakespeare. He shows some restraint, and
especially he sets his 'wit' to play with the situation. In sonnet
XXX he says,

My love is like to ice, and I to fire;

and he exclaims,

What more miraculous thing may be told
That fire which all things melts, should harden ice :
.   .   .   .   .   .
Such is the power of love in gentle mind,
That it can alter all the course of kind.

Here love performs the miracle of altering the natural quality of things, somewhat like Shakespeare's friend. Or, to come closer still to Shakespeare, in sonnet LV he says,

> I marvel of what substance was the mould
> The which her made at once so cruel fair.

He then explains that as she is none of the elements there must be a fifth element that she is. This suggests the quintessence, and that suggests Plato's ideal essence or substance. And here we are at Shakespeare's question.

Sonnet 54

> Oh how much more doth beauty beauteous seem,
> By that sweet ornament which truth doth give,
> The rose looks fair, but fairer we it deem
> For that sweet odour, which doth in it live:
> The canker blooms have full as deep a dye,
> As the perfumed tincture of the roses,
> Hang on such thorns, and play as wantonly,
> When summer's breath their masked buds disclose:
> But for their virtue only is their show,
> They live unwooed, and unrespected fade,
> Die to themselves. Sweet roses do not so,
> Of their sweet deaths, are sweetest odours made:
> And so of you, beauteous and lovely youth,
> When that shall vade, by verse distills your truth.

Shakespeare introduced a new aspect of his friend in the last line of sonnet 53, 'the constant heart'. In this sonnet he now compares the outward beauty that all sonnet ladies have with the inward essence or character of his friend that this suggests. Imagery from the scent of the rose pervades the whole sonnet. Beauty, he says, is more beautiful when it wears the ornament that truth gives it. The sense of this being not an extraneous ornament but an inner quality carries over from sonnet 53 where the constant heart is contrasted with 'all external grace'. Truth is like the scent of the rose. 'Canker blooms'—that is roses that have 'canker'—have as deep a dye, but not the scent of healthy roses: they have no real virtue since they have no fragrance. When sweet roses die, scent is made from them. So when his friend dies, Shakespeare's verses will perpetuate his truth, his real worth. 'Vade' means 'fade', and 'by' is an obvious misprint for 'my'. We can be sure it is Shakespeare's verse that will distil his friend's real worth for this makes the theme of the next sonnet. Sonnet 54 is a bridge linking the theme of his friend's virtues with that of perpetuating him in verse—the main topic of his sonnets, which he now picks up again.

The next group of sonnets makes fun of Ovid. As Shakespeare has already incorporated him into his parody, we are not unprepared for this. Ovid influenced the sonnet tradition, but apart from this indirect background, Shakespeare made an original contact. He must have read at least parts of the *Metamorphoses* at school. A copy survives with his initials, although this is very far from proof that the book was his. Whether or not he was a good enough Latin scholar to remember details of what he read at school, Sir Sidney Lee[75] showed that it is Golding's translation that the sonnets reflect, or as I see it, react to. Shakespeare does with Ovid what he did with Erasmus, integrates him into the sonnet parody. And of this fusion we could not have a better illustration than sonnet 45, already discussed.

Sonnet 55

> Not marble, nor the gilded monuments,
> Of princes shall outlive this powerful rhyme,
> But you shall shine more bright in these contents
> Than unswept stone, besmeared with sluttish time.
> When wasteful war shall statues overturn,
> And broils root out the work of masonry,
> Nor Mars his sword, nor war's quick fire shall burn:
> The living record of your memory.
> 'Gainst death, and all obvious enmity
> Shall you pace forth, your praise shall still find room,
> Even in the eyes of all posterity
> That wear this world out to the ending doom.
> So till the judgment that yourself arise,
> You live in this, and dwell in lovers' eyes.

Poets promising their friends immortality in their verse originally copied Horace. His monument, however, was more enduring than brass, not marble, as in this sonnet, where Ovid is more relevant. Ovid was concerned with the changes that time works through decay and destruction rather than, like Horace with the mere passing into oblivion. Thus he refers to Troy once 'great and strong' destroyed by war and having[76]

> nothing left of all her wealth to show,
> Save ruins of the ancient works which grass doth over-
> grow,
> And tombs wherein their ancestors lie buried on a row.

Shakespeare's 'gilded monuments of princes' probably reflects the tombs where ancestors are buried; and the 'unswept stone, besmeared with sluttish time' could be a re-creation of ruins where 'ancient works' are overgrown with grass. This shows recollection of a general impression rather than makes a verbal echo. The sonnet as a whole confirms that a *Road to Xanadu*-like process was at work in its creation. From this point of view

> Nor Mars his sword, nor war's quick fire

rewards a close analysis. Ovid as Golding has it at the end of his *Metamorphoses* says,

> Now I have brought a work to end which neither Jove's
> fierce wrath,
> Nor sword, nor fire . . .
> Are able to abolish quite.

This has been recognised as Shakespeare's source, but the question asked is where does Mars come from. This is of particular interest as Meres in his *Palladis Tamia* uses 'Mars' as a mis-quotation from Ovid. Since he had read Shakespeare's sonnets he may have been misled by a memory of them. To account for Shakespeare's use of the word is not difficult. As the sonnet is saturated with Golding's Ovid, an explanation may reasonably be looked for there. It is clear that Ovid had war in mind when he referred to sword and fire, for about twenty lines later than the reference to Troy just quoted, Aeneas is told,

Both fire and sword shall unto thee thy passage freely
give,

indicating a passage to victory in war. Shakespeare certainly
infers that the reference is to war. He seems to have recollected
a contrast in neither Jove nor war being able to abolish Ovid's
verse. Ovid does not use the word 'war', but indicates it by the
two concrete symbols, sword and fire. Shakespeare's creative
memory appears to have seized on the conjunction of a god
and war. Ovid's Jove has, so to say, no content, no concrete-
ness. It is not surprising if he slipped Shakespeare's memory
except in so far as he was a Greek god. The two devastating
facts were sword and fire in that order. This gives god and war,
sword and fire. Remembered in this way Mars becomes
obvious. Shakespeare's imagination supplied him with 'Mars
his sword' and 'war's . . . fire' to fill the rhythm of Ovid's line.
For 'neither Jove's fierce wrath, Nor sword and fire', he wrote
'Nor Mars his sword, nor war's quick fire.'

Golding goes on to,

And all the world shall never
Be able for to quench my name. For look how far so
ever
The Roman Empire by the right of conquest shall extend,
So far shall all folk read this work. And time without all end
(If poets as by prophesy about the truth may aim)
My life shall everlastingly be lengthened still by fame.

Shakespeare asserts with an even greater confidence that nothing will outlive his work, and this will perpetuate his friend's
name. He could not use his common method of turning
extravagant hyperbole into prose to parody, for Ovid writes
with a strong sense of reality; he might reasonably assume that
his verse was read all over the Roman Empire, and he qualified his further claim with an apology for prophesy. To
parody, therefore, Shakespeare has to boast more grandly. He
neither qualifies nor apologises. His verse is 'The living record'
of his friend's memory and defends him ''Gainst death, and all

oblivious enmity'. He will live 'in the eyes of all posterity' 'till this world' comes to 'the ending doom'. Golding's 'everlastingly' and 'time without all end' is given an emotional stress.

All sonneteers reflect this ending of the *Metamorphoses*. Shakespeare is doing no more than, as a sonneteer, was expected of him. From at least two of them, he may have got some of his phrases. Daniel's sonnet XXXIV says his verse

> may remain thy lasting monument,
> Which happily posterity will cherish :
> These colours with thy fading are not spent.

This may have given Shakespeare 'monument' and 'posterity' : Spenser's sonnet LXIX has also contributed :

> The famous warriors of the antique world,
> Use trophies to erect in stately wise :
> In which they would the records have enrolled,
> Of their great deeds and valorous emprize.
> What trophy then shall I most fit devise,
> In which I may record the memory
> Of my love's conquest, peerless beauty's prize
>
>   .   .   .   .   .   .
>
> Even this verse vowed to eternity,
> Shall be thereof immortal monument :
> And tell her praise to all posterity.

The last line has given Shakespeare 'praise' in the eyes of 'all posterity'. Spenser's sonnet certainly sprang out of Ovid and was perhaps influenced by *Delia*. By itself it is enough to have given Shakespeare his impetus. He parodies by introducing 'eyes' in posterity and in lovers, which seem absurd in Ovid's context of monuments in ruin, war's sword and fire, the ravages of time. Spenser's sonnet was not absurd, for he asks what trophy he can give comparable with past records. He has a solid enough sense. But Shakespeare's sonnet follows magnificent ruin with a promise that is not only bathos but evaporates into an unreal mist.

Sonnet 56

> Sweet love renew thy force, be it not said
> Thy edge should blunter be then appetite,
> Which but to-day by feeding is allayed,
> To-morrow sharpened in his former might.
> So love be thou, although to-day thou fill
> Thy hungry eyes, even till they wink with fullness,
> To-morrow see again, and do not kill
> The spirit of love, with a perpetual dullness:
> Let this sad interim like the ocean be
> Which parts the shore, where two contracted new,
> Come daily to the banks, that when they see:
> Return of love, more blest may be the view.
> As call it winter, which being full of care,
> Makes summer's welcome, thrice more wished, more rare.

This makes a 'sad interim' indeed after the confidence of sonnet 55, which claimed to eternise love and to last till doomsday. Here Shakespeare presents unchanging permanence as dulling, as satiety. He is not 'famished for a look', as he said he was in sonnet 47; his 'hungry eyes' go to sleep, or 'wink with fullness', and he asks when he wakes again in the morning that 'the spirit of love' should not be killed by a 'perpetual dullness'. This is a parody of Daniel's sonnet XXI, where he complains of Delia,

> I sacrifice my youth, and blooming years,
> At her proud feet, and she respects not it:
> My flower untimely's withered with my tears,
> And winter woes, for spring of youth unfit.
> She thinks a look may recompense my care,
> And so with looks prolongs my long-looked ease:
> As short that bliss, so is the comfort rare,
> Yet must that bliss my hungry thoughts appease.

Delia thinks a look will be enough recompense, and so with 'looks prolongs' his 'long-looked ease'. This is all she offers to appease his 'hungry thoughts'; this is all he has given his youth for, as he now withers in winter woes. Shakespeare says his situation is the opposite. He is not complaining that all he gets is looks to feed his hunger. He is asking love not to treat

H

him as if he just wanted to be fed, satisfied today and given more tomorrow. Although he goes to sleep bored with Daniel's long-looked ease today, he wants to awake in the morning not killed with 'perpetual' boredom. Let love be romantic he says in the sestet, so that lovers come and look at each other across a distance every day, or let winter, when love is absent make summer welcome. So, using Daniel's imagery, he is really saying that periods of absence are not a bad thing for love.

Sonnet 57

> Being your slave what should I do but tend,
> Upon the hours, and times of your desire?
> I have no precious time at all to spend;
> Nor services to do till you require.
> Nor dare I chide the world without end hour,
> Whilst I (my sovereign) watch the clock for you,
> Nor think the bitterness of absence sour,
> When you have bid your servant once adieu.
> Nor dare I question with my jealous thought,
> Where you may be, or your affairs suppose,
> But like a sad slave stay and think of nought
> Save where you are, how happy you make those.
> So true a fool is love, that in your Will,
> (Though you do any thing) he thinks no ill.

Sonnet 58

> That god forbid, that made me first your slave,
> I should in thought control your times of pleasure,
> Or at your hand the account of hours to crave,
> Being your vassal bound to stay your leisure.
> Oh let me suffer (being at your beck)
> The imprisoned absence of your liberty,
> And patience tame, to sufferance bide each check,
> Without accusing you of injury.
> Be where you list, your charter is so strong,
> That you yourself may privilege your time
> To what you will, to you it doth belong,
> Yourself to pardon of self-doing crime.
> I am to wait, though waiting so be hell,
> Not blame your pleasure be it ill or well.

Ridiculous though it may seem, these sonnets have been taken seriously to show that Shakespeare's friend was so much above him in rank that he had to accept a servile role. They are of course parodies of the love as 'servant' that he made fun of in *The Two Gentlemen of Verona,* and besides provide a second argument against love's permanence. Sonnet 56 dealt with the boredom that too much of one's love may bring. This deals with the opposite misery. It shows another 'world without end hour' that is undesirable. Shakespeare deals bitterly and sarcastically with his servitude, not at all in the cheerful way a lover should. He comes to a climax in the first sonnet of 'So true a fool is love' that, punning on his own name, he says whatever his friend does he will 'think no ill'. In the second sonnet he makes a climax of not being allowed to blame his friend although waiting is hell. The attitude parodied is too pervasive to need illustrating, but there may be identifiable echoes. In his first sonnet in *The Passionate Centurie,* Watson says that

> Cupid hath clapped a yoke upon my neck
> Under whose weight I live in servile kind :

and ends,

> Some comfort yet I have to live in thrall
> In whom as yet I find no fault at all.

Constable in the second sonnet of decade 5 says he does not complain, among other things, 'of the hour, season, time nor place' which Shakespeare echoes at the beginning of sonnet 57. And possibly Spenser's sonnet XLIII is a special reference :

> Shall I then silent be or shall I speak?
> And if I speak, her wrath renew I shall :
>
>   .   .   .   .   .
>
> What tyranny is this both my heart to thrall,
> And eke my tongue with proud restraint to tie?
> That neither I may speak nor think at all,
> But like a stupid stock in silence die.

Shakespeare links the not thinking at all with waiting.

After dealing with these objections to the Ovidian ecstasy of sonnet 55, Shakespeare turns to another theme of Ovid's.

Sonnet 59

> If there be nothing new, but that which is,
> Hath been before, how are our brains beguiled,
> Which labouring for invention bear amiss
> The second burden of a former child?
> Oh that record could with a backward look,
> Even of five hundred courses of the sun,
> Show me your image in some antique book,
> Since mind at first in character was done.
> That I might see what the old world could say,
> To this composed wonder of your frame,
> Whether we are mended, or whether better they,
> Or whether revolution be the same.
> Oh sure I am the wits of former days,
> To subjects worse have given admiring praise.

Ovid had a theory that nothing perishes but everything returns in cycles, so that what appears fresh is only a new recurrence of what was before. Golding uses the word 'revolution' for this circular movement. Shakespeare makes the humorous comment, if this is so how deceived we are when labouring to invent something new. He seems to have Sidney's first sonnet in mind :

> But words came halting out, wanting invention's stay,
> Invention nature's child, . . .
> .   .   .   .   .
> Thus great with child to speak, and helpless in my throws,
> Biting my tongue and pen, beating myself for spite :
> Fool said my muse to me, look in thy heart and write.

And all this 'labouring for invention' of Sidney's, Shakespeare adds, is to bring forth a child that was born before. And not only Sidney. He may suggest that all sonneteers are in the same fix—so killing both them and Ovid with the same stone. Then again he asks to be shown any image of his friend in some old book; if he could see this, he would know if Ovid had spoken truth, for he would then see if his friend were better or worse now, or whether 'revolution be the same'. He adds a couplet tag : the one fact he knows is that in former days worse subjects have been highly praised, possibly by sonneteers. And again he scores a double hit.

Sonnet 60

> Like as the waves make towards the pebbled shore,
> So do our minutes hasten to their end,
> Each changing place with that which goes before,
> In sequent toil all forwards do contend.
> Nativity once in the main of light,
> Crawls to maturity, wherewith being crowned,
> Crooked eclipses 'gainst his glory fight,
> And time that gave, doth now his gift confound.
> Time doth transfix the flourish set on youth,
> And delves the parallels in beauty's brow,
> Feeds on the rarities of nature's truth,
> And nothing stands but for his scythe to mow.
> And yet to times in hope, my verse shall stand
> Praising thy worth, despite his cruel hand.

This makes almost a point by point précis of Golding, beginning with,[77]

> As every wave drives other forth, and that that comes behind
> Both thrusteth and is thrust itself : even so the times by kind
> Do fly and follow both at once, and evermore renew.

Golding goes on to show how 'dame nature' 'brought us out to air' from our mother's womb. Shakespeare translates, 'Nativity once in the main of light', the ocean of light, as Dover Wilson suggests. Ovid then takes man's progress to maturity from the time when he crawls 'four footed' to old age, which 'doth undermine the strength of former years, and throws it down'. Shakespeare makes the child once born crawl to maturity, and 'Time that gave, doth now his gift confound'. Ovid refers to Helen weeping because of 'her aged wrinkles'. Shakespeare says time 'doth transfix the flourish set on youth, And delves

the parallels in beauty's brow'. This leads to Ovid's 'eater-up of
things', time that destroys everything. Shakespeare says it
'Feeds on the rarities of nature's truth, And nothing stands'
against it. All he adds is the final tag, which itself has certainly
not altered, that he hopes his verse will stand, despite time's
'cruel hand'.

Sonnet 61

> Is it thy will, thy image should keep open
> My heavy eyelids to the weary night?
> Dost thou desire my slumbers should be broken,
> While shadows like to thee do mock my sight?
> Is it thy spirit that thou send'st from thee
> So far from home into my deeds to pry,
> To find out shames and idle hours in me,
> The scope and tenure of thy jealousy?
> Oh no, thy love though much, is not so great,
> It is my love that keeps mine eye awake,
> Mine own true love that doth my rest defeat,
> To play the watchman ever for thy sake.
> For thee watch I, whilst thou dost wake elsewhere,
> From me far off, with others all too near.

This has no connection with the sonnets immediately preceding. It relates rather with 44 and 45, and the last line may
recollect sonnet 57 line 12. It gives a direct comment on
Wyatt's sonnets XLI, and XLII in Tottel. In the former he
says that his thought

> Makes me from company to live alone,
> In following her whom reason bids me flee.
> And after her my heart would fain be gone :

and in XLII he asks for the fulfilment of a dream that has
brought him to embrace his love. He agrees that

> By good respect in such a dangerous case
> Thou broughtest her not into these tossing seas,
> But madest my sprite to live my care to encrease,
> My body in tempest her delight to embrace.
> The body dead, the sprite had his desire.

But he complains that his dream 'where it was at wish, could not remain'. Shakespeare disbelieves that his friend has mysterious powers of this sort to disturb his sleep by mocking him with his image, or that he could send his spirit far from home to follow him about and see what he is doing. Oh no, it is his own worry that keeps him awake, with the obvious conclusion that

> Sin of self-love possesseth all mine eye,
> And all my soul, and all my every part;
> And for this sin there is no remedy,
> It is so grounded inward in my heart.
> Methinks no face so gracious is as mine,
> No shape so true, no truth of such account,
> And for myself mine own worth do define,
> As I all other in all worths surmount.
> But when my glass shows me myself indeed
> Beated and chopt with tanned antiquity,
> Mine own self love quite contrary I read
> Self, so self loving were iniquity.
> 'Tis thee (my self) that for myself I praise,
> Painting my age with beauty of thy days.

(Sonnet 62)

After the quatrain stressing his self-love Shakespeare gives a fantasy result. Since all he does is to love himself he thinks himself the most beautiful and true of all people and superior to everyone else. But as presumably what one *sees* in love is the important thing, he gives all these qualities to his face, which he can see in his glass. He contrasts this idea of himself with what the glass really shows him, and realises that since by definition as a sonnet lover he is identical with his friend, it is his friend he sees in the perfect image of himself. We have already seen that sonneteers like referring to themselves as old. Shakespeare takes the prize here. He is 'beated and chopped with tanned antiquity', and not only because of his natural age but with the 'antiquity' that the word suggests Ovid would attribute to him when he is doing what lovers and poets did in the past. This may explain the apparent irrelevance of sonnet

61 in the context. It makes a way to lead his friend back into the heart of Ovid, as we can see by the development in sonnet 63.

The next three sonnets form a closely integrated group, paraphrasing the same passages in Ovid already reflected in sonnets 55 and 60. Against the inevitable course of nature Shakespeare promises that the beauty of his friend shall live 'in these black lines'. In 65 he refers to this as a miracle, 'That in black lines my love may still shine bright'. Ink makes the climax of both 63 and 65. It is incongruous on more than one score. It is black, ugly; it is man made; it is perishable, fading in the course of time; and especially it is highly incongruous poetically.

Sonnet 63

> Against my love shall be as I am now
> With time's injurious hand crushed and o'erworn,
> When hours have drained his blood and filled his brow
> With lines and wrinkles, when his youthful morn
> Hath travelled on to age's steepy night,
> And all those beauties whereof now he's king
> Are vanishing, or vanished out of sight,
> Stealing away the treasure of his spring.
> For such a time do I now fortify
> Against confounding age's cruel knife,
> That he shall never cut from memory
> My sweet love's beauty, though my lover's life.
> His beauty shall in these black lines be seen,
> And they shall live, and he in them still green.

From the same passage in Ovid about youth growing to maturity and old age, paraphrased in sonnet 60, Shakespeare remembered man continuing his journey at last 'Through drooping age's steepy path', where he ends or 'runneth out his race'. And here he condenses it to, 'travelled on to age's steepy night'. Time's injurious hand is illustrated by Ovid, as we have seen, filling the brow with lines and wrinkles, beauty vanished, the treasure of spring gone. Here 'Against confounding age's cruel knife' Shakespeare pits 'these black lines'. A similar devaluation occurs in substituting the common knife for the more classical image of time's scythe.

Sonnets 63, 64 and 65 are closely linked by their imagery, and perhaps particularly by imagery suggested by 'confounding age'. The epithet is repeated in 64 in 'state itself confounded'. It seems to carry a submerged metaphor of a castle attacked and its walls threatened and ruined. This is not expressed or followed up in 63, for all that 'confounding age' is given is a 'cruel knife'. But in sonnet 64 'lofty towers' are 'down rased' and 65 has the 'wrackful siege of battering days'.

Sonnet 64

> When I have seen by time's fell hand defaced
> The rich proud cost of outworn buried age,
> When sometime lofty towers I see down rased,
> And brass eternal slave to mortal rage.
> When I have seen the hungry ocean gain
> Advantage on the kingdom of the shore,
> And the firm soil win of the watery main,
> Increasing store with loss, and loss with store.
> When I have seen such interchange of state,
> Or state itself confounded, to decay,
> Ruin hath taught me thus to ruminate
> That time will come and take my love away.
> This thought is as a death which cannot choose
> But weep to have, that which it fears to lose.

This like the last sonnet is turgid with the Ovidian past, but whereas that dealt with decay at the personal level, this laments the ruin of man's great works and of nature's sublimities—'The rich proud cost' of perhaps buried cities, 'lofty towers down rased' like Ovid's[78] 'Athens and Amphions towers in honour once', even Horace's brass, the most durable of metals, 'the hungry ocean' and 'the firm soil' at eternal interchange, and even this interchange, and 'state itself confounded'. All but the couplet make one magnificent Latin period, with three sonorous, parallel clauses of time, leading to the conclusion of what ruin has taught him, that time will come and take his friend away—a bathos. But he says the thought is like a death and makes him weep. It is a magnificent statement to end in such simplicity, not to say sentimentality, for does anyone with a friend not directly threatened, weep for his inevitable death? And does not time come in too familiar terms after this magniloquence, to take his friend away.

In its grammatical structure and by verbal echoes this sonnet reflects both Ovid and the parodied sonneteers. The tune in parallel clauses is Constable's, but Ovid also uses a similar parallelism to emphasise the interchange of sea and land. In Golding's translation the passage[79] begins, 'For I have seen', and 'I have seen' is repeated :

> For I have seen it sea which was substantial ground alate,
> Again where sea was, I have seen the same become dry
> land.

Although the imagery with its change and flux is Ovid's, the contrast of love perpetuated by the poet's fame comes from the sonneteers. And the final reduction to ink is Sidney's. In sonnet VI he scoffs at the poet whose 'tears pour out his ink'. The perpetuating of love in verse is so taken for granted in the sonnet tradition that it comes to seem dull fact. And indeed this may have encouraged Shakespeare to turn it to bombast. Possibly the most pedestrian hyperbole is Watson's in sonnet LXXVII of *The Passionate Centurie*, where he says that time consumes everything—youth, beauty, trees, pleasures, princely state, the calm sea. After this list with its selection from the usual items, he concludes as one expects in the final couplet that it cannot make him cease to love. It is of course a variation on the old theme which has lost its reality in artifice, that of loving

> Till a' the seas gang dry, my dear,
> And the rocks melt wi' the sun.

Sonnet 65

> Since brass, nor stone, nor earth, nor boundless sea,
> But sad mortality o'ersways their power,
> How with this rage shall beauty hold a plea,
> Whose action is no stronger than a flower?

Oh how shall summer's honey breath hold out,
Against the wrackful siege of battering days,
When rocks impregnable are not so stout,
Nor gates of steel so strong but time decays?
Oh fearful meditation, where alack,
Shall time's best jewel from time's chest lie hid?
Or what strong hand can hold his swift foot back,
Or who his spoil or beauty can forbid?
Oh none, unless this miracle have might,
That in black ink my love may still shine bright.

This continues with a music made out of parallels, but of parallel questions instead of parallel clauses. They are answered by 'Oh none' unless there is a miracle in black ink. The sonnet begins by summing up Ovid's universal ravage and asking how beauty that is so frail can stand against it. Sonnets 55 and 64 are recollected in the first line, and beauty as a flower, as the summer scent of honey, is measured against time's battering rams tearing down the walls of a fortress under siege. The submerged metaphor of sonnet 63, which came to clear expression as actual towers in 64, is used here in summing up. Neither rocks that the sea wears down, nor steel gates that feel the battering ram can stand. In the sestet Shakespeare emphasises that nothing can stand against time. He uses his old imagery again of the jewel in the chest and asks if it can escape. The only hope is the miracle that will let his love shine in black ink—a final bathos after the 'boundless seas', 'immortality', impregnable rocks, and the rest. And it is not only the sublime but poetry, the scent of honey, that founders in black ink.

Sonnet 66

Tired with all these for restful death I cry,
As to behold desert a beggar born,
And needy nothing trimmed in jollity,
And purest faith unhappily forsworn,
And gilded honour shamefully misplaced,
And maiden virtue rudely strumpeted,
And right perfection wrongfully disgraced,
And strength by limping sway disabled,
And art made tongue-tied by authority,

And folly (doctor-like) controlling skill,
And simple-truth miscalled simplicity,
And captive-good attending captain ill.
Tired with all these, from these would I be gone,
Save that to die, I leave my love alone.

Here begins a group of sonnets on the present age as degener-
ate, which reflects pagan attitudes. In the first sonnet Shakespeare expresses his disgust with what he finds around him.
'Art tongue-tied by authority' might suggest a personal experience, but Leslie Hotson has pointed out[80] that there was a
censorship of books from 1586 to 1593, when it 'tapered off'; if
we can presume some criticism and distaste of it then, this may
be a topical observation helping to date the sonnets. 'Simple
truth miscalled simplicity' also has a personal feel about it. But
this occurs in every age.

The next sonnet follows up by discussing why his friend
should live in this bad age. In sonnet 66 Shakespeare refrains
from calling for 'restful death' for himself in order not to desert
his friend. So the question naturally follows.

Sonnet 67

Ah wherefore with infection should he live,
And with his presence grace impiety,
That sin by him advantage should achieve,
And lace itself with his society?
Why should false painting imitate his cheek,
And steal dead seeing of his living hue?
Why should poor beauty indirectly seek,
Roses of shadow, since his rose is true?
Why should he live, now nature bankrupt is,
Beggared of blood to blush through lively veins,
For she hath no exchequer now but his,
And proud of many, lives upon his gains?
Oh him she stores, to show what wealth she had,
In days long since, before these last so bad.

Shakespeare's friend is the one true rose, the only real beauty
in a corrupt age. Why should nature have made him when
apart from him she has made an 'infected age'? Sin because of

his presence intertwines itself with real beauty to its advantage, and so becomes a sort of false beauty. Why should what is false imitate and steal from him? Why should those searching for beauty have to look to this shadow or unreal beauty? His friend's rose is true. Why should he live now that nature is bankrupt and has no real life, no reality? There is only his truth. Nature is proud of having created many things, but they live on his reputation. Then Shakespeare answers his questions: nature has preserved him to show what she once had.

This reflects Ovid in that nature is thought of as the creator, and in presuming the golden age of perfection 'In days long since'. But there was no need to go to Ovid for this view. Sidney in sonnet CI makes nature interested in Stella's sickness because she, like Shakespeare's friend after her, is the essence of beauty in a world not her equal. Nature is concerned,

> Knowing worlds pass, ere she enough can find
> Of such heaven stuff to clothe so heavenly mind.

The ideas are similar. Both Stella and Shakespeare's friend stand out for their quality, and nature is concerned to preserve them. Stella was sick, and Shakespeare's friend lives 'with infection'. Shakespeare does not comment. He asks why, since Stella and therefore his friend were so difficult to create and are so different from her other creations nature should have created them. There is a hint of incredulity, and his answer is sarcastic, its mood being suggested by the opening 'Oh'.

Sonnet 68

> Thus is his cheek the map of days outworn,
> When beauty lived and died as flowers do now,
> Before these bastard signs of fair were born,
> Or durst inhabit on a living brow:
> Before the golden tresses of the dead,
> The right of sepulchres, were shorn away,
> To live a second life on second head,
> Ere beauty's dead fleece made another gay:
> In him those holy antique hours are seen,
> Without all ornament, itself and true,

> Making no summer of another's green,
> Robbing no old to dress his beauty new,
> And him as for a map doth nature store,
> To show false art what beauty was of yore.

This has the same theme as the last sonnet. Shakespeare complains of the artificiality of beauty now, as compared with in the old days when it was as natural and unaffected as that of a flower. Dover Wilson in his edition of the sonnets suggests that the previous one shows concern about make up, and this about wigs, and says these were especially repugnant to Shakespeare. But this is to overstress illustrative imagery as if it were the theme itself. He is more likely to have thought it comic than repugnant.

Incidentally the form of this sonnet is interesting with the opening imagery repeated at the end.

Sonnets 69 and 70 carry on the argument, showing the infection that may harm the natural rose in a false world. Beauty attracts envy and slander. The beautiful are suspected of not being good. Shakespeare implies a background of beautiful sonnet ladies suspected of having a vile nature by their sonnet lovers. He defends his friend against such imputations:

Sonnet 69

> Those parts of thee that the world's eye doth view,
> Want nothing that the thought of hearts can mend:
> All tongues (the voice of souls) give thee that end,
> Uttering bare truth, even so as foes commend.
> Thy outward thus with outward praise is crowned,
> But those same tongues that give thee so thine own,
> In other accents do this praise confound
> By seeing farther than the eye hath shown.
> They look into the beauty of thy mind,
> And that in guess they measure by thy deeds,
> Then churls their thoughts (although their eyes were kind)
> To thy fair flower add the rank smell of weeds,
> But why thy odour matcheth not thy show,
> The soil is this, that thou dost common grow.

This parodies Sidney's sonnet **LXXX** :

> Sweet swelling lips well mayst thou swell in pride,
> Since best wits think it best thee to admire,
> Nature's praise, virtue's stall, Cupid's cold fire,
> Whence words, not words but heavenly graces slide,
> The new Parnassus where the graces bide :
> Sweetness of music, wisdom's beautifier,
> Breather of life, the fastness of desire,
> Where beauty's blush in honour's grain is died.
> Thus much my heart my mouth compelled to say :
> But now, spite of my heart my tongue will stay,
> Loathing all lies, doubting this flattery is.

The sonnet ends by saying he will test whether it is true by a kiss.

A series of abstract nouns gives character to Sidney's sonnet. The only concrete thing is lips, for 'tongue' is used to mean speech. Even 'mouth' is personified. Sidney seems to be making general statements about abstract qualities. He says that Stella's lips are justified in their pride because best wits admire all her qualities, including the cold fire of her love, her honour. From this admiration it comes that words which are not words but heavenly graces, find a new inspiration or Parnassus, where the graces dwell, and of which he gives examples. This is where beauty's blush is dyed in indelible honour. His mouth has been compelled by his heart to say this, but his tongue, which loathes lies, doubts it may be flattery.

Shakespeare parodies by making statements about abstract things too, most of them the same abstractions. He gives them a further remoteness by making them plural, dissociating them from himself, making it appear almost as if they had a separate existence unattached to people. There are 'parts of thee', 'thought of hearts', 'all tongues', 'churls their thoughts (although their eyes were kind)'. Just as Sidney qualified 'words' as not words but heavenly graces, so Shakespeare qualifies 'tongues'. He deduces from Sidney's tongue which loathed lies and doubted the flatteries it was compelled to say, that tongues are 'the voices of souls'. He plays with his impersonal *dramatis personae* by adding to the common heart-eye conflict an inward-outward contrast which is there in Sidney's sonnet, where Stella's lips, her beauty, are justified in their pride because of her inward qualities—her honour, her wisdom, her cold virtue-controlled love. Shakespeare parodies by making his friend's beauty unjustified, by giving his 'tongues' and 'thought of hearts' something more substantial to cavil at than Sidney does. But he follows him in making them at first agree that his friend was beautiful outwardly. It was only when they looked deeper that they became churlish and added the rank smell of weeds to his beauty's flower. Sonnet 54 suggested that his friend's flower was a rose, and that the scent of a rose is its inward truth. The scent of the weed is rank. By ending the parody with his pun on 'soil' and 'common' he binds it to his context. The reason, ground, soil of his friend's rankness comes from his growing common, as the weed's quality depends on its soil in the common where it grows. Thus whereas the sonnets immediately preceding protested the uniqueness of his friend's quality he now says that his inward qualities are those of the 'infected' world or soil he has grown in.

Sonnet 70

> That thou art blamed shall not be thy defect,
> For slander's mark was ever yet the fair,
> The ornament of beauty is suspect,
> A crow that flies in heaven's sweetest air.
> So thou be good, slander doth but approve,
> Their worth the greater being wooed of time,
> For canker vice the sweetest buds doth love,
> And thou present'st a pure unstained prime.
> Thou hast passed by the ambush of young days,
> Either not assailed, or victor being charged,
> Yet this thy praise cannot be so thy praise,
> To tie up envy, evermore enlarged,
> If some suspect of ill masked not thy show,
> Then thou alone kingdoms of hearts shouldst owe.

As in sonnet 54 'the ornament of beauty' was said to be truth, and the scent of a rose its soul or essence, with these associations still in mind, Shakespeare is saying that the truth of a beautiful person is always suspect. But this does not mean that he must be to blame. Slander is not attached to the suspect, but like a crow flies apart through 'heaven's sweetest air'. Provided it is undeserved, it merely confirms one's virtue for it is like canker that attacks the sweetest buds, such as his friend's unstained youth. Although he has passed through his youth safely, unhurt by anyone who might lie in wait to attack, he could not expect to escape for ever, as people's good opinions do not stop envy, and if some did not suspect him, then he alone of all men would have whole kingdoms in love with him.

There is ample background for these two sonnets. Nearly all the sonneteers condemn their beautiful ladies, whose actions show that their essence is bad. But they all find excuses for them. Here is a complaint from Wyatt's sonnet LXIX of Tottel:

> My grievous pain how little she regardeth,
> The solemn oath, whereof she takes no cure,
>   .   .   .   .   .   .
> Broken she hath : ...
> To the disdainful, all her life she leadeth :
> To me spiteful, without just cause, or measure.

Sidney makes play with the contrast between looks and reality in sonnet LXXX which we have already dealt with. Spenser suspects deceit in sonnet XLI :

> But if her nature and her will be so,
> That she will plague the man that loves her most :
> And take delight to increase a wretch's woe,
> Then all her nature's goodly gifts are lost.
> And that same glorious beauty's idle boast,
> Is but a bait such wretches to beguile :
>   .   .   .   .   .
> Oh fairest fair let never it be named,
> That so fair beauty was so foully shamed.

Shakespeare does not let it happen. The important thing for all sonneteers as he says of his friend is

> That thou art blamed shall not be thy defect,

and to prove this is the purpose of the sonnet. This must be shown at all costs. His friend has no fault, whatever his actions may suggest. Indeed in the end, the sonneteer can only blame himself, and this Shakespeare does in sonnets 71 and 72, where he contemplates what would happen if he died and left this vile world where his friend's beauty is unquestioned, but his inward or essential nature is either affected by the soil in which it grows, or else slandered.

Sonnet 71

No longer mourn for me when I am dead,
Than you shall hear the surly sullen bell
Give warning to the world that I am fled
From this vile world with vilest worms to dwell:
Nay if you read this line, remember not,
The hand that writ it, for I love you so,
That I in your sweet thoughts would be forgot,
If thinking on me then should make you woe.
Oh if (I say) you look upon this verse,
When I (perhaps) compounded am with clay,
Do not so much as my poor name rehearse;
But let your love even with my life decay.
Lest the wise world should look into your moan,
And mock you with me after I am gone.

When a sonneteer dies it is usually because his lady has murdered him. Shakespeare does not make his friend do this. But he is afraid his death may embarrass him. He cannot accuse his friend of his death so he makes the shame his own; and his love for him is so great that he asks him not even to mourn in case someone should discover why he is moaning and then mock him. It is said in an elegiac music. The emotional, 'Nay if you read this line, remember not' is itself mocked in, 'Oh if (I say) you look upon this verse'.

Probably several sonneteers go to make these parodies. Constable cautions his lady in decade 2, sonnet IV,

Of murder's guilt (dear lady) then beware.
My loss of life a millionfold were less,
Than the least loss should unto you befall.

In his next sonnet his heart is found murdered. Although it is not related with this incident, he ends sonnet II of decade 5 :

My death is such as I may not complain.

Spenser concludes sonnet XXXVI by warning his lady that when she has slain him,

some perhaps will moan,
Ye shall condemned be of many a one.

A sonnet of Daniel's printed in the pirated edition of *Astrophel and Stella*, tells how he died and went to Elysium :

If any ask, why that so soon I came?
I'll hide her fault, and say it was my lot,
In life and death I'll tender her good name,
My life and death shall never be her blot.
Although the world this deed of hers may blame,
The Elysian ghosts shall never know the same.

Similarly in sonnet 71 Shakespeare shields his friend from any hurt his death might do to him. He does it

Lest the wise world should look into your moan

—a line compounded of Daniel and Spenser.

Sonnet 72

Oh lest the world should task you to recite,
What merit lived in me that you should love
After my death (dear love) forget me quite,
For you in me can nothing worthy prove.
Unless you would devise some virtuous lie,
To do more for me than mine own desert,
And hang more praise upon deceased I,
Than niggared truth would willingly impart:
Oh lest your true love may seem false in this,
That you for love speak well of me untrue,
My name be buried where my body is,

And live no more to shame nor me, nor you.
For I am shamed by that which I bring forth,
And so should you, to love things nothing worth.

This parodies another sonnet of Daniel's, no. XXXVI :

Oh be not grieved that these my papers should,
Bewray unto the world how fair thou art :

. . . . . .

Think not sweet Delia, this shall be thy shame,
My muse should sound thy praise with mournful warble :
How many lives the glory of whose name,
Shall rest in ye, when thine is graved in marble.
Thou mayst in after ages live esteemed,
Unburied in these lines reserved in pureness;

. . . . . .

Yet count it no disgrace that I have loved thee.

Shakespeare presumes that he has disgraced his friend by writing in praise of him. He imagines him challenged to prove the contrary, and tells him not to invent some lie in praise of his verse. Rather than this he would be forgotten, for he is shamed by what he has written and so should his friend be if he praised it.

Daniel's sonnet obviously stimulated Shakespeare for he mocks at the lines I have omitted in sonnet 81, and in this sonnet makes a close parody of what I have quoted. Daniel pleads 'Oh be not grieved' that he has betrayed 'unto the world' how fair his lady is. Shakespeare takes this up in 'Oh lest the world' should task his friend to say what merit his poet has to deserve his love. Daniel asks Delia not to think it shall be her 'shame' to receive his praise. Shakespeare says he is 'shamed' by what he brings forth. Daniel asks the lady to remember how long 'the glory of her name' will live when she is 'graved in marble' and Shakespeare asks his friend to forget him when his 'name is buried with his body'. Daniel adds, 'Yet count it no disgrace that I have loved thee', and Shakespeare ends that his friend would be disgraced 'to love things nothing worth'.

In sonnet 73 Shakespeare again writes on approaching death, but in a different mood. We should not forget that he was a young man when he wrote it.

Sonnet 73

> That time of year thou mayst in me behold,
> When yellow leaves, or none, or few do hang
> Upon those boughs which shake against the cold,
> Bare ruined choirs, where late the sweet birds sang.
> In me thou seest the twilight of such day,
> As after sunset fadeth in the west,
> Which by and by black night doth take away,
> Death's second self that seals up all in rest.
> In me thou seest the glowing of such fire,
> That on the ashes of his youth doth lie,
> As the death-bed, whereon it must expire,
> Consumed with that which it was nourished by.
> This thou perceiv'st, which makes thy love more strong,
> To love that well, which thou must leave ere long.

Sonneteers ask their ladies to love while it is summer before winter comes, the argument for love lying in the short time it can last. Shakespeare has gone one better. He says it is already winter with him. He is at death's door. His time is *very* short. Since you can see this, he tells his friend, you should love me more.

Some of the credit for this sonnet must go to Daniel, who in sonnet XXXII combines the arguments in the first two quatrains, asking Delia to love while it is summer and in the morning before night comes, and in sonnet XXXIV where he requests her to read his verse on her

> When winter snows upon thy golden hairs,
> And frost of age hath nipped thy flowers near :
> When dark shall seem thy day that never clears,
> And all lies withered that was held so dear.

Barnes in sonnet LIX brings together

> The leafless branches of the lifeless boughs
> Carve winter's outrage in their withered barks.

and

> The withered wrinkles in my careful brows.

And although he is saying something different, Constable in decade 6, sonnet VI may have contributed to the imagery in the third quatrain, where he refers to

> Thy beauty so, the brightest living flame,
> Wrapped in my cloudy heart by winter pressed.

He exclaims,

> Oh that my heart might still contain that fire,
>
> . . . . . .
>
> For as the fire through freezing clouds doth break,
> So, not myself, but thou in me would speak.

The fire is linked with frost and winter, although it is the sun that Constable is writing about. His imagery, however, relating fire with winter may have been in Shakespeare's mind. But all these are common sonnet images. Shakespeare has geared the 'bare ruined choirs', the twilight and the ashes to death and created the most unforgettable of all the sonnets, ridiculous only in the implication that the strength of love is in inverse ratio to the length of time remaining for it, or in this being used as a relevant argument for love.

Sonnet 74

> But be contented when that fell arrest,
> Without all bail shall carry me away,
> My life hath in this line some interest,
> Which for memorial still with thee shall stay.
> When thou reviewest this, thou dost review,
> The very part was consecrate to thee,
> The earth can have but earth, which is his due,
> My spirit is thine the better part of me,

So then thou hast but lost the dregs of life,
The prey of worms, my body being dead,
The coward conquest of a wretch's knife,
Too base of thee to be remembered,
The worth of that, is that which it contains,
And that is this, and this with thee remains.

Shakespeare begins with the bailiff carrying him off in death. He says there will be some interest in this line ('interest' of course being a pun) that will remain to his friend as a memorial. 'Memorial' may have remained in his mind from Daniel's

The sad memorials of my love's despair:

in sonnet IX although it was only his lady's disdain that made him despair. Leishman[81] suggests that Shakespeare may be thinking of the passage in Ovid already quoted, where he says that his 'better part' will be carried up in immortality above the stars when he dies. But he may also be remembering Spenser's sonnet XIII, where he compares the fair proud face of his lady raised to the sky, with her humble

looking on the earth whence she was born :
Her mind remembereth her mortality,
What so is fairest shall to earth return.
But that same lofty countenance seems to scorn
Base thing, and think how she to heaven may climb :
Treading down earth as loathsome and forlorn,
That hinders heavenly thoughts with drossy slime.

Shakespeare not only says that the best part of him—his verse —was consecrated to his friend but that what his friend has lost—his dregs, the prey of worms—is too 'base', using Spenser's identical word to be 'remembered', also Spenser's word. His spirit is his friend's. What is contained in his dregs, or his body, gives him his only worth and what is contained is his sonnet, which remains with his friend. Mixed with this is the recollection of the burial service, which Spenser's sonnet suggests. His lady looks on the earth from which she came and

remembers 'her mortality'. She treads down earth as loathsome, and hindering 'heavenly thoughts'. Shakespeare in effect
says earth to earth, but his 'spirit', his 'better part', his poetry
to his friend.

The literary historian in search for facts has with some
excuse seen a reference to Marlowe in

> The coward conquest of a wretch's knife,

which, although applicable to Marlowe, would destroy both the
meaning and the structure of this sonnet. The theme is that
though death will put an end to Shakespeare's body, which is a
worthless, a base thing, it cannot touch his verse, which being
his better part, his spirit, will survive. Death, the executioner as
every Elizabethan reader would remember has a scythe. This is
not the only sonnet in which Shakespeare robbed the image of
its poetic cloud by calling it a 'knife'. So too to call death a
'coward' fits this context. Shakespeare is denegrating the whole
set up. Death involves the loss of dregs, makes the body the
prey of worms, comes from the knife of that coward who does
not give one the chance to hit back. The first image in the
sonnet was of a 'fell' arrest. This makes the bailiff death despicable, for he allows no argument or bail. 'Conquest' too is the
right word, for the poet is at war with time's inexorable
destruction. The body is too base to be remembered. It, the
bailiff, and the coward knife are all base. But the poet's better
part remains as his memorial. To think of Marlowe at this
point would be to think of something of great value destroyed,
which would make nonsense of the meaning and ruin a perfectly constructed sonnet.

Sonnet 75

> So are you to my thoughts as food to life,
> Or as sweet seasoned showers are to the ground:
> And for the peace of you I hold such strife,
> As 'twixt a miser and his wealth is found.
> Now proud as an enjoyer, and anon
> Doubting the filching age will steal his treasure,
> Now counting best to be with you alone,
> Then bettered that the world may see my pleasure,

Sometime all full with feasting on your sight,
And by and by clean starvéd for a look,
Possessing or pursuing no delight
Save what is had, or must from you be took.
Thus do I pine and surfeit day by day,
Or gluttoning on all, or all away.

This returns to the old theme of, as Daniel calls it in sonnet XV, 'Hunger-starven thoughts'. The feverish turning now to one thing, then its opposite, is common in the sonnets.

Sonnet 76

Why is my verse so barren of new pride?
So far from variation or quick change?
Why with the time do I not glance aside
To new found methods, and to compounds strange?
Why write I still all one, ever the same,
And keep invention in a noted weed,
That every word doth almost tell my name,
Showing their birth, and where they did proceed?
Oh know sweet love I always write of you,
And you and love are still my argument:
So all my best is dressing old words new,
Spending again what is already spent:
For as the sun is daily new and old,
So is my love still telling what is told.

This sonnet prepares the way for what has been called the rival poet. Shakespeare says his verse is inadequate; he always says the same thing monotonously. The reason is, as stated in the couplet, that his theme never varies. In fact he is doing what Sidney says in sonnet LVI that he has decided to do, no longer to call on the muses,

No other sugaring of speech to try,
But on her name uncessantly to cry.
For let me but name her whom I do love,
So sweet sound straight my ears and heart do hit,
That I well find no eloquence to it.

With this no doubt in mind Shakespeare makes two comments.

He says in effect this leads to barren repetition, 'dressing old words new', 'spending again what is already spent'. Sidney lays emphasis on his incessantly calling her name, but Shakespeare quietly insinuates 'That every word doth almost tell' his own name, that this is the real aim of the sonneteer—a point he makes more than once.

Sonnet 77

Thy glass will show thee how thy beauties wear,
Thy dial how thy precious minutes waste,
The vacant leaves thy mind's imprint will bear,
And of this book, this learning mayst thou taste.
The wrinkles which thy glass will truly show,
Of mouthed graves will give thee memory,
Thou by thy dial's shady stealth mayst know,
Time's thievish progress to eternity.
Look what thy memory cannot contain,
Commit to these waste blacks, and thou shalt find
Those children nursed, delivered from thy brain,
To take a new acquaintance of thy mind.
These offices, so oft as thou wilt look,
Shall profit thee, and much enrich thy book.

This sonnet has presented difficulties. 'Blacks' has been taken to be a misprint for 'blanks', and it has been supposed that Shakespeare gave a blank book to his friend to use as a diary. But one must say first that there is no need to presume this misprint, and secondly that then his friend is apparently being told to write what his 'memory cannot contain'—an absurdity with no point. The third reason is not inherent in the sonnet, but in its context. Shakespeare dedicates both the preceding and the following sonnets to writing about his friend. An interpretation that presumes that he is doing that also in this sonnet should be given preference to any other doubtful interpretation. On the face of it he seems to say his friend's glass will show him his wrinkles, his dial remind him of his mortality, and that this 'book' that Shakespeare is writing will bear the print of his mind. If he reads it he will discover what he does not remember about himself at all. He is told to attend to these wasted, or unread black lines and he will find things about himself that he has experienced but forgotten, delivered again as if new. This would both profit him and also add to the value of the book, for (as Shakespeare assumes he need not say) the value of writing lies in communication. To this interpretation 'thy' book and 'commit' may be obstacles. But a book written by Shakespeare about his friend could well be offered to him as 'thy book'. And if he accepts that what he reads is his own although he did not remember it, this might be thought of as committing himself to its acceptance.

Perhaps the best argument for this reading lies in the sonnets that Shakespeare is parodying. Daniel in sonnet **XXIX** writes:

> Oh why doth Delia credit so her glass,
> Gazing her beauty deigned her by the skies:
> And doth not rather look on him (alas)
> Whose state best shows the face of murdering eyes.
>
> . . . . . .
>
> Then leave your glass, and gaze yourself on me,
> That mirror shows what power is in your face:
> To view your form too much, may danger be,
> Narcissus changed to a flower in such a case.

After him Constable wrote in sonnet V of decade 5:

> His shadow to Narcissus well presented
> How fair he was by such attractive love:
> So if thou would'st thyself thy beauty prove,
> Vulgar breath-mirrors might have well contented,
>
> . . . . . .
>
> But more thou forc'st, making my pen approve
> Thy praise to all, . . .
> With this hath wrought, you which before wert known
> But unto some, of all art now required,
> And thine eyes' wonders wronged, because not shown
> The world, with daily orisons desired.
>
> . . . . . .
>
> And thus my pen hath made thy sweets admired.

Daniel, and imitating him, Constable presume their ladies admiring themselves like Narcissus. Daniel makes his lady do this in her glass, and Constable offers his a 'breath-mirror' in his pen. He offers to make her beauty, which is not well enough known, perceived generally. Shakespeare parodies by saying his friend sees another sort of truth about himself in his glass. Presumably he is as anxious that the truth about him should be known, as the ladies that they should be admired. His glass tells him, says Shakespeare, that he is ageing and his dial that this is a minute by minute progress to eternity. Shakespeare's pen, his unread 'blacks' will tell him what he does not know, not what he does. It will show him what he has perhaps forgotten, but which Shakespeare has remembered and now makes known afresh. The parody suggests that the sort of truth Shakespeare wants to tell his friend is far from being what he wants to know about himself, what he wants to be told, or what is flattering or pleasant. The truth is not that he is a beautiful Narcissus, but that he is fast growing old.

The next three sonnets write of rival poets, and this has been taken to be autobiographical. But writing about their rivals was a traditional sonnet practice. It takes two forms. The Italians had a convention of praising their rivals. From the other angle, Du Bellay, among the French, ridicules what is ridiculous in sonnet writing, but says he will do anything to please his lady, even use Petrarchan phrases.[82] Some similarities in Shakespeare's sonnets might perhaps suggest that he had read the Italian and French sonneteers, but any evidence of this sort is so tenuous, that certainly at this moment in history it seems wisest to presume only English sonneteers as his background. And there is an English background to the rival.

Sonnet 78

> So oft have I invoked thee for my muse,
> And found such fair assistance in my verse,
> As every alien pen hath got my use,
> And under thee their poesy disperse.
> Thine eyes, that taught the dumb on high to sing,
> And heavy ignorance aloft to fly,
> Have added feathers to the learned's wing,
> And given grace a double majesty.
> Yet be most proud of that which I compile,
> Whose influence is thine, and born of thee,

In others' works thou dost but mend the style,
And arts with thy sweet graces graced be.
But thou art all my art, and dost advance
As high as learning, my rude ignorance.

Sonnet 79

Whilst I alone did call upon thy aid,
My verse alone had all thy gentle grace,
But now my gracious numbers are decayed,
And my sick muse doth give another place.
I grant (sweet love) thy lovely argument
Deserves the travail of a worthier pen,
Yet what of thee thy poet doth invent,
He robs thee of, and pays it thee again,
He lends thee virtue, and he stole that word,
From thy behaviour, beauty doth he give
And found it in thy cheek: he can afford
No praise to thee, but what in thee doth live.
Then thank him not for that which he doth say,
Since what he owes thee, thou thyself dost pay.

Sonnet 80

Oh how I faint when I of you do write,
Knowing a better spirit doth use your name,
And in the praise thereof spends all his might,
To make me tongue-tied speaking of your fame.
But since your worth (wide as the ocean is)
The humble as the proudest sail doth bear,
My saucy bark (inferior far to his)
On your broad main doth wilfully appear.
Your shallowest help will hold me up afloat,
Whilst he upon your soundless deep doth ride,
Or (being wrecked) I am a worthless boat,
He of tall building, and of goodly pride.
Then if he thrive and I be cast away,
The worst was this, my love was my decay.

In sonnet 78 Shakespeare says he has received inspiration from
his friend and written so much about him that every other poet
has copied him. His eyes that taught the dumb Shakespeare to
sing and gave him the know-how have added qualities of style

to the poetry of those who already have the art. He asks his friend to think more of what he writes, however, since he owes everything to him, than of the others who only learnt from him how to add grace to their art. In the first sonnet then, as condensed in the couplet, Shakespeare says his friend has so inspired him that he has become the equal of others.

Things have grown worse by the second sonnet. Whereas when only he wrote of his friend, he received all his favour, now he has to give place to another. He admits that his friend deserves 'a worthier pen'. All the same, what this rival pays his friend in compliment he must first have stolen from him, since he can praise only what is there to praise. Do not thank him for this, Shakespeare ends, since 'thou thyself dost pay'.

In the third sonnet Shakespeare 'faints with jealousy' but consoles himself with the thought that the ocean has room for humble little boats like his verse, as well as for great ships. At worst he has failed because he loved.

None of these sonnets implies a real rival. They are unmistakable parodies of Sidney's third sonnet.

> Let dainty wits cry, on the sisters nine,
>
> . . . . .
>
> Or Pindar's apes flaunt in their phrases fine,
>
> . . . . .
>
> Ennobling new found tropes, with problems old :
> Or with strange similes, enrich each line,
>
> . . . . .
>
> Phrases and problems from my reach do grow,
> And strange things cost too dear for my poor sprites,
> How then? Even thus, in Stella's face I read,
> What love and beauty be, then all my deed.
> But copying is, what in her nature writes.

Here are rival poets. They rely on the nine muses, copy Pindar, use art and devices of style, while Sidney finds such things strange and beyond him. All he knows is what he reads in Stella. Shakespeare parodies this in his three sonnets. He begins with a plain statement as if it were of a fact, that he has invoked his friend so often for his muse (as Sidney did Stella) that every writer has copied him (as happened to Sidney?).

Those who are already learned, like Sidney's rivals who studied
Pindar and used art and devices of style such as tropes and
strange similes, have 'added feathers' to their wings, but he asks
his friend to be prouder of him, for he is even more naïve than
Sidney. His 'ignorance' is 'heavy' and 'rude', but as Stella
taught her poet, his friend has taught him. In his second sonnet
Shakespeare takes up Sidney's next point. And here he
complains not of many rivals, but of one. This allows him to
make his joke more pointedly. Sidney said he 'read' in Stella's
face 'what love and beauty be' so that all he did was to copy
what nature wrote in her. Shakespeare follows up the consequences of his rival doing this. He says that when he 'invents'
to praise his friend, all he does is to steal the 'word' he found
written in his 'virtue'. He can therefore well afford to praise
since he robbed what he pays. So he tells his friend not to
thank him for what he says, 'Since what he owes thee, thou
thyself dost pay'. Although Sidney gave the framework of the
parody, Spenser and Constable add details. Spenser in his third
sonnet has

> The sovereign beauty which I do admire,
> Witness the world how worthy to be praised :
> The light whereof hath kindled heavenly fire,
> In my frail spirit by her from baseness raised.
> That being now with her huge brightness dazed,
> Base thing I can no more endure to view :
>
> .   .   .   .   .   .
>
> So when my tongue would speak her praises due,
> It stoppéd is with thought's astonishment :
> And when my pen would write her titles true,
> It ravished is with fancy's wonderment :
> Yet in my heart I then both speak and write,
> The wonder that my wit cannot endite.

Spenser has learnt from his lady's beauty so that his 'frail spirit'
is 'from baseness raised'. In sonnet 78 Shakespeare says his
friend's eyes taught him, 'the dumb' 'on high to sing' and his
ignorance 'aloft to fly'. The lady being 'worthy to be praised'
may be echoed in sonnet 79 where the friend 'Deserves the
travail of a worthier pen'; when Spenser's pen would write it

was 'stoppéd by astonishment'. Shakespeare therefore says a worthier 'pen' than his was needed. Finally Constable, who is himself an offshoot from Sidney, in decade 8 sonnet IV contributes verbal echoes:

> My tears are true, though others be divine,
> . . . . . .
> And I though disaccustoming my muse,
> And sing but low songs in an humble vein,
> May one day raise my style as others use.

The last line may have given Shakespeare the echoes of 'others' and 'style' for 'In others' works thou dost but mend the style' in sonnet 78.

The imagery of the ship in sonnet 80 is one of the commonest from Petrarch onwards. Shakespeare has given it an individual slant to fit his purpose. He makes the point that although 'the better spirit' in this sonnet in contrast with Spenser's 'frail spirit', makes him 'tongue-tied' as Spenser's was 'stoppéd', since his 'worth' (also Spenser's word) bears the 'humble' (Constable's word) as well as the proudest sail, his small boat will float on the shallowest water his friend allows, while his rival's proud ship needs an ocean of favour too deep to sound. That is to say his love, if inferior, at least has one finer aspect. Shakespeare, however, defines that quality as 'saucy'.

Sonnet 81

> Or I shall live your epitaph to make,
> Or you survive when I in earth am rotten,
> From hence your memory death cannot take,
> Although in me each part will be forgotten.
> Your name from hence immortal life shall have,
> Though I (once gone) to all the world must die,
> The earth can yield me but a common grave,
> When you entombed in men's eyes shall lie,
> Your monument shall be my gentle verse,
> Which eyes not yet created shall o'er-read,
> And tongues to be, your being shall rehearse,
> When all the breathers of this world are dead,
> You still shall live (such virtue hath my pen)
> Where breath most breathes, even in the mouths of men.

This sonnet summarises what has already been said. Shakespeare has written on both his own death and his friend's, and on preserving his friend's memory in his verse. But it also makes a comment on Daniel's no. XXXVI, which I have already partially quoted, and which he parodied in sonnet 72. There he found that the poet would 'unbury' Delia, and in the passage I omitted from my previous quotation, he says that his lines

> shall entomb those eyes, that have redeemed
> Me from the vulgar, thee from all obscureness.

This is the reference for Shakespeare's friend being 'entombed in men's eyes', which one might call an intentional misquotation. The ending of the sonnet with his friend's memory lasting till 'all the breathers of the world are dead', 'Where breath most breathes, even in the mouths of men' might perhaps be a parody of Constable's 'breath-mirrors' in the sonnet I have already quoted when dealing with Shakespeare's sonnet 77.

Sonnets 82 to 86 return to the theme of the rival poet. On the whole they repeat what has already been said.

Sonnet 82

> I grant thou wert not married to my muse,
> And therefore mayst without attaint o'erlook
> The dedicated words which writers use
> Of their fair subject, blessing every book.
> Thou art as fair in knowledge as in hue,
> Finding thy worth a limit past my praise,
> And therefore art enforced to seek anew,
> Some fresher stamp of the time bettering days.
> And do so love, yet when they have devised,
> What strained touches rhetoric can lend,
> Thou truly fair, wert truly sympathized,
> In true plain words, by thy true telling friend.
> And their gross painting might be better used,
> Where cheeks need blood, in thee it is abused.

This expresses Shakespeare's acceptance of the situation, although he has a mildly cynical reference to dedications and

I

to patrons on the outlook for promising new writers. However, his friend he says, is not married to his muse, and as his worth exceeds Shakespeare's praise, he must look for a poet of the new generation, which has improved on the past. He tells his friend to do this, but when the new poets have given what 'strained touches rhetoric can lend', like Sidney's rivals, to remember that Shakespeare wrote of him truthfully in plain words. Their coarse painting of him is an insult to his friend, and would be better used of those who need flattery.

There are obvious links with Shakespeare's own sonnets here. The gross painting of bloodless faces made a prominent image in sonnet 67, and the contrast between others who use rhetoric and style, compared with Shakespeare's plain words we have also heard. Indeed all sonneteers are sure they speak truth whereas their rivals use art. No matter whether in fact they practise it, they agree in theory with what Shakespeare demonstrated in his plays that honest kersey speech is the right one for love. Shakespeare leaves no doubt what he thinks about it, as he emphasises in the next two sonnets.

Sonnet 83

> I never saw that you did painting need,
> And therefore to your fair no painting set,
> I found (or thought I found) you did exceed,
> The barren tender of a poet's debt:
> And therefore have I slept in your report,
> That you yourself being extant well might show,
> How far a modern quill doth come too short,
> Speaking of worth, what worth in you doth grow.
> This silence for my sin you did impute,
> Which shall be most my glory being dumb,
> For I impair not beauty being mute,
> When others would give life, and bring a tomb.
> There lives more life in one of your fair eyes,
> Than both your poets can in praise devise.

This begins by recapping the end of sonnet 82. Shakespeare has not flattered his friend since he thinks it would not add to his beauty to offer him repayment of his debt in this way, and the modern rhetorical poet comes short of his friend's worth.

But his friend has complained of this silence. Shakespeare answers that it is to his credit that he has remained dumb, for by silence he has not impaired his friend's worth. With another hit at Daniel entombing his love's eyes, he says his rival attempts to give life to his loved one, but instead has entombed him, whereas there is more life in one of his eyes than both Shakespeare and his rival together can adequately praise.

Sonnet 84

Who is it that says most, which can say more,
Than this rich praise, that you alone, are you,
In whose confine immured is the store,
Which should example where your equal grew,
Lean penury within that pen doth dwell,
That to his subject lends not some small glory,
But he that writes of you, if he can tell,
That you are you, so dignifies his story.
Let him but copy what in you is writ,
Not making worse what nature made so clear,
And such a counterpart shall fame his wit,
Making his style admired everywhere.
You to your beauteous blessings add a curse,
Being fond on praise, which makes your praises worse.

This carries on the theme of sonnet 83 and reflects what Sidney wrote about Stella. Shakespeare says that neither he nor his rival can say more than that his friend is himself. Anything that would show his equal lies within himself; that is, he has no equal. As a rule, he is a poor writer who cannot lend some glory to his theme, but anyone who writes in praise of his friend merely talks the truth about him. If a poet just copies him and does not spoil what nature has so clearly given, it is enough to bring him fame. But Shakespeare reserves his couplet to deliver a shock. His friend, he says, is fond of praise and that is to add a curse that vitiates it.

Sonnet 85

My tongue-tied muse in manners holds her still,
While comments of your praise richly compiled,

Reserve their character with golden quill,
And precious phrase by all the Muses filed.
I think good thoughts, whilst other write good words,
And like unlettered clerk still cry Amen,
To every hymn that able spirit affords,
In polished form of well refined pen.
Hearing you praised, I say 'tis so, 'tis true,
And to the most of praise add something more,
But that is in my thought, whose love to you
(Though words come hindmost) holds his rank before,
Then others, for the breath of words respect,
Me for my dumb thoughts, speaking in effect.

The theme of Shakespeare's dumbness is carried over. He picks out 'tongue-tied' from sonnet 80, dumbness from 83, and the 'precious phrase' and 'Muses filed' may refer to 82. The first quatrain is difficult, but Professor Mahood[83] explains it neatly :

> My muse, by her reticence, remains well-mannered whatever excesses of affectation other poets may commit in their praise of you.

The rest is straightforward. Shakespeare concludes that his friend should respect others for their words, ridiculed as 'breath', and him for not expressing his thoughts, which in itself is an expression.

All this contrasting of the poet's silence with the writing of others has a considerable background but no clear reference to any one sonnet. Shakespeare relates it with the other sonnet theme of the tongue-tied poet. Perhaps I should give some possible sources for the imagery and ideas. Spenser's sonnet XXII may have suggested the temple where the service is performed that he says 'amen' to :

> This holy season fit to fast and pray,
> Men to devotion ought to be inclined :
> Therefore, I likewise on so holy day,
> For my sweet saint some service fit will find.
> Her temple fair is built within my mind,
> In which her glorious image placéd is,

> On which my thoughts do day and night attend
> Like sacred priests that never think amiss.

Barnes in sonnet XVII asks why he persists

> In framing tuneful elegies, and hymns
> For her whose name my sonnet's note so trims . . .

Sidney seems likely to be in the background with sonnet LIV, where we find,

> Dumb swans, not chattering pies do lovers prove,
> They love indeed, who dare not say they love.

If there is a direct parody, it may be of Wyatt's sonnet XLVIII in Tottel:

> Because I still kept thee fro lies, and blame,
> And to my power always thee honouréd,
> Unkind tongue, to ill hast thou me rendered.
>
> .   .   .   .   .
>
> In need of succour most when that I am,
>   . . . thou standest like one afraid,
> Alway most cold: and if one word be said,
> As in a dream, unperfect is the same.
>
> .   .   .   .   .
>
> And only doth my look declare my heart.

Shakespeare, however, defends his silence. He says it is better than words. By this he might perhaps imply that if you really love you do not write sonnets about it.

Sonnet 86

> Was it the proud full sail of his great verse,
> Bound for the prize of (all too precious) you,
> That did my ripe thoughts in my brain inhearse,
> Making their tomb the womb wherein they grew?
> Was it his spirit, by spirits taught to write,
> Above a mortal pitch, that struck me dead?
> No, neither he, nor his compeers by night

Giving him aid, my verse astonished.
He nor that affable familiar ghost
Which nightly gulls him with intelligence,
As victors of my silence cannot boast,
I was not sick of any fear from thence.
But when your countenance filled up his line,
Then lacked I matter, that enfeebled mine.

This sonnet has been taken to refer to Chapman's *Shadow of Night*, which *Love's Labours Lost* has also been said to parody. It was first published in 1594 but might have been in circulation before that date. The sonnet seems to have some particular reference, and the particulars seem to fit Chapman better than any other poet. But it may parody something that I have missed. In any case if it does refer to him, it is a parody of a mystical experience that Shakespeare was out of sympathy with, and does not necessarily imply animosity or a sense of his being a rival.

Sonnet 87 begins a series on the poet out of favour with his friend, yet determined to go on loving him. We have already met this situation in the sonnets of both Shakespeare and of sonneteers generally. Sonnet 87 parodies Sidney's LXIX, which however, expresses an ecstasy of love :

Oh joy, too high for my love still to show,
Oh bliss, fit for a nobler seat than me,
Envy put out thine eyes, lest thou do see
What oceans of delight, in me doth flow.
My friend that oft saw'st through all masks, my woe,
Come, come, and let me pour myself in thee :
Gone is the winter of my misery.
My spring appears, lo see what here doth grow,
For Stella hath with words (where faith doth shine)
Of her high heart given me the monarchy :
And Io, I may say that she is mine.
And though she give but this conditionally,
This realm of bliss, while virtues course I take;
No kings be crowned, but they some covenant make.

This rings with joy; it is like an epithalamion. The lady is far

above the poet's deserts, 'fit for a nobler seat'. He tells envy to
put out its eyes so that it will not see the delight that flows in
him. He then says that his 'friend' saw his woe and gave
herself. So he asks her to come and let him pour himself into
her; his winter of misery has gone. He ends by saying Stella has
made him monarch of her heart, given this realm of bliss on
condition; the king is not crowned yet but the covenant is
made.

Here is Shakespeare :

Sonnet 87

> Farewell thou art too dear for my possessing,
> And like enough thou know'st thy estimate,
> The charter of thy worth gives thee releasing:
> My bonds in thee are all determinate.
> For how do I hold thee but by thy granting,
> And for that riches where is my deserving?
> The cause of this fair gift in me is wanting,
> And so my patent back again is swerving.
> Thyself thou gav'st, thy own worth then not knowing,
> Or me to whom thou gav'st it, else mistaking,
> So thy great gift upon misprision growing,
> Comes home again, on better judgement making.
> Thus have I had thee as a dream doth flatter,
> In sleep a king, but waking no such matter.

Shakespeare like Sidney writes with a singing tune. We might
say it is a marriage music but with a feminine rhyme which
adds a plaintive note, and this in itself makes part of the
parody. He follows Sidney's statement point by point. Both
have a legal contract or covenant. Both are in some way
undeserving and dependent on the will of their love. But the
situations have worked out differently. It is as if Shakespeare
had retorted to Sidney, 'My experience is quite different'.
Sidney begins, 'Oh joy'; his love has given herself although she
is 'too high', 'fit for a nobler seat'. Shakespeare begins, 'Farewell'; his friend is 'too dear', 'And,' he adds cynically, 'like
enough' he knows his estimate. All Sidney need fear is envy.
With Shakespeare it was a matter not of giving, but of the law,
and the charter of his friend's worth allows him to break the

bond. Whereas Stella gave herself because Sidney was sad, and all he has to do is to give himself in return and rejoice, Shakespeare's lack of desert leads to his friend ending the contract. Sidney is made rich by Stella. Shakespeare's friend 'on better judgement' takes his gift back. Finally, where Sidney has been made monarch of Stella's heart, with every hope that he will not forfeit the contract (as Shakespeare did) and that he will be crowned king, Shakespeare was a king only in a dream, on 'waking no such matter'.

Although the parody of Sidney's sonnet is close, we can detect suggestions from other sonnets. Possibly Watson's *Centurie of Love* may have contributed something, for in **LX** we find :

> Love is the lord and signor of my will,
> How shall I then dispose of any deed?
> By forced bond, he holds my freedom still.

Here is a suggestion for 'My bonds in thee are all determinate'. Wyatt has sonnets of farewell. No. **XC** of Tottel begins very like Shakespeare's sonnet :

> Farewell, love, and all thy laws for ever.

Wyatt's love's rejection of him taught him that the pursuit of it was not worth it. It is the friend who discovers this in Shakespeare's situation. Sonnet **XLII** of Tottel might conceivably have suggested the dream, with its ending,

> Such mocks of dreams do turn to deadly pain.

There is perhaps also a possible suggestion from Constable's second decade, sonnet **I** where he says,

> too much worth hath made thee too much coy.

Sonnet 88

> When thou shalt be disposed to set me light,
> And place my merit in the eye of scorn,

Upon thy side, against myself I'll fight,
And prove thee virtuous, though thou art forsworn:
With mine own weakness being best acquainted,
Upon thy part I can set down a story
Of faults concealed, wherein I am attainted:
That thou in losing me, shalt win much glory:
And I by this will be a gainer too,
For bending all my loving thoughts on thee,
The injuries that to myself I do,
Doing thee vantage, double vantage me.
Such is my love, to thee I so belong,
That for thy right, myself will bear all wrong.

We have seen Shakespeare adopt this typical sonnet pose before. Here he brings it to an absurd extreme. In order to 'vantage' his friend he will say that whatever he scorns him for is true. So he himself will have a double advantage, since he so loves his friend, so belongs to him, is so identified with him, that he will bear any wrong that sets him right. It is important to note that Shakespeare has not said he did anything to merit scorn, for the sonnet has been taken to prove that he did. His friend is 'forsworn', and Shakespeare says he will 'set down a story' to justify him.

Daniel's sonnet VII may have suggested the first line of this sonnet. It begins,

Oh had she not been fair and thus unkind,
Then had no finger pointed at my lightness.

Shakespeare says his friend sets him light. Daniel continues to explain,

Then had no censor's eye these lines surveyed,
Nor graver brows have judged my muse so vain;
No sun my blush and error had bewrayed,
Nor yet the world had heard of such disdain.

This may be the origin of Shakespeare's whole trouble, why his merit is placed 'in the eye of scorn'. In other words, his sonnet may be a parody of this. But Constable also may have contributed something to the taking over of suffering that is his friend's fault. In sonnet VIII of the first decade he blames himself:

> That my own folly did procure my pain,
> Then shall I say to give myself content,
> Obedience only made me love in vain.

In the first sonnet of decade 3 he asks sickness to leave his love and let him bear her suffering:

> Harbour thou in me:
> Whom love long since hath taught to suffer pain
> So she which hath so oft my pain increased,
> .   .   .   .   .
> By my poor pain, might have her pain released.

Shakespeare has concentrated all this love-play into a real life situation, which is psychologically incredible.

Sonnet 89

> Say that thou didst forsake me for some fault,
> And I will comment upon that offence,
> Speak of my lameness, and I straight will halt:
> Against thy reasons making no defence.
> Thou canst not (love) disgrace me half so ill,
> To set a form upon desired change,
> As I'll myself disgrace, knowing thy will,
> I will acquaintance strangle and look strange:
> Be absent from thy walks and in my tongue,
> Thy sweet beloved name no more shall dwell,
> Lest I (too much profane) should do it wrong:
> And haply of our old acquaintance tell.
> For thee, against myself I'll vow debate,
> For I must ne'er love him whom thou dost hate.

Shakespeare makes the theme of the previous sonnet even more ridiculous here for he says he will act out any fault his friend has accused him of and quarrelled over. If his friend says he is lame, he will halt, or do anything else that does not really belong to him, all for the fantasy that if his friend hates him, then he must hate himself. And he will avoid him and not even mention his name for fear of bringing disgrace on him.

Sonnet 90

> Then hate me when thou wilt, if ever, now,
> Now while the world is bent my deeds to cross,
> Join with the spite of fortune, make me bow,
> And do not drop in for an after loss:
> Ah do not, when my heart hath 'scaped this sorrow,
> Come in the rearward of a conquered woe,
> Give not a windy night a rainy morrow,
> To linger out a purposed overthrow.
> If thou wilt leave me, do not leave me last,
> When other petty griefs have done their spite,
> But in the onset come, so shall I taste
> At first the very worst of fortune's might.
> And other strains of woe, which now seem woe,
> Compared with loss of thee, will not seem so.

This sonnet ends the section. It begins with the conclusion of 89, 'For I must ne'er love him whom thou dost hate.' Since you must hate me, it says, do it now, add your hate to what I already suffer. Do not wait till that is over and make your hate an 'after loss'. If you do as I ask, the other woes will seem light in comparison. This reads like a parody, but I have not found the original.

Sonnet 91 begins a new group where the couplet presents a contradiction which is resolved in the next sonnet, that in its turn ends with a contradiction, and so on. They parody a selection of Sidney's.

In sonnet XXIII Sidney says he is suspected of all sorts of obsessions such as politics and personal ambitions but all his

> thoughts have neither stop nor start,
> But only Stella's eyes, and Stella's heart.

In the next he continues that fools who pursue such things as wealth have some sense, but the richest fool whose only wealth lies in his love, if he loses it, is rich only in his folly. Shakespeare writes,

Sonnet 91

Some glory in their birth, some in their skill,
Some in their wealth, some in their body's force,
Some in their garments though new-fangled ill:
Some in their hawks and hounds, some in their horse.
And every humour hath his adjunct pleasure,
Wherein it finds a joy above the rest,
But these particulars are not my measure,
All these I better in one general best.
Thy love is bitter than high birth to me,
Richer than wealth, prouder than garments' cost,
Of more delight than hawks and horses be:
And having thee, of all men's pride I boast.
Wretched in this alone, that thou mayst take,
All this away, and me most wretched make.

'Bitter' in line 9 is of course a misprint for 'better'. The sonnet states Sidney's theme in terms of an extraverted life. Shakespeare says he has everything he could boast of except for the fear of what Sidney says leaves one rich in folly. In sonnet 92 he proves it not folly since even if his friend did steal himself away, as this would kill him there is nothing to fear. But then he adds the contradiction in the couplet.

Sonnet 92

But do thy worst to steal thyself away,
For term of life thou art assured mine,
And life no longer than thy love will stay,
For it depends upon that love of thine.
Then need I not to fear the worst of wrongs,
When in the least of them my life hath end,
I see, a better state to me belongs
Than that, which on thy humour doth depend.
Thou canst not vex me with inconstant mind,
Since that my life on thy revolt doth lie,
Oh what a happy title do I find,
Happy to have thy love, happy to die!
But what's so blessed fair that fears no blot,
Thou mayst be false, and yet I know it not.

The final couplet may be suggested by Sidney's sonnet LXVII, where he says he hopes Stella is true and does not flatter him, but unlike Shakespeare he ends that if Stella does deceive,

> I am resolved thy error to maintain :
> Rather than by more truth to get more pain.

In sonnet 93 Shakespeare gives pseudo-serious thought to this situation of his friend looking as if he loved, but actually deceiving :

Sonnet 93

> So shall I live, supposing thou art true,
> Like a deceived husband so love's face,
> May still seem love to me, though altered new :
> Thy looks with me, thy heart in other place.
> For there can live no hatred in thine eye,
> Therefore in that I cannot know thy change,
> In many's looks, the false heart's history
> Is writ in moods and frowns and wrinkles strange.
> But heaven in thy creation did decree,
> That in thy face sweet love should ever dwell,
> Whate'er thy thoughts, or thy heart's workings be,
> Thy looks should nothing thence, but sweetness tell.
> How like Eve's apple doth thy beauty grow,
> If thy sweet virtue answer not thy show.

This parodies Sidney's sonnet XXV where he discusses the virtue that shines in Stella's face. He considers

> That virtue if it once meet with our eyes,
> Strange flames of love it in our souls would raise.

Consequently as this can be too much for our sight,

> Virtue of late with virtuous care to stir
> Love of himself, take Stella's shape, that he
> To mortal eyes might sweetly shine in her.
> It is most true, for since I did her see,
> Virtue's great beauty in her face I prove.

In sonnets 93 and 94 Shakespeare makes great game of the idea in this sonnet. Since his friend has this virtue in his face, if he has hate in his heart, it will not be possible to discern it. Many people who are false show it in their face by their expression. But just as Stella's face was given this strange virtue, so heaven gave it to Shakespeare's friend at his creation. Sweet love dwells in his face whatever his thoughts or feelings. Its expression does not change whatever he thinks. Then in the couplet he adds but if his thoughts and feelings have not this 'sweet virtue' also, then he is like a temptress.

The most heroic efforts have gone into making sense of sonnet 94. Understood as part of the parody we have been tracing it is not difficult, for it makes fun of Sidney's beautiful face created to express virtue so that everyone will fall in love with it. In that case, Shakespeare deduces, if the thoughts and feelings of the person whose it is do not influence or become visible in it, it is so to say, a detached face, a thing with the most profound significance in itself, but not related to the personality behind it. He is interested in what it must be like to be that person.

Sonnet 94

> They that have power to hurt, and will do none,
> That do not do the thing, they most do show,
> Who moving others, are themselves as stone,
> Unmoved, cold, and to temptation slow:
> They rightly do inherit heaven's graces,
> And husband nature's riches from expense,
> They are the lords and owners of their faces,
> Others, but stewards of their excellence:
> The summer's flower is to the summer sweet,
> Though to itself, it only live and die,
> But if that flower with base infection meet,
> The basest weed outbraves his dignity:
> For sweetest things turn sourest by their deeds,
> Lilies that fester, smell far worse than weeds.

We can interpret thus : Those who have power to hurt like the sonnet lady and Shakespeare's friend, but who neither do so,

nor act out the virtue they show in their face, who only move
others by their beauty, but behind it have no feelings, no
temptations, are quite right to look the virtue that heaven gave
them and keep it safe. They can be said to own their faces, in
contrast with other people who, if they act virtuously, can do
so only as agents or stewards of excellence. This beautiful face
is like a flower, sweet although it has no other significance than
its beauty. Then turning to the opposite, to end his sonnet,
Shakespeare adds that if behind the lovely face there is evil, it
is 'far worse' than that of one who does not carry this beauty.

Shakespeare has combined his parody of Sidney with that of
another poet, whom I shall discuss later, John Davies of Hereford. Sonnet XXIX among those 'In praise of Poesie' in his
Wittes Pilgrimage goes thus:

> They that have skill to keep, and nourish bees
> Do hold that hives wherein most noise they make
> To be the best, or with them best agrees
> Who, to the same, most honied riches rake:
> But they that have the charge of human swarms:
> Do hold them happiest when they quietest be:
> And furthest off from uproars, and alarms,
> As having honied sufficiency!
> Sufficiency, the nurse of rest, and peace:
> For excess breeds excess of sin, and shame:
> And sin, and shame do wars, and woes increase:
> Where wasps make honied rich's spoil, their game:
> Then, in our treble hives of treble realms,
> We want no peace, because we want extremes.

Davies says that human beings are unlike bees in that the
quieter they are and the less they run to extremes the better.
Shakespeare makes fun by agreeing that human beings are best
if they do not do the harm they could, if they remain 'Unmoved
cold and to temptation slow'. Then they 'nourish heaven's
riches' as the bees their 'honied riches', and their 'summer's
flower is to the summer sweet', also a matter of interest to bees.
In other words he is saying the less you do, the less harm you
do. This combines well with the virtue of faces that remain
unmoved no matter what lies behind them. The two confirm
each other to make a parody doubly loaded. We can be sure

that the resemblance of Davies's sonnet is not just coincidence since their similar openings could not be a matter of chance. Not only are the shapes of the sentences the same, both have 'skill' or its near synonym 'power'—'skill to keep' and 'power to hurt'. Both 'do' or 'do not'.

The next sonnet works out the situation of the infected rose.

Sonnet 95

> How sweet and lovely dost thou make the shame,
> Which like a canker in the fragrant rose,
> Doth spot the beauty of thy budding name?
> Oh in what sweets dost thou thy sins enclose!
> That tongue that tells the story of thy days,
> (Making lascivious comments on thy sport)
> Cannot dispraise, but in a kind of praise,
> Naming thy name, blesses an ill report.
> Oh what a mansion have those vices got,
> Which for their habitation chose out thee,
> Where beauty's veil doth cover every blot,
> And all things turns to fair, that eyes can see!
> Take heed (dear heart) of this large privilege,
> The hardest knife ill used doth lose his edge.

Here Shakespeare is still parodying Sidney. If virtue chooses to create a beautiful face to dwell in, then vice must choose the body that is its mansion too. He begins with the situation introduced at the end of the last sonnet. The rose quality of his friend makes the sins enclosed within his beauty sweet. Those who talk lasciviously of him cannot help praising although they are discussing his evil qualities. What a beautiful mansion evil has chosen in him! It turns everything 'to fair'. Having thus disproved the criticism with which he ended sonnet 94, Shakespeare offers another caution. Take heed, he says; if his friend trades on his beauty to veil his vices, he may find it loses its power like a knife which, even if of the hardest steel, when not reserved for cutting what it was made for, will have its edge destroyed.

Sonnet 96

> Some say thy fault is youth, some wantonness,
> Some say thy grace is youth and gentle sport,
> Both grace and faults are loved of more and less:
> Thou mak'st faults graces, that to thee resort:
> As on the finger of a throned queen,
> The basest jewel will be well esteemed:
> So are those errors that in thee are seen,
> To truths translated, and for true things deemed.
> How many lambs might the stern wolf betray,
> If like a lamb he could his looks translate.
> How many gazers mightst thou lead away,
> If thou wouldst use the strength of all thy state?
> But do not so, I love thee in such sort,
> As thou being mine, mine is thy good report.

As this is the last sonnet in the series, Shakespeare has given it a different structure. It begins, as we expect, with the fault excused. The contradiction occurs with the opening of the sestet; his friend's lamb-look, which a wolf lacks, could lead many astray if he used his beauty in the service of his failings. The couplet resolves the problem by a plea that he will not misuse his beauty, since as love identifies them, their reputation is the same.

Sidney is still in Shakespeare's mind as he excuses his friend. In sonnet XXI Sidney said his friends

> me causely do blame
> My young mind marred whom love doth menace so :
> .   .   .   .   .   .
> That Plato I have read for nought, but if he tame
> Such coltish years; ...
> .   .   .   .   .
> If now the May of my years much decline,
> What can be hoped my harvest time will be.

Some say this of Shakespeare's friend, that his fault is youth. And Daniel provides the excuses of the others. In sonnet V he tells us that

> Whilst youth and error led my wandering mind,
> And set my thoughts in heedless ways to range,

he met a goddess who 'turned' his 'sport into a heart's despair'. Hence the 'wantonness' or 'wandering . . . in heedless ways', and the 'gentle sport' that some others attribute to Shakespeare's friend.

Sonnets 97 and 98 make a complete break, unless an association of May lingered in Shakespeare's memory from Sidney's sonnet just quoted. They express the very common situation of the poet absent from his love in the mood of winter, although May all around him rejoices in spring and love. Here is a sample from Surrey's second poem in Tottel :

> The sweet season, that bud and bloom forth brings,
> With green hath clad the hill and eke the vale :
> The nightingale with feathers new she sings :
> The turtle to her make hath told her tale :
> Summer is come, for every spray now springs,
> The hart hath hung his old head on the pale :
> The buck in brake his winter coat he flings :
> The fishes float with new repaired scale :
> The adder all her slough away she slings :
> The swift swallow pursueth the flies small :
> The busy bee her honey now she mings :
> Winter is worn that was the flowers' bale :
> And thus I see among these pleasant things
> Each care decays, and yet my sorrow springs.

This has the song quality of Troubadour love, as old and as fresh as ever. Shakespeare civilises it, writing it out of a winter's mood in sonnet 97, and from the angle of summer in 98.

Sonnet 97

> How like a winter hath my absence been
> From thee, the pleasure of the fleeting year?
> What freezings have I felt, what dark days seen?
> What old December's bareness everywhere,
> And yet this time removed was summer's time,
> The teeming autumn big with rich increase,

Bearing the wanton burden of the prime,
Like widowed wombs after their lords' decease:
Yet this abundant issue seemed to me,
But hope of orphans, and unfathered fruit,
For summer and his pleasures wait on thee,
And thou away, the very birds are mute.
Or if they sing, 'tis with so dull a cheer,
That leaves look pale, dreading the winter's near.

Sonnet 98

From you have I been absent in the spring,
When proud pied April (dressed in all his trim)
Hath put a spirit of youth in everything:
That heavy Saturn laughed and leaped with him.
Yet nor the lays of birds, nor the sweet smell
Of different flowers in odour and in hue,
Could make me any summer's story tell:
Or from their proud lap pluck them where they grew:
Nor did I wonder at the lily's white,
Nor praise the deep vermilion in the rose,
They were but sweet, but figures of delight:
Drawn after you, you pattern of all those.
Yet seemed it winter still, and you away,
As with your shadow I with these did play.

The first line of sonnet 97 seems a memory of Sidney's 'Gone is the winter of my misery' in sonnet LXIX which Shakespeare has already parodied. But Watson's *Tears of Fancie* gives the real background. Sonnet XLVII begins a short series on Shakespeare's theme :

Behold dear mistress how each pleasant green,
Will now renew his summer's livery

and flowers 'will flourish'. But he alas in 'whose mourning mind'

The grafts of grief are only given to grow :
Cannot enjoy the spring which others find,
But still my will must wither all in woe.

Spring seems strange to him now. His

> winter's woe therefore can never cease.

In the next sonnet he says,

> The tender buds whom cold has long kept in,
> And winter's rage enforced to hide their head :
> Will spring and sprout as they do now begin,
> That everyone will joy to see them spread.
> But cold of care so nips my joys at root,
> There is no hope to recover what is lost :
>
>   .   .   .   .   .
>
> Needs must I fall, I fade both root and rind,
> My branches bow at blast of every wind.

Sonnet LI has the same imagery :

> Each tree did boast the wished spring time's pride.
>
>   .   .   .   .   .
>
> No tree whose branches did not bravely spring.
> No branch whereon a fine bird did not sit :
> No bird but did her shrill notes sweetly sing
>
>   .   .   .   .   .
>
> Trees, branches, birds, and songs were framed fair.
> Fit to allure frail mind to careless ease :
> But careful was my thought, yet in despair
> I dwelt.

And in the next sonnet he possibly contributed to Shakespeare's no. 98. It begins,

> Each creature joys Apollo's happy sight,

and ends with his lady as his glorious sun,

> That lights the world but shines to me in clouds.

This ancient classical theme of sadness while nature rejoices has travelled down through the sonnet tradition.

Shakespeare's second sonnet on this theme dances with the spirit of youth. It literally does so in his rhythm. It so dances that even the heavy god of melancholy, Saturn, must laugh and leap. Critics, more interested perhaps in trying to anchor Shakespeare's sonnets in incidents of his actual life than in listening to what he is saying, have tried to date the sonnet by Saturn, taking him to be a planet, and calculating in which years Saturn would shine brightly in the April sky. But the god Saturn is the relevant image in this context. It belongs with Watson's Apollo. And Shakespeare out-Apollos Apollo by making even Saturn rejoice. He makes him 'heavy' with the double meaning of being heavy in heart and heavy in body, and he is chosen as the least likely of all gods to be affected with the spirit of youth; but even he leaps for joy. There is nothing star-like in the imagery. But Shakespeare might also have in mind the other association of Saturn's age as the golden time of innocent and undiluted joy. Greville in sonnet XLIV explains:

> The golden age was when the world was young,
> Nature so rich as earth did need no sowing,
> Malice not known, the serpents had not stung.

He ends by saying that in the golden age 'Saturn ruled alone', but in this one every planet has its influence. Though this may have remained in Shakespeare's memory, the general sense of the sonnet seems to indicate the interpretation I have given. However, while I doubt if Shakespeare was thinking of the star Saturn, bright in the sky as leaping about, it may be fair to note that Barnes has a series of sonnets relating his love with the night sky by going through the successive stages of the zodiac. In sonnet XXIV we find,

> But when in May my world's bright fiery sun
> Had past in zodiac with his golden team.

But this is merely to indicate what time of year it was. Saturn is not involved.

As to the rest of Shakespeare's sonnet, Constable's decade I sonnet IX may be an influence. There Diana is said to make the roses red and the lilies pale.

> In brief, all flowers from her their virtue take;
> From her sweet breath, their sweet smells do proceed.

Similarly Shakespeare says that all flowers, different in odour and hue, have their quality from his friend. He particularises the rose and lily, but says his friend is the 'pattern' that all were 'Drawn' from. He concludes the Platonic situation that this expresses by saying that all the spring was like the shadow of his friend, reflecting him. This may echo Spenser's sonnet XXXV, where he says he loathes everything when absent from his love :

> All this world's glory seemeth vain to me,
> And all their shows but shadows saving she.

If there is one sonnet that makes the climax of Shakespeare's background for this sonnet it is Watson's XXVI of *The Passionate Centurie*. It gave Shakespeare his tune :

> When May is in his prime, and youthful spring
> Doth clothe the tree with leaves, and ground with flowers,
>
> .   .   .   .   .
>
> And lovely nature smiles, and nothing lours :
> Then Philomela most doth strain her breast.

Although Shakespeare does not refer to Philomel till sonnet 102, he adds the 'lays of birds' to the sweet smell and colours of the flowers that Constable suggests. It is the nightingale too that has the most memorable 'Summer's story'.

Sonnet 99 parodies Constable's sonnet IX of the first decade :

> My lady's presence makes the roses red,
> Because to see her lips, they blush for shame :
> The lily's leaves (for envy) pale became,
> And her white hands in them this envy bred.
> The marigold the leaves abroad doth spread,

Because the sun's, and her power is the same :
The violet of purple colour came,
Dyed in the blood she made my heart to shed.

This continues with the lines already quoted where he says the 'sweet smells of flowers proceed from her sweet breath'.
Here is Shakespeare :

Sonnet 99

The forward violet thus did I chide,
Sweet thief whence didst thou steal thy sweet that smells
If not from my love's breath, the purple pride,
Which on thy soft cheek for complexion dwells?
In my love's veins thou hast too grossly dyed,
The lily I condemned for thy hand,
And buds of marjoram had stol'n thy hair,
The roses fearfully on thorns did stand,
One blushing shame, another white despair:
A third nor red, nor white, had stol'n of both,
And to his robbery had annexed thy breath,
But for his theft in pride of all his growth
A vengeful canker eat him up to death.
More flowers I noted, yet I none could see,
But sweet, or colour it had stolen from thee.

This reflects Constable's sonnet closely. He created a flattering mythology about the flowers taking their qualities from his lady, the rose blushing for shame when it saw her lips, the lily pale with envy of her hands, the marigold spreading its leaves since its power is like that of his lady, and the violet dyed purple in the blood which she shed. In brief all flowers take their virtue from her, and smell with her breath. Shakespeare deduces that the flowers must be thieves. He begins with the violet, Constable's last one, and accuses it particularly of stealing its 'sweet that smells' from his love's breath, so mocking Constable's general statement about flowers, that immediately follows : 'From her sweet breath their sweet smells do proceed'. The double 'sweet' is parodied by being turned into a noun as 'thy sweet that smells'. He may intend two meanings for its petals being 'too grossly' dyed. Not only is the purple a grosser shade but the theft is too obvious to be missed. The lily is 'condemned' for its action in taking its colour from his friend's hands. Instead of the marigold that does not give an image for theft, 'marjoram' is substituted, which alliterates and has the same rhythm. The myth of the roses is geared to theft and made too fanciful. They all stand in fear because of their guilt. One blushes for shame, another is white with despair, not for envy, but because of the theft. A third has stolen both red and white and also his friend's breath. But for this outrageous theft a canker took vengeance and 'eat him up to death'. To complete the nonsense Shakespeare says he looked at other flowers but found that they too had all stolen their colour and their 'sweet' from his friend. With this mock amazement he ends.

We have enjoyed three spring-time, flowery sonnets as a relief from intricate wit. Now we return to it in sonnet 100 as if after a holiday.

Sonnet 100

> Where art thou muse that thou forget'st so long,
> To speak of that which gives thee all thy might?
> Spend'st thou thy fury on some worthless song,
> Darkening thy power to lend base subjects light.
> Return forgetful muse, and straight redeem,
> In gentle numbers time so idly spent,
> Sing to the ear that doth thy lays esteem,
> And gives thy pen both skill and argument.
> Rise resty muse, my love's sweet face survey,
> If time have any wrinkle graven there,
> If any, be a satire to decay,
> And make time's spoils despised everywhere.
> Give my love fame faster than time wastes life,
> So thou prevent'st his scythe, and crooked knife.

How pleasant it would be if we could feel justified in taking a glimpse into Shakespeare's actual life in the real world between sonnets 99 and 100, if we could say, here Shakespeare ended his sequence for a time, and after a gap began again with sonnet 100. But if so, Constable had certainly been there before him, and Sidney. In decade 7 sonnet II the former says he has fallen from the grace of the muse of all muses, which

one need not be told is his lady. So the muses that inspire verse
fly from him too. Shakespeare begins as if he had heard this, or
as if the same thing had happened to him, and asks where his
muse (his creative impulse) is that he has not written of his
muse (his friend) that gives it all its power. The difference is
significant. As with all sonneteers, the lady is the fount of
Constable's creative spirit or muse. It is quite otherwise with
the truthful Shakespeare. It is his creative impulse that makes
him write of his friend, and not vice versa. He asks this forgetful muse, meaning the muse that has forgotten his friend, to
return. One questions what he means by the 'worthless song'
which the muse of his creative impulse has been spending its
fury on. Presumably it is the three sonnets we have just been
considering, for we may remember that in his plays he appears
not much impressed by the pretty ditty that all this May-day .
stuff runs to. It is even likely that he wrote them to have this
'worthless song' to refer to, as part of his parody. Anyhow this
is only introductory to his theme which Joan Grundy[84] found
the spoor of, when she noted that 'skill and argument' in line 8
reflects 'love and skill' in Sidney's sonnet XV. Sidney refers to
sonneteers who have skill but lack Stella as

> You that do dictionary method bring
> Into your rhymes, running in rattling rows,
> You that old Petrarch's long deceased woes
> With new born sighs, and wit disguised sing,

and says they take 'wrong ways'. Skill is not enough; love also
is needed, so,

> if both for your love and skill you name,
> You seek to nurse at fullest breast of fame,
> Stella behold and then begin to write.

This is obviously what Shakespeare parodies. Just as Sidney
begins by illustrating sonnets that have only skill, so Shakespeare begins by regretting his muse spending its fury on his
'rhymes, running in rattling rows', which he has just composed
as 'worthless songs'. He therefore tells his 'forgetful muse' to
return and say what gives his pen both 'skill and argument'.

He urges his resty muse, therefore to look at his 'love's sweet face'. One interpretation of 'resty' is 'restive', as of a horse, perhaps a Parnassian steed, that of the poet seeking fame, and as he has just referred to its 'fury', this would seem to fit. His creativeness is impatient, it has been writing worthless songs, so it is urged, after Sidney's, to look at the other element than skill, necessary to fame. Having dealt with skill, he now investigates this other, his 'love's sweet face'. Unfortunately it has wrinkles. This must seem like a satire on the poet's theme, for that is to immortalise his love's beauty. Wrinkles present themselves as the real truth about time. In fact they may be called time's spoils, despised everywhere—a deplorable situation from the poet's angle. But he quickly turns away and ends with an urgent and ironic expression of his aim as a poet:

> Give my love fame faster than time wastes life,
> So thou prevent'st his scythe, and crooked knife.

I take it 'prevent' has the double meaning which includes its original sense of getting there first. The last line mocks the dignity of time's scythe with his 'crooked knife'.

Sonnet 101 links the two previous ones, that perhaps need their coherence made obvious. It certainly makes clear that we are not to think there is a gap between sonnets 99 and 100.

Sonnet 101

> O truant muse what shall be thy amends,
> For thy neglect of truth in beauty dyed?
> Both truth and beauty on my love depends:
> So dost thou too, and therein dignified:
> Make answer muse, wilt thou not haply say,
> Truth needs no colour with his colour fixed,
> Beauty no pencil, beauty's truth to lay:
> But best is best, if never intermixed.
> Because he needs no praise, wilt thou be dumb?
> Excuse not silence so, for it lies in thee,
> To make him much outlive a gilded tomb:
> And to be praised of ages yet to be.
> Then do thy office muse, I teach thee how,
> To make him seem long hence, as he shows now.

This sonnet besides uniting beauty and truth with the truant muse, (the three things discussed in the previous sonnet) echoes a number of other sonnets. It throws back to no. 54 where also beauty and truth are united. Here Shakespeare asks his muse what is its excuse for neglecting the truth that is dyed in beauty, as the flowers were in 99. Both beauty and truth depend on his friend, as so does his muse. The muse answers that truth has its colour fixed, perhaps as the colours of a regiment are, but also it does not derive its colour, as flowers have been said to do. Nor does beauty need to be related with truth by describing it. In answer Shakespeare replies that the poet should not therefore deduce that he need say nothing, as indeed he himself did in sonnet 83, where he said that those who describe his friend only bring a tomb not immortality. Here, however, he says his muse could make his friend outlive a gilded tomb. He orders it to do its office, and says he teaches it how to make his friend seem as he is now, to those who will live a long time hence.

The next sonnet also, links previous themes—that of 85 with 98, 100 and 101.

Sonnet 102

> My love is strengthened though more weak in seeming,
> I love not less, though less the show appear,
> That love is merchandised, whose rich esteeming,
> The owner's tongue doth publish everywhere.
> Our love was new, and then but in the spring,
> When I was wont to greet it with my lays,
> As Philomel in summer's front doth sing,
> And stops his pipe in growth of riper days:
> Not that the summer is less pleasant now
> Than when her mournful hymns did hush the night,
> But that wild music burdens every bough,
> And sweets grown common lose their dear delight.
> Therefore like her, I sometime hold my tongue:
> Because I would not dull you with my song.

This begins with a direct criticism of love that is 'merchandised', which 'The owner's tongue doth publish everywhere'. Shakespeare then shows that he himself has done precisely this in sonnets 97 to 99 like all the other sonneteers, and he uses the imagery of Philomel which belongs in the context they suggest. But, he says, our love was new then. It is not less now, however, than when Philomel sang mournfully. But he is tired of the sonneteers, whose 'music burdens every bough' and has become common. So he says he sometimes holds his tongue, suggesting that the other sonneteers never do, and ought to. He does not take his own advice, however, but proceeds to sonnet 103 with its not unrelated theme.

Sonnet 103

Alack what poverty my muse brings forth,
That having such a scope to show her pride,
The argument all bare is of more worth
Than when it hath my added praise beside.
Oh blame me not if I no more can write!
Look in your glass and there appears a face,
That over-goes my blunt invention quite,
Dulling my lines, and doing me disgrace.
Were it not sinful then striving to mend,
To mar the subject that before was well,
For to no other pass my verses tend,
Than of your graces and your gifts to tell.
And more, much more than in my verse can sit,
Your own glass shows you, when you look in it.

From Petrarch onwards this is a sonnet theme; no sonneteer feels he can do justice to his love's beauty. Watson in sonnet XXIV of *The Passionate Centurie* expresses amazement at the image in his lady's mirror, and this might be relevant. He addresses her glass,

I marvel how her beams that are so bright
Do never cause thy little sides to craze:
. . . . . .
For when she first with seeming stately grace
Bestowed on me a loving sweet regard,
The beams, which then proceeded from her face
Were such, as for the same I found no word.

Barnes is finally struck dumb by his lady's beauty, after writing one hundred and three sonnets, and says in his last, that he is

> with beauty's excellence unable
> To write, or bear, my pens, and books refuse,
> Thine endless graces are so amiable,
> Passing the spirit of mine humble muse,
> So that the more I write more graces rise
> Which mine astonished muse cannot comprise.

This seems in the spirit of Shakespeare's sonnet. Both poets are unable to write of their love's 'graces'.

Sonnet 104 has a fresh theme. It makes fun of the lover seeing youthful beauty in his lady even in her imagined old age. In an elegiac tune Shakespeare sings, 'To me fair friend you never can be old', 'as you were when first' I saw you, so 'seems your beauty still'. And then we learn that this was only three years ago.

Sonnet 104

> To me fair friend you never can be old,
> For as you were when first your eye I eyed,
> Such seems your beauty still: three winters cold,
> Have from the forests shook three summers' pride,
> Three beauteous springs to yellow autumn turned,
> In process of the seasons have I seen,
> Three April perfumes in three hot Junes burned,
> Since first I saw you fresh which yet are green.
> Ah yet doth beauty like a dial hand,
> Steal from his figure, and no pace perceived,
> So your sweet hue, which methinks still doth stand
> Hath motion, and mine eye may be deceived.
> For fear of which, hear this thou age unbred,
> Ere you were born was beauty's summer dead.

The idea of a three years' testing may have come from Daniel's sonnet XXVI, where he complains that his heart flew to the sanctuary of Delia's heart, but there she slew it, and

> My privilege of faith could not protect it,
> That was with blood and three years' witness signed.

Shakespeare stresses the three years by repeating it as if it had great significance, and sentimentalising its spring and summer. Then in the sestet he says he fears that since time's movement is imperceptible, he may be deceived. So he calls aggressively to future generations to note that 'beauty's summer' died before they were born. The phrase 'beauty's summer' seems to hold the whole experience of sonnet love, a life-span perhaps of three years.

Sonnet 105

> Let not my love be called idolatry,
> Nor my beloved as an idol show,
> Since all alike my songs and praises be
> To one, of one, still such, and ever so.
> Kind is my love to-day, to-morrow kind,
> Still constant in a wondrous excellence,
> Therefore my verse to constancy confined,
> One thing expressing, leaves out difference.
> Fair, kind, and true, is all my argument,
> Fair, kind, and true, varying to other words,
> And in this change is my invention spent,
> Three themes in one, which wondrous scope affords.
> Fair, kind, and true, have often lived alone.
> Which three till now, never kept seat in one.

This parodies two of Constable's sonnets, although Daniel and perhaps Spenser may be involved too. At first it seems a sonnet of unrelated bits. What have the 'songs and praises' being always 'to one', to do with making love an idol? Why this switching off onto love being kind and constant and the not having differences? Why the odd conclusion about three separate things living alone as a rule, but uniting in his friend and keeping seat in one? Constable provides the idol and the kindness with which the sonnet begins, in decade 4, no. IV. He says that 'she' to whom he prays is Mahomet, 'The iron idol that compassion wants', where 'wants' means 'lacks'. She is all gold except for her heart; 'Her face, limbs, flesh and all' are gold, although her heart is iron. Shakespeare protests, 'Let not my love be called idolatry' since his friend is not made of many things like gold and iron but of one, repeated three times. So

far from lacking compassion is he and having an iron heart
that he is 'kind'. This also is iterated thrice. He is kind today,
'tomorrow kind, Still constant', as he was 'one, of one, still
such, and ever so'. This echoes Constable's 'face, limbs, flesh
and all'. There is a tradition in the sonnets of having things in
threes, but Daniel's sonnet XI may have given Shakespeare his
tune for the octave, and be associated with Constable in his
mind, since it too has its idol, and its flinty heart:

> Tears, vows, and prayers win the hardest heart:
> Tears, vows, and prayers have I spent in vain;
> Tears, cannot soften flint, nor vows convert,
> Prayers prevail not with a quaint disdain.
> I lose my tears, where I have lost my love,
> I vow my faith, where faith is not regarded;
> I pray in vain, a merciless to move:
> So rare a faith ought better be rewarded.
> Yet though I cannot win her will with tears,
> Though my soul's idol scorneth all my vows;
> Though all my prayers be to so deaf ears:
> No favour though the cruel fair allows.
> Yet will I weep, vow, pray to cruel she;
> Flint, frost, disdain, wears, melts, and yields we see.

It is just possible that Shakespeare remembered Spenser's
sonnet XVIII, though by no means certain. He says he weeps,
wails and pleads in vain.

> Whiles she as steel and flint doth still remain.

Although it is clear enough that there is a tradition of threes
in sonnet-writing to be parodied, to see what Shakespeare is
doing we must go to the second sonnet of Constable, (decade 1,
sonnet X) which he parodies. Indeed it is his first target. Here
are the relevant lines:

> Heralds at arms do three perfections quote,
> To wit, most fair, most rich, most glittering:
> So when those three concur within one thing,
> Needs must that thing of honour be a note.

Shakespeare begins his sestet with, 'Fair, kind and true, is all my argument', which he repeats in the next line, saying it can vary 'to other words'; this refers to Constable, the first of whose triplets is 'fair', followed by 'other words'. Constable seems to be saying that their significance is much less when separate, but when they 'concur within one thing' 'that thing' is a 'note' of honour, or a sign of honour. Shakespeare has seized on this. In the octave he stressed that his verse expressed 'One thing' although he said so in threes. In the sestet he elaborates Constable's point from heraldry, which concerns social status, or signs of it. When fair, kind and true are separate, they have no importance; they live alone in separate little houses. But now for the first time they are one; so they have become noble and 'keep seat in one'. The phrase suggests keeping court. Only the main residence of a noble or important person is called his seat of residence. So Shakespeare's love must live in a great castle. But why stop there, he seems to suggest, for he now reminds us of his 'Three themes in one' stressed in the octave. He says this 'affords wondrous scope'. His friend, as he has already shown, has a trinity of oneness and of kindness, the opposite of an idol of gold with an iron heart, and unkindness. This can be relevant as an argument against his love being an idol only if the trinity has a theological significance, and this is suggested at the end of the sonnet by the reference to 'Three themes in one'. Three in one, when everyone had to be a member of the Church of England, would inevitably have suggested the Trinity. So we are told that Shakespeare's love cannot be an idol because he is ... And it just stops short of blasphemy. Parody could go no further.

Sonnet 106

> When in the chronicle of wasted time,
> I see descriptions of the fairest wights,
> And beauty making beautiful old rhyme,
> In praise of ladies dead, and lovely knights,
> Then in the blazon of sweet beauty's best,
> Of hand, of foot, of lip, of eye, of brow,
> I see their antique pen would have expressed,
> Even such a beauty as you master now.
> So all their praises are but prophecies

Of this our time, all you prefiguring,
And for they looked but with divining eyes,
They had not skill enough your worth to sing:
For we which now behold these present days,
Have eyes to wonder, but lack tongues to praise.

Shakespeare has been attempting to find words to praise his
friend, and indeed gone to extremes to do so, but he realises
that all those who attempt to express this wonder must 'lack
tongues to praise'. The sonnet reflects one of Constable's in
the Todd manuscript which opens,

> Miracle of the world I never will deny
> That former poets praise the beauty of their days
> But all those beauties were but figures of thy praise
> And all those poets did of thee but prophesy.

Then he says he learnt from her 'What Petrarch's Laura
meant'. 'His songs were hymns of thee'.

Sonnet 107

> Not mine own fears, nor the prophetic soul,
> Of the wide world, dreaming on things to come,
> Can yet the lease of my true love control,
> Supposed as forfeit to a confined doom.
> The mortal moon hath her eclipse endured,
> And the sad augurs mock their own presage,
> Incertainties now crown themselves assured,
> And peace proclaims olives of endless age.
> Now with the drops of this most balmy time,
> My love looks fresh, and death to me subscribes,
> Since spite of him I'll live in this poor rhyme,
> While he insults o'er dull and speechless tribes.
> And thou in this shalt find thy monument,
> When tyrants' crests and tombs of brass are spent.

In this and the following sonnets Shakespeare follows up the
classical theme he has returned to. He sets out to show that his
rhyme will be his friend's 'monument', when at length the
crests of tyrants and tombs of brass 'are spent'. In the first
quatrain, just as in sonnet 106 he thought of the antique,

K

perhaps medieval, world with its knights and ladies 'prefiguring' his friend, so he now, as it were, escalates his claim and looks on all prophecies of the future. He says that fears that his friend will die, and that he thus is doomed to a limited future are unfounded, that this fear does not control the 'lease' that his true love has of the whole world of the future. The second quatrain has been much discussed. Poets often called Queen Elizabeth 'the mortal moon', and this has been taken to refer to her. But other referents have been suggested by which to date the sonnet, and nothing has been agreed. Its place in the argument is to suggest that fearful prognostications do not always come true, for the mortal moon is no longer threatened and there is promise of peace. The sestet concludes that it therefore looks as if death has acknowledged that Shakespeare's rhymes will live, although it still brings oblivion to those dull ('dim' as we might say) people who are not poets. So he concludes that his friend will find his monument in his sonnets, and so live on. We in the twentieth century may agree that this has happened. But, as we have already seen, Shakespeare had a greater respect for what death and decay can do than to claim this conquest; also as a man not yet thought to be a giant, he was unlikely to make a serious claim of this sort for himself, while spurning everyone else as of the common herd. He is mocking the sonnet tradition, saying with irony that death subscribes to him. And this ironic intention is enough to account for the 'most balmy time' that he announces, a sort of second age of innocence when 'love looks fresh' and 'peace proclaims olives of endless age', the sort of time in which such a miracle might happen.

There is a verbal echo in this sonnet that should be noted, from Constable's decade 7, sonnet IV. 'The prophetic soul . . . dreaming on things to come' reflects 'yet when posterity in time to come'. Indeed the sonnet floats on a Constable-like inflation.

Sonnet 108

> What's in the brain that ink may character,
> Which hath not figured to thee my true spirit,
> What's new to speak, what now to register,
> That may express my love, or thy dear merit?

Nothing sweet boy, but yet like prayers divine,
I must each day say o'er the very same,
Counting no old thing old, thou mine, I thine,
Even as when first I hallowed thy fair name.
So that eternal love in love's fresh case,
Weighs not the dust and injury of age,
Nor gives to necessary wrinkles place,
But makes antiquity for aye his page,
Finding the first conceit of love there bred,
Where time and outward form would show it dead.

This is interesting coming after sonnet 105, for it too almost makes Shakespeare's friend God. He says that although he has nothing new to say, he goes on repeating his praise just as one repeats the Lord's prayer without change. So he goes on saying of his friend, 'hallowed be thy name'. No matter how often one says this, it retains its first significance. This 'eternal love' whose name one hallows, when it appears in each fresh instance of love in time, as Plato and Ovid confirms, does not respect the outward decay, the dust, injury and wrinkles of the individual copy, but makes the written page find its archetypal meaning where it first existed, in antiquity. This is true although in time and in its outward form or body the love as shadowed in each loved person dies.

Sonnet 109

Oh never say that I was false of heart,
Though absence seemed my flame to qualify,
As easy might I from myself depart,
As from my soul which in thy breast doth lie:
That is my home of love, if I have ranged,
Like him that travels I return again,
Just to the time, not with the time exchanged,
So that myself bring water for my stain,
Never believe though in my nature reigned,
All frailties that besiege all kinds of blood,
That it could so preposterously be stained,
To leave for nothing all thy sum of good:
For nothing this wide universe I call,
Save thou my rose, in it thou art my all.

This sonnet begins a new group on the faults of the lover, ending with no. 112. It starts by recalling ideas already expressed—the identity of the lovers, the image of the lover's heart dwelling in the loved one's breast, absence not diminishing love. The octave ends with the lover's faults or guilt. Shakespeare says he brings water to wash his 'stain', and this has been taken to refer to some actual fault. But surely in this context the reference is to his 'absence'. Indeed 'absence' seems to be used metaphorically in the sonnet sequence to indicate an unfeeling period or attitude quite as frequently as to refer to absence from the loved one's presence. The meanings often fuse, as in this sonnet which is making amends. It climaxes in the hyperbole of his love as the rose being the only thing of value in the universe.

Sonnets 110 and 111 have been taken to refer to Shakespeare as an actor. Dover Wilson[85] uses them as sufficient evidence 'for a particularly notorious i.e. popular exhibition of himself on the stage, shown in different noble houses as well as at Blackfriars ("here and there")'. On the contrary sonnet 110 is a palpable parody of Greville's sonnet LX, which has Sidney's XXVII as its background. Here is Sidney's:

> Because I oft in dark abstracted guise,
> Seem most alone in greatest company,
> With dearth of words, and answers quite awry,
> To them that would make naked speech arise;
> They deem, and of their doom the rumour flies,
> That poison foul of bubbling pride doth lie
> So in my swelling breast, that only I
> Faun on myself, all others do despise:
> Yet pride (I think) doth not my soul possess,
> (Which looks too oft in this unflattering glass)
> But one worse fault, ambition I confess,
> That makes me oft my best friends overpass,
> Unseen unheard, while thought to highest place
> Bends all his powers, even unto Stella's grace.

Sidney describes himself as an abstracted, introverted man, a bad mixer with no general conversation, inattentive, giving the impression, as shy people often do, that their social awkwardness or reserve is a deliberate pose expressing pride. He says, however, that it is not pride that makes him like this, but the worse fault of ambition. This makes him neglect his best friends, and keep himself aloof, since he gives all his energy to gaining the highest place there is, namely Stella's favour.

Greville in sonnet LX presents himself discussing a similar situation with Caelica. She has accused him of this fault, and he agrees, yes, "tis true':

> Caelica, you said, I do obscurely live,
> Strange to my friends, with strangers in suspect,
> For darkness doth suspicion ever give
> Of hate to men or too much self-respect;
> Fame, you do say, with many wings doth fly;
> Who leaves himself, you say, doth living die.
>
> Caelica, 'tis true I do in darkness go,
> Honour I seek not nor hunt after fame;
> I am thought-bound, I do not long to know,
> I feel within what men without me blame;
> I scorn the world, the world scorns me, 'tis true;
> What can a heart do more to honour you?
>
> Knowledge and fame in open hearts do live,
> Honour is pure heart's homage unto these;
> Affection all men unto beauty give,
> And by that law enjoined are to please;
> The world in two I have divided fit;
> Myself to you, and all the rest to it.

Greville's behaviour is the same as Sidney's. Both keep themselves apart, secret, in darkness; they behave strangely. This makes them suspect. But the truth is that they are obsessed by their lady.

Shakespeare parodies this by describing himself in opposite terms as the average man, the good mixer, socially adequate. He deals with it in mock solemnity and poetic abstractions. Although he probably has Sidney in mind, we can be sure that Greville is his target by his opening with the admission, "tis true', which like Greville he repeats later in the sonnet.

Sonnet 110

> Alas 'tis true, I have gone here and there,
> And made myself a motley to the view,
> Gored mine own thoughts, sold cheap what is most dear,
> Made old offences of affections new.
> Most true it is, that I have looked on truth
> Askance and strangely: but by all above,
> These blenches gave my heart another youth,
> And worse essays proved thee my best of love.
> Now all is done, have what shall have no end,
> Mine appetite I never more will grind
> On newer proof, to try an older friend,
> A god in love, to whom I am confined.
> Then give me welcome, next my heaven the best,
> Even to thy pure and most most loving breast.

Shakespeare apologises for not having kept himself secret and abstracted as the man in love should, thinking only of his friend. He has gadded about, played the fool as the social success often does. He has killed his own thoughts like a clumsy bull, behaved without integrity, given friendship easily, or sold it cheaply. He has fallen into new affections and behaved with all his old faults as a friend. Alternatively 'old' may mean common generally. He has looked at truth 'askance and strangely'. This he takes from both poets parodied. They have this strangeness in common. Shakespeare mocks by calling normal superficialities a strange way of treating truth. Then he adds, in the most unsonnet-like fashion that 'by all above' he has enjoyed this promiscuous fellowship, that it has given his heart another youth. In any case, the worst of his new friendships has proved his friend of the sonnets his 'best of love'. So he remains quite unrepentant. But with a sudden change, he renounces all that and offers his friend 'what shall have no end'. He promises no longer to sharpen his appetite or increase his desire for friendship by making new friends to try his old one. His old friend is his god, as already indicated in sonnets 105 and 108, and he is contained within this worship. Then he asks his friend to welcome him home from all these wanderings in the society of others (his metaphorical absence) by a pure and loving embrace.

All three sonnets give a picture of the poets acting a social role unacceptably and end by putting their love in a unique position as the one thing important in life. Shakespeare mocks by apologising for good social behaviour, which he has most shamelessly enjoyed and found refreshing, and he overtops all claims of the lovers by making his friend a god.

Sonnet 111 begins with the situation created in 110, of living an extroverted life in society, behaving in a friendly way with other people and not being obsessed by his friend. He now says what this has led him to.

Sonnet 111

> Oh for my sake do you with fortune chide,
> The guilty goddess of my harmful deeds,
> That did not better for my life provide,
> Than public means which public manners breeds.
> Thence comes it that my name receives a brand,
> And almost thence my nature is subdued
> To what it works in, like the dyer's hand,
> Pity me then, and wish I were renewed,
> Whilst like a willing patient I will drink,
> Potions of eisel 'gainst my strong infection,
> No bitterness that I will bitter think,
> Nor double penance to correct correction.
> Pity me then dear friend, and I assure ye,
> Even that your pity is enough to cure me.

Shakespeare asks his friend to scold fortune, as responsible for his manners being socially conditioned, for his social habits do not reflect his real nature. But if his friend will pity him, he will do anything or suffer anything to cure himself of his 'infection'. He ends with the common refrain that if his friend pities him this will cure him, which we could say shows his hand dyed in the sonnet medium.

Greville's sonnet XLIII gives background to this and the next sonnet :

> Caelica, when you look down into your heart,
> And see what wrongs my faith endureth there,
> Hearing the groans of true love, loathe to part,

> You think they witness of your changes bear.
> And as the man that by ill neighbours dwells,
> Whose curious eyes discern these works of shame,
> Which busy rumour to the people tells,
> Suffers for seeing those dark springs of fame.

Greville puts the blame into Caelica's heart. Living in this environment of shame and scandal has led to his faults. This may have given Shakespeare his theme of 'nature subdued by what it works in'; Greville being in his lady's heart might have suggested its red dye. It may be some justification for this guess, or at least it confirms that Greville was in his mind, that Shakespeare comments on 'busy rumour' in his next sonnet, or as he calls it 'vulgar scandal'.

Sonnet 112

> Your love and pity doth the impression fill,
> Which vulgar scandal stamped upon my brow,
> For what care I who calls me well or ill,
> So you o'er-green my bad, my good allow?
> You are my all the world, and I must strive,
> To know my shames and praises from your tongue,
> None else to me, nor I to none alive,
> That my steeled sense or changes right or wrong,
> In so profound abysm I throw all care
> Of others' voices, that my adder's sense,
> To critic and to flatterer stopped are:
> Mark how with my neglect I do dispense.
> You are so strongly in my purpose bred,
> That all the world besides me thinks ye are dead.

This carries on directly from the previous sonnet. The pity that cured the poet now fills the impression that scandal stamped on his brow. It is 'vulgar' because public, that of the people, one's neighbours. But since his friend is all his world, he will value only his judgement of the situation. Lines 7 and 8 are difficult to paraphrase in detail, but the general sense is that no one else's opinion matters, nor does Shakespeare matter to anyone else alive. This may mean that he matters only to his friend whom everyone else thinks dead. Thus his feeling is steeled against criticism, whether it changes to right or wrong, for or against. His acutest hearing is stopped against the voices of others whether they criticise or flatter. Notice, he says, how he dispenses with, or liquidates neglect of himself. The couplet is difficult. It has been suggested that the last line is a misprint for 'That all the world besides methinks are dead'. But this fails to respect a reference to 'none alive' in line 7, and it still leaves the problem of his friend being 'bred' in his purpose, which gives the basis for the deduction in the last line. If we take the last line as printed, we could paraphrase that his friend owes his existence so strongly to being bred in Shakespeare's purpose, which is parody, that everyone besides himself thinks he is dead, or does not exist. This ties in with contrasting his friend with 'none alive' earlier in the sonnet.

The next sonnet makes game of a very common sonnet conceit.

Sonnet 113

> Since I left you, mine eye is in my mind,
> And that which governs me to go about,
> Doth part his function, and is partly blind,
> Seems seeing, but effectually is out:
> For it no form delivers to the heart
> Of bird, of flower, or shape which it doth lack,
> Of his quick objects hath the mind no part,
> Nor his own vision holds what it doth catch:
> For if it see the rud'st or gentlest sight,
> The most sweet-favour or deformedst creature,
> The mountain, or the sea, the day, or night:
> The crow, or dove, it shapes them to your feature.
> Incapable of more replete, with you,
> My most true mind thus maketh mine untrue.

It is easy to find illustrations of poets making everything they see relevant to their love. Sidney in a sonnet printed as Constable's decade 3, sonnet VIII says

> in each thing whereto my eye doth range,
> Part of my pain meseems engraved lies.

Thus the rocks show his lady's 'hard refusal', the woods seem to darken his sun

And stately hills disdain to look so low.

So on he goes till he sums up with,

> Rocks, woods, hills, caves, dales, meads, brooks answer
> me,
> Infected minds infect each thing they see.

This may have contributed to the sonnet. So may Spenser's LXXVIII. He says that he goes 'from place to place' trying to find where last he saw his love's face, but cannot find it anywhere,

> Yet field and bower are full of her aspect,
> But when mine eyes I thereunto direct,
> They idly back to me return again,
> And when I hope to see their true object,
> I find myself but fed with fancies vain.
> Cease then mine eyes, to seek herself to see,
> And let my thoughts behold herself in me.

Similarly Shakespeare expresses concern that his mind is too full of his friend to see the 'true object', or as he has it 'quick objects', thus his mind makes itself 'untrue'. Nor does he find that bird or flower gives his heart what it lacks, any more than it gives Spenser what he seeks. The epithet for objects in the real world as 'quick' seems to confirm the contrast I suggested for the last sonnet, of all Shakespeare's interests lying in his friend who does not exist or is 'dead', to the exclusion of what is alive or 'quick'.

Sonnet 114

> Or whether doth my mind being crowned with you
> Drink up the monarch's plague this flattery?
> Or whether shall I say mine eye saith true,
> And that your love taught it this alchemy?
> To make of monsters, and things indigest,
> Such cherubins as your sweet self resemble,
> Creating every bad a perfect best
> As fast as objects to his beams assemble:

Oh tis the first, 'tis flattery in my seeing,
And my great mind most kingly drinks it up,
Mine eye well knows what with his gust is 'greeing,
And to his palate doth prepare the cup.
If it be poisoned, 'tis the lesser sin,
That mine eye loves it and doth first begin.

Here Shakespeare comments on the experience described in the previous sonnet. He likens his mind to a monarch whom his friend has crowned, and asks whether this seeing everything in terms of him is flattery and therefore a false vision, or should he say that his friend taught him how to transform these base metals to gold, making monsters and things not easy to accept resemble him, so that even bad 'objects' become perfect in his beams. He concludes it is flattery and he drinks it all up. His eye, knowing what he likes, provides it to prepare a welcome cup. If it is false, and so poisoned, that would make the sin of his falsehood the lesser, since he could say that his eye deceived him, and not he himself.

The suggestion from this sonnet comes from Constable's first decade, sonnet VIII :

Falsely doth envy of your praises blame
My tongue, my pen, my heart of flattery
Because I said there was no sun but thee,
It called my tongue the partial trump of fame;
And saith my pen hath flatteréd thy name,
Because my pen did to my tongue agree;
And that my heart must needs a flatterer be,
Which taught both tongue and pen to say the same.
No, no, I flatter not, when thee I call
The sun, sith that the sun was never such :
But when the sun thee I compared withal,
Doubtless the sun I flatteréd too much.
Witness mine eyes I say the truth in this :
They have seen thee, and know that so it is.

Shakespeare gives pseudo-serious consideration to this, but it is monsters that he says are like his friend. This is all the greater compliment of course, as the alchemy is then the greater wonder; why be content with just the sun? He comes to a different conclusion from Constable; he thinks it better to assume that what has happened is flattery. Constable ends by calling his eyes to witness it is true. Shakespeare says on the contrary that it was his eyes that began the falsehood.

Sonnet 115

> Those lines that I before have writ do lie,
> Even those that said I could not love you dearer,
> Yet then my judgment knew no reason why,
> My most full flame should afterwards burn clearer,
> But reckoning time, whose millioned accidents
> Creep in 'twixt vows, and change decrees of kings,
> Tan sacred beauty, blunt the sharp'st intents,
> Divert strong minds to the course of altering things:
> Alas why fearing of time's tyranny,
> Might I not then say now I love you best,
> When I was certain o'er incertainty,
> Crowning the present, doubting of the rest:
> Love is a babe, then might I not say so
> To give full growth to that which still doth grow.

Shakespeare says that he lied when he said he could not love his friend better. In a world where millions of unforeseen happenings ('accidents') change even the decrees of kings (which is the state he assumed in the previous sonnet) he asks why he should fear to say he now loves his friend better. Of course no sonneteer fears to do this, but he is pointing out a flaw in the usual assumption, of which we might take Watson's sonnet LXXVII of *The Centurie of Love* as an example:

> Time doth consume fame, honour, wit and strength.
> Time kills the greenest herb and sweetest flowers,

and so on it goes, ending,

> And yet no time prevails in my behoof,
> Nor any time can make me cease to love.

Shakespeare sees a snag in this. Translated into human terms where people have 'strong minds' and make vows and yet change, not only must time's tyranny be acknowledged in general; if an exception is made of love, this cuts out possibility of development as well as of change; if love is to be allowed to increase such lines will have to be unsaid.

Sonnet 116

> Let me not to the marriage of true minds
> Admit impediments, love is not love
> Which alters when it alteration finds,
> Or bends with the remover to remove.
> Oh no, it is an ever fixed mark
> That looks on tempests and is never shaken;
> It is the star to every wandering bark,
> Whose worth's unknown, although his height be taken.
> Love's not time's fool, though rosy lips and cheeks
> Within his bending sickle's compass come,
> Love alters not with his brief hours and weeks,
> But bears it out even to the edge of doom:
> If this be error and upon me proved,
> I never writ, nor no man ever loved.

Taken seriously this sonnet has given many readers a moving experience. It is perfectly said. But not only is the tone sarcastic, the form of the sentences suggests doubt. It begins with the church declaration of marriage banns, where anyone who knows 'just cause or impediment' is asked to come forward now and say so. Shakespeare takes the position of one considering the matter, who is not going to admit impediment. 'Let me not' is the opening of the debater making a point. The first point is that love which alters 'when it alteration finds' is not love. This is a backhanded admission that some love does alter. 'Oh no,' Shakespeare continues. The words imply that he has been contradicted, or envisages a contradiction. But he asserts emphatically that love is an 'ever-fixed mark' like a lighthouse steady in tempest, or the lodestar, whose value is mysterious beyond knowledge, although mathematicians calculate its height. 'Love is not time's fool' he emphasises, perhaps implying that someone has said it is. Love lasts till the day of judgement. Shakespeare seems to be protesting too much. Then finally, on any reading the couplet makes one feel uneasy about its sincerity. It is a trite commonplace.

Let me now look at Shakespeare's evidence. Spenser's sonnet XXXIV is very much to the point:

> Like as a ship that through the ocean wide,
> By conduct of some star doth make her way.
> When as a storm hath dimmed her trusty guide.
> Out of her course doth wander far astray:
> So I whose star, that wont with her bright ray,
> Me to direct, with clouds is overcast,
> Do wander now in darkness and dismay,
> Through hidden perils round about me plast.
> Yet hope I well, that when this storm is past
> My Helice the lodestar of my life
> Will shine again, and look on me at last,
> With lovely light to clear my cloudy grief,
> Till then I wander careful comfortless,
> In secret sorrow and sad pensiveness.

With this in mind Shakespeare can support himself in doubt. 'Oh no, love is this star, this light in the storm.'
Greville in sonnet LXXXVI says:

> Love is the peace whereto all thoughts do strive,
> Done and begun with all our powers in one;
> The first and last in us that is alive,
> End of the good and therewith pleased alone.
>
> .　　.　　.　　.　　.　　.
>
> Constant, because it sees no cause to vary,
> A quintessence of passions overthrown,
> Raised above all that change of objects carry,
> A nature by no other nature known;
> For glory's of eternity a frame,
> That by all bodies else obscures her name.

Oh no, love is this fixed mark, 'whereto all thoughts do strive'. Here is love with 'no cause to vary', 'End of the good', the moral philosopher's goal. Or Shakespeare may find support in

Surrey, who makes an impassioned statement in sonnet XII of
Tottel :

> Set me whereas the sun doth parch the green,
> Or where his beams do not dissolve the ice :
> In temperate heat where he is felt and seen :
> In presence pressed of people mad or wise.
> Set me in high, or yet in low degree :
> In longest night, or in the shortest day :
> In clearest sky, or where clouds thickest be :
> In lusty youth, or when my hairs are gray.
> Set me in heaven, in earth, or else in hell,
> In hill, or dale, or in the foaming flood :
> Thrall, or at large, alive where so I dwell :
> Hers will I be, and only with this thought
> Content myself, although my chance be nought.

All sonneteers illustrate this constancy in one form or another,
no matter what they suffer from the disdain and discourage-
ment they receive. And even if we remember such apostate
sonneteers as Wyatt, we can say he made himself notorious
merely by 'altering' because of his lady's attitude.

What we could call 'external' proof of the ironic character
of Shakespeare's sonnet can be seen in that not only the one
immediately preceeding, but the series of sonnets immediately
following, present love as far from being fixed and constant.
That this sonnet appears precisely in this place suggests irony.

Sonnet 117

> Accuse me thus, that I have scanted all,
> Wherein I should your great deserts repay,
> Forgot upon your dearest love to call,
> Whereto all bonds do tie me day by day,
> That I have frequent been with unknown minds,
> And given to time your own dear purchased right,
> That I have hoisted sail to all the winds
> Which should transport me farthest from your sight.
> Book both my wilfulness and errors down,
> And on just proof surmise, accumulate,
> Bring me within the level of your frown,

But shoot not at me in your wakened hate:
Since my appeal says I did strive to prove
The constancy and virtue of your love.

Shakespeare admits practically everything he is accused of, and
they make quite an array. He gives as his excuse that he was
testing his friend to prove his constancy, which the previous
sonnet said the virtue of love implied. In other words this
sonnet delivers a knock-out blow to sonnet 116. Dover Wilson
noting their inconsistency said that the sonnet must be misplaced. But this is to miss the point. Actually it is a parody of
Barnes' sonnet XI:

Why did thou then in such disfigured guise
Figure the portrait of mine overthrow?
Why manlike didst thou mean to tyrannise,
No man but woman would have sinned so:
Why then inhuman and my secret foe
Didst thou betray me, yet would be a woman?
From my chief wealth out weaving me this woe,
Leaving thy love in pawn till time did come on
When that thy trustless bonds were to be tried,
And when (through thy default) I thee did summon
Into the court of steadfast love, then cried
As it was promised, here stands his heart's bail:
And if in bonds to thee my love be tied:
Then by those bonds, take forfeit of the sale.

Shakespeare presumes that he is the accused in 'the court of
steadfast love', and has not repaid the debt. Barnes' lady when
taken to court for her unsuitable behaviour 'cried' 'here stands
his heart's bail'. But Shakespeare says he 'Forgot . . . to call' on
his friend's love, 'Whereto all bonds do tie me day by day'—a
line that echoes Barnes', 'And if in bonds to thee my love be
tied'. He admits his unsuitable behaviour as a lover; it is
inconsistent with that reported in sonnet 116. But his plea is
that he was trying to prove his friend's constancy in love.
Barnes' lady got away with it by her clever defence. So Shakespeare too may be presumed to have won his argument by an
appeal to whether his friend's love meets the test promulgated

in the previous sonnet. It seems a fair enough rejoinder. If the claim of sonnet 116 stands, Shakespeare's testing it by seeing if his friend's love 'removes' when he 'alters' may be justified.

Sonnet 118

> Like as to make our appetites more keen
> With eager compounds we our palate urge,
> As to prevent our maladies unseen,
> We sicken to shun sickness when we purge.
> Even so being full of your ne'er cloying sweetness,
> To bitter sauces did I frame my feeding;
> And sick of welfare found a kind of meetness,
> To be diseased ere that there was true needing.
> Thus policy in love to anticipate
> The ills that were not, grew to faults assured,
> And brought to medicine a healthful state
> Which rank of goodness would by ill be cured.
> But thence I learn and find the lesson true,
> Drugs poison him that so fell sick of you.

This makes a follow on from the previous sonnet where Shakespeare tried out the sonnet ideal of love as constancy. Here he reports another experiment suggested by a sonneteer. He says that just as one's appetite is stimulated by bitter ('eager') sauces, or purges are used to prevent illness, so to prevent himelf becoming cloyed by his friend's sweetness, even though he is not yet cloyed, he pretended faults that 'grew to faults assured', and this state of sickness brought back a healthful state to his attitude towards his friend, as a purge does. It was as if goodness could grow rank, and the way to cure it was to do ill. The lesson he learnt was that this poisoned his nature by establishing faults in him that he originally feigned.

This extraordinary phantasy parodies one of Sidney's sonnets that appeared in *Diana* as no. VII of decade 3 :

> When love puffed up with rage of high disdain,
> Resolved to make me pattern of his might,
> Like foe, whose wits inclined to deadly spite,
> Would often kill to breed more feeling pain.
> He would not armed with beauty only reign,
> On these affects which easily yield to sight :

But virtue sets so high, that reason's light
For all his strife can only bondage gain;
So that I live to pay a mortal fee,
Dead-palsy sick of all my chiefest parts,

.   .   .   .   .   .

To stammering minds such is good Cupid's dish.

Sidney says that Cupid in order to increase the pain of love adds to the binding quality of beauty, virtue or chastity. Shakespeare leaves out this sense-making item in his sonnet. He writes on Cupid's dish, with its 'bitter sauces' and adds the more drastic image of a purge that makes one feel ill in order to cure. His motive is to prevent his friend's sweetness from cloying, but he resorts to Cupid's prescription before it does cloy, and he says he is 'sick of welfare' perhaps thinking of chastity, so making a parallel with Cupid not relying only on beauty which has an easy conquest. Thus he makes himself suffer like Sidney who was 'sick' of all his 'chiefest parts'. Unfortunately what Shakespeare learnt was that this dish of love poisoned him—not the effect intended by Cupid or Sidney. We may take it then that this was a prescription that did not make sense.

Sonnet 119 begins with this poison and errors made in the cause of love.

Sonnet 119

What potions have I drunk of siren tears
Distilled from limbecks foul as hell within,
Applying fears to hopes, and hopes to fears,
Still losing when I saw myself to win?
What wretched errors hath my heart committed,
Whilst it hath thought itself so blessed never?
How have mine eyes out of their spheres been fitted
In the distraction of this madding fever?
Oh benefit of ill, now I find true
That better is, by evil still made better.
And ruined love when it is built anew
Grows fairer than at first, more strong, far greater.
So I return rebuked to my content,
And gain by ills thrice more than I have spent.

The potion he drank was of siren's tears, of love made up of
fearing he would not see what he hoped for, and hoping his
fears would not be realised. He asks what wretched errors his
heart committed, all the while thinking it loved or was loved.
This fever has made his eyes go mad too. But he concludes with
the ironic situation, rejected in the previous sonnet, that what
is better is made still better by evil, and that ruined love built
anew, is fairer and stronger and greater than before. Actually
this may be true. But if so what about sonnet 116? Anyhow,
Shakespeare concludes that he has gained three times more
than the ills he suffered.

This parody is quite difficult to disentangle. Sidney provides
a group of sonnets that seem the main target, although the first
two lines certainly come from Barnes, who in sonnet XLIX
calls love a 'siren' and rhymes

From my love's 'lembic still 'stilled tears, Oh tears!

with 'oh fears', where the tears 'quench mine heat'. This
combination of 'siren' ''lembic' ''stilled', 'tears' 'fears' and
'heat' is conclusive. But apart from these concentrated echoes
the two sonnets have not much in common. One must say too
that most sonnet lovers are fevered at one time or another—a
sickness derived from Plato—and suffer from hope and fear,
but conclude that love is worth the suffering. Thus Spenser in
sonnet XXV writes,

How long shall this like dying life endure,
And know no end of her own misery:
But waft and wear away in terms unsure,
Twixt fear and hope depending doubtfully.

. . . . .

But yet if in your hardened breast ye hide,
A close intent at last to show me grace:
Then all the woes and wrecks which I abide,
As means of bliss I gladly will embrace.
And with that more and greater they might be,
That greater need at last may turn to me.

Although we have here hopes and fears and suffering and a

happy ending, only the couplet seems to have suggested any very definite detail to Shakespeare. Spenser writes 'More and greater' suffering may turn to the 'greater need', and Shakespeare that ruined love, built anew, 'Grows fairer ... more strong, far greater'. But what one wants to discover is the point of Shakespeare's odd statements. Why should he have drunk 'siren tears', or is it enough to say these are tears that lead one astray. Barnes's were the tears of his lady. What 'errors' has his heart committed? Whatever can his eyes being fitted 'out of their spheres' mean? Who 'rebuked' him and what for, and why return to 'my content'? One can find reasons for all these in Sidney, if one culls from several sonnets. In sonnet LXII we are told that Stella loves 'with a love not blind'. Here as elsewhere she scolded or 'rebuked' her lover for not being virtuous. This is Sidney's error that his heart committed, but Shakespeare does not seem to know what his was. Sidney ends his sonnet

> Dear, love me not, that you may love me more.

Shakespeare parodies,

> Better is, by evil still made better.

In sonnet LXVI Sidney writes,

> And do I see some cause of hope to find?
>
> .   .   .   .   .
>
> Desire, still on stilts of fear doth go.
> And yet amidst all fears, a hope there is
> Stolen to my heart : since last fair night (nay day)
> Stella's eyes sent to me the beams of bliss,
> Looking on me, I look another way :
> But when mine eyes black to their heaven did move :
> They fled with blush, which guilty seemed of love.

If 'black' is a misprint for 'back' which would seem to make the better sense, here are the poet's eyes having left their spheres and moving back again. Finally in the next sonnet we may discover why the siren is in tears :

Hope art thou true or dost thou flatter me?
Doth Stella now begin, with piteous eye
The reign of this her conquest to espy?

. . . . . .

What blushing notes dost thou in margin see?
What sighs stolen out . . .

. . . . .

Well how so ere thou dost interpret my contents,
I am resolved thy error to maintain :
Rather than by more truth to get more pain.

Here is a piteous eye that may be false or true. Shakespeare
gives it Barnes' sinister quality, as he also does to his heart's
'wretched errors'. At the end he accepts the implied reconciliation without reserve. He has been rebuked but returns to his
'content'. Presumably if Sidney knows what his 'contents'
means, so will Shakespeare's readers. Just as in the previous
parody he omitted the chastity that would have made sense of
the imagery, so here he omits desire which was Sidney's theme.
He may have intended this as a comment on sonnet language,
which makes the play of images more important than the sense.

Sonnet 120 translates Sidney's sonnet LVII into pseudo-
fact.
Here is Sidney :

Woe having made with many sighs his own
Each sense of mine; each gift, each power of mind
Grown now his slaves, he forced them out to find
The throwest words, fit for woe's self to groan
Hoping that when they might find Stella alone,
Before she could prepare to be unkind,
Her soul (arméd with such a dainty rind,)
Should soon be hurt with sharpness of the moan.
She heard my plaints, and did not only hear,
But them so sweet, she did most sweetly sing,
With that fair breast, making woe's darkness clear,
My privy cares I holp to her to bring,
To tell my grief, and she with face and voice,
So sweets my pains, that my pains me rejoice.

There are three actors in this story; woe and Stella are the first
two and the poet the subsidiary third. Woe made all the poets
'senses' his, and forced all his powers of mind to groan, hoping
by this means to hurt Stella before she could 'prepare to be
unkind'. She fell for this and sang his 'plaints' so sweetly,
'making woe's darkness clear', that he could tell her his grief,
which she soothed so that he rejoiced in his pains.
Here is Shakespeare:

Sonnet 120

> That you were once unkind befriends me now,
> And for that sorrow, which I then did feel,
> Needs must I under my transgression bow,
> Unless my nerves were brass or hammered steel.
> For if you were by my unkindness shaken
> As I by yours, ye have passed a hell of time,
> And I a tyrant have no leisure taken
> To weigh how once I suffered in your crime.
> Oh that our night of woe might have remembered
> My deepest sense, how hard true sorrow hits,
> And soon to you, as you to me then tendered
> The humble salve, which wounded bosoms fits!
> But that your trespass now becomes a fee,
> Mine ransoms yours, and yours must ransom me.

Shakespeare starts with the unkindness of his friend in the past,
just as Sidney started with his woe. But he himself is unkind
now, as woe was unkind preparing to hurt Stella before she
was ready to strike. Shakespeare realises that they must both
have 'passed a hell of time'. Stella made 'woe's darkness clear'
so that reconciliation became possible. And Shakespeare comments, 'Oh that our night of woe' might have remembered
'My deepest sense, how hard true sorrow hits' and he had
tendered the salve, as Stella and his friend did. But Shakespeare then turns it into a relationship of law and debts. He
says his friend's trespass has become 'a fee'. His fee ransoms his
friend, and his friend's must ransom him. Fees and ransoms are
common coinage of sonneteers. Shakespeare has also parodied
by translating the personification into a quarrel where each has
tried deliberately to be unkind (which is Sidney's word) to the

other. He has made a serious business out of what was a sonnet phantasy.

Sonnet 121 ends the series on Shakespeare's errors and, as he often does to end a series, puts it in the superlative, or brings it to a climax.

Sonnet 121

> 'Tis better to be vile than vile esteemed,
> When not to be, receives reproach of being,
> And the just pleasure lost, which is so deemed,
> Not by our feeling, but by others' seeing.
> For why should others' false adulterate eyes
> Give salutation to my sportive blood?
> Or on my frailties why are frailer spies,
> Which in their wills count bad what I think good?
> No, I am that I am, and they that level
> At my abuses, reckon up their own,
> I may be straight though they themselves be bevel
> By their rank thoughts, my deeds must not be shown
> Unless this general evil they maintain,
> All men are bad and in their badness reign.

Needless to say this makes good evidence for some real fault of Shakespeare's in the eyes of those who seek for biographical details. But taken as the end of a series of sonnets parodying Sidney's response to Stella's dislike of the desirous element in his love, it does not seem personal. In the previous sonnets Shakespeare conspicuously omitted referring to desire or its opposite, chastity. He now, having danced around the theme avoiding attack, suddenly deals a stunning blow to accusations like Stella's. He says it would be better to be vile and have the pleasure of this impermissible desire, than to lose all the pleasure of love not because of what he actually feels, but because of what others see in him. Why should someone whose own eyes are unclean hail his blood as sportive. I take his 'frailer spies' to be women critics. If men critics hail him as an adulterous boon companion, the 'frailer spies' may well be women who count as bad what the poet thinks good. In this indirect way he strikes a blow at Sidney's puritanism. He is

what he is and not what others project on to him. He is bad only
in the sense that all men are, and rule their life by it.

Sonnet 122

> Thy gift, thy tables, are within my brain
> Full charactered with lasting memory,
> Which shall above that idle rank remain
> Beyond all date even to eternity.
> Or at the least, so long as brain and heart
> Have faculty by nature to subsist,
> Till each to razed oblivion yield his part
> Of thee, thy record never can be missed:
> That poor retention could not so much hold,
> Nor need I tallies thy dear love to score,
> Therefore to give them from me was I bold,
> To trust those tables that receive thee more,
> To keep an adjunct to remember thee,
> Were to import forgetfulness in me.

Here Shakespeare returns to the theme of making his friend
immortal in his verse. He may have Daniel's thirteenth sonnet
in mind. Daniel 'figured' Delia

> on the table of my heart :
> The fairest form, the world's eye admires.

But he worked 'on flint'. 'Hard is her heart', 'Unhappy I to
love a stony heart'. Shakespeare's experience is different. His
friend gave him the 'tables' that record him and they are in his
brain. What is written in his memory will remain 'Beyond all
date even to eternity'. Or at least, taking care to speak truthfully in contrast with the usual practice, it will last as long as
heart and brain survive. Until these yield to oblivion, the
record will not fail. His memory, however, could not hold
everything worth remembering, but he does not need tallies to
keep the score. Therefore he takes courage to 'give them from'
himself by writing them in his sonnets and in doing so he trusts
the tables of his memory that receive more than he could write.
To keep an actual diary of him would imply that he could
forget.

Sonnet 123

> No! time, thou shalt not boast that I do change,
> Thy pyramids built up with newer might
> To me are nothing novel, nothing strange,
> They are but dressings of a former sight:
> Our dates are brief, and therefore we admire,
> What thou dost foist upon us that is old,
> And rather make them born to our desire,
> Than think that we before have heard them told:
> Thy registers and thee I both defy,
> Not wondering at the present, nor the past,
> For thy records, and what we see doth lie,
> Made more or less by thy continual haste:
> This I do vow and this shall ever be,
> I will be true despite thy scythe and thee.

An attempt has been made to date this sonnet by taking 'thy pyramids' to refer to actual pyramids or obelisks of topical interest, but the evidence is inconclusive. A reference that cannot be doubted is that to the *Metamorphoses*. Shakespeare repudiates Ovid's claim that time continually changes everything, on the grounds that it does not change his love. However willing he is to accept the idea that ancient pyramids reappear in later generations, he says this is not novel or strange. They are, he accepts it, re-creations of what has been before. We live a short time and therefore are surprised that we should have foisted on us what is old as if it were new; we rather think our works express what we want and are new, not realising, he says ironically, that we heard of their existence long ago. In the sestet both the old records and time are defied. Shakespeare is not impressed by what he sees in the present or reads about in the past, for both are deceptive, having only a contemporary truth, which is short since time is always hastening off. Then he swears in the face of time that he will be true in spite of its destruction. As we have heard him on this before, I need not comment further.

Sonnet 124

> If my dear love were but the child of state
> It might for fortune's bastard be unfathered,

As subject to time's love or to time's hate,
Weeds among weeds, or flowers with flowers gathered.
No it was builded far from accident,
It suffers not in smiling pomp, nor falls
Under the blow of thrallèd discontent,
Whereto the inviting time our fashion calls:
It fears not policy that heretic,
Which works on leases of short numbered hours,
But all alone stands hugely politic,
That it nor grows with heat, nor drowns with showers.
To this I witness call the fools of time,
Which die for goodness, who have lived for crime.

Here Shakespeare strikes a more personal note. In the previous sonnet he defied time, the great abstraction. He now looks at his personal love among mutable things. He says that if his dear love (which I take to be his feeling rather than his friend) were subject to expediency like a political matter, it might be proved a child of chance and therefore a bastard. But on the contrary it has an eternal, immutable quality. If it were like a child of state then it would be subject to both the good and the bad in time, its hate and love; it might be a weed or a flower. No, he protests, his love was built in a realm far from chance, untouched by happenings in time. It suffers neither the pomp of greatness, nor is it like a discontented and miserable slave—the extremes in the contemporary state that time calls everything to. His love does not fear expediency—that heretic to love—which is concerned only with interests that are short-lived. It stands alone with a philosophy that is unassailable, neither increasing in good fortune, like a flower in warm weather, nor drowning in bad. He calls on the fools of time (that is perhaps those who die, or more likely those who are time-servers) to witness his statement, or possibly his signature to his long-dated lease. These ordinary people have lived in the crime of their heresy, but make a good end, or die as ordinary people are usually said to do. The meaning of the couplet, however, is not at all clear.

Although this sonnet has been taken to have a topical reference, there is no agreement as to what. However, it has certainly a literary background. To begin with, Constable in decade 3, sonnet X says to Diana,

Of fortune as thou learned'st to be unkind,
So learn to be inconstant to disdain.

If Shakespeare's love were a child of state it might be made a
bastard by 'fortune'. 'Unkind' in Shakespeare's day could
mean unnatural, or not behaving like a good relative, and
therefore might suggest a bastard. Diana learnt from fortune to
be unnatural. Shakespeare's child was 'unfathered' and thus
treated 'unkindly'. Constable tells Diana to be 'inconstant to
disdain', and constancy is Shakespeare's theme; his love is
beyond all mutable things. But there is not a close similarity
between the sonnets. If Constable's is relevant it is as a verbal
memory of something in the same context. Shakespeare's
parody seems to be rather of Sidney, who opens sonnet
XXVIII,

You that with allegories curious frame
Of other's children changlings use to make,
With me those pains for God-sake do not take,
I list not dig so deep for brazen fame.

'Other's children' means the creations or writings of others.
This may have suggested to Shakespeare his love as a child,
changed to a bastard by being treated with this importance.
The idea of its being a child of state also comes from this
context, for Sidney continues that he loves Stella alone in 'simplicity' because of whose beauty he finds joy, 'though nations
count it shame'. He follows with sonnets about states. The first
refers to 'Lords, neighbours by mighty kings', and in the next
come Turkey, Poland, Muscovy, Holland, Ulster, Scotland.
Shakespeare parodies by saying his love is not at all this sort of
child; politics or expediency has nothing to do with it; it
belongs to a world out of time. Also relevant is Sidney's sonnet
XXIV, which I have already referred to, and which has 'fools'
subject to 'fortune's lot', who value the wrong things and
therefore would be heretics in Shakespeare's sense and 'fools of
time'.

Sonnet 125 is similar to this in stressing an inward reality as
against an outward.

Sonnet 125

> Were it aught to me I bore the canopy,
> With my extern the outward honouring,
> Or laid great bases for eternity,
> Which proves more short than waste or ruining?
> Have I not seen dwellers on form and favour
> Lose all, and more by paying too much rent
> For compound sweet; forgoing simple savour,
> Pitiful thrivers in their gazing spent.
> No, let me be obsequious in thy heart,
> And take thou my oblation, poor but free,
> Which is not mixed with seconds, knows no art,
> But mutual render, only me for thee.
> Hence, thou suborned informer, a true soul
> When most impeached, stands least in thy control.

Unless one refers this sonnet to its literary background it is difficult to interpret, for it seems a jumble of incompatible images, with the couplet making a climax of irrelevance. It makes good sense, however, as a parody of four of Constable's sonnets To begin with, in decade 4, sonnet VII, he announces,

> The richest relic Rome did ever view,
> Was Caesar's tomb.

But 'what Rome shaped, hath living light in you' he says to Diana. In sonnet V of the same decade he says,

> With one sole look you leave in me no soul,
>
> . . . . . .
>
> Would God that I might hear my last bell toll,
> So in your bosom I might dig my grave.

If we put these together we get a contrast between a grave in his love's bosom with her living quality and the great, material outward monument to Caesar. Constable has also made his lady deprive him of his soul, hence his death. The contrast in Shakespeare's sonnet is of this sort; that between a living reality, a spiritual attitude contrasted with an outward. He says his friend is buried in his heart, where he pays his respects, 'obsequies' being the last rites for the dead. The oblation is the sacrament, the sacrifice which, says Shakespeare, is of the best elements not mixed with anything second rate, and what he gives in this interior sacrifice to the memory of his friend is himself in exchange for his friend's love. From the other angle, and in parody also, Shakespeare asks if it could mean anything to him to carry the canopy over his friend at his burial, honouring him in this outward way with his 'extern', or exterior, as if he were to lay concrete 'bases for eternity' like that of Caesar's tomb that time ruins, the tomb that Constable said was the richest relic in Rome. There is a new intention here, significant in the parody, for not only is stress laid on paying respects to a great man, but on one's own importance in doing so. Carrying the canopy implies some dignity derived from the personality one serves. Shakespeare says that he has seen people who receive favour from the great, lose everything by paying too much for it; they do without the simple heart to heart experience, in paying for the complex pleasure of being gazed at, like those who carry the canopy. Constable in sonnet VI of decade 5 gave Shakespeare the idea for obsequies (or being obsequious) and 'simple savour'. He says he is care's 'essence' since Diana disdains him :

> Within thine arms sad elegies I sing.
>
> . . . .
>
> Thou smellest from me the savours sorrows bring.

This combines funeral rites or elegies and 'savour'. Being care's essence also gives the clue to Shakespeare's couplet with its very surprising image, looking as if it were something out of a quite different context. Indeed it suggests that the point of the parody may partly lie in the incongruity of the imagery. Shakespeare has developed and given weight to Constable's suggestion of 'elegies' and the 'grave'. Paying rent for a 'compound sweet', for which they forgo 'simple savour' takes Constable's absurd 'savours of sorrows' which Diana 'smells' into the pseudo-serious prose situation of paying too much rent for it. And then there is this quite unrelated image of the 'suborned informer' in the couplet. It has found a way here through association with Constable's 'care'. In his next sonnet to that with care's essence and the smell, he writes this, which includes

besides care and the suborned informer the bastard of sonnet
124, and a lackey that runs 'by death':

> But being care, thou flyest me as illfortune.
> Care the consuming canker of the mind,
> The discord that disorders sweet heart's tune,
> The abortive bastard of a coward mind:
> The light-foot lackey that runs post by death,
> Bearing the letters which contain our end,
> The busy advocate that sells his breath,
> Denouncing worst to him is most his friend.
> Oh dear, this care no interest holds in me,
> But holy care, the guardian of thy fair,
> Thine honour's champion, and thy virtue's fee,
> The zeal which thee from barbarous times shall bear.
> This care I am, this care my life has taken.
> Dear to my soul, then leave me not forsaken.

Constable's suborned informer is care. It is significant that
Shakespeare dismisses it with the same words as he dismisses
'fear' in sonnet 107, which deals with his friend's monument in
verse in contrast with tombs of brass; both fear in 107 and the
informer are said to be not able to control the lease of love, the
image being expressed in 107 and implied by 'rent' in this
sonnet. It is very interesting to find this association suggested
by 'care'. Constable's word is not used, but the association of
dismissing it in the context of external monuments, brings back
the rhyme of 'soul' and 'control' from 107. This seems the same
sort of 'recurrent association' that Edward Armstrong[86] shows
prevailing throughout Shakespeare's plays.

Out of Constable's association of images Shakespeare has
created a 'story' with its own form and sense, but not quite
Constable's sense. The parody partly consists in using images
deprived of their referents, the implication perhaps being that
images mean more to sonneteers than their meaning, or that
the meaning does not make sense. We have already seen him
parody in this way in sonnets 118 and 119. The parodies can
be understood only if we have the sonnets parodied fresh in our
minds as we read.

Sonnet 125 ends the series on the man with the imagery of
his death and burial. Sonnet 126 is a sort of epitaph. So, a

rational end is provided for one who exists only as a parody. This sonnet also makes a final comment on the sonneteers' aim of giving their loves an eternity in spite of time.

Sonnet 126

O thou my lovely boy who in thy power,
Dost hold time's fickle glass, his fickle, hour:
Who hast by waning grown, and therein show'st,
Thy lovers withering, as thy sweet self grow'st.
If nature (sovereign mistress over wrack)
As thou goest onwards still will pluck thee back,
She keeps thee to this purpose, that her skill
May time disgrace, and wretched minutes kill.
Yet fear her Oh thou minion of her pleasure,
She may detain, but not still keep her treasure!
Her audit (though delayed) answered must be,
And her quietus is to render thee.
( )
( )

Sonnet 126 was printed with two blank lines in brackets as above. There seems absolutely no reason for this. The sonnet is of course in couplets and complete as it stands. Its twelve lines need not be filled up to make fourteen. Perhaps this represents a printer's misconception. It could conceivably be a joke of Shakespeare's; Constable, for instance, writes a decade of decades, 100 sonnets, but the sum is completed only by omission.

The 'lovely boy' of the sonnet can be interpreted either as Shakespeare's friend or as Cupid. In either case Shakespeare makes the final comment on his main theme of preserving his love from time's destruction. If we take the boy as his friend, then he tells him that he holds time's fickle, fragile, changeable glass for an uncertain period of time—a time that is insecure. And he reminds him that he has developed by growing older or waning from his prime, and that this has shown him his lovers withering. So, if nature who ruins, and in that sense is wrack's mistress, is always trying to prevent his progress to old age, she keeps him young in order to disgrace time and neutralise the ruin caused by its creeping minutes. Yet he tells his friend to fear nature. She may favour him, detain him, but not keep him for ever. Her day of reckoning, her audit, must be answered. And her quietus, which is to say the payment due to her, the settlement of Shakespeare's account, is to give her his friend. And, he implies, in this his last sonnet to his friend, that is precisely what he is doing.

It would make a better design if Cupid were the 'lovely boy' (and this description suits him as well, or better than it suited the friend of the Erasmus sonnets) since the sonnets on the dark lady end with Cupid, and are written in a more conventional idiom also. But it is not easy to find a meaning for Cupid waning, or for nature trying to pluck him back, although it makes good sense that she should leave him to kill time's 'wretched minutes'. The result of nature's audit may be to end love not just with the death of Shakespeare's friend, but with each particular death, or at doomsday with the death of love itself.

To sum up: I have shown that many of Shakespeare's sonnets to the man friend certainly parody specific sonnets and that many others are certainly parodies of prevailing sonnet attitudes. I have also shown by implication that difficulties in interpretation are best cleared up by referring them to a source in other sonneteers. I believe I have also shown that there is no sonnet that cannot be referred to this background and does not allow of an explanation as parody, particularly as to say to a man what is commonly said to a woman is itself to parody. Everything that characterises the man friend reflects the lady love of the sonneteers. He is given no masculine characteristics at all. Indeed sonnet 20, which we could almost say introduces him, expressly states that Shakespeare is interested only to the extent that he is a woman, or that he has not any male sex. Not only so, the attitudes and reactions of Shakespeare to his friend are precisely a selection of those of the other sonneteers to their ladies. The sonnet theme is enriched by being coupled with other literary parodies in the Erasmus and Ovidian sonnets, and particularly with the poetic convention of verses to perpetuate the memory of his friend to all eternity, but these are orientated to the sonnet tradition.

As to method, Shakespeare gets fun out of such things as making play with the imagery or the situation, with exaggerating and mocking, with naive explanations or expressions of surprise that his experience is different, with translating sonnet situations into terms of reality and by treating them seriously showing how absurd they are.

This interpretation of the sonnets must inhibit projection into them of the reader's own deep desires or experiences, and so deprives them of more than just a sentimental significance. But it does not deprive Shakespeare of his quality. The parody has a sort of greatness, which I should say is sensed chiefly in its music. It mimics in a dance that has its own breadth, dignity and grace, if we except some of the sonnets, particularly some of those to the woman. Shakespeare's artistry and design contribute to this impression, by giving his sonnets shape. His imagination too, by catching reality-experience in a verbal structure with layers of association, contributes to the 'tones of voice' of his music, and gives great variety to it. This seems to have been the quality that struck his contemporaries, if we can take Meres as speaking for them, and since he compares this music with Ovid's, he must have intended something not just superficial. One could say the sonnets have the sound of great poetry. We are aware all the time of a quality that belongs essentially to Shakespeare. They reveal a new aspect of his genius.

L

V

POSTSCRIPTS

1. THORPE'S DEDICATION

Shakespeare did not publish his sonnets. Perhaps we should guess why not, since he dedicated his other poems, *Venus and Adonis* and *The Rape of Lucrece* to the Earl of Southampton. It may be that as parodies they lacked sufficient dignity to be used for this sort of compliment. Their readers were his private friends until Thomas Thorpe printed them in 1609.

Thorpe's dedication is interesting:

> TO. THE. ONLIE. BEGETTER. OF.
>
> THESE. INSUING. SONNETS.
>
> MR. W.H. ALL. HAPPINESSE.
>
> AND. THAT. ETERNITIE.
>
> PROMISED.
>
> BY.
>
> OUR. EVER-LIVING. POET.
>
> WISHETH.
>
> THE. WELL-WISHING.
>
> ADVENTURER. IN.
>
> SETTING.
>
> FORTH.
>
> T.T.

This appears to be a dedication to the author by the publisher, in which he calls himself 'the well-wishing adventurer in setting forth'. He is an adventurer since he is not publishing for the poet, but adventuring on his own, as a pirate in fact. 'In setting forth' may be the sort of pun that Shakespeare often used.

Thorpe set forth as an adventurer, but even more, he set forth the sonnets, or printed them. A pun would be in character, for in his dedication of Marlowe's *First Book of Lucan translated*, which he also published, he says to Edward Blount,

Blount : I propose to be blunt with you.

He is facetious. But it carries a friendly, complimenting tone. He expresses himself warmly, wishing Shakespeare well and dedicating his book to him. For this he could have received the poet's permission, and indeed it would be cheek to steal the work from him and then present him with it. The tone of the dedication besides being appreciative is ingenious and playful. He wishes the poet 'that eternity' promised by himself in the sonnets. He noticeably omits to say to whom he promised this. In fact Shakespeare claimed it ironically both for himself and his friend. So he wishes Shakespeare the eternity that he promised himself, 'our ever-living poet'. To call him 'only' begetter was suggestive. Who else might beget? It strikes an overtone from the first seventeen sonnets where the friend is urged to marry and beget, but as Thorpe accepts, does not. This, however, is only his fun. He had a practical reason, as publisher, for assuring his public that all the sonnets here were by Shakespeare. It may be remembered that the pirate edition of *Astrophel and Stella* included sonnets by Daniel, and Constable's *Diana* sonnets of Sidney and of other still unidentified poets, although this was expressly stated. But quite disgracefully, *The Passionate Pilgrim,* purporting to be written by Shakespeare, included only seven of his sonnets. So it is not in the least surprising that Thorpe should think it necessary to stress that Shakespeare is their only begetter. He does it pleasantly, complimenting Shakespeare at the same time by using the image of begetting from the sonnets themselves, just as he promises their 'eternity'.

All is not as straightforward as this, however. It seems odd that the begetter should be referred to as 'Mr W.H.'; but a fashion for anonymous publication existed at this time, as if writers were coy; and they often used identifying initials so that they could claim their work if they wished, or so that their friends would recognise it. Sometimes the initials were not those of the first letters of their names. Thus S.W. was used to indicate Southwell, with S. for 'South' and W. for 'Well', and S.P.L. for James Sempill, using the first, last and middle letters of his surname.[87] Thorpe may be doing the same sort of thing, using H. instead of S. for 'Shakespeare'. To represent the initial sound of the word requires H. as well as S. and since the intention was to hide identity, this would seem a reasonable substitute. If this was the idea, Thorpe is still being facetious, for Shakespeare's name was on the title page. That is to say it would make his bit of parody of a fashion that pretended anonymity but actually revealed identity. To parody would continue the complimentary reference to the contents of the book. This may be a feeble sort of wit, but it is still used by the compliment-paying chairman introducing a well-known writer. There is contemporary evidence that Thorpe was understood to be dedicating his pirate printing to the author in this facetious way, for a very few years later, in 1613, the poet George Wither parodied it in his own dedication to *Abuses Stript and Whipt*:

To himself, G. W. wisheth all happiness.

Not only is this an obvious parody of Thorpe's dedication, but one of the characteristics high-lighted is the use of initials that hide nothing. The German critic, D. Barnstoff, noticing this, even went so far in 1860 as to suggest that 'W.H.' stood for 'William himself', which is not the most far-fetched of the explanations that have been suggested.

At the end of the eighteenth century, once the literary background of Shakespeare's sonnets had been forgotten, it became reasonable to think that he wrote to a real man, and when eventually historians set themselves to find some known character who might be the friend of the sonnets, 'Mr W.H.', as the only clue, became important. I need not attempt to investigate this, although if any of the claimants to the title were proved genuine it would invalidate all I have written. From my point of view the weak spot in Thorpe's dedication is 'Mr W.H.', but I hope I have given at least a possible explanation.

Another detail needs clarification. It is now being said (for instance it is still maintained by A. L. Rowse[88]) that in Shakespeare's day 'beget' could be used as synonymous with 'get'. In that case the begetter might be anyone who obtained the sonnets for the publisher. If this were so it would not prove the existence of a real friend and a dark lady, but it would leave a chink, through which something might be spied. Happily, for this statement there is no justification at all. It is based on an error in *The Oxford English Dictionary*. There we find that 'beget' was one form of the verb 'get', meaning to obtain. An example from *Beowulf* is given. This form of the word gradually fell into disuse, the last entry justified in the dictionary being for Gower in 1393. But Shakespeare is credited with its usage, and *Hamlet*, Act III, sc. 2, line 8 is quoted: 'You must acquire and beget a temperance'. Anyone who knows the play will recognise the quotation as part of Hamlet's advice to the players, where neither 'acquire' nor 'beget' can be interpreted as 'procure' or 'obtain' in the sense required if Thorpe intended to refer to Mr W.H. as someone who provided him with his copy. Here is the complete sentence:

> Nor do not saw the air too much with you hand, thus; but use all gently: for in the very torrent, tempest, and, as I may say, whirlwind of your passion, you must acquire and beget a temperance that may give it smoothness.

It is not Shakespeare's usual practice when he couples words in this way to use exact synonyms; his second word adds a new dimension to the meaning rather than repeats it. A few examples to hand in the second scene of *Hamlet* will show this. The King explains how his enemies hope to take advantage of Denmark,

> thinking by our late dear brother's death
> Our state to be disjoint and out of frame.

'Disjoint' and 'out of frame' differ in meaning although they are near enough to reinforce each other in a way that is not precise but carries an emotional charge. So also when Laertes asks him for his 'leave and favour to return to France', or he asks Hamlet to remain at court 'in the cheer and comfort of our eye', the words couple to add diverse meanings which relate with each other to give a two-dimensional quality to the sentence. Possibly the most memorable example in this scene is Horatio's reference to the ghost's appearance 'In the dead vast and middle of the night'. 'Dead vast' and 'middle' are far from being synonyms. 'Dead vast' is more like an epithet giving a horrific quality to 'middle of the night'. 'The dead of night' would have come nearer to the same sense as 'middle of the night', although it too has frightening associations. We might translate 'vast' as 'void', a region opening on limitlessness, and with suggestions of terror. By this conjunction of a factual phrase with a parallel carrying a numinous quality, the sense of an unblessed time when ghosts may come, is conveyed. It is to give such a fullness of meaning that Shakespeare couples words. So with 'acquire' and 'beget'. 'Acquire' is used in the sense in which one talks of acquiring a skill: the boys must learn to act with temperance. But no art is just a skill that one acquires or learns, Shakespeare comes nearer his meaning by coupling 'beget' with it. To beget a temperance in acting is to bring it into being as a result of the activity of one's feelings and intuition; it is a creative act. Indeed any art is a matter of this fusion of skill and creation, which the two words suggest. Nothing could be further from Shakespeare's meaning than to interpret either word as 'obtain' or 'get'. Not only so, Shakespere could not have used the word to mean 'get'. Although 'beget' occurs often in his plays, used both literally and metaphorically, he never uses it with this sense. I need hardly run through all the passages where the word occurs for proof. It should be enough to examine the instance where it comes nearest to meaning 'get'. In *Pericles,* Act IV, sc. 2, line 129 the bawd giving advice says,

> To weep that you live as ye do makes pity in your lovers: seldom but that pity begets you a good opinion, and that opinion a mere profit.

In the mouth of his bawd Shakespeare cheapens 'beget' until it ends in meaning to obtain money. The first begetting is a creation of pity, which brings into being its offspring, a good opinion, and that in turn is, a 'mere profit'. The joke consists in reducing what is begot by degrees into something that begets profit, which is as close as the image can come to meaning 'obtain', but it would not be the cynical joke it is, if something of the real meaning did not remain at the end.

To return to Thorpe, he could not have used 'beget' to mean 'get', and if that was what he meant, there seems no reason why he should not have used the word that would convey this sense. His obscurity comes from trying to be witty, or clever as we should say. At all events 'Mr W.H.' and 'beget' (used wrongly) make very unsafe keystones to support the autobiographies that have been built on them.

II. GULLING SONNETS

Sir John Davies, not to be confused with John Davies of Hereford, wrote a tiny sonnet sequence which he called *Gulling Sonnets,* as if this were a special brand. Not all mocking poems could be called gulling. Davies's have a special quality. The difference can be appreciated if we contrast them with Gabriel Harvey's mockery of the sonnets. Harvey was less poet than pedant, and his view is that of the philistine. Thus, he writes disparagingly in a long amorphous 'verse-letter' dated 1573, and called,

> An amorous odious, sonnet intituled The Student's
> Love or Hatred, or both or neither, or what
> shall please the loving or hating reader, either
> in sport or earnest to make of such contrary passions
> as are here discoursed.

From this we can see that he is thinking of students writing sonnets. Both Sidney and Spenser were among his young friends about this time. Although sonnet writing was old in European history, it was fairly new in England, made possible by a growing interest in Italian and French. Harvey, a classicist, writes as a scholar of the old tradition who dislikes this newfangledness. His mocking verse might be considered good as undergraduate stuff, making fun of some professorial aberration. How it should be characterised in the reverse position I do not know. He shows no understanding of sonnet writers, or sympathy with their youthfulness. Here is a sample :

> Oh delicate mistress,
> Oh very goddess,
> Oh heavenly night,
> Oh blissful wight,
> Such a semblance of Deity
> Must needs provoke idolatry.

He continues like this at great length, and includes,

> I took her for a saint
> She rhymes to a door.

His wit in general is immature; it belongs to the type where a point can be scored by calling one's opponent an ass. His attack is not gulling. The gulling sonnet is urbane, like parody where a poet who both understands and respects the form which he parodies, exercises his skill in creating the thing he ridicules. Both Shakespeare and Davies belong in this class, the one using his supreme quality as a poet the other his very considerable art.

It seems likely that Davies may have learnt to gull from Shakespeare. Thus the second sonnet tells a little story in serious tones of voice, opening with a skyscape :

> As when ye bright Cerulian firmament
> Hath not his glory with black clouds defaced,

meaning 'One fine morning', but implying that the sonneteer's sky is normally defaced by gloom. Shakespeare uses this art of the superficially innocuous statement phrased to mock. In other sonnets Davies, like Shakespeare, writes what is hardly at all less ridiculous than what he parodies, relying on flood-lighting by mere copying, to show up its absurdity. Thus he uses common devices like making the first line of a sonnet repeat the last of the previous one. Or in sonnet V he writes,

> Mine eye, mine ear, my will, my wit, my heart
> Did see, did hear, did like, discern, did love :
> Her face, her speech, her fashion, judgment, art.

This is very little more ridiculous than sonnet XLVII in Griffin's *Fidessa* :

> I see, I hear, I feel, I know, I rue
> My fate, my fame, my pain, my loss, my fall.

An incongruity introduced into the mirroring is enough in sonnet VII, where love dwelling in the heart of the lover is gulled. Cupid admits himself 'Into the Middle Temple' of the poet's heart; there he breaks the rules and is condemned to depart 'Out of the Middle Temple of my heart'. This might have a particular reference, but love in the heart, even the temple with hymn-singing, Amen-saying and obsequies, is where it can usually be found. Only the Middle Temple is unexpected and absurd with its incongruity and yet, since lovers seem obsessed by legal images, its particular aptness. Another of Shakespeare's methods which Davies uses is treating a metaphor as if it were a prose fact. He does this in sonnet VI, only a little more crudely and obviously. It goes thus :

> The sacred muse that first made love divine
> Hath made him naked and without attire,
> But I will clothe him with this pen of mine.

He proceeds to do so, giving him 'a hat of hope' and equally incongruous stockings, gaiters, pumps and so on. This could have originated in a recollection of Shakespeare's sonnet 26, and may parody the same sonnet of Surrey which it does. Davies indicates the target of his last two sonnets :

> My case is this I love Zepheria bright.

So he writes as a lawyer dealing with her case. She is the lady of an anonymous sonnet series that indulges in legal imagery, and where sonnets tend to be concerned with an accusation or judgement. His parody is quiet and matter of fact like some of Shakespeare's. Thus sonnet XXXVII of *Zepheria* begins with the serving of a 'parent's writ' and indulges in what to us at least are recondite legal terms. In the first of his two parodies Davies deals with Zepheria as his feudal lady in terms suitable to that legal set up, and in the second with love as his lord, thus:

> To love my lord I do knight's service owe
> And therefore now he hath my wit in ward,
> But while it is in his tuition so
> Methinks he doth entreat it passing hard;
>
> .   .   .   .   .
>
> But why should love after minority
> When I am past the one and twentith year
> Preclude my wit of his sweet liberty;
>
> .   .   .   .   .
>
> I fear he hath another title got
> And holds my wit now for an idiot.

The sonnets in Davies's other parody, *Ten Sonnets to Philomel*, are even more like Shakespeare's than those in *Gulling Sonnets*. He does not label it 'gulling' although by making it 'Ten' he may suggest parody of Watson's *Centurie*, or more likely, of Constable's decades. It is interesting, and probably significant, that several of the sonnets parodied are those that Shakespeare did. Among them Daniel's stand out. They begin with an unmistakable parody of his twenty-fourth, which Shakespeare parodied in sonnets 146 and 151. Daniel stopped 'the passage' of his heart, but while he guarded that,

> Another passage opens at her voice.

Davies tells the same story and echoes this sentence almost exactly, only substituting 'ear' for voice, thus making it literal and therefore absurd—a trick of Shakespeare's:

> Oft did I hear our eyes the passage were,
> By which love entered to assail our hearts;
> Therefore I guarded them, and void of fear,
> Neglected the defence of other parts.
> Love knowing this, the usual way forsook:
> And seeking found a by-way by mine ear.
> At which he entering, my heart prisoner took,
> And unto thee sweet Philomel did bear.

This like others in the series might almost be taken seriously, as Shakespeare's parody has been. His second sonnet also mocks others of Daniel's which Shakespeare parodied, especially numbers VI and VII, the latter quoted when I was dealing with Shakespeare's no. 88. Daniel ends VI,

> Oh had she not been fair and thus unkind,
> My muse had slept, and none had known my mind.

And in VII he says the world would never have known what he found, or 'have heard of such disdain', but alas his 'degraded hopes' forced him to 'groan out griefs'. Davies echoes not just the sense; he has caught his tune as distinctly as Shakespeare did. Here he is:

> Oh why did fame my heart to love betray,
> By telling my dear's virtue and perfection?
>   .   .   .   .   .   .
> Had I been deaf, or fame her gifts concealed,
> Then had my heart been free from hopeless love.

Although he is distracted 'twixt hope and dreadful fear' he concludes,

> Yea I could quietly death's pains abide,
> So that she knew that for her sake I died.

But Drayton's Amour IV must have as good a claim to Davies's parody, and not only because it also obviously copies Daniel's:

> My fair, had I not erst adorned my lute,
> With those sweet strings stolen from thy golden hair,
>   .   .   .   .   .   .
> Had not mine eye seen thy celestial eye,
> Nor my heart known the power of thy name
> My soul had ne'er felt thy divinity,
> Nor my muse been the trumpet of thy fame.
> But thy divine perfections . . .

And Constable's decade 7 sonnet V, quoted with reference to Shakespeare's sonnet XIV, may be relevant also.

Not all the parodies in *Ten Sonnets* are of Daniel's. Thus in sonnet III the lover who would relieve his lady of her sickness and bear it himself is gulled, and in sonnet VI the miraculous work of the lady's eyes, where she looks at her lover as he passes her window, but keeps herself hidden. It would have been easy and obvious to make her eyes have the usual effect although the poet had not seen them. But he does not do this. He is more subtle, suggesting only a mutual sympathy.

> Alas, my dear, couldst thou suppose, that face
> Which needs not envy Phoebus' chiefest pride,
> Could secret be, although in secret place,
> And that transparent glass such beams could hide?
> But if I had been blind, yet love's hot flame,
> Kindled in my poor heart by thy bright eye,
> Did plainly show when it so near thee came.
>
> . . . . . .
>
> So though thou hidden wert, my heart and eye
> Did turn to thee by mutual sympathy.

Sonnet VII parodies the same sonnets as Shakespeare in 24. Davies says that when he could not see his love,

> Her lively picture in my heart I drew,
> That I might it behold both day and night.

But she commanded love

> To burn the picture which was in my heart,

and his heart was turned to ruin and decay.

> Love could not burn the spirit, it was divine,
> And therefore fired my heart, the saint's poor shrine.

The lines about love not being able to 'burn the spirit' since it was divine, echo Shakespeare's sonnet 74, and perhaps suggest the shrine in 125. It may then have a direct reference to

Shakespeare himself, not just to the sonnets he parodies, although this cannot be taken as certain.

To conclude: Whether or not Davies copied details from Shakespeare he certainly selected many of the same sonnets for parody, and even more interestingly, used the same methods. We may perhaps say that he learnt from him how to dance sonnet steps in mockery and with some sophistication. I have shown how near he is to Shakespeare by contrast with the bumbling Harvey. Some civilising influence divides them. Davies's is true parody; he writes a good sonnet criticising itself. He belongs to the same genre as Shakespeare, writing considered art not philistine passion, teasing rather than condemning. If both poets aim to kill—but I am not sure that Shakespeare does, or Davies for that matter—they do it with a *coup de grâce* in a mannered dance.

Although I conclude that Davies learnt from Shakespeare, this may not be everyone's opinion. So let us look at all possible consequences of their resemblance. If both poets happened on this gulling method independently, then we must conclude that Shakespeare's parody was inherent in the culture of his age, a natural, perhaps inevitable outcome. If it is possible that Shakespeare could have learnt from Davies, the reason for his gulling needs no other explanation, while if Davies learnt from him, it confirms that Shakespeare's intention was perceived by him as parody. But more than this. Davies has an interesting dedication to his *Gulling Sonnets,* from which we can draw two conclusions. It was written to Sir Anthony Cooke (to whom Drayton had dedicated his 1594 edition of *Idea's Mirrour*). He says,

> Here my chameleon muse herself doth change
> To diverse shapes of gross absurdities.
>
> .   .   .   .   .   .
>
> Your judgment sees with pity, and with scorn
> The bastard sonnets of these rhymers base,
> Which in this whisking age are daily born
> To their own shame, and poetry's disgrace.
> Yet some praise those and some perhaps will praise
> Even these of mine: ...
>
> .   .   .   .   .   .

Yet if some rich rash gull these rhymes commend
Thus you may set this formal wit to school,
Use your own grace, and beg him for a fool.

This sonnet shows that when he was not gulling, Davies could be as censorious as anyone. Shakespeare does not look on sonneteers 'with scorn' and superior 'pity'. And Davies, when he gulls, uses a different approach and mood from that of his dedication. It is Shakespeare's.

Secondly, we may ask who was the 'rich rash gull' who might 'these rhymes commend'? Davies seems to have set out to gull, or make a fool of, the reader who might take him seriously; he is leg-pulling. It is just possible he wrote his sonnets to be used in this way. There is more to Shakespeare's sonnets than this, for they reflect a deeper experience of what they mock. Indeed the depth of feeling reflected in them makes one of their characteristics. By comparison Davies's are superficial. But it is conceivable that Shakespeare's sonnets have some leg-pulling intention. Perhaps this is a wild suggestion. Or is it? It would explain Thorpe's mystery-making dedication as his way of proving that he had not been fooled, and yet not giving the game away. At least the suggestion—for it is no more—is less wild than some that have been made. It is not more fantastic than Dover Wilson's[89] that the dark lady provided Thorpe with his copy. He argues it thus:

> it must have been one of three persons: and, since it is incredible that either Shakespeare or the Friend could ever have countenanced the publication of the liaison sonnets . . . I am left with the Dark Woman herself, unless some pirate unknown had been at work. All or most of the sonnets in section II presumably belonged to her, for if she was the woman I take her for she would have enjoyed the hating sonnets as much as the tender-amorous ones, for they were an even greater testimony to her power; . . . Thus, either because she was in want of money in 1609 or because she had been got at by the smart young stationer Thorpe who somehow learned of her hoard, a bargain was struck.

It may not seem fair to take such a baseless sample of scholarly

guess-work for contrast. Yet many others have as little founda-
tion. On the other hand Thorpe was undoubtedly indulging in
some sort of facetiousness, and even if we take this as merely
characteristic of him, we still have to ask what precisely are the
hidden implications. Does it not look as if some sort of gulling
might be involved, and if Shakespeare wrote a parody for the
quick-witted, whether he intended it or not, the slower-witted
were gulled.

III. THE DATE

What one has looked for in dating the sonnets has depended on
one's theory about them. Those who believed they were
addressed to a real man and woman identifiable in history,
dated according to their history, but this is unsatisfactory without agreement on who these individuals were. Those who took
the sonnets to be a miscellaneous collection, looked for references to external events within particular sonnets and dated
only them, but this view has lost favour, and indeed been
discredited by more careful studies of the sonnets, so that dates
that do not corroborate each other have become unconvincing.
However, two new consequences result from the close inter-
relationship now seen to exist between the sonnets, and their
over-all designing, form and coherence. It would not now be as
wild to assume, as it might have seemed a few years ago, that if
we can date one sonnet for certain, we have dated the whole
sequence. And even more important, arguments long used for
dating the plays become valid when applied to the sonnets.

On my theory the natural thing to do is to date by 'borrowings'. Thus I should say that my study has shown that Shakespeare's sonnets must have been written later than 1591.
Wyatt, Surrey, Watson, Sidney and Daniel had certainly
written all that he parodies by then. The relevant Greville
sonnets are generally agreed to be contemporaneous with
Sidney's. Joan Grundy suggests that 'many, perhaps all' Constable's were written by the end of 1591;[90] *Diana* was published in 1592. Barnes returned to London from his participa-
tion in Essex's adventure on the continent, in October 1591,
although if we can take *Parthenope and Parthenophil* to have
any autobiographical significance, he wrote it when he was
twenty-one, for he says he was fourteen when he fell in love

with Laya and is writing seven years later, and his twenty-first birthday was in March 1592. On the other hand seven is a number hallowed by imagination; if he had said 'six' it would certainly be literal. It is relevant that *The Two Gentlemen of Verona* has an obvious reference to Barnes' sonnet VI, as I have shown when dealing with the play; but this might indicate either that the play was written after 1591 or that Barnes wrote his sonnets before he was twenty-one. Spenser also was in London from roughly 1589 to 1591 and certainly wrote under the stimulation of that sonnet year, when they could have gone from hand to hand in manuscript. Shakespeare's parodies show a close memory of details, which suggests that they were written not long after his reading. This would put his earliest possible date very late in 1591 or soon after March 1592. But we have still to consider John Davies of Hereford, one of whose sonnets I showed Shakespeare parodied in his ninety-fourth.

Davies would perhaps have justified a place in my earlier chapters, but I shall consider him at some length now. Shakespeare's most obvious parody of him is in sonnet 151,* where he parodies more than one of Davies's including sonnet XXIV of the 'amorous' sonnets that make the first section of his *Wittes Pilgrimage*. Here it is:

> So, art thou (cruel!) like a balance-scale
> For, when I sink with bale, thou mount'st with bliss;
> And when I rise with bliss, thou sink'st with bale:
> So, still thou art mine opposite by this.
> And why all this? (Oh froward fair!) oh why
> In mine annoy dost thou so much delight?
> Can I not live, but thou forthwith must die?
> Or doth my death give thy life, life, and spright?
> There's no necessity herein at all,
> Unless thou be the same: who, (Parchas-like)
> Doth never rise, but by another's fall:
> That is, their thread of life quite off to strike:
> For while I weigh them wounded by thy beams
> Their number, rising, falls into extremes.

* See p. 134.

Imagery of rising and falling appears also in sonnet XV, where the lady's eyes are said to be stars,

> Who are the presidents of peace, or wars,
> And either cause, as either fall, or rise.

And again in sonnet XCII, which ends,

> May charge thee with my fall, when I shall rise
> To meet thee, to have justice in the skies.

The parody of this image in Shakespeare's sonnet 151 cannot be missed, but there is a not quite so devastating parody of other sonnets in the same context. Thus Davies ends sonnet XXII saying that he would choose to be 'blinded by the light of his lady's sun', and Shakespeare in sonnet 148,*

> The sun itself sees not, till heaven clears.
> Oh cunning love, with tears thou keep'st me blind,
> Lest eyes well seeing thy foul faults should find.

Shakespeare's reason for wishing to be blind is of course quite different. Sonnet 149 also ends with blindness. Davies's sonnet XXIII includes,

> Then, let me love thee, in thy better case,
> That in thy worst, so much should grieved be.

This has a similarity with Shakespeare's 150, which includes 'in my mind thy worst all best exceeds', where he asks, 'Who taught thee how to make me love thee more', and which ends,

> If thy unworthiness raised love in me,
> More worthy I to be beloved of thee.

Davies's XXIV questions in hurt, and Shakespeare's 149 opens, 'Canst thou oh cruel, say I love thee not'. In answer it protests that he takes part against himself for her sake and worships even her defect. The metaphor of the balance in

---

* See p. 138.

sonnet XXIV corresponds with the implied metaphor of 'sway' in 150. The question is how the lady has power to 'sway' his heart with 'insufficiency', 'insufficiency' being a word of Davies's. Sonnet 150 also says that her 'unworthiness raised love' in him. When we come to 151 itself we find the poet betraying his 'nobler part' to his 'body's treason', his soul given permission to love and therefore 'flesh' staying no further reason, 'But rising at thy name' to 'point out thee'; he therefore is content to 'stand in thy affairs, fall by thy side', and he ends,

> No want of conscience hold it that I call,
> Her love, for whose dear love I rise and fall.

There can be no doubt of a very close similarity between the two poets.

Possibly this and the sonnet I dealt with in chapter IV are such obvious parodies that they could not be questioned, but as there is not such massive evidence for the parodying of Davies as for all the other poets whose sonnets I have examined, perhaps I should discuss further. Our first question in determining which is the original when two sonnets like Davies's XXIV and Shakespeare's 151 are similar, must be whether either could have been written but for the other. Davies's sonnet XXIV certainly could. His interest comes out of a different background from Shakespeare's. He is patently as interested in Greek philosophy as in sonnet love, and his thinking about body and soul comes directly from Plato. Thus in sonnets XXIV and XXV of the little series 'In praise of Poesie', which makes part of the section of 'Other Sonnets upon other Subjects' that follows his 'amorous' sonnets in *Wittes Pilgrimage,* he discusses one of Plato's theories, and bases the argument on our consisting in body and soul, 'And that my body for my soul was made'. Similarly the background of sonnet XXIV of the 'amorous' sonnets was the Greek philosophy of the opposites. He explains in sonnet XC, of the amorous sonnets,

> In nature are two supreme principles :
> As namely, unity, and binary :

The first doth form all beauty's miracles :
The last's the fount of all deformity :

The contrast of rising and falling in sonnet XXIV, is led up to
in the previous sonnet from the angle of all creation being a
matter of opposites. Therefore his lady is made like this :

If thou can'st be thine own true antitype,
(That's most deformed, sith most well formed thou art !)
If thou can'st rotten be, now, thou art ripe,

.   .   .   .   .   .

Then do I smart for love of (graceful) thee :
Then, let me love thee, in thy better case,
That in thy worst, so much should grieved be.

So sonnet XXIV is presented as an elaboration of her duality,
or opposites. Her contrariness naturally results. Rising and falling are opposites proving one thing heavier or lighter. Not only
is the lady a duality, the poet attuned to her is her opposite :
when one falls the other rises and vice versa. The sestet says
that besides having this essential principle of life which consists
in being a One composed of opposites, she is the giver of
opposites herself and determines life and death. 'Parchas' is
obviously a misprint for 'Parchae', the goddesses who hold the
threads of life, and determine the birth of one while they cut
the thread of life of another. But, he continues, as her unity
falls into numbers, they increase until they fall into extremes.
We can see his point from sonnet XXIX 'In praise of Poesie',
which Shakespeare parodied in sonnet 94,* and where he got
the word 'sufficiency', which is said to bring peace, whereas
excess breeds sin and shame.

We want no peace, because we want extremes.

It is clear, therefore, that the contrast of rising and falling is a
detail that has arisen naturally out of an interest in Greek
philosophy. The sonnet, indeed the context where it occurs, is
closely argued, and explicable within itself.

If we now turn to Shakespeare we may note that when I was

* See p. 271.

discussing sonnet 151 in chapter III, although I found a background for other details there was nothing whatever to suggest the image of rising and falling. It seemed to come out of the blue as a gratuitous sex joke. Gratuitous sex-joking is a feeble type of wit, not that this makes it unShakespearean as his punning on 'lie' shows. But to suddenly tumble the pseudo-philosophy of Davies's sonnet into a matter of sex like this was really funny. It makes Davies's imagery seem quite ridiculous. Not only does there seem no other origin for the joke, this is adequate as a source. And more, after Shakespeare's parody, no other writer could possibly risk using this image, let alone copy it. Its metal is indelibly tarnished.

That Shakespeare should think of Davies when dealing with the soul-body contrast of love was natural. He already had in mind the sonnet tradition with love a matter of contradictions, the lady perverse and the lover happily unhappy. Even the suggestion of balance in 'sway' was there in Daniel. So also 'Can'st thou oh cruel' needs no Davies. But his rising and falling was new. In this context of sex-joking it was nearly inevitable that Shakespeare should have thought of its irreverent application to Davies's solemn philosophy. That is to say Davies's sonnet is not only necessary but obvious as the background to Shakespeare's wit.

Sonnet 151 has much more relevance to Davies than this, however. We may notice that 'conscience' is quite as much of an intruder in it as the rising and falling joke. The first line is very puzzling. Why should love be too young to know what conscience is? What can the sense be? Yet this appears the theme of the sonnet; it is coupled with rising and falling for love and they are reconciled formally at the end. Davies's sonnet XVI of those 'In praise of Poesie' gives the answer. Indeed the primary purpose of sonnet 151 was to parody it, with the joke against sonnet XXIV of the 'amorous' sonnets as only ancillary. Let us look at Davies's sonnet:

> When will doth long to effect her own desires
> She makes the wit (as vassal to the will)
> To do what she (howe'er unright) requires,
> Which wit doth (though repiningly) fulfil.
> Yet, as well pleased (oh temporising wit!)

He seems to effect her pleasure willingly;
And all his reasons to her reach doth fit;
So, like the world, gets love by flattery.
That this is true, a thousand witnesses
(Impartial conscience) will directly prove;
Then, if we would not willingly transgress,
Our will should swayed be by rules of love :
Which hides the multitude of sins because
Her sire, thereby, to him his servants draws.

Here I take 'will' to mean not sex desire, but whatever one wishes, what the worldly man he is writing about wishes. Davies is saying that when we desire anything, we use our wits to do whatever is necessary to achieve it, whether that is right or not. And our wit, which temporises even if it knows better, appears to do so willingly, finding good reasons, every reason, for aiding and abetting. It fits itself to the world and obtains love by flattery. A concensus of opinion, the equivalent of an impartial conscience, witnesses to this. Therefore if we do not want to transgress, we should determine our actions not by what we want but by rules of love. The reason that love is said to cover a multitude of sins is because by it God draws his servants to him, in contrast with wit's servants. Shakespeare treats Davies's morality as irreverently as his philosophy. He says that love is a dubious guide; it is too innocent and irresponsible to know anything about conscience, yet everyone 'knows' (at least Davies said) that conscience is born of love. But he asks gentle love not to cheat him by giving him advice that will prove bad, or betray his 'nobler part' to his 'gross body's treason' for when his soul says love may triumph, his body needs no other reason (like Davies's wit with 'all his reasons') to do what it likes. So he concludes that it is not for lack of conscience or love with her rules that he lets his flesh triumph.

I must refer to just one other example of Shakespeare's parody. Sonnet XIX of Davies's 'amorous sonnets' has this :

The Stoics, in their strange philosophy,
Make all, and nothing, nothing but all one :

.   .   .   .   .   .

> For, thou, being all, art mine, that nothing am,
> I nothing am that is not all thy due,
> So, all and nothing's nothing but the same!
> Then sith my nothing and thy all all's one,
> Thou, all, I, nothing, make an unity:
>
> .   .   .   .   .
>
> But all, and nothing still shall one appear.

Sonnet XXXIII ends,

> Only, for thee, I life, in show, retain:
> And if thou wilt have that, sith that's for thee
> Then take thou all, and leave the rest for me.

We have already seen him playing with nature's two principles of unity and 'binarity' in sonnet XC, where he suggests,

> Let's not be two (fair sweet) but fast embrace
> The mean whereby we may be still conformed:

Although the similarity between the poets depends on each being grounded in a not too dissimilar past, Davies with the emphasis on Greek philosophy and Shakespeare on the sonnets, yet there may be a direct echo of all this in Shakespeare's sonnet 36* *Let me confess that we two must be twain,* where he draws a ridiculous conclusion from his premise, and sonnet 40†, *Take all my loves, my love, yea take them all,* where he stresses the all that will leave him nothing: 'All mine was thine, before thou hadst this more.'

If we now turn to the aspect of parody that involves mocking the other's voice, we find a distinct resemblance between Davies's style and tunes and Shakespeare's, and not only as tunes that characterise the English tradition. Even from the little that I have quoted from Davies a close likeness in their way of writing may be seen. Both have as their basis prose idioms, not to say conversational, with inversions mainly to accomodate rhyme. An easy way to illustrate the likeness may be to quote some of Davies's opening lines and ask

* See p. 198.
† See p. 203.

whether, given the difference in imagination, Shakespeare could not have written some of them.

Weary of rest, thus resting in the clift (20)

When first I learnt the A,B,C of love, (9)

The sweetness (sweet) which in thy love I feel, (26)

Some say they love, because their loves are fair; (45)

Where shall I hide me from love's power? Oh where? (66)

Fool that I am to seem so passionate (97)

I hope it may be concluded that Shakespeare's parody of Davies is as clear as that of the sonneteers whose influence I have already examined. We now come to the difficult question of dates. It would seem that the other poets parodied by Shakespeare are known to have written before 1592 or to have been in London in 1591 and to have some link with the Pembroke family or connections. The date when *Wittes Pilgrimage* was published is not known, but a reference to James I in the introductory poems proves that it must be after 1603. This, however, is no argument for the date of the 'amorous' sonnets. Greville's love sonnets were not printed till 1633 many years after they are presumed to be written. This seems so of Davies also. His first published book was not printed till 1602 and it is very unlikely indeed that he only began writing then. Moreover the 'amorous' sonnets begin *Wittes Pilgrimage* which suggests that his journey started with them. It looks as if he might even have written about the same time as Sidney and Greville. Grossart says he was 'intimate' with Sidney, although there are degrees of intimacy. At any rate Sidney admired his penmanship, which it was his job to teach, and the beauty of which eventually brought him a wide reputation. He wrote sonnets to the Earl of Pembroke and Sidney's sister among other famous people. This would seem to make him old enough to have written sonnets before Sidney died in 1586, easily by

1592. The first evidence of his being in London dates from 1608, but he ends his 'amorous' sonnets thus:

> Now, to this sea of city-commonwealth
> (Limitless London) am I come obscured;
> Where twofold plagues endanger may the health
> Of soul, and body of the most secured:
> The body's plague's an ill which God can do
> For, is ill in the city he doth not?
> But sin (the plague which doth the soul undo)
> He cannot do, though how he well doth wot.
> Then, now my soul stand stiffly on thy guard
> Sith many mortal dangers thee surround
> Let grace, thy guide, thy house still watch, and ward
> To keep thy habitation clean, as sound:
> And, if thou can'st with Lot, live chastely here
> Angels will fetch thee hence when plagues are near.

This sonnet has a young and innocent air as of the provincial youth come to town for the first time. He writes, 'I am come', so must be referring to his present state and not be writing from recollection. It ends his 'amorous' sonnets, so seems to be connected with them. If he wrote this final sonnet after completing his sequence, the reference to the plague may date it. How long after finishing the sequence he wrote this postscript, we cannot know. But since 1592–3 are the plague-years, there seems no argument for putting Shakespeare's date later than 1592, especially since Davies's is uncertain and that of other sonneteers well founded.

Let us now see what borrowings from Shakespeare's sonnets by other poets indicate as the latest date by which he must have finished them. It is easy to find correspondences, but may be difficult to decide which is the borrower, or even if neither need have borrowed, and the resemblance merely shows a common influence. The most impressive evidence I have found comes from Claes Schaar, although I am far from accepting all his judgements. Out of great industry he concludes,[91] that whereas the 1592 edition of *Delia* shows no influence of Shakespeare at all, the 1594 does. He says that Shakespeare was the first sonneteer to use imagery from stealing in the way he does in sonnets 63, 75 and 77. Daniel although he has no instance of this in his 1592 edition, or in any sonnet printed before 1594, uses this imagery in that edition. Another possible but not certain influence occurs in *Willobie His Avisa,* published in 1594. In canto LXVI after saying that his lady thought it good 'with cruelty to kill' him, the poet says to her,

> You still did loath my life, my death shall be your gain
> To die to do you good, I shall not think it pain.
>
> .　　.　　.　　.　　.　　.
>
> Yet love doth make me say, to keep you out of blame,
> The fault was only mine, and that you did but right,
> When I am gone, I hope my ghost shall show you plain
> That I did truly love, and that I did not fain.

Shakespeare's sonnets 88 and 89 could have inspired this. The poet had read *The Rape of Lucrece* and might have known the sonnets. But I can feel no certainty of it. The ghost does not suggest him and it does indicate the sonnet of Daniel's which I quoted when dealing with Shakespeare's sonnet 71. Likewise Claes Schaar[92] has demonstrated a massive background for faults and pains being only the lover's and the praise being only for the loved, from Petrarch onwards.

The most convincing evidence of borrowings from Shakespeare in work published 1594 is that in *Idea's Mirrour.* Drayton appears to have composed love sonnets from time to time, so not all need have been written at one time. In his dedicatory sonnet he says that they 'long . . . have slept in sable night'. How long he does not say. But it might be reasonable to take late 1592 or early 1593 as a possible date for some of them. This comes close to Shakespeare's earliest possible date. But it would not be surprising if Drayton had read Shakespeare's sonnets soon after they were written.

I have already shown that amour VIII reflects Shakespeare's sonnet 38 and XLIII sonnet 129. But perhaps I should consider some others. Sonnets VI and XVII are comparable with 59* and 106. The former runs:

* See p. 228.

Stay, stay, sweet time, behold or ere thou pass
From world to world, thou long hast sought to see,
That wonder now wherein all wonders be,
Where heaven beholds her in a mortal glass,
Nay, look thee time in this celestial glass,
And thy youth past, in this fair mirror see :
Behold world's beauty in her infancy,
What she was then, and thou or ere she was.
Now pass on time, to after-worlds tell this,
Tell truly time what in thy time hath been,
That they may tell more worlds what time hath seen,
And heaven may joy to think on past world's bliss.
Here make a period time, and say for me,
She was, the like that never was, nor never more shall be.

Drayton must have been familiar with Ovid's theory of time as
the mover, and its revolution bringing back what was. Shakespeare added to Ovid in sonnet 59 by making fun with a play
of his friend re-appearing in each revolution. If Ovid is right,
he says, then his friend must do so. This is what Shakespeare
stresses. Not so Drayton. He is not looking freshly, as Shakespeare was, at the implications of Ovid's theory for his love. He
assumes Shakespeare's situation of the lady as a given and
accepted part of the revolving system. In fact his sonnet presumes Shakespeare's. Time, he says, passes from world to
world; it has long sought to see the wonder 'wherein all
wonders be', where heaven, which holds the ideal, sees her
reflected in a mortal glass—the Platonic situation. In the
second quatrain time is told to look in the celestial glass and see
the world's beauty as she first was in her infancy before it and
she were created. Finally it is told to pass on to after worlds
and say what she was like then, so that each age in turn may
hand on what she has always been. In the couplet he calls a
halt at the present moment and asks time to show him (not
others but him) what she is like in his eyes, something unlike
what has ever been, or will be. What Drayton got from Shakespeare was the idea of this progression of time showing his lady
age after age. He writes as if the connection between Ovid and
the lady were an accepted fact, something belonging together.
Since he takes Shakespeare for granted, there can be no doubt

that he was the borrower. But his debt is even more fundamental than this. In sonnet 59 Shakespeare asks to be shown
his friend's image 'in some antique book, Since mind at first in
character was done'. Drayton asks this, that time should reveal
his lady even before the infancy of the world, 'or ere she was',
in her first celestial state. Shakespeare's reason for wanting to
see his friend's image was 'That I might see what the old world
could say, To this composed wonder'. The 'composed' or
created wonder is Drayton's theme.

It is interesting that English sonnets published around 1593
to 1596 show an outburst of the sonnet lady as a 'wonder'. (I
have not tracked down the reason.) Drayton makes it the
theme of amour XVII where the word occurs seven times in
the fourteen lines, with arithmetic that is perhaps significant :

> If ever wonder could report a wonder,
> Or tongue of wonder worth could tell a wonder thought,
> Or ever joy express, what perfect joy hath taught,
> Then wonder, tongue, then joy, might well report a
>   wonder.
> Could all conceit conclude, which past conceit admireth,
> Or could mine eye but aim, her object's past perfection,
> My words might imitate my dearest thought's direction :
> And my soul then obtain which so my soul desireth.
> Were not invention stalled, treading invention's maze,
> Or my swift-winged muse tired by too high flying,
> Did not perfection still on her perfection gaze,
> Whilst love (my phoenix bird) in her own flame is dying,
> Invention and my muse, perfection and her love,
> Should teach the world to know the wonder that I prove.

We can be sure that Drayton got his 'wonder' from Shakespeare, not only because it and the question of its impression on
the world are in sonnet 59, but since his sonnet develops the
last line of 106,* where it is said that we

> Have eyes to wonder, but lacks tongues to praise.

Drayton begins by considering 'If ever wonder could report a

* See p. 288.

wonder, Or tongue ... could tell', and ends that it 'should
teach the world to know the wonder that I prove'. Shakespeare
says he went to 'the chronicle of wasted time' and discovered
that 'their antique pen would have expressed, Even such a
beauty' as his friend.

These are far from being the only borrowings in the 1594
edition of *Idea's Mirrour,* some more convincing in their own
right than others. Of the less certain, we can say as we said of
Shakespeare's parodies, that cumulating coincidences may in
the end amount to certainty. As an example we might take the
sestet of amour XLIX, which could conceivably have been
written exactly as it is even if Shakespeare had never existed,
but which we can accept as a reflection of sonnet 33 on
account of many other resemblances between the poets and the
certainty of Drayton's debt in some of them. Thus Drayton
writes,

> Behold the clouds which have eclipsed my sun,
> And view the crosses which my course doth let,
> Tell me, if ever since the world begun,
> So fair a morning had so foul a set?
> And by all means, let black unkindness prove,
> The patience of so rare divine a love.

In sonnet 33 Shakespeare says, 'Full many a glorious morning
have I seen, ... permit the basest clouds' to hide the sun and
make it steal 'unseen to west'. He continues,

> Even so my sun one early morn did shine,
> With all triumphant splendour on my brow,
> But out alack, he was but one hour mine,
> The region cloud hath masked him from me now.
> Yet him for this, my love no whit disdaineth,
> Suns of the world may stain, when heaven's sun staineth.

Drayton reads like a shortened version of Shakespeare. Not
only have both poets the glorious morning and the foul set,
both end with the experience leaving their love unstained.

So far then, I hope we may conclude that borrowings prove
that Shakespeare must have written before 1594. We may get

closer than that however, for one of Giles Fletcher's sonnets shows the unmistakable influence of Shakespeare. This is the Giles who was father of the better known poet, Giles Fletcher. He dates the dedication of his sonnet sequence *Licia* as 4 September, 1593. Sonnet XII goes thus:

> I wish sometimes, although a worthless thing,
> Spurred by ambition, glad for to aspire,
> Myself a monarch, or some mighty king:
> And then my thoughts do wish for to be higher.
> But when I view what winds the cedars toss,
> What storms men feel that covet for renown;
> I blame myself that I have wished my loss:
> And scorn a kingdom, though it give a crown.
> A'licia thou, the wonder of my thought,
> My heart's content, procurer of my bliss;
> For whom, a crown I do esteem as nought:
> And Asia's wealth, too mean to buy a kiss.
> Kiss me sweet love! This favour do for me;
> Then crowns and kingdoms shall I scorn for thee.

This resembles Shakespeare's sonnet 29, *When in disgrace with fortune and men's eyes*. Let us look at what the two sonnets have in common. Most obviously, both have 'scorn', Shakespeare's of 'kings' and Fletcher's of 'crowns and kingdoms'. Shakespeare says that his friend's

> sweet love remembered such wealth brings,
> That then I scorn to change my state with kings.

Fletcher ends,

> Kiss me, sweet love! This favour do for me;
> Then crowns and kingdoms shall I scorn for thee.

Both have 'sweet love', that in one when 'remembered' and in the other when she kisses him, 'then' (in both) lead them to scorn kings. Both wish to have better fortune than they have; Fletcher wishes to be a king, and then 'to be higher'; Shakespeare is more specific, wishing to be richer than one man,

have the features of another and so on. That is to say, both
poets compare their lot with that of others and neither is
content with it. Shakespeare is 'with what I most enjoy contented least'. Fletcher when he sees 'What storms men feel that
covet for renown' says, 'I blame myself that I have wished my
loss'. Shakespeare does not actually blame himself, but he is not
only in disgrace and beweeping his 'outcast state', he describes
himself as 'in these thoughts myself almost despising'. The
resemblance between the sonnets is obvious. The question is,
which has influenced which. So let us ask whether either sonnet
could have been written as it is but for the other.

Shakespeare's sonnet follows a logic inherent in itself, each
part naturally related with other parts. It has a natural
development, and can be explained within itself, given influences I have already investigated, and without reference to
Fletcher's sonnet. The scorning to be a king makes its natural
climax. In comparison with his friendship, Shakespeare scorns
everything, the very top of other experience; that is to say
being a king. The image of the king is subordinate to the
general thought. It is not even a striking expression in the
sonnet; its use is merely functional, almost as functional as a
preposition or a conjunction, for it signifies merely the topmost
desire, whatever that is. Indeed both 'scorn' and 'state of kings'
appear in the sonnet because they are superlatives. Their significance lies in this alone, and they need no other explanation.
It would be quite absurd to say that they appear because
Shakespeare found them in someone else's sonnet. If the
reader will look back at my explanation of what Shakespeare
did borrow, and accepts it, it will be seen that the sonnet
sprang out of a background which it parodies, of the poet out
of favour with his lady, in disgrace because of this, and that it
is structured to reach a climax in the resolution of this misery
by the conventional means of being compensated by his loved
one's favour. Shakespeare parodies this by making the disgrace
that of fortune so that he is led to compare his general fortune
with that of others; and by substituting men's eyes, and thus
the estimate of others for those of his lady, he comes almost to
despise himself.

If we now turn to Fletcher we see that his sonnet can best be
explained as a re-working of Shakespeare's, that his ideas had

their origin in Shakespeare's sonnet, and that it can more easily be explained in this way than accounted for in any other. It can hardly be explained by inter-relating parts within itself, for the ideas have not an internal coherence. But they are explicable if we take Shakespeare's sonnet as their source. It looks as if Fletcher had begun with the idea of the scorning of a monarch for the sake of his lady. That is to say he starts from the last statement in Shakespeare's sonnet. He prepares for it by creating a monarch which he can scorn, so to say. There seems no reason why he should wish to be a king although Shakespeare's sonnet 114 might have influenced him. Indeed this seems to have struck him as he wrote, for he immediately apologises, saying he does so, although he is 'a worthless thing' (as Shakespeare was). To work out his idea on the model of Shakespeare he has to blame himself, not be contented with his desire to be a king. So he says he wishes to be even higher than a king. Then he considers the storms that men feel who covet renown, and by this means he can blame himself for wanting something that really would be a loss rather than a gain. The only reason for wishing to be higher than a king seems to be to engineer a situation where he can place himself in the wrong, as Shakespeare almost despises himself. Fletcher blames himself for wishing 'the loss' that aiming too high brings. In this way he recreates Shakespeare's mood. From this experience, says Fletcher, he learnt to scorn a kingdom, though it give a crown. There is not much sense in this statement. But his scorning the kingdom 'though' it give a crown, leaves the crown with a special virtue. The truth is that he had never any reason for desiring the crown at all, except so that he could scorn it for his lady. Now at the sestet he has to bring the argument round to that. He has scorned the kingdom in the mood of Shakespeare's despair, and he leaves the crown as the apex of the kingdom so that he can reject it for his lady. He does this by saying she is the real 'procurer' of his bliss and for her he esteems a crown as nothing. He has said what Shakespeare says, borrowing clothes that do not hang together on himself. The explanation of the sonnet cannot lie in its own inherent meaning for it has no real interior logic. But it is easy to explain as a reflection of Shakespeare.

I have shown that Shakespeare's sonnet has gained nothing

from Fletcher's, and that it cannot have copied his since its progression is not in any way determined by it. I have also shown how Fletcher's sonnet can reasonably be explained as taking shape under Shakespeare's influence, and that this is enough to account for the similarity. While Shakespeare's sonnet could have been written exactly as it is without pre-supposing that he had read Fletcher's, it is extremely unlikely that Fletcher's would have been written in the form in which it is, or indeed have ever been written at all, if he had not read Shakespeare's. It certainly seems that he started from the idea in Shakespeare's last line, and that he worked it out with echoes of Shakespeare's sonnet in his mind. On the other hand, Shakespeare finishing with Fletcher's statement has nothing to do with him, and his general attitude and argument have been conditioned by others as I have already shown, in contrast with Fletcher's main and dominating image, which comes from what was merely functional in Shakespeare's sonnet. I hope I have shown that an examination of the sonnets puts beyond doubt that their likeness is to be attributed to Fletcher's borrowing rather than to Shakespeare's. One can also say that Fletcher would not think such imitation anything to apologise for, since the alternative title for *Licia* is 'Poems of Love . . . To the imitation of the best Latin poets, and others'.

I take it, then, that *Licia* proves that early 1593 is the latest possible date for Shakespeare's sonnets, and that this is pretty closely confirmed by Daniel's and Drayton's borrowings in their 1594 sonnet series, and perhaps by reflections in *Willobie his Avisa*. We can now say that a comparison with contemporary sonnets suggests that Shakespeare's were written in 1592, or at least between late 1591 and early 1593.

No one date is generally accepted for the sonnets, although some scholars favour 1592. Probably not enough emphasis has been laid on dates suggested by correspondences between the sonnets and Shakespeare's other works. E. K. Chambers[93] takes into account in dating the plays, that out of all his work *Venus and Adonis* and *The Rape of Lucrece* have most passages resembling others in the sonnets. They have fifty each. Some of these are so similar as to put beyond doubt that Shakespeare's creativeness was coursing the same ground when he wrote them. But the significant fact is that his plays with many correspondences can be put into groups according to the number of resemblances to the sonnets they contain, and in such a way as to suggest that the sonnet influence made a very strong impact on Shakespeare's mind, that faded only gradually as time went on. This makes an important pointer for dating the plays. In the first group come *Love's Labours Lost, The Two Gentlemen of Verona, Romeo and Juliet* and *A Midsummer Night's Dream,* with a hundred and fifty correspondences between them, then another with *As you like it, Much Ado About Nothing, The Merchant of Venice* and *Twelfth Night* with about fifty between them. Chambers gives this and other elements of style the fullest value in dating the plays. Since however, there is no certainty over their precise dates, all we can deduce with respect to the sonnets is that they were written during Shakespeare's early romantic period,[94] and that they made an element in their creation. This is given support by an interesting link with the sonnets noted by A. O. Fox[95] who quotes a list of contraries in love from Lodge's *Rosalynde* which Shakespeare echoes in sonnet 129. It includes,

> A heaven in show, a hell to them that prove.
> A gain, in seeming, shadowed still with want,
>
> . . . . .
>
> A minute's joy to gain a world of grief.

Shakespeare says this of lust in sonnet 129 with its expense and waste, its ending in

> To shun the heaven that leads men to this hell,

and its list of contradictions including,

> A bliss in proof, and proved a very woe.

Although this does not mean that Shakespeare wrote the sonnets and *As you like it* at the same time, it shows that both had a common influence in Lodge's novel published in 1590. Now we also have proof that Shakespeare read Brooke's version of *Romeus and Juliet* roughly about the same date. We

M

can be sure of it since he makes Queen Margaret use imagery from Brooke in her opening speech of the fourth scene of Act V of *Henry VI*, part 3, which Chambers[96] dated 1590–1. Her image of the shipwreck was suggested by Friar Lawrence's speech scolding Romeus for despairing, and urging him to summon up his courage. It is likewise interesting that Sidney's *Arcadia* was published in 1590. We have already seen a reflection of it in Shakespeare's opening sonnets. We can therefore say that *As you like it, Romeo and Juliet* and the sonnets were contributed to by reading of romantic literature in 1590 or thereafter.

Although it is beside the point, I cannot refrain from commenting on Shakespeare's using the shipwreck from Brooke for Queen Margaret's speech rather than where it belongs, in Friar Lawrence's to Romeo. It fits both the Queen's character and the situation in which she uses it, where it is not only magnificent, but psychologically right. Since he used it there, Shakespeare could not of course let his Friar Lawrence have it. But it was psychologically wrong in Brooke's poem. He had not the dramatist's instinct of how the imagination works in the human situation. He writes as a poet indulging in imagery for its own sake, not creating what is suitable for an old man of religion scolding the passionate misery of a boy, whereas Shakespeare's sense of dramatic fitness is seen everywhere in his selection from his sources. It makes an element in his sense of humour also, and contributes to his parody of the sonnets. The image of a terrific storm tearing a great ship to bits, fits only a disaster that is more than personal. So, at the other end of the emotional scale, his criticism of sonnet psychology, since it was only a game, is made in the anti-game of parody.

To return to dating, although nothing precise can be deduced from a comparison with the plays, we have dates for the publication of *Venus and Adonis* and *The Rape of Lucrece*. The former was registered in Stationers' Hall on 18 April 1593 and the latter in May 1594. I shall show in the next section of this chapter that a comparison of similarities in *Venus and Adonis* and the sonnets suggests that they were written first, so confirming 1592 or early 1593 as the latest date for their composition. Likewise, considering the almost overwhelming evidence I have given that Shakespeare's sonnet imagery had its source in the sonnet tradition, which flowered in 1591, it does not seem unreasonable to place it first in the phenomenon of a great sonnet resonance in his work which gradually faded.

IV. SHAKESPEARE NOT HOMOSEXUAL

Putting Shakespeare's sonnets in their literary background leaves no chink for a real man and woman. It was not till the end of the eighteenth century, after their background had been forgotten, that this possibility was suggested, as in these circumstances was bound to happen sometime. But given that background, the idea of a real man and woman being involved, becomes ridiculous. As it is, some of the situations and suggestions provided by historians who believe they have identified Shakespeare's 'friend', add to the humour, making perhaps the last aspect of Shakespeare's joke. It is not merely that there are such eventualities as that of the dark lady, Mary Fitton, whose discovery excitingly confirmed one story, at last turning out to be fair, Rowse's hope[97] that his commentary on the sonnets would give some of the pleasure of a novel proves only too true, while Dover Wilson's notes on a *different* friend and lady is if anything more novelesque.

Here is Wilson on sonnet 57, *Being your slave*[98] :

> taken with 58 and 61 it gives us a vivid picture, steeped in irony, of the unhappy player-poet, waiting into the night for a meeting with this young noble who fails to keep his appointment, and does so because, as the player comes to realize, his lordship is engaged in bed with the player's mistress. Giving it up at last the Poet goes off to his own bed, but not to sleep, for there follows the night described in 61.

To return to the world of fact, I doubt if much of the evidence submitted to identify 'the friend' as an actual man recorded in history, even where coincidences are proved, would carry much weight in a court of law if something important such as the inheritance of some large estate, or even a title, were at stake. It is not even circumstantial evidence, merely conjectural. As E. K. Chambers noticed[99] there is a remarkable resemblance between relevant incidents in the lives of the two most distinguished claimants, the Earls of Southampton and Pembroke, one Shakespeare's first patron, the other his posthumous. This in itself shows that the incidents are worthless as evidence. And there are of course many other claimants. It gives some indication of the tenuousness of the proofs, that qualifying for being a plain 'Mr' has seemed worth mentioning.

Since the sonnets, given their literary background, do not of themselves suggest that Shakespeare was homosexual, a previous question must be whether there is any other evidence that might do so, and open up this possibility in the sonnets. The question has of course been asked, but no evidence of this sort has been found. And that makes the strongest argument against.

Perhaps the best way to investigate this may be to compare Shakespeare with two other poets of the day, who were self-admitted homosexuals—Richard Barnfield and Marlowe. Barnfield published a little series of sonnets to *Ganymede* in 1595, a date that would have allowed him to know Shakespeare's sonnets. In many of them he says what sonneteers usually say to their ladies, and in this is not unlike Shakespeare except that he does not give it a comic twist. But his sequence also includes passages where a physical attraction is apparent. Thus in sonnet VIII he says he sometimes wishes he were his friend's pillow to steal a kiss and yet not be seen, and that bees are foolish since they sip only flowers. In XIII he says his 'kisses make thee oft thy red to lose', in XVII he refers to his friend's 'love enticing delicate soft limbs', and asks,

> Oh how can such a body sin-procuring,
> Be slow to love, and quick to hate, enduring.

Shakespeare never refers to his friend's body desirously like this. He may love his friend's beauty, but gives no sign of desiring physical contact. He also contrasts with Marlowe, whose interest in boys was self-declared, well-known, and if he had not been murdered, could have involved him in a trial on a very serious criminal charge. Nothing of this sort has ever been suggested of Shakespeare. Before comparing them, however, it may be interesting to look at *Venus and Adonis* which has been cited against him, and which must be compared with Marlowe's *Hero and Leander*.

Venus and Adonis blends two stories from Ovid's *Metamorphoses*—that of Hermaphroditus, the son of Hermes and Aphrodite, who was embraced and fondled by a woman as he bathed in a pool, but who rejected her, and the story of Venus and Adonis. It has been claimed that Shakespeare chose this theme so that he could identify with Venus and indulge in phantasy wooing of a youth. But we do not *know* that this was why he chose the story, and we have no more reason to think he identifies with Venus than that he identifies with all the characters in his plays that reveal understanding. His genius as a dramatist is seen as clearly in the poem as it is in his plays. And more, he could with as much reason be said to identify with Adonis, the boy not sexually awake, who is bored and embarrassed. Indeed, if we had to find something in Shakespeare's own experience to account for the poem, the obvious place to look for it would be in experience that led him when a youth of nineteen to marry a woman eight years older than himself. If we need to presume that he is drawing on his own experience, here surely is where we should look first. But we need not presume it, considering the psychological imagination that lights up his plays. And the final word must be that Venus, although goddess-size, does not appear like a man. She could hardly be more feminine. Shakespeare's presentation of her does not support the view that she is himself in disguise.

To compare the poem with the sonnets will throw up their different qualities. *Venus and Adonis* has a sensuous richness and warmth quite different from the cool intellectuality of the sonnets. As Leishman[100] notes, these show a 'continuous intellectual activity'. And it belongs in the tradition, where poets are wits, where conceits flourish, where the mind plays with its material. *Venus and Adonis* on the other hand is a story told for its physical passion, fleshy, urgent and dramatic. The poet is not exercising a brilliant play of mind, but imagining in a series of sense impressions.

As is his habit in the plays, Shakespeare opens the poem with a statement of his theme in colourings that give its character.

He starts with Adonis, 'rose-cheeked', 'more lovely than a man',

> Hunting he loved, but love he laughed to scorn:

—and Venus, 'trembling in her passion', pulling him from his horse and kissing him. Adonis 'blushed, and pouted in a dull disdain'.

> She red, and hot, as coals of glowing fire,
> He red for shame, but frosty in desire.

The fleshiness of Venus, however, is seen in proportion only if we remember that the whole story is presented as experienced by the senses. Thus it has been pointed out that Shakespeare seems as interested in Adonis's horse as in the lovers. In the opening lines, as Venus begs the boy to dismount and play with her, she indicates his horse and asks him to 'rein his proud head to the saddle bow', giving an image which suggests as definite a shape as any Keats was later to create.
Shakespeare continues,

> The studded bridle on a ragged bough,
> Nimbly she fastens.

He is certainly not all-absorbed by the sex in the situation. His observation of all three, of Venus, Adonis and the horse, shows delight in them as visualised in the detail suitable for a stage production :

> So soon was she along, as he was down,
> Each leaning on their elbows and their hips:
> Now doth she stroke his cheek, now doth he frown,
> And gins to chide, but soon she stops his lips,
> And kissing speaks, with lustful language broken,
> If thou wilt chide, thy lips shall never open.

Other signs of her passion are noted :

> Look how a bird lies tangled in a net,
> So fastened in her arms Adonis lies,
> Pure shame and awed resistance made him fret,
> Which bred more beauty in his angry eyes.

When she would kiss he 'turns his lips another way'. Venus commends herself by all possible means. 'My flesh is soft, and plump' she says. Her hand is smooth and moist. But she suddenly bursts into a sort of song :

> Bid me discourse, I will enchant thine ear,
> Or like a fairy, trip upon the green.

This change of key takes one's breath away. Shakespeare, young like his nearest imitator Keats, is getting everything he can out of the story. His sonnet 'wit' has abdicated in favour of a more basic approach.

Let us now look at some of the sonnet imagery that one might not expect in this context and see how Shakespeare integrates it. The first idea in the sonnets, the idea that young men should love and beget children is used by Venus as she tries to seduce Adonis. If she cannot do it by sex appeal and enchantment, she will try moral argument. To find Erasmus's reasoning in her mouth, the scholar's words on her sensual lips, is surprising. This cannot be where Shakespeare first met them. Like all the sonnet images that appear in this poem they must have originated in the sonnets where they naturally belong, many of them being commonplaces. I have traced their source and shown how Shakespeare came to use them in the sonnets. They could hardly have leapt to his mind as most applicable to Venus if they had not remained in it after he had finished his sonnets. Thus they do not express her feeling so much as forward the dramatic action. Their function is to tie together. Or if we look from the other angle, in *Venus and Adonis* they are like ready-made balls pitched about, whereas in the sonnets they crystallised out of Shakespeare's background material.

The first recollection from the sonnets goes thus :

> Torches are made to light, jewels to wear,
> Dainties to taste, fresh beauty for the use,
> Herbs for their smell, and sappy plants to bear.
> Things growing to themselves, are growth's abuse,
>   Seeds spring from seeds, and beauty breedeth beauty,
>   Thou wast begot, to get it is thy duty.

Upon the earth's increase why shouldst thou feed,
Unless the earth with thy increase be fed?
By law of nature thou art bound to breed,
That thine may live, when thou thyself art dead:
    And so in spite of death thou doest survive,
    In that thy likeness still is left alive.

By this the love-sick Queen began to sweat,
For where they lay the shadow had forsook them,
And Titan tired in his midday heat,
With burning eye did hotly over-look them,
    Wishing Adonis had his team to guide,
    So he were like him, and by Venus' side.

And now Adonis with a lazy sprite,
And with a heavy, dark, disliking eye,
His louring brows o'er-whelming his fair sight.
Like misty vapours when they blot the sky,
    So wring his cheeks, cries, fie, no more of love,
    The sun doth burn my face I must remove.

We smile at Venus's discomfiture. This Erasmus argument does not belong in love. What has Venus to do with propagating a family? It serves as persuasion at her wit's end. Here is another sonnet image she uses:

Art thou obdurate, flinty, hard as steel?
Nay more than flint, for stone at rain relenteth.

In its place in the sonnets this describes that sort of love. Venus does not accept it. She uses it as an opening for feminine complaining that is more in character:

What am I that thou shouldst contemn me this?
Or what great danger, dwells upon my suit?
What were thy lips the worse for one poor kiss?

This is the sort of plaint that comes naturally out of the situation. The image from flint only decorates the fact of Adonis's coldness. In the same way the next sonnet imagery is turned from its original associations:

Well painted idol, image dull, and dead,
Statue contenting but the eye alone,
Thing like a man, but of no woman bred.

You could say of this, that the idea of the idol had been perverted from its sense. In the sonnets the woman as idol is deified, a thing to worship and adore. That is what an idol is for and why the image is used in the sonnets. But it has remained in Shakespeare's mind when its real meaning is no longer relevant. To Venus an idol is not to be worshipped. It is a piece of sculpture with no significance for love. She wants flesh and blood. She complains that Adonis is as unresponsive as a statue, not a divine thing but something less than man, inhuman. It does not relieve her feeling at all. 'This said, impatience chokes her pleading tongue,' 'and fiery eyes blaze forth her wrong'. She behaves like a real woman frustrated, not a poet playing at being in love. But it is as if Shakespeare were defining her by throwing up her quality against a sonnet background in his memory. On another occasion she pours out a whole series of sonnet images to express impetuous pleading. She says that Adonis kills her, disdains her, has 'murdered this poor heart of mine', that their lips have 'crimson liveries'. She asks,

Pure lips, sweet seals in my soft lips imprinted,
What bargains may I make still to be sealing?
. . . . . .
Set thy seal manual, on my wax-red lips.

She says,

A thousand kisses buys my heart from me,
And pay them at thy leisure, one by one.
. . . . . .
Say, for non-payment, that the debt should double,
Is twenty hundred kisses such a trouble?

These sonnet commonplaces are naturalised in the new context by becoming a passionate torrent, whose purpose is to make Adonis promise one kiss before the sun sets :

> Now let me say goodnight, and so say you,
> If you will say so, you shall have a kiss.

It was a dangerous and innocent promise. She wins at kissing.

> Her lips are conquerors, his lips obey,
> Paying what ransom the insulter willeth:
>   .   .   .   .   .   .
> ... she will draw his lips' rich treasure dry.

This again originated in the sonnets, but its purpose here is to make part of the dramatic outburst that expresses Venus's impetuous and irresistible pleading and lets her conquer by mere superior force of feeling. However, as she has won by will-force alone, it is not a real conquest. She loses at last, for in the morning the boy prefers boar-hunting. His rejection is made absolute by his condemning her love as lust, an idea from the sonnets possibly, but it has been realised by Adonis from her kissing assault:

> Love comforteth like sunshine after rain,
> But lust's effect is tempest after sun,
> Love's gentle spring doth always fresh remain,
> Lust's winter comes, ere summer half be done:
>   Love surfeits not, lust like a glutton dies:
>   Love is all truth, lust full of forged lies.
>
> More I could tell, but more I dare not say,
> The text is old, the orator too green,
> Therefore in sadness, now I will away,
> My face is full of shame, my heart of teen,
>   Mine ears that to your wanton talk attended,
>   Do burn themselves, for having so offended.

Although this is a sonnet theme the dramatist has expressed it as a boy might, in general presenting the orator as 'too green'.

The passion of Venus portrayed with such gusto, by comparison throws light on Shakespeare's restraint both in his sonnets and in his plays. For the one it suggests that his purpose in the sonnets could not be to express passion, or even deep feeling, whether his own or imaginary. For the other it shows how much the plays were conditioned by his stage, where boy actors made passionate love impossible, but where equally an over-sophisticated mind-play would be out of place. The sonnets belong in an intellectually brilliant world of their own where ideas live, and not to that of real life passion, or human drama, although they have their own lively play.

A comparison of *Venus and Adonis* with Marlowe's *Hero and Leander* is as interesting and relevant as that between it and the sonnets. Caroline Spurgeon[101] has compared the imagery of the poets in general. Marlowe is more ethereal, stimulated by thought, Shakespeare down to earth, stimulated by feeling; he has the widest range and images from all the senses. But the important difference between the poems from our point of view lies in Marlowe's frankly homosexual imagery, although there was no necessity for it. It is obvious that he found a man's body more interesting than a woman's. Thus in the opening, one cannot miss the greater interest in Venus's clothes than in her physical appearance. She has lawn garments lined with purple silk, wide green sleeves, a 'kirtle blue', a veil of 'artificial flowers and leaves'. It takes two pages to describe the effect she made. She was courted by 'young Apollo' 'for her hair'. Cupid loved her in detail, nature wept,

> Because she took more from her than she left,
> And of such wondrous beauty her bereft.

But of direct description of herself, nothing. On the other hand Leander's clothing is neglected, but we are told,

> His body was as straight as Circe's wand,
> Jove might have sipped out nectar from his hand.
> Even as delicious meat is to the taste,
> So was his neck in touching, and surpassed
> The white of Pelop's shoulder, I could tell ye,
> How smooth his breast was, and how white his belly,
> And whose immortal fingers did imprint,
> That heavenly path, with many a curious dint,
> That runs along his back, but my rude pen,
> Can hardly blazon forth the loves of men.

When Leander is crossing the Hellespont, however, he seizes the opportunity for his 'rude pen' to do what it can :

> Leander being up began to swim,
> And looking back, saw Neptune follow him,
> Whereat aghast, the poor soul gan to cry,
> Oh let me visit Hero ere I die.
> The god put Helles' bracelet on his arm,
> And swore the sea should never do him harm.
> He clapped his plump cheeks, with his tresses played,
> And smiling wantonly, his love bewrayed.
> He watched his arms, and as they opened wide,
> At every stroke, betwixt them would he slide,
> And steal a kiss, and then run out and dance,
> And as he turned, cast many a lustful glance,
> And threw him gaudy toys to please his eye
> And dive into the water, and there pry
> Upon his breast, his thighs, and every limb,
> And up again, and close beside him swim.

But we must accede that Chapman also, who finished the poem after Marlowe's death, carries forward the sea's love :

> Off went his silken robe, and in he leapt;
> Whom the kind waves so licorously cleapt,
> Thickening for haste one in another so,
> To kiss his skin.

It has not been suggested that Chapman was homosexual in consequence, although we may notice that his images are of the waves caressing, not the man-like Neptune. We must also allow that Marlowe, although it almost looked as if he avoided describing Hero in his introduction, is by no means coy over the heterosexual love involved by the poem. And one would expect Hero to be less fleshy and rumbustious than Venus, although Leander's praises as, 'So young, so gentle, and so debonair' may be too diaphanous. Incidentally Marlowe, like Shakespeare and perhaps copying him leans on sonnet love, even using Erasmus's argument :

> But this fair gem, sweet, in the loss alone,
> When you fleet hence, can be bequeathed to none.

If we consider the treatment of homosexuality in plays we must remember that this theme was not shocking on the Elizabethan stage, and although the practice was both against the law and taken as immoral, it also appeared natural, just as any other sin is natural. Both Shakespeare and Marlowe illustrate this, and its appearance in their plays does not necessarily mean that they were either homosexual or attracted by the theme. Shakespeare does not condone it, although he may take it lightly in Oberon's 'lovely boy', who however was a changeling that Titania wanted for herself, rather than was jealous of. Similarly the opening scene of *The Tragedy of Dido,* with Jove bribing Ganymede, does not without other evidence, show Marlowe's approval.

Wherever we find the homosexual situation in Shakespeare's plays, we can see that it is not exploited for its own sake, but contributes to forward a dramatic action with an overriding interest. Thus the innocent love of the boy Arthur for Hubert in *King John* is there not because Shakespeare delights in the love of boys, but for its pathos. His children tend to be colourless; Shakespeare exploits their innocence. Thus Hubert in an aside says of Arthur,

> If I talk to him, with his innocent prate
> He will awake my mercy which lies dead.
>
> *Arthur:*   Are you sick, Hubert? You look pale to-day :
> In sooth, I wish you were a little sick,
> That I might sit all night and watch with you;
> I warrant I love you more than you do me.

Shakespeare is playing on our feelings; this is 'sob-stuff' not sex. So also, King John's expression of love for Hubert in Act III lacks conviction. The king dissembles to trap him into doing away with Arthur.

> *King John:* Come hither, Hubert. Oh my gentle Hubert,
> We owe thee much! Within this wall of flesh
> There is a soul counts thee her creditor,
> And with advantage means to pay thy love :
> And, my good friend, thy voluntary oath
> Lives in this bosom, dearly cherished.
> Give me thy hand. I had a thing to say,

> But I will fit it with some better time.
> By heaven, Hubert, I am almost ashamed
> To say what good respect I have of thee.

Hubert replies respectfully, not lovingly,

> I am much bounden to your majesty.

The King needs to be assured of his loyalty and suggests,

> I love thee well;
> And, by my troth, I think thou lovest me well.

I take the last line to have the inflection of a question, to which Hubert, not in the least deceived, replies,

> So well, that what you bid me undertake,
> Though that my death were adjunct to my act,
> By heaven, I would do it.

Thus the King's motive is to persuade Hubert to murder the boy and keep faith over it, and Shakespeare's to forward the action of the play.

The most relevant, and most interesting comparison between Shakespeare and Marlowe concerns *Richard II* and *Edward II*. Both histories come from Holinshed and in general are to be taken as factual. Homosexuality contributed to the ruin of both kings. It enraged their nobles thus contributing to their tragic end. But this is treated quite differently in the plays, Marlowe enlarging on the homosexual motive, Shakespeare pruning it to almost nothing. And this seems the more significant since Shakespeare borrowed much that was dramatically powerful from Marlowe. Let us look at the plays more closely.

Marlowe made homosexuality the theme of *Edward II*. Its main emphasis falls on the King's infatuation. It opens with Gaveston reading a letter from Edward announcing the death of his father, and therefore his accession to the throne, and expressing their love-relationship as the most important thing in the situation. Gaveston responds,

Sweet prince I come, these these thy amorous lines,
Might have enforced me to have swum from France,
And like Leander gasped upon the sand,
So thou wouldst smile and take me in thy arms.

He does not love London,

But that it harbours him I hold so dear,
The king, upon whose bosom let me die,
And with the world be still at enmity.

He plans to provide all sorts of musical and poetic entertain-
ments. 'Sometime a lovely boy' will play Diana and bathe in
the lake. An important step in the play is taken when the king
refuses to give Gaveston up; the plot hinges on it. We see
Edward besotted, showering Gaveston with more than all he
could wish. A climax comes when he rejects his wife. We are
told that he

dotes upon the love of Gaveston.
He claps his cheeks, and hangs about his neck,
Smiles in his face, and whispers in his ears.

Later, Mortimer senior advises his nephew,

Nephew, I must to Scotland, thou stayest here,
Leave now to oppose thyself against the king,
Thou seest by nature he is mild and calm,
And seeing his mind so dotes on Gaveston,
Let him without controlment have his will.
The mightiest kings have had their minions,

. . . . . .

Then let his grace, whose youth is flexible,
And promiseth as much as we can wish,
Freely enjoy that vain light-headed earl,
For riper years will wean him from such toys.

Mortimer junior does not grieve over 'his wanton humour',
only that Gaveston is 'basely born' and riots it 'with the

treasure of the realm'. We see the homosexual emphasis again when the King greets Gaveston after his absence :

> Thy absence made me droop, and pine away,
> For as the lovers of fair Danae,
> When she was locked up in a brazen tower,
> Desired her more, and waxed outrageous,
> So did it sure with me : and now thy sight
> Is sweeter far, than was thy parting hence
> Bitter and irksome to my sobbing heart.

Marlowe uses the King's weakness not to alienate or make us critical, but to create pity for him. He is the one selfless character in the play, if his devotion to his favourites can be called this, and why not. And he is deprived of them, deserted by all, and ends suffering a Marlowesque cruelty.

Although Shakespeare had the homosexual motive to hand in the story of Richard II if he had wished, he lays no stress on it. His favourites have minor parts. The play is not about a harmless young king destroyed by homosexuality. Richard II is much more complex than Edward II, and although presented as a weakling, and even more unrelated with the reality of the situation he has created, he has enough conventional morality to retain a sort of dignity. In fact it might almost seem that Shakespeare deliberately planned his play so as not to need this motive. Richard's destroying sin was his murder of Gloucester, and this is kept to the fore throughout. In place of the pity and softness that Edward's love of his favourites contributes to Marlowe's play, Shakespeare invented the love between Richard and his queen, which he did not find in Holinshed. It became necessary only because he rejected the King's love of his favourites as a means of creating pity. As it is, we hardly notice the homosexual in the play. In the fourth scene where we first see the King alone with his friends, there is no hint of it. Their function is to bring him (and us) up to date with the news, to let us hear of Richard's intention of going to Ireland, and of his farming the land out to provide money for the expedition. In the first scene of the next act, York's list of Richard's faults does not include boys or immorality in the narrow sense of the word. He is frivolous rather than vicious, although he listens to 'Lascivious metres'; he is said to be running after foreign fashions, while 'A thousand flatterers sit within his crown'. His favourites even to Bolingbroke are at first only 'upstart unthrifts'; this is the harm they do in his court. The first suggestion of any sex relationship with the King is made by Bolingbroke in the opening scene of Act III, where he explains why he has condemned Bushy and Green to death. And his statement is a series of lies. Firstly we have seen the King and Queen together and know that his favourites have not led to their alienation; on the contrary the relationship between them is tender and moving. Nor have we seen any justification for the accusation that he was involved in the 'filthy sin of lechery and fornication', as indicated by Holinshed. Shakespeare seems to have judged that this would have destroyed our pity for the King or sullied our respect too much. Or perhaps he had a scruple over showing this on the stage, for the well known relationship of Achilles and Patrocles is only referred to in *Troilus and Cressida*. Patrocles is quite objective about it :

> To this effect, Achilles, have I moved you.
> A woman impudent and mannish grown
> Is not more loathed than an effeminate man
> In time of action. I stand condemned for this:
> They think my little stomach to the war
> And your great love to me restrains you thus.
> Sweet, rouse yourself; and the weak wanton Cupid
> Shall from your neck unloose his amorous fold,
> And, like a dew-drop from the lion's mane,
> Be shook to air.

Perhaps I should say something about *As you like it* since it has recently been taken as a calculated presentation of transvestism. But to exploit the fact of boy actors for women's parts like this would have been absolutely impossible on the Elizabethan stage as it would have undermined the illusion that boys with their unbroken voices were used to create. The first essential of a drama that holds the mirror up to life is to create an impression of reality. Any dramatist who tampered with this, or made game of its weakness would risk cutting the ground from under his feet. This must have precluded Shakespeare's making fun out of it. An audience carried away in a dramatic illusion forgets that the actors are acting, that the women are really boys. Nowhere do we find a more willing 'suspension of disbelief' than in a good theatre production. To suggest that *As you like it* and *Twelfth Night* exploit a fundamental falseness in the representation is to suggest a sophistication, and even a decadence that is incredible in the Elizabethan theatre. It is particularly incredible of Rosalind. The comedy depends on our accepting her as a real woman. In the production on the London stage where she was played by a full-grown man and where it was intended we should remember this, the illusion of her as a woman was still complete. Shakespeare's Celia was destroyed by this experiment, but it seemed that Rosalind could not be. The fun of Shakespeare's Rosalind depends on her assured femininity. She is a woman in disguise, laughing at Orlando because she has him at a disadvantage. His wooing of Ganymede, not knowing he is Rosalind, is presented as awkward. This is the joke, Rosalind's joke not less because her laughter is sometimes rueful, as when his kisses have no feeling.[102] She says,

> his kissing is as full of sanctity as the touch of holy bread.

To this Celia replies, to agree with her and to mock her,

> He has bought a pair of cast lips of Diana: a nun of winter's sisterhood kisses not more religiously, the very ice of chastity is in them.

Shakespeare obviously intends no love of any sort in the kisses the man gives thinking it is a boy he kisses. There is not the faintest suggestion of anything homosexual.

However this is not the most doubtful joke in the play. The most telling argument for Shakespeare being aware of an aspect of transvestism in the *As you like it* situation lies in Rosalind's coupling the behaviour of women and boys when as Ganymede she actually proposes that Orlando woos her. She explains how she once cured a man of the madness of love:[103]

> He was to imagine me his love, his mistress; and I set him every day to woo me; at which time would I, being but a

moonish youth, grieve, be effeminate, changeable, longing and liking, proud, fantastical, apish, shallow, inconstant, full of tears, full of smiles; for every passion something, and for no passion truly anything, as boys and women are for the most part cattle of this colour.

If this coupling of women and boys were Shakespeare's joke, it might show where his thoughts lay. But it is Lodge's, who wrote his romance to be read, and was very well aware of this aspect of the situation. Rosalind was not Shakespeare's creation, but Lodge's, charm, naughtiness, daring and all. And his Rosalynde is certainly aware that in boy's clothes she assumes another attraction. She says,

all women have desire to tie sovereign to their petticoats, and ascribe beauty to themselves, where if boys might put on their garments, perhaps they would prove as comely.

And when she blushes to hear Rosader read his poem describing her, she hides her embarrassment by braving it out as a boy, protesting,

Believe me . . . it makes me blush, to hear how women should be so excellent, and pages so unperfect.

But Shakespeare has not carried any overtone of homosexuality into his dramatising of Lodge's story, although a vestige remains in this joke. On the contrary Rosalind can trade on the very obvious innocence of Orlando. Without giving herself away, she goes as far as she safely can to provoke him into flirting with her. It is only too apparent that she has nothing to fear from her attraction as Ganymede. No doubt her coupling boys and women might have produced a laugh in the theatre. But she said it to confirm her disguise as a boy, and it does not endanger her illusion of femininity.

To sum up, Marlowe's plays do not necessarily prove him homosexual. We must allow the dramatist to create other than from his own personal viewpoint. But given the evidence of his love of boys both in his own life and in *Hero and Leander,* the homosexual in his plays appears in a new light. On the other hand there is neither external evidence that Shakespeare was interested in boys, nor any indication of this from his poems or plays. Indeed, very few historians or critics, even of those who presume a real man was involved in the sonnets, consider that the relationship had a physical basis. They treat them as expressions of an extraordinarily ideal friendship. But there is as little to justify this as to justify a physical attraction to boys. Finally, Shakespeare let us know what he thought of Platonic friendship in *The Two Gentlemen of Verona*, where he presents it as extraordinary nonsense.

NOTES

Chapter 1

The edition of Meres used is that of the Scholar's Facsimiles and Reprints, New York.

1. Philip Sidney, *Astrophel and Stella,* sonnet LVI.
2. Giles Fletcher, *Licia,* sonnet LII.
3. Thomas Watson, *Passionate Centurie of Love,* sonnet XCIV.
4. Richard Linche, *Diella,* sonnet IV.
5. L. F. Mott, *System of Courtly Love* (Ginn, 1896), for early troubadours pp. 1–21, for Chrétien de Troyes pp. 26–52.
6. J. B. Broadbent, *Poetic Love* (Chatto, 1964), p. 30.
7. J. J. Parry, *The Art of Courtly Love* (Records of Civilization, Sources and Studies, No. 33, 1941), p. 21.
8. J. J. Parry's book is a translation.
9. Ibid., pp. 200–9.
10. Ibid., p. 184.
11. Ibid., pp. 184–6.
12. Mott, op. cit., pp. 112–28.
13. Plato, *Symposium,* trans. W. Hamilton (Penguin, 1951), pp. 45–7, 50–3, 59–64, 76–82, 92–5.
14. Translation in Loeb's Classical Library by H. N. Fowler (Heinemann, 1914), pp. 465, 487–505, 531–5.
15. Translation in Loeb's Classical Library by R. G. Bury (Heinemann, 1929), pp. 59–61.
16. Ibid., p. 55.
17. Margaret Schlauch, *Some Medieval Literature and its Social Foundations* (Oxford University Press, 1967), p. 119.
18. Lu Emily Pearson, *Elizabethan Love Conventions* (Allen & Unwin, 1967), p. 10.
19. Ibid., pp. 32–9, 319–24.

20. For a good general introduction to English sonneteers, I suggest J. W. Lever, *The Elizabethan Love Sonnet* (Methuen, 1956).

21. Richard Puttenham, *Arte of English Poesie,* 1589 edition, p. 48.

22. Printed in John Stevens, *Music and Poetry in the Early Tudor Court* (Methuen, 1961).

23. Ibid., p. 13.

24. Ibid., No. 13 of the Fairfax Manuscript, p. 357.

25. Ibid., No. 126.

26. Ibid., the Henry VIII Manuscript, pp. 388–428.

27. Pearson, op. cit., pp. 44, 58–9.

28. Sergio Baldi, *Sir Thomas Wyatt,* translated by F. T. Prince for the British Council and the National Book League, 1961.

29. Sidney Lee, *Elizabethan Sonnets* (Constable, 1904), Vol. I, p. xxxix.

30. Katharine M. Wilson, *Sound and Meaning in English Poetry* (Cape, 1930), pp. 120–5, 145–53.

31. Philip Sidney, *Arcadia,* edited by A. Feuillerat (Cambridge, 1922), p. 57.

32. Ibid., p. 82.

33. Ibid., p. 90.

34. Ibid., p. 98.

35. Claes Schaar, *An Elizabethan Sonnet Problem* (Lund Studies in English, No. 28, 1960).

36. B. H. Newdigate, *Drayton and his Circle* (Blackwell, 1941), p. 42.

37. Hebel's edition of *Works,* Vol. V (introduction and notes by Kathleen Tillotson and B. H. Newdigate) does not mention that he was.

38. M. H. Dodds in *Archaellogia Æliana,* Vol. XXII (1946), p. 8.

39. Henry Constable, *Poems,* edited by Joan Grundy (Liverpool University Press, 1960), pp. 26–33.

40. Ibid., p. 51.

41. Edmund Spenser, *Works,* edited by J. C. Smith and E. de Selincourt (Oxford University Press, 1912), pp. xxviii–xxxi.

Chapter II

The text of the quotations from *The Two Gentlemen of Verona, Love's Labours Lost, As You Like It* and *Romeo and Juliet* is that of the New Shakespeare editions, except that I have printed all nouns which have what to us seem unnecessary capitals (like personifications) without them, given an "h" to the ejaculation "O" and not retained elisions. For other plays I quote from the Temple Shakespeare. The quotations from Lodge's *Rosalynde* are from Vol. I of the Collected edition, printed by the Hunterian Club, 1883. The original spelling of *Love's Labours Lost* had no apostrophe. On my interpretation the 's' of 'Labours' indicates the plural, not an elision for 'is'.

42. E. K. Chambers, *William Shakespeare—A Study of the Facts and Problems,* Vol. I (Oxford University Press, 1930), pp. 9–10.

43. Foster, Watson, *The English Grammar Schools to 1660* (Cass, 1968), pp. 91, 490–500.

44. Laurence Stone, *The Crisis of the Aristocracy 1558–1641* (Oxford University Press, 1965), p. 682.

45. Ibid., pp. 670–709.

46. *Shakespeare Quarterly,* Vol.XV, Spring 1964, pp. 25–7.

47. Frances Yates, *A Study of Love's Labour's Lost* (Cambridge University Press, 1936), p. 34. I have modernised the spelling. The author gives a full background for the play. She promulgates theories that some (including myself) do not accept, but the general background is relevant to any theory. So also of Dover Wilson in the New Shakespeare edition of the play.

48. Ibid., pp. 114–15.

49. Ibid., p. 43.

50. P.4 of the 1589 edition.

51. *Shakespeare: The Early Comedies.* Writers and Their Works Series (published by the British Council and the National Book League, 1960), p. 25.

52. John Stevens, *Music and Poetry in the Early Tudor Court* (Methuen, 1961), pp. 167–9.

53. C. L. Barber, *Shakespeare's Festive Comedy* (Oxford University Press, 1959).

Chapter III

The text of Shakespeare's, Daniel's and Spenser's sonnets is that of the Scolar Press facsimile editions, that of Wyatt's and Surrey's is from the Scolar Press facsimile edition of Tottel's Miscellany of *Songes and Sonettes,* 1557. Constable's and Barnes's sonnets and Watson's *Passionate Centurie* are quoted from the first editions. Sidney's text is that of the Cambridge English Classics, 1922, edited by A. Feuillerat. Watson's *Tears of Fancie* is that of the Arber reprints. I have modernised the spelling (including not giving capital letters for personifications) and set all sonnets with unindented lines, although many, including Shakespeare's, indent the final couplet. I have kept the original punctuation, however unhelpful.

54. M. C. Bradbrook, *Shakespeare and Elizabethan Poetry* (Chatto, 1951), p. 40.
55. *Sonnets,* New Shakespeare edition, 1969, pp. cx and cxiv.
56. Henry Constable, *Poems,* edited by Joan Grundy (Liverpool University Press, 1960), p. 125.
57. E. A. Bloom, *Shakespeare 1564–1964* (Brown University Press, U.S.A., 1964), pp. 134–5.
58. Frances A. Yates, *A Study of Love's Labour's Lost* (Cambridge University Press, 1936), p. 105.
59. Patrick Cruttwell, *The Shakespearean Moment* (Chatto, 1954), p. 14.
60. David Kalstone, "Sir Philip Sidney: The Petrarchan Vision", in Paul Alpers (ed.), *Elizabethan Poetry* (Oxford University Press, 1968), p. 190.
61. As in Hyder E. Rollins' edition (Harvard University Press, 1965).

Chapter IV
62. Folios 22–34 in the first edition.
63. J. B. Leishman, *Themes and Variations in Shakespeare's Sonnets* (Hutchinson, 1961), p. 137.
64. Ibid., p. 62.
65. Golding's translation of the *Metamorphoses,* edited by W. H. D. Rouse (De La More Press Folios, 1904), Bk XV, lines 93–4.
66. Ibid., line 433.
67. Ibid., line 258.
68. Ibid., line 229.
69. Sidney Lee, *Life of William Shakespeare* (Murray, 1931), pp. 155–6n.
70. M. M. Mahood, *Shakespeare's Word Play* (Methuen, 1957), p. 106.
71. George Wyndham, *Poems of Shakespeare* (1898), p. 284.
72. Golding, op. cit., line 265.
73. Mahood, op. cit., pp. 93–4.
74. Seymour-Smith (ed.), *Shakespeare's Sonnets* (Heinemann, 1963), note on the sonnet.
75. *Quarterly Review,* April 1909, also *Elizabethan and Other Essays* edited by Boas (1929).
76. Golding, op. cit., line 467.
77. Ibid., line 201.
78. Ibid., line 471.

79. Ibid., line 228.
80. *Mr. W. H.* (Hart-Davis), p. 99.
81. Leishman, op. cit., p. 33.
82. Lu Emily Pearson, *Elizabethan Love Conventions* (Allen & Unwin, 1967), pp. 270, 211–12.
83. Mahood, op. cit., p. 107.
84. "Shakespeare's Sonnets and the Elizabethan Sonneteer", *Shakespeare Survey*, 1962 (Cambridge University Press), p. 47.
85. Note on sonnet 110 in the New Shakespeare edition of the *Sonnets.*
86. Edward Armstrong, *Shakespeare's Imagination* (Lindsay Drummond, 1946), p. 107.

Chapter V
Quotations from *Venus and Adonis* and *Hero and Leander* are from the Scholar Press facsimiles. The text of Sir John Davies's sonnets is Grossart's and of John Davies of Hereford that of the original edition of *Wittes Pilgrimage* with the spelling modernised.

87. Franklin B. Williams Jnr, in *Studies in Bibliography*, 1957.
88. A. L. Rowse, *William Shakespeare* (Macmillan 1964), p. 200.
89. *Sonnets*, New Shakespeare edition, 1967, pp. xl–xli.
90. Henry Constable, *Poems* edited by Joan Grundy (Liverpool University Press, 1960), p. 60. *Diana* was published in 1592.
91. Claes Schaar, *An Elizabethan Problem* (Lund Studies in English, No. 28, 1960), p. 175. Incidentally, Daniel's sonnet is No. XXI not XX as stated.
92. Claes Schaar, *Elizabethan Sonnet Themes* (Lund Studies in English, No. 32, 1962), pp. 37–9.
93. E. K. Chambers, *William Shakespeare—A Study of the Facts and Problems*, Vol. 1 (Oxford University Press, 1930), p. 564.
94. R. M. Alden, *Sonnets of Shakespeare* (Variorum, 1916), p. 450.
95. *Notes and Queries*, 1956, p. 190.
96. Chambers, op cit., p. 270.
97. A. L. Rowse, *Shakespeare's Sonnets* (Macmillan, 1964), pp. xxi–xxii.
98. *Sonnets*, New Shakespeare edition, 1967, p. lvii.
99. Chambers, op. cit., p. 565.
100. J. B. Leishman, *Themes and Variations in Shakespeare's Sonnets* (Hutchinson, 1967), p. 190.
101. Caroline Spurgeon, *Shakespeare's Imagery* (Cambridge University Press, 1935), pp. 13–15, 35–6, 78–85.
102. Act III, sc. 4, line 13.
103. Act III, sc. 2, line 400.

INDEX